S0-AUJ-762

Daily Struggles

Daily Struggles

THE DEEPENING RACIALIZATION AND FEMINIZATION
OF POVERTY IN CANADA

Edited by Maria A. Wallis and Siu-ming Kwok

Canadian Scholars' Press Inc.
TORONTO

Daily Struggles: The Deepening Racialization and Feminization of Poverty in Canada
edited by Maria A. Wallis and Siu-ming Kwok

First published in 2008 by
Canadian Scholars' Press Inc.
180 Bloor Street West, Suite 801
Toronto, Ontario
M5S 2V6

www.cspi.org

Copyright © 2008 Maria A. Wallis, Siu-ming Kwok, the contributing authors, and Canadian Scholars' Press Inc. All rights reserved. No part of this publication may be photocopied, reproduced, stored in a retrieval system, or transmitted, in any form or by any means, electronic, mechanical, or otherwise, without the written permission of Canadian Scholars' Press Inc., except for brief passages quoted for review purposes. In the case of photocopying, a licence may be obtained from Access Copyright: One Yonge Street, Suite 1900, Toronto, Ontario, M5E 1E5, (416) 868-1620, fax (416) 868-1621, toll-free 1-800-893-5777, www.accesscopyright.ca.

Every reasonable effort has been made to identify copyright holders. CSPI would be pleased to have any errors or omissions brought to its attention.

Canadian Scholars' Press Inc. gratefully acknowledges financial support for our publishing activities from the Government of Canada through the Book Publishing Industry Development Program (BPIDP).

Library and Archives Canada Cataloguing in Publication

    Daily struggles : the deepening racialization and feminization of poverty in Canada / edited by Maria A. Wallis and Siu-ming Kwok.

Includes bibliographical references.
ISBN 978-1-55130-339-0

    1. Poor women—Canada. 2. Minorities—Canada—Economic conditions. 3. Poverty—Social aspects—Canada. I. Kwok, Siu-ming, 1965– II. Wallis, Maria A. (Maria Antoinette), 1960–

HC120.P6D34 2008   362.5082'0971   C2007-906219-9

Designed and typeset by Em Dash Design
Cover photograph by Vika Valter, "Crossed Hands with Stress 2819036,"
    from www.istockphoto.com.

08   09   10   11   12   5   4   3   2   1

Printed and bound in Canada by Marquis Book Printing Inc.

Table of Contents

Acknowledgements

Producing a collection of articles requires considerable teamwork and dedication by all involved. Therefore, we would like to express our appreciation to those involved directly and indirectly in the production of this edited book.

Maria Wallis:
I owe a debt of gratitude to my co-editor, Dr. Siu-ming Kwok. His dedication and friendship have sustained me in many ways. I thank you, Siu-ming, for the privilege of working with you on this project. Thanks to David MacGregor and Tania Das Gupta for their feedback on selected sections of the manuscript. Special thanks to my students, Erin O'Neill and Tarek El Morsy, for their contributions to this project. Finally, a special thank you to my mother, Esmeralda Wallis, and my daughter, Rose Mansi Wallis, for their love and support.

Maria Wallis can be reached at wallismariarose@hotmail.com

Siu-ming Kwok:
I am grateful to Dr. Maria Wallis, who is my best friend and colleague and is the chief editor of this book. She gave me the opportunity to work with her on this book project. Thank you to my students, Poonam Chhabra and Xin Chen, for their contributions to this project. Lastly, special thanks to my wife, Dora, who is always on my side and offers me endless support.

Maria Wallis and Siu-ming Kwok:
Many thanks to Megan Mueller at Canadian Scholars' Press Inc., who skilfully guided this project every step of the way. We would also like to thank the three reviewers, Sunera Thobani, Sylvia Hale, and Dennis Raphael, for valuable suggestions on our book proposal.

A NOTE FROM THE PUBLISHER

Thank you for selecting *Daily Struggles: The Deepening Racialization and Feminization of Poverty in Canada*, edited by Maria A. Wallis and Siu-ming Kwok. The editors and publisher have devoted considerable time and careful development (including meticulous peer reviews) to this book. We appreciate your recognition of this effort and accomplishment.

TEACHING FEATURES

This volume distinguishes itself on the market in many ways. One key feature is the book's well-written and comprehensive part openers, which help to make the readings all the more accessible to undergraduate students. The part openers add cohesion to the section and to the whole book. The themes of the book are very clearly presented in these section openers.

The general editors have also greatly enhanced the book by adding pedagogy to close and complete each section. Each part ends with chapter-specific annotated Further Readings and Related Web Sites, also annotated.

For the university and college market, critical thinking questions pertaining to each section of the book can be found on the CSPI web site at www.cspi.org

Introduction

Maria A. Wallis and Siu-ming Kwok

Take a moment to reflect on how our society is represented back to us. Is there discussion of the latest technological gadget on the market? The new movie in town? The sports scores? Some incident in the life of a celebrity? Or another trivial conversation on the radio? Such "news" items are so common that they tend to constitute the imagined "normal" day. Discussions then of the growing gap between the rich and poor, and the increasing racialization and feminization of poverty in Canada sound jarring, and maybe even unbelievable or unreal to some. The gap in Canadian society between the representation of how we are living, and what the majority experience as daily struggles to live a quality life, is very wide. This book bears witness to this increasing depth of poverty in Canadian society. We have a national crisis—the breadth and depth of poverty—in Canada. Too many Canadians in this wealthy nation are being deprived of fundamental human rights—that is, the right to be treated with respect and dignity as human beings. This respect includes adequate food, shelter, and a decent quality of life, a standard of life a wealthy nation can afford for all its citizens.

However, the reality of this wealth gap in Canada is coupled with the illusion of a content population. This illusion is constructed, along with other factors, by the increasing concentration of media control in the hands of a few. News is created in the interests of those in power and includes fear mongering of "Others," a selective focus on stock figures, and narratives of a prosperous Canada that requires, in order to be competitive or so it is claimed, free trade and less government intervention. Currently, poverty is rarely discussed substantively on any level of government in Canada. Occasionally, one may hear of homelessness, or child care, or food banks. However, the illusion of a prosperous Canada *for all* persists. The denial of the deepening and widening poverty in Canada is deafening.

Structural poverty is a violence that diminishes us all. This violence gets reinforced when discussions begin and end with the very definition of poverty. According to the National Council of Welfare:

> Statistics Canada has consistently maintained that it does not regard the LICOs [the Low Income Cut-Off] as poverty lines, presumably because the federal government does not want to give official recognition to poverty. Most social policy groups in Canada have consistently disagreed with the position of the federal government and continue to use the LICOs as poverty lines. (1999:4)

Rather than attempting, as the Canadian government did, to change methods to measure poverty in secrecy and without consultation with anti-poverty organizations, Canada needs to have an official poverty indicator. This is currently non-existent. Instead, Canadian officials have made attempts to "lower" poverty by erasing it on paper. Such manoeuvres need to be exposed and rejected. In addition, the LICOs needs to be revised to ensure that *all* Canadians are counted. According to the National Council of Welfare, "one of the Statistics Canada surveys used to get data on poverty every year is done in conjunction with the Labour Force Survey, which specifically excludes Indian reserves and territories" (1999:16). Poverty among the First Nations' communities is a national disgrace and requires urgent attention, not denial.

This book focuses on poverty in relation to gender and race. However, to do so, poverty has to be contextualized within the reality of increasing poverty in general, and the fragmented documentation of such poverty. So when we reflect on poverty, questions emerge: How many people are we talking about? And how do they live under such circumstances?

POVERTY IN GENERAL

In March 2007, Armine Yalnizyan, a research associate with the Canadian Centre for Policy Alternatives, published a report titled: "The Rich and the Rest of Us: The Changing Face of Canada's Growing Gap." The report presents the following list of findings: the income gap is at a 30-year high; there is greater polarization; the rich are getting richer; the bottom half are shut out of economic gains; and people are working longer to maintain their earnings (2007:3–4).

These disparities are being reported at a time when the Canadian economy is growing. In 2005, Canada's GDP was the ninth largest of 183 nations (Yalnizyan, 2007:9). However, this prosperity is not being equitably distributed. The data show a significant difference when one compares earnings to after-tax incomes (includes government income supports and income taxes): "The poorest 10% of families earned less than $9,400. Five percent of families earned less than $1,050 that year.... The poorest 10% of families raising children—more than 376,000 households in Canada—lived on less than $23,300, after taxes, in 2004. Half of these families lived on less than $17,500 a year" (2007:7–8).

In addition to the income gap, most Canadian families are working longer in the paid labour force than families in the late 1970s, but their incomes are lower today than they were a generation ago. As a result, today even jobs are not enough. According to the National Council of Welfare, "Half of poor two-parent families relied primarily on employment earnings and did not receive any welfare payments or employment insurance in 2001. Their average earnings were a paltry $15,000. Child benefits helped push their average total income up to $22,000. In comparison, the average income for all non-poor two-parent families was $86,000" (2004). Canada's system of taxes and transfers have helped families in the last 10 years (Yalnizyan, 2007:26). However, this system of social supports is weakened by cuts to taxes and cuts to social services, the former benefiting the wealthy and the latter disadvantaging all other citizens. According to Yalnizyan, "the fact that the after-tax income gap is growing should be of concern. Strong economic conditions and rising employment rates of the working-age population should be pointing to more opportunities for those at the bottom. Government measures to redistribute incomes through taxes and transfers should be further closing the gap. Clearly something is going on" (2007:16).

The real value of Canadians' earnings is falling. Even with a strong economy and increasing productivity, Canadians are not receiving their share of this prosperity. Social inequality in Canada—specifically the income gap—is growing. Armine Yalnizyan concludes:

> The rich are getting richer, the poor aren't going anywhere and there are fewer people in the middle to mediate the two extremes. We ignore these trends at our collective peril.
>
> When you see that pattern repeat itself between neighbourhoods, regions, and nations, you know that inequality has become to social and economic life what climate change has become to our physical world. The trend lines in both cases are unsustainable. (2007:31)

This overall picture of poverty in Canada achieves even greater depth when we focus on women, racialized peoples, and then specifically racialized women.

WOMEN AND POVERTY

The feminization of poverty is increasing in Canada. In *A Report Card on Women and Poverty* (2000), Monica Townson writes, "As Canada enters the 21st century, almost 19% of adult women are poor—the highest rate of women's poverty in two decades. About 2.2 million adult women are now counted as low-income compared with 1.8 million who had low incomes in 1980" (2000:1). Women's poverty is often caused by discrimination that results in the wage gap between men and women, gender segregation, lack of an effective national child-care program, and other policies that affect women negatively. Government cutbacks of social programs such as child care and unemployment insurance are another cause of women's poverty. Women's jobs now include non-standard jobs such as temporary, part-year, and contract work (2000:5). According to Townson, "It has been estimated that 40% of women's paid jobs, compared with 27% of men's jobs, are now of this type" (2000:5).

Cuts in social assistance generally lack any form of gender analysis by government. Monica Townson focuses on the Canada Pension Plan:

> For example, in the February 1996 Information Paper that served as the basis for consultation on changes to the Canada Pension Plan, the government's proposals included cutting benefits for surviving spouses; changing the structure of the child-rearing dropout; limiting inflation indexing; increasing the age of eligibility for retirement pensions; and eliminating the year's basic exemption so that even low-income workers would be required to contribute to the CPP from the first dollar of their earnings. (2000:9)

With these proposed measures, older women and single women would face an increased risk of a future of poverty.

Another illustration of the lack of gender analysis is the cuts the federal government made to unemployment insurance. Townson writes: "In its 1999 report *Left out in the Cold: The End of UI for Canadian Workers*, the [Canadian Labour] Congress found that the percentage of unemployed workers covered by UI in 1997 was less than half of what it was in 1989—falling from 74% of the unemployed to 36%. But UI coverage for women is even lower. Only 32% of unemployed women received UI in 1997" (2000:9–10). Women are being systematically made ineligible for what is now euphemistically called Employment Insurance (EI) because of the revised requirements. Women were simply not qualifying for EI benefits and were left to fend for themselves.

The irony, and yet another scaffolding in the illusion of prosperity, is the United Nations' ranking of Canada as one of the best countries in which to live. The indicators used in this ranking are: "life expectancy at birth; literacy; and per capita income, which it suggests reflects a "decent standard of living" (Townson, 2000:12). However, the gross domestic product (GDP) is an average and does not reflect the distribution of the nation's wealth. Another indicator shows a different story. An index of social health (ISH) focuses on health, mortality, poverty, unemployment, inequality, and access to services: "[The] ISH constructed by Setya Brink and Allen Zeesman of Human Resources Development Canada showed that, while Canada's GDP per capita continued to climb throughout the period from 1970 to 1995, the ISH did not follow the same pattern" (Townson, 2000:12). Unemployment remained high and real value of wages fell (Townson, 2000:12).

While poverty, inequality, and a deteriorating quality of life are worsening in Canada, the depth of poverty is most particularly experienced by women:

> Statistics Canada produces a measure that gauges the depth of poverty and is referred to as the "average income deficiency." ... It shows that "poverty gap," or how much additional income would be needed to raise them above the low-income line.
>
> For example, 49% of older women on their own were poor in 1997, and their average incomes were $3,000 below the poverty line. But, while 56% of women heading lone-parent families were poor in the same year, their depth of poverty, at just over $9,000, was three times greater. (Townson, 2000:2)

Women—that is, half of the citizens in Canada—are not being adequately represented and served by their government and the various institutions in this country. Their very rights as equal citizens are being denied. This social exclusion is also being experienced by racialized groups. Current research is also documenting the racialization of poverty.

RACE AND POVERTY

The globalization of the world economy and resulting consequences of transnational migration have increased Canada's population of racialized communities. Canada's racist and exclusionary immigration policies that made up Canada's social imaginary as a "White" settler society were finally opened up in the late 1960s with the establishment of the point system. With the focus shifting from national origin to levels of education, skills, and language, immigrants from African, South Asia, and East Asia, among others, finally began immigrating to Canada.

Along with opportunities in this new land, however, racialized groups in Canada confront systemic racial discrimination in many aspects of their lives. The extent and depth of racial discrimination in Canada, along with poverty, is also denied. Instead, Canada is portrayed as a multicultural showcase, a society to be envied for its diversity management.

Canada's racialized communities were defined as "visible minorities" by the federal Employment Equity Act of 1986. Statistics Canada, in 1986, included the following as visible minorities: Blacks, Indo-Pakistani, Chinese, Korean, Japanese, South East Asian, Filipino, Other Pacific Islanders, West Asian and Arab, and Latin American, excluding Argentinean and Chilean (Li, 2003 quoted in Galabuzi, 2006:1). In *Canada's Economic Apartheid: The Social*

Exclusion of Racialized Groups in the New Century (2006), Grace-Edward Galabuzi noted the following:

> The percentage of racialized groups in the Canadian population, under 4% in 1971, grew to 9.4% by 1991, then 11.2% by 1996, and had reached 13.4% by 2001. The immigrant population accounted for 18.4% of the Canadian population in 2001. Both racialized groups and immigrants are projected to rise to 20% and 25% respectively by 2015.… In a number of major Canadian urban centers, racialized group members and recent immigrants now make up majorities in the population. (2006:3)

Canada's racialized group members included immigrants (68 percent) and, even more significantly, 32 percent of this group are Canadian-born citizens (Galabuzi, 2006:4).

John Porter, in 1965, characterized Canadian society as a "Vertical Mosaic," a nation stratified by ethnicity. Class and ethnicity were intertwined in Canada. These social hierarchies are now racialized and references are being made to a colour-coded vertical mosaic (Galabuzi, 2006:8). According to Grace-Edward Galabuzi:

> … data, based on individual earnings before taxes, shows that in 1996, racialized Canadians earned an average of $19,227; non-racialized Canadians made $25,069, or 23% lower. The 1996 median before-tax income gap at 29% ($13,648 to $19,111) shows an even more profound inequality because it factors out the highest and lowest earners. This gap grew in 1997 as earnings of racialized individuals increased slightly to $19,558, a gap of 25% when compared to the $25,938 earned by other Canadians. The median before-tax income again betrays a widening inequality, with earnings of $13,413 for racialized groups and $19,602 for others, or a gap of 32%. The tax and government transfers' effect was marginal in terms of closing the gap. (2006:92)

Higher education levels within racialized communities did not translate into equivalent incomes. "Race" mediated the earnings also of Canadian-born racialized group earners. Galabuzi writes, "According to Statistics Canada data, in 1995, just over 253,000 earners in the racialized group population were born in Canada. Their average employment income of $18,565 was almost 30% below the level reported by all other earners who were Canadian-born" (2006:104–105). This situation exists even when racialized groups' educational levels are higher than that of other Canadian-born earners.

In addition, racialized individuals are segregated in low-paying sectors and occupations, and underrepresented in high-status occupations (Galabuzi, 2006:111). This segregation exists even with a university degree (Galabuzi, 2006:111). Unemployment levels—apart from precarious, part-time, contract work—also characterize the racial discrimination experienced by racialized groups.

> [W]hile racialized groups made up 11% of Canada's population in 1996, they had an average unemployment rate of 16%, compared to 11% for the general population in 1995" (2006:107). Michael Ornstein's analysis of the 1996 Census regarding ethno-racial inequality in the City of Toronto highlighted what can only be described as a crisis. Despite their educational qualifications, unemployment rates for Africans, Blacks, and South Asians have skyrocketed. Among Ethiopians, Ghanaians, Somalis, and "other African nations," the overall unemployment rates respectively are 24, 45, 24, and 23 percent, while the

> Pakistani and Bangladeshi, Sri Lankan, Tamil, and "Multiple South Asian" groups have unemployment rates above 20 percent. This is in stark contrast to the Toronto average unemployment rate of 11 percent. (Ornstein, 2000:52–60)

As a result, the racialization of poverty is an ugly Canadian reality. According to Galabuzi, "In 1996, the rate of poverty among racialized group members in Canada's urban centres was 37.6%, compared to 20.9% for the rest of the population" (2006:17). In Ornstein's analysis, the percentage of ethno-racial families living below the LICO in the city of Toronto are: "14.4 percent of all the European groups, 29.6 percent for the East and Southeast Asians and Pacific Islanders, 32.1 percent of Aboriginals, 34.6 percent for South Asians, 41.4 percent for Latin Americans, 44.6 percent of Africans, Blacks and Caribbeans, and 45.2 percent of Arabs and West Asians" (Ornstein, 2000:97). These figures are very high and only hint at the degree of devastation in people's lives.

RACIALIZED WOMEN AND POVERTY

Yet, even these figures get worse when one focuses on women from racialized groups. The total numbers of racialized women increased by 50 percent from 1986 to 1996. In 1996, they were 11 percent of all women in Canada and 51 percent of all racialized group members (Galabuzi, 2006:126). In 1996, among racialized women between the ages of 15 and over, 17 percent had university degrees compared to 12 percent of other Canadian women. However, this high level of educational attainment did not translate into jobs with good incomes. Many, in fact, are unemployed. In 1996, only 53 percent of racialized women were employed or self-employed, compared to 63 percent of non-racialized women (Jennifer Chard quoted in Galabuzi, 2006:109). Using 1996 Census data, Galabuzi calculated that for racialized women, average earnings were $16,621 in 1996, compared to $23,635 for racialized men, $19,495 for other women, and $31,951 for other men (2006:91).

Racialized women are segregated into low-paying sectors and occupations. The work they do is often precarious employment that is part-time, contract, with little or no benefits. Many take on more than one job to survive. As a result, many racialized women make up the growing working poor in Canada. According to Galabuzi's calculations, "in 1995, 37% of racialized women lived below the low-income cut-off, compared with 19% for other women and 35% for racialized men" (2006:126–127). In addition to this national data, Punam Khosla's report titled *If Low-Income Women of Colour Counted in Toronto* (2003) provides important insight into the poverty among women of colour in Toronto:

> There are 1.3 million women living in Toronto and a good half of them are women of colour.... Women make up 60% of Toronto's caseload for Ontario Works, and are over-represented among low-wage earners living below the poverty line, including the unemployed and under-employed.... The median income of single parent families in Toronto fell by 17.7% during the nineties. Sole support mothers face deep poverty with incomes below the poverty line.... Recorded poverty rates for Ethiopian, Ghanaian, Somali, Tamil, Vietnamese, and Central American single mothers are well above eighty percent. (2003:19)

These figures signal a crisis. Instead of directly dealing with poverty specifically among women, racialized communities, and racialized women, the move is toward denial and erasure. Children's poverty is taken out of context of families and women living in poverty too. The rationalizations and denial legitimize the lack of any action to deal with this social injustice. Khosla reinforces this point:

> Masking single mothers as gender neutral: "lone parents," burying women in discussions of "families," and reducing the persistent concerns of all people of colour as only tempo-rary settlement issues facing recent immigrants, is more than mere word-play. It allows the insidious dismantling of important equity policies and programs to proceed [with] relatively little resistance. Generic proposals for change, which render those most seriously affected by growing poverty and inequality faceless and invisible, are unlikely to address their real needs. (2003:9)

In this way poverty in general, but specifically among women and racialized people, is reinforced and known as "structural poverty." This is feminized and racialized when it is combined with systemic gender and racial discrimination.

STRUCTURAL SOCIAL INEQUALITY

The term "structural" here implies issues or social problems that are built into our society. Institutions operate in a way that exclude people along class, gender, race, disability, sexual orientation, and other grounds. The cause of the problem then is not the individual but the structures of society. Usually this approach to social injustice does not place these different forms of exclusion in any hierarchy, but rather as intersecting in the total system of oppression within the Canadian capitalist economy.

All complex societies have a division of functions, so differentiation exists within society. However, differentiation does not automatically mean social stratification or social inequal-ity. Structured inequality includes the distribution of both material and symbolic resources in society that have critical consequences for individual lives. According to Celia S. Heller, "the term *structured* indicates an arrangement of elements: the inequality is not random but follows a pattern, displays relative constancy and stability, and is backed by ideas that legitimize and justify it. The various forms of patterning, the degree of stability, and the extent of institution-ization vary from one system to another" (1987:5). Consequences of structured inequality include the very chance to survive, the shelter one lives in, the quality of education, access to society's resources, and the way one can participate in society to provide a quality of life for oneself as an individual, for families, and for communities.

STRUCTURED GENDER DISCRIMINATION AND SOCIAL EXCLUSION

Structural inequality is both gendered and racialized. Initially, the issues of gender and social inequality were depersonalized and non-gendered by analyses that focused on *class* as *relation-ships* and *positions* in the social organization of production (Crompton and Mann, 1986:2–3). Eventually Marxist theory shifted to focus on "domestic labour":

> It has been argued (Dalla Costa, Himmelweit, Zaretsky) that even though production has been shifted from the home to the "public" sphere, women's labour in the home, (although not offered on the market) makes an indirect contribution to the extraction of surplus value from the working class as a whole. That is, by caring for and reproducing the labour force both on a day to day basis and over the generations, women's work reduces the overall cost of labour to capital. (Crompton and Mann, 1986:4)

In the 1970s and 1980s, the "dual-systems" theory emerged to treat capitalist and patriarchal structures (including racialized structures) as separate but interrelated systems: "Capitalist development creates the places for a hierarchy of workers, but traditional Marxist categories cannot tell us who will fill which places. Gender and racial hierarchies determine who fills the empty places" (Hartmann, 1976:18 quoted in Crompton and Mann, 1986:5). Women's social position and evaluation as human beings is structured by both the "public" and "private" spheres in society. This perspective emphasizes the importance of gender and race to an in-depth understanding of society and social inequality.

STRUCTURED RACIAL DISCRIMINATION AND SOCIAL EXCLUSION

Similarly, structured racial inequality begins with the social construction of race that is used to justify inequality. In *The Mismeasure of Man* (1981), Stephen Jay Gould documents the way superiority of the Caucasian standard was legitimated. The various grounds of justification included divine creation, Whites as a separate (and superior) biological species, the innate inferiority of non-White races, innate ability, and "scientific" racism, including IQ testing (1981:70–79 quoted in Wallis, 1998:25). However, the way the term "race" is used today in Canada to justify inequality tends to be more subtle and systemic.

The sophisticated form of racism that exists in Canada is known as "systemic racism." Here Frances Henry distinguishes between institutional and systemic racism:

> Institutional racism is manifested in the policies, practices, and procedures of various institutions, which may, directly or indirectly, consciously or unwittingly, promote, sustain, or entrench differential advantage or privilege for people of certain races.... Systemic racism, although similar to institutional racism, refers more broadly to the laws, rules, and norms woven into the social system that result in an unequal distribution of economic, political, and social resources and rewards among various racial groups. It is the denial of access, participation, and equity to racial minorities for services such as education, employment, and housing. (1995:48 quoted in Wallis, 1998:30–31)

Similarly, Tania Das Gupta highlights the lack of any "checks" or system of accountability with respect to racial discrimination (1996:12 quoted in Wallis, 1998:31). This process of racial exclusion now takes place without the use of the word "race."

Robert Miles suggests that systemic racism can be gauged from two sets of circumstances: "First, there are circumstances where exclusionary practices arise from, and therefore embody, a racist discourse but which may no longer be explicitly justified by such a discourse. Second, there are circumstances where an explicitly racist discourse is modified in such a way that the explicitly racist content is eliminated, but other words carry the original meaning" (Miles, 1989:84). In the Canadian context, the first set of circumstances Miles suggests can be illustrated by the example of explicit racism in Canadian immigration policy going underground by the adoption of the point system or the use of "neutral" categories such as language, education, and skills to select immigrants. An example of the second set of circumstances would be the criteria used in the past such as "continuous journey" (when this was impossible), or the discretionary use of "not suitable for the Canadian climate," and the current use of the word "terrorists" to eliminate or cause suspicion about certain groups of immigrants. These current forms and expressions of racialization are now also the focus of the Critical Race perspective:

> Critical anti-racism interrogates the historical institutionalization of racial discrimination through legal and customary sanctions that uphold the economic supremacy of one group or groups in society over another or others. The group(s) benefiting from this institutionally imposed privilege defend those institutionalized or normalized rules and sanctions by perpetuating them through systemic processes, policies, and practices. The resulting structures reproduce themselves and ensure that the processes of privilege production endure. (Loomba, 1998:20 quoted in Galabuzi, 2006:49–50)

In this way exclusion and privilege in Canada is institutionalized and systemically structured along race, gender, and class. The intersection of these three structural, exclusionary social processes—race, gender, class—is an important aspect of poverty in Canada.

The high levels of poverty among women and racialized groups including racialized women, coupled with the lack of policy attention to these issues, indicate a class, gender, and race war that is disguised in various ways, including as democratic racism (Henry et al., 1995). Systemic racism—the way institutional policies and society's assumptions work, without explicit racial intent, to exclude racialized groups—is increasing in Canada. The official denial of its existence further absolves individuals' and society's accountability and responsibility to address this grave injustice experienced by Canadian citizens. In the conclusion, we will address the vision and actions required to move forward to make democracy and freedom real and substantive for all Canadian citizens.

THE ORGANIZATION OF THE BOOK

In Part I some theoretical frameworks are presented to examine the racialization processes in Canada with attention to gender consequences. The social construction of "race" and its subsequent devaluation and marginalization has several consequences for racialized individuals, especially racialized women. In Part II, we will examine the economic consequences of "race" and gender. In Part III, we will examine how poverty, "race," and gender are criminalized. In addition to the economic consequences of "race" and gender, there are other social ways that racialized people, specifically women, are socially constructed to experience their lives as second-class Canadian citizens. In Part IV, we will examine some other consequences of the racialized and gendered nature of poverty. These consequences fundamentally affect people's quality of life. Then with the last article in this part, we begin our reflections, continued in the conclusion, on how we can address these structural forms of poverty in Canada.

BIBLIOGRAPHY

Crompton, R., and M. Mann. (eds.). (1986). *Gender and Stratification*. Cambridge: Polity Press.

Das Gupta, T. (1996). *Racism and Paid Work*. Toronto: Garamond Press.

Galabuzi, G.-E. (2006). *Canada's Economic Apartheid: The Social Exclusion of Racialized Groups in the New Century*. Toronto: Canadian Scholars' Press Inc.

Heller, C. (1987). *Structured Social Inequality: A Reader in Comparative Social Stratification*. New York: Macmillan Publishing Company.

Henry, F. et al. (1995). *The Colour of Democracy: Racism in Canadian Society*. Toronto: Harcourt Brace Canada.

Hermer, J., and J. Mosher. (eds.). (2002). *Disorderly People: Law and the Politics of Exclusion*. Halifax: Fernwood Publishing.

Khosla, P. (2003). *If Low-Income Women of Colour Counted in Toronto*. Toronto: Community Social Planning Council of Toronto (CSPT).

Miles, R. (1989). *Racism*. New York: Routledge.

National Council of Welfare. (1989–1999). *A New Poverty Line: Yes, No, or Maybe?* Retrieved from http://www.ncwcnbes.net/htmdocument/reportnewpovline/newpovline_e.htm.

National Council of Welfare. (2004). *Even Jobs Are No Guarantee against Poverty* [Press release].

Ornstein, M. (2000). *Ethno-racial Inequality in the City of Toronto: An Analysis of the 1996 Census*. Toronto: City of Toronto. http://ceris.metropolis.net.

Townson, M. (2000). *A Report Card on Women and Poverty*. Ottawa: Canadian Centre for Policy Alternatives.

Wallis, M. (1998). *The Social Imaginary of Systemic Racism Versus the Human Spirit: "Back of the Bus" Social Practices and the Aesthetics of Everyday Resistance*. Doctoral dissertation, York University, Canada.

Yalnizyan, A. (2007). *The Rich and the Rest of Us: The Changing Face of Canada's Growing Gap*. Ottawa: Canadian Centre for Policy Alternatives.

PART ONE

Theoretical Framework

OBJECTIVES

To understand the social value of "race" in Canada and its economic consequences

To understand the social processes that create an "immigrant"

To critically reflect on issues of "diversity" and how it continues to shape Canadian society

To critically analyze how arbitrary criteria for establishing "Indianness" created both control over all Aboriginal peoples and White supremacy and privilege simultaneously

INTRODUCTION

To comprehend the consequences of poverty among racialized and Aboriginal communities, and especially the women in these communities, it is essential to examine the social construction of "race." Racialized communities, Aboriginal peoples, and other groups such as people with disabilities and gays and lesbians are categorized as "Other" and then assessed as "inferior." This social stigmatization and devaluation is then legitimized in various ways.

In this part some theoretical frameworks are presented to examine the racialization processes in Canada with attention to gender consequences. The part begins with Peter Li's article in Chapter 1, which makes the argument that there is a social hierarchy of races, and this hierarchy is associated with unequal earnings in the labour market, with those of European origin having higher average earnings than non-White Canadians. Using quantitative analysis from Statistics Canada's data, Peter Li theorizes the link between the social value of "race" in Canada and the resulting devaluation—the market value of "race."

This analysis of social structures in Canadian society explains the way racial inequality and poverty are socially reproduced and legitimized in Canada in the way that non-White origin creates a penalty for all visible minorities, both native-born or foreign-born, in the Canadian labour market.

Rose Folson, in Chapter 2, provides a perspective into the social construction of the experience of an "immigrant," in particular women immigrants. She provides an overview of the research of scholars of migration studies and notes that they agree that different groups of migrants are regulated by a matrix of economic, political, sexual, and cultural factors. These theories of migration help contextualize the Canadian construction of an immigrant woman. Folson's perspective also traces the linkages between "race," "immigrant," gender, and poverty. She argues that Western countries, including Canada, still hold a constructed image of being exclusively White nations, despite the presence of a large number of non-White citizens. White immigrants are often constructed as citizens, while non-White citizens are constructed as immigrants. Drawing also on the work of Roxana Ng, Folson further argues that migrant women in Canada are systematically constructed as someone who is dependent on a spouse or other sponsor and has no access to language schools or to professional advancement institutions. This process is a sure path to the creation of a "type" of woman who becomes part of an unskilled, cheap, exploitable labour force. As a result, the social construction of the immigrant women—one who is socially devalued and economically exploited—is complete.

In Chapter 3, Yasmeen Abu-Laban and Christina Gabriel examine Canada's policies of immigration, employment equity, and multiculturalism to examine how "diversity" in Canada is socially constructed. The authors argue that under the initial call in 1986 that "multiculturalism means business," the policy focus since the 1990s especially emphasized the economic exploitation of Canada's racial and ethnic diversity to capture markets at home and abroad at the probable expense of gender equality and other equity initiatives. For example, this market-oriented emphasis effectively sidelines issues of systemic discrimination that employment equity was intended to address. These trends they call "selling diversity" can and are being resisted. Transnational struggles open the possibility of being linked to peoples and struggles in other parts of the world to add new dimensions to the sense of citizenship rights, belonging, identity, and social justice. Such struggles challenge a profoundly narrow vision of diversity that, the authors argue, is basically a selling out of an agenda based on pursuing substantive equality for those marginalized by race/ethnicity, gender, and class. In this way local and global resistances offer alternative visions of equality and justice and illuminate the fact that "selling diversity" is but one approach to chart in the 21st century.

Finally, in Chapter 4, the last article in this part, Bonita Lawrence critically analyzes Canadian legislation under which Aboriginal peoples must organize their lives. She argues that a central aspect of the colonization process in Canada was breaking the power of Aboriginal women within their nations. As a result of arbitrary regulations and standards of "Indianness," Aboriginal communities have had to invent themselves as new groupings of individuals with no organic link to one another in settings that are often radically different from their places of origin. In this way the very existence of White settler societies is therefore predicated on maintaining racial apartheid, on emphasizing racial difference, both White superiority and Native inferiority. According to Lawrence, the extent of penalties and lack of compensation for losses suffered by Indian women is "retribution, not restitution," what Justice Bora Laskin, in his dissenting opinion in *Lavell and Bedard*, termed "statutory banishment." This alienation from Native culture transformed Native women's rights as "individual rights" and not collective Native rights that must survive colonization. Lawrence concludes that because the subordination of Aboriginal women has been a central nexus through which colonizers have sought to destroy Aboriginal societies, contemporary gender divisions created by the colonizer continue to subvert sovereignty struggles in Canada today.

The four articles in this first part provide an insight into "structural" poverty by demonstrating the historical and contemporary social relations that construct "race," "immigrant," "diversity," and "Indianness." Race and gender are evaluated as inferior in Canadian society, and in the next part we will focus specifically on the economic consequences of this devaluation and social marginalization.

CHAPTER ONE

The Market Value and Social Value of Race

Peter S. Li

The notion of *race* is commonly accepted as an ascribed feature of people in that it signifies certain physical and cultural characteristics which are associated with people at birth. One of these characteristics is skin colour, which is often seen to provide a logical basis for classifying people, and for understanding why people behave differently. In reality, there is nothing rational about using superficial physical features to sort people into groups. Thus, the social import of race has to do with society giving significance to people according to selective phenotypic characteristics, and treating the resulting groupings as though they are naturally constituted in and of themselves.

The process by which society attributes social significance to groups on superficial physical grounds is referred to by social scientists as *racialization*; people so marked may be referred to as racialized minorities in terms of their relation to a dominant group, which has the power to set the terms and conditions of racial accommodation. Over time, racialization systematically pairs superficial features of people with social characteristics that are often undesirable to give the false appearance that the social import of race comes from a natural origin, and not society's attribution.

This paper shows that racialization, or the social construction of race, produces two major outcomes in Canadian society. First, there is a social hierarchy of races, which is manifested in Canadians' view of which groups are socially desirable or undesirable according to racial origin. Second, racial groupings are associated with unequal earnings in the labour market, with those of European origin having higher average earning than non-White Canadians. The disparity persists even after intergroup differences in schooling and other factors are taken into account. The social value and market value associated with racial origins are indications of how a society has developed concrete manifestations of what otherwise would be an abstract notion of race.

RACE AND ITS SOCIAL AND MARKET VALUE

Many authors have pointed out that there is no scientific basis to justify using superficial features such as skin colour to categorize people as though the resulting groupings are logical genetic classifications (Rex, 1983:1–5; Miles, 1989:41–50; Bolaria and Li, 1988:14–25). However, since the term *race* is used both as a folk and scientific concept, there is confusion between the phenotypic traits used to justify the construction of race on the one hand, and the social attributes given to racial groupings on the other (Banton, 1979). Some authors prefer to use the term *social race* to highlight the fact that selected phenotypic attributes are important only in the social construction of racial categories, but otherwise trivial in genetic classifications (Banton, 1979; Miles, 1989:69–73). In other words, physical and cultural traits of people being racialized take on special meanings such that race becomes what Banton (1979:129) calls a "role sign," and that superficial physical variations serve as markers of racial roles.

In short, while superficial physical features of people do not provide the scientific grounds for classifying them into logical genetic groups, phenotypic features are used in the social construction of race. Over time, as it becomes socially acceptable to consider people on racial grounds, physical and cultural characteristics which are originally trivial become socially significant, since they represent convenient markers by which people and groups, and their implied characteristics, can be distinguished.

To the extent that it is socially meaningful to regard people on racial grounds, it implies that society has attributed normative values and expectations to people of certain identifiable features that are primordial in origin. Such a normative scheme provides people with a rationale and a guide for evaluating race and racial origin. Over time, as certain ideas of race take root in the minds and hearts of people, and as social actions continue to reflect the meaning of race, the normative order associated with race becomes a part of the culture which people internalize in their way of life and perpetuate through socialization.

The racially based normative order is also manifested in many aspects of life; for example, as racism in the ideological realm and as social practice embedded in social institutions of society. In short, racialization makes it socially meaningful to regard people on racial grounds, and it attributes social value to people according to racial origin. In this sense, race can be considered as having a social value, not so much as deriving from the essential nature of race, but from society's placing relative social worth on superficial physical and cultural characteristics of people.

The social worth placed on race is only one manifestation of how race has assumed social importance in the lives of people. After all, the idea of race cannot sustain itself as a meaningful concept unless it is also supported by social actions which reflect the relevance of race. In this respect, racial ideas and social practices mutually reinforce each other. Thus, in addition to its articulation in the ideological domain, race can be manifested as a social feature in politics, the economy, and other aspects of society.

One social context in which the relevance of race is articulated is the labour market. The unequal market worth given to people of different racial origins is one indication of how the labour market has come to recognize the relative economic value of race. In this sense, race can be seen as having a market value in that the origin of some people adversely affects their economic returns in the labour market, while that of others improves the outcomes of their market participation. Hence, the earning differentials attributed to race provide a basis for assessing the market worth of race in a society which upholds its social importance.

THE SOCIAL VALUE OF RACE

Historically, Canada has maintained discriminatory policies and practices towards people of certain racial origins, with the result that the racial origin of members of such groups and their social conditions became inseparable in defining the meaning of race. In this way, race was given social importance in that it provided the ground for segregating people for differential treatment as well as for justifying such actions. The history of Canadian Aboriginal peoples, for example, was characterized by the domination of Europeans, which led to the destruction of their livelihood and the loss of autonomy (Patterson, 1972). The Indian Act of 1876 legalized the distinction between Indians and the rest of the population, since the Act formally established what Indian status was, and placed Indians under the legislative and administrative control of the state. With the decline of the fur trade and agricultural expansion into western Canada, the Aboriginal peoples lost further control over their land, their livelihood, and their political future. Even today, the marginal social and economic position of Aboriginal peoples in Canadian society makes them dependent on the state for survival (Frideres, 1993; Satzewich and Wotherspoon, 1993). Thus, the term *Indians* or *Native peoples* becomes associated not only with a racial origin of a remote past, but also signifies a contemporary people which is economically deprived, socially marginal, and politically militant. Canada's past policies and treatment of Asian Canadians also reflect how the public and the state resorted to using the notion of a foreign race to manage and control a marginalized segment of the population (Li, 1998). Throughout the latter half of the nineteenth century and early twentieth century, Asians in Canada were viewed as an inferior race, with loathsome values, customs, and behavioural standards that would corrupt the morality and culture of Europeans (Anderson, 1991; Li, 1998; Roy, 1989; Satzewich, 1989). By the early part of the twentieth century, the notion of Asians in general, and Chinese in particular, as racially distinct and culturally inferior was well entrenched in the ideology and practice of Canada; as well, the view of a racial hierarchy that favours Occidental culture and the White race was prevalent in Canadian society (Anderson, 1991; Berger, 1981; Li, 1998). Canada's historical treatment of racial minorities has imputed many deep-seated symbols and meanings to the notion of race in Canadian society. However, in the decades after the Second World War, Canada also developed legal protection and public policies to safeguard basic human rights. Some of the major statutes include the Canadian Charter of Rights and Freedoms in Part I of the Constitution Act of 1982 (Statutes of Canada, 1982, c. 11), the Employment Equity Act of 1986 (Statutes of Canada, 1986, c. 31), and the Multiculturalism Act of 1988 (Statutes of Canada, 1988, c. 31). These statutes in particular formally affirm the fundamental rights of the individual to equality without discrimination; the Multiculturalism Act endorses the policy of the federal government to recognize and to promote cultural and racial diversity of Canadian society as the individual's freedom of choice. At the same time, there are some indications that racialized minority groups, such as the Chinese and Japanese, which historically were marginalized and discriminated, have been upwardly mobile in terms of educational level and occupation status (Li, 1990). As well, the First Nations became more assertive in their claims of Aboriginal recognition and constitutional entitlement in the post-war decades; consequently, they have gained some political concessions from both federal and provincial governments when it comes to Aboriginal title and Aboriginal rights (Boldt, Long, and Little Bear, 1985). On the surface, it would appear that the post-war social conditions are more favourable towards racial minorities than the historical ones. As a result, the social import of race may have receded as human rights are entrenched in Canadian society.

Some authors have argued that despite the legal protection of human rights and the general acceptance of the principle of equality in Canadian society, racism continues to be manifested in the ideas of people and in practices of social institutions (Henry et al., 1995; Li, 1995; Zong, 1994). Henry et al. (1995:17) use the term *democratic racism* to refer to the contradictory way in which racist ideologies are articulated in Canadian society, which also upholds egalitarian values of justice and fairness. Democratic principles and racist ideologies can co-exist, especially when some people rely upon their stereotypes of race to make sense of their everyday experiences, since they provide the grounds for simplistic but convenient explanations of complex economic and social problems. Ironically, the entrenchment of individual rights and freedoms in Canadian society in the post-war decades also gives added legal ammunition to extremists to advocate racial supremacism in the name of freedom of speech (Li, 1995). As Canadians face an uncertain future due to economic re-structuring, it is appealing to accept a rationale which allows those who feel their traditional economic and social security being eroded to blame racial minorities and immigrants for their woes (Li, 1995). In this way, the historical construction of race in Canada is given contemporary reality, as it offers a simplistic but meaningful solution to people in dealing with the hardships and contradictions they face (Li, 1995).

There is substantial empirical evidence to indicate that Canadians continue to attribute unequal social worth to people of different racial origin despite the public's awareness and general acceptance of democratic principles of equality and justice. For example, Berry, Kalin, and Taylor (1976) reported data from a 1974 national survey to show that Canadians tended to rank people of European origin much higher than racial minorities in terms of whether they were considered "hardworking," "important," "Canadian," "clean," "likable," "interesting," and other qualities. Among the groups with the lowest ranking were "Chinese," "Canadian Indian," "Negro," "East Indian" (Berry, Kalin, and Taylor, 1976:106).

Other studies have also produced evidence to show that Canadians tend to project a lower social image on racial minorities (Driedger and Peters, 1977; Filson, 1983; Li, 1979; Pineo, 1977; Richmond, 1974). For example, Pineo (1977) reported findings from a national study to show that English Canadians regarded "Negroes," "Coloureds," "Canadian Indians," "Chinese," and "Japanese" to have the lowest social standing, while French Canadians gave "Chinese," "Negroes," "Coloureds," and "Japanese" the lowest social ranks. Filson (1983) indicated that Canadian respondents in a 1977 national survey showed most hostility towards immigrants from India and Pakistan, followed by those from the West Indies; in contrast British and American immigrants received the least hostility. Foschi and Buchan (1990) studied perceptions of university male subjects to see how much they perceived their partner as competent to perform a task on the basis of the racial origin of the partner, and found that the subjects were more influenced from a partner portrayed as White than from one portrayed as East Indian.

In 1991, a national attitudinal survey was conducted by Angus Reid Group on behalf of Multiculturalism and Citizenship Canada to find out how Canadians felt about multiculturalism and ethnic diversity (Angus Reid Group Inc., 1991). The results indicate strong public support for various elements of the Multiculturalism Policy; as well, they suggest the notion of race is meaningful to Canadians in two major ways. First, as many as 45 percent of the respondents agreed that discrimination against non-Whites is a problem in Canada, and 36 percent agreed that it is more difficult for non-Whites to be successful in Canadian society than Whites (Angus Reid Group, 1991:50). In other words, a substantial segment of the general population thought that race was a barrier for non-Whites in Canadian society. Second, respondents themselves displayed different degrees of "comfort" towards individuals of various ethnic groups. Ethnic groups of European origin had higher social rankings than those of non-White origin, mostly Asians and Blacks, in terms of having a larger percentage of respondents report the highest comfort levels while being with them (Table 1.1). For example, 83 percent of respondents said they had the highest comfort levels with immigrants of British origin, as compared to 69 percent who said so for Chinese, and 48 percent for Indo-Pakistani. The lower rankings of non-White ethnic groups relative to White ethnic groups held true irrespective of whether individuals of the group being evaluated were immigrants or native-born. This kind of public opinion surveys indicates that racial minorities have a lower social standing in Canadian society than those of European origin.

The same survey also indicates that Canadians showed contradictory tendencies with respect to the principle of equality and support of minority rights. For example, 85 percent of the respondents indicated that they support a multiculturalism policy which promotes equality among all Canadians, regardless of racial or ethnic origin (Angus Reid Group, 1991:24). At the same time, 28 percent of the people surveyed said "people who come to Canada should change to be more like us" (Angus Reid Group, 1991:35). Another survey, conducted by Ekos Research Associates in 1994, found that most respondents agreed that there are too many immigrants, especially from visible minority groups, and 60 percent of respondents agreed that "too many immigrants feel no obligation to adapt to Canadian values and way of life" (*Globe and Mail*, 1994). These results confirm that a segment of the Canadian public sees visible minorities as being the major problem of immigration, and that their alleged unwillingness to adapt to Canadian values and lifestyle is threatening Canadians' traditional way of life.

The findings from the foregoing studies also suggest that despite the existence of multicultural policy and the legal entrenchment of human rights in the post-war decades, Canadians continue to consider it meaningful to use race as a basis to evaluate the social standing, competence, and desirability of others.

THE MARKET VALUE OF RACE

The social importance of race is manifested in many facets of life in Canadian society. One such facet is in the labour market, where race affects the opportunities of individuals and their economic outcomes. Many studies have reported findings which indicate that there are differences in occupation and earnings associated with the racial and ethnic origin of Canadians. Historically, members of racialized minorities, such as the Chinese, were systematically paid less than White workers, and they were hired in labour-intensive projects when White workers were hard to find (Li, 1998). But as soon as White workers became readily available, Chinese labourers became the targets of racial exclusion and were blamed for taking away the jobs of White Canadians and depressing their wages (Li, 1998).

Porter's systematic study of the relationship between ethnic origin and occupational status shows that certain racial and ethnic groups were underrepresented in professional, managerial, and technical occupations, but overrepresented in labouring jobs, and that the occupational disadvantages associated with racial and ethnic origins persisted from 1931 to 1961, the period being studied (Porter, 1965). A number of people have reconsidered Porter's thesis and have since found that he overstated the magnitude of the relationship between ethnic affiliation and social class (Brym with Fox, 1989; Darroch, 1979). However, despite disagreements over the precise magnitude of influence of ethnic origin on socio-economic performance, many studies have shown that race affects one's market outcomes such that non-Whites are often disadvantaged in occupational status and earnings (Lautard and Loree, 1984; Lautard and Guppy, 1990; Li, 1988; Satzewich and Li, 1987; Geschwender, 1994).

TABLE 1.1

Ranking of Selected Immigrant Ethnic Groups and Canadian-Born Ethnic Groups According to the Percent of Respondents Who Indicated Having the Highest Comfort Levels Being around Individuals from Each Group

	RESPONDENTS INDICATING THE HIGHEST COMFORT LEVELS TOWARD:	
ORIGIN BEING EVALUATED	IMMIGRANT ETHNIC GROUP (%)	CANADIAN-BORN ETHNIC GROUP (%)
British	83	86
Italian	77	83
French	74	82
Jewish	74	78
Ukrainian	73	79
German	72	79
Portuguese	70	76
Chinese	69	77
Native Canadian	—	77
West Indian Black	61	69
Moslem	49	59
Arab	52	63
Indo-Pakistani	48	59
Sikh	43	55

Source: Multiculturalism and Canadians: Attitude Study 1991 National Survey Report, submitted by Angus Reid Group, Inc. to Multiculturalism and Citizenship Canada, August, 1991, p. 51.

For example, using data from the 1981 Census, Li (1988) showed that Canadians of European origin had an income advantage over those of Black origin or Chinese origin, even after differences in education and other factors had been taken into account. Data from the 1986 Census also indicated that an earning disadvantage was associated with non-White origin, while an advantage was linked to White origin, despite controlling for social class, and adjusting for differences in education and other variables (Li, 1992). Non-White women in particular were most affected by income disadvantage that could be attributed to race and gender (Li, 1992). These studies show that there is a market value being attached to racial origin, and that people of different origins are being remunerated in unequal terms in the Canadian labour market.

The 1991 Census provides further evidence for estimating the market value of race. The 1991 Census allowed respondents to be classified according to whether they belong to the visible minority category or not. A person is defined as belonging to the visible minority category if the person claims a single or multiple origin of the following groups: Black, South Asian, Chinese, Korean Japanese, South East Asian, Filipino, Other Pacific Islanders, West Asian, and Arab and Latin American (Statistics Canada, 1994b:56). On the basis of the 1991 Census data on origin, respondents can be classified as White Canadians, visible minority, and Aboriginal peoples.

The 1991 Census shows that White Canadians account for 87 percent of the total population; Aboriginal peoples, 3.7 percent; and visible minorities, 9.3 percent. White Canadians and visible minorities can be further classified into those born in Canada (native-born) and those born outside of Canada (foreign-born).

The data show that there are marked income differences among these groups. For example, the average earnings for Aboriginal peoples is $5,992 below the national mean of $23,740, and that for native-born and foreign-born visible minorities is $4,894 and $2,710 below the mean, respectively. In contrast, foreign-born White Canadians' average income is $4,171 above the national average; and native-born White Canadians earn just marginally below the national average.

Although these income disparities indicate how much each group actually earns on average in the labour market, some of the differences are due to groups having unequal levels of education and other individual and market characteristics. However, when inter-group differences in education, age, gender, occupation, industry of work, and duration of work have been statistically adjusted, the data still show that there are residual income differences that can be attributed to the racial origin and nativity of groups. Foreign-born visible minorities have the lowest average income, which is over $3,000 below the national average, followed by the income of Aboriginal peoples, which stands at $1,122 below the mean. As well, native-born visible minorities also have below average earnings, but not to the same extent as those born outside of Canada. White Canadians, both foreign-born and native-born, show an income advantage over other groups.

It should be pointed out that the gross income differences are the actual income disparities among the various groups, and the statistics clearly show that non-White Canadians, irrespective of nativity, earn less than White Canadians. However, some of the earning disparities can be attributed to differences in educational levels and other demographic and market factors. Thus, the net differences are produced under the hypothetical condition that the five racial groups have similar levels in other variables, and the residual earning gaps can be attributed to racial origins as defined by nativity and origin. The net differences suggest that native-born visible minorities would have less income disadvantage if they were to have the same educational level and the same average demographic and market characteristics as others. Similarly, foreign-born visible minorities would have earned less if their educational level were not higher than others, and their other characteristics were not the same as other groups.

About 87 percent of White Canadians were native-born, whereas about 86 percent of visible minorities were foreign-born. These demographic differences reflect the historical bias in the immigration system in favouring European immigrants over those from Asia and Africa, and that it was only after the changes in the immigration policy of 1967 that racial minorities were able to immigrate to Canada under the same selection criteria as others. The unequal demographic distribution between White Canadians and visible minorities means that comparisons between the two groups are necessarily confounded by nativity. Furthermore, in a society which evaluates racial minorities on a lower standing than the White majority, there are many grounds to believe that visible minority status and foreign-born status together would produce an interaction effect, placing persons in this situation at a greater disadvantage than the sum total disadvantage of what nativity and race would produce. For example, foreign accents would affect non-White immigrants more negatively than White immigrants due to the unequal way racial origin is being evaluated in Canadian society (Scassa, 1994). These subtle differences would explain why there are substantial earnings disparities between foreign-born and native-born visible minorities. Even though both groups earn less than the average when other differences are accounted for, foreign status probably interacts with racial origin in such a way as to make it easier for racial minorities to be discriminated against on the basis of language problems, the lack of Canadian experience, and other stereotypes about many alleged incapacities of non-White immigrants. In the case of native-born visible minorities, discrimination on the grounds of language and Canadian experiences become more difficult to justify.

The data indicate that, even before any differences in education and other factors are taken into account, all non-White groups, whether of visible minority or Aboriginal origin, have average earnings which fall below the national average; in most cases the differentials are substantial. White Canadians, except those with South European origins (such as Greek, Portuguese, and Spanish), have average income levels above the national average. These differences are actual disparities among groups according to origin. Again, some of the income gaps are probably due to differences in the levels of human capital and demographic characteristics of the groups.

When inter-group differences in education, occupation, industry of work, and other job-related features are artificially adjusted, non-White groups still have income levels substantially below the national average. For example, those of Latin American origin have an average income $5,894 below the Canadian average, while those of Arab or West Asian origin have earnings over $4,000 below the national mean. As well, those of Chinese, Filipino, or Vietnamese origin earn, on average, over $3,000 less than what an average Canadian earns, even after educational and other differences have been accounted for.

Although all visible minorities earn less than the national average after inter-group differences are adjusted, some earn more than before while others earn less. For example, the Chinese and the Arabs earn even less, and those of Filipino, Vietnamese, Latin American, or Black origin earn relatively more after other variations are controlled. One reason for these changes has to do with the differences in educational levels of various groups. The reason that some groups, such as the Chinese, earn more before controlling for other variations is because they have relatively high educational levels. But when their educational level is assumed to be the same as the national average, they suffer a larger income disadvantage. In other words, the reason the Chinese earn only $2,074 (gross) less than the national average is because they have higher average education; but if their educational advantage is removed, then they would earn even less (net). Conversely, a group such as Blacks earn less than the national average in part because of their relatively low education level. When their educational level is assumed to be the same as others, their income improves, but not to the extent that it matches the national average. The data are unequivocal in showing that non-White origin creates a penalty for all visible minorities in the labour market.

In contrast, White Canadians tend to have an average income level above the national average, except for those of certain Southern European and Eastern European origins. For example, those of Polish, Greek, or Spanish origin show an income disadvantage that is over $1,000 below the national average. However, those of Portuguese origin show an income advantage of $2,451 after other differences are adjusted, suggesting that some of the original income disadvantage may be due to their lower educational level and other demographic variations. It is not entirely clear why some European groups from southern and eastern Europe earn less than those from western and northern Europe, although in the past, those from southern and eastern Europe also tended to do less well than those from western European origin in occupational status and income level (Porter, 1965; Li, 1988). By and large, White Canadians' average income tends to be above the national mean. Even in those European-origin groups whose income falls below the average, the deviation tends to be much less than non-White Canadians.

These data clearly indicate that there are unequal market values associated with different racial origins in the Canadian labour market. Since these income differentials are maintained after adjusting for other differences, it can be said that non-White Canadians, both Aboriginal peoples and visible minorities, are penalized in terms of receiving a lower income that is attributed to their origin. By comparison, most White Canadians enjoy an income premium due to their origin.

Pendakur and Pendakur (1996) also analyzed the 1991 Census data using a different model, but came to similar conclusions with respect to earning disparities between White Canadians and visible minority Canadians. The authors wrote: "Even when controlling for occupation, industry, education, potential experience, CMA (Census Metropolitan Area), official language knowledge and household type, we find that visible minorities earn significantly less than native-born White workers in Canada" (Pendakur and Pendakur, 1996:19).

Many other studies have produced evidence to suggest that life chances for various racial and ethnic groups are not the same, and that visible minorities such as Asians and Blacks have lower earning returns in the Canadian labour market than White Canadians (Reitz and Breton, 1994; Satzewich and Li, 1987; Abella, 1984). Several factors have been identified as creating barriers of employment and social mobility for non-White Canadians, especially those who are immigrants. These factors include the difficulty faced by many non-White immigrants in having their credentials fully recognized in Canada (McDade, 1988), and employment discrimination against racial minorities with identifiable linguistic characteristics and racial features (Henry and Ginsberg, 1985; Henry, 1989; Scassa, 1994).

The point about foreign credentials was also made by Basavarajappa and Verma (1985), who, based on their analysis of Asian immigrants in Canada in the 1981 Census, argued that the insistence by employers on having Canadian experience as a condition of employment and the fact that foreign credentials were not being fully recognized would explain why Asian immigrants were less likely to be in professional and managerial jobs despite their relatively high educational attainment. Rajagopal (1990) produced data from the 1986 Census to indicate that although Indo-Canadians in Ontario were more likely than the general population in Toronto to have completed university, Indo-Canadians in Toronto had a lower annual income level than immigrants and non-immigrants in Toronto. Rajagopal (1990) suggested that one of the barriers had to do with Indo-Canadians' foreign credentials being highly discounted or not recognized by business and educational institutions, and evaluators using prejudicial opinions and not objective criteria in assessing Indian applicants.

Henry and Ginsberg (1985) conducted a field study in Toronto and found that non-White Canadians were less likely to be hired than White Canadians in the Toronto job market. Their study used matched Black and White job seekers to apply for entry positions advertised in a newspaper, and White job seekers received three times more job offers than Black job seekers. Furthermore, Henry and Ginsberg (1985) reported that telephone callers with an Asian or Caribbean accent were often screened out when they called about a job vacancy. A follow-up study of employers and personnel managers of large businesses and corporations in Toronto revealed that 28 percent of the respondents felt that racial minorities had less ability than White Canadians to meet performance criteria (Billingsley and Muszynski, 1986).

Beside direct job discrimination, Canadians of non-White origin often face other obstacles in the labour market. Scassa (1994) argued that non-native speakers of the dominant language encounter discrimination in employment and in access to services because of their language characteristics, and that their lack of fluency, their accent of speech, and their deviation from the language standard of the dominant group can be used as bases of unfavourable treatment and as surrogates of racial discrimination. Ethnographic accounts by immigrant women in Fredericton also indicated that their accent and "colour" set them apart from mainstream society, despite their ability to speak English (Miedema and Nason-Clark, 1989). These studies offer some explanations as to how those of non-White origins are associated with a lower market value; in essence, it has much to do with racial minorities being disadvantaged in the labour market as a result of racial discrimination, or differential treatment based on superficial differences.

CONCLUSION

Superficial physical differences such as skin colour do not provide sound scientific grounds for classifying people into logical genetic groupings. Nevertheless, phenotypic traits are used in the social construction of race, with the result that superficial physical and cultural characteristics are systematically associated with social features to produce racial categories which are meaningful to people. Canada has a long history of maintaining discriminatory policies and practices towards Canadians deemed to be racial minorities based on skin colour and other superficial features. Over time, differential treatment and unfavourable polices targeted towards racial minorities became in themselves identifiable characteristics of these groups. In this way, superficial characteristics of racial minorities are inseparable from unfavourable social features attributed to them. Throughout the nineteenth and twentieth centuries, White people, mainly of European origin, were socially accepted in Canadian society as more desirable than non-White minorities.

There is substantial evidence to indicate that this is still the case today. Canadian society continues to attribute unequal social value to people of different origins. Many studies have shown that Canadians regard non-White minorities as socially less desirable and less favourable than people of European origin, and that the notion of race remains meaningful to many people as a means to make sense of their everyday experiences.

Several studies have also indicated that there are unequal market values attached to various racial origins, and that people of non-White origin suffer an income disadvantage in the labour market, while those of European origin enjoy an income advantage that can be attributed to their origin. Data from the 1991 Census confirm that such a hierarchy of market value exists in accordance to White and non-White racial origins, and that non-White groups suffer an income penalty while most White Canadians receive an income premium as a result of their racial origin. Other studies have argued that discrimination based on racial origin, language standard, and credentials tends to adversely affect the job opportunities or racial minorities. Consequently, they suffer from having lower remuneration as a result of their racial origin being negatively evaluated and discounted in the Canadian labour market.

Finally, it should be recognized that the social value and market value attached to racial origin are related. It can be seen that economic disadvantages associated with certain racial origins reinforce their low social standing since people so marked carry a lower market worth. In the long run, economic disparities according to racial origins help to maintain the social reality of race by giving a discounted market value to certain racial groups. In turn, the low social value given to certain racial origins creates obstacles which further limit the market outcomes for people racialized.

ACKNOWLEDGMENT

Research for this paper was funded by a grant from the Social Sciences and Humanities Research Council of Canada. The 1991 Census data used in this paper are based on the 1991 Public Use Microdata File on Individuals supplied by Statistics Canada and made available to the author through the University Library of the University of Saskatchewan as a member of a consortium of the Canadian Association of Research Libraries. The author is solely responsible for the use and interpretation of the Census data. The helpful comments of Vic Satzewich and three anonymous reviewers are gratefully acknowledged.

REFERENCES

Abella, Rosalie S. 1984. *Report of the Royal Commission on Equality in Employment.* Ottawa: Minister of Supply and Services.

Anderson, Kay J. 1991. *Vancouver's Chinatown: Racial Discourse in Canada, 1875–1980.* Montreal and Kingston: McGill-Queen's University Press.

Angus Reid Group. 1991. *Multiculturalism and Canadians: Aattitude Study 1991 National Survey Report.* Submitted to Multiculturalism and Citizenship Canada.

Banton, Michael. 1979. "Analytical and folk concepts of race and ethnicity." *Ethnic and Racial Studies* 2:127–138.

Basavarajappa, K.G., and R.B.P. Verma. 1985. "Asian immigrants in Canada: Some

findings from 1981 Census." *International Migration* 23(1):97–121.

Berger, Thomas R. 1981. *Fragile Freedoms: Human Rights and Dissent in Canada.* Toronto and Vancouver: Clarke, Irwin and Company Limited.

Berry, John W., Rudolf Kalin, and Donald Taylor. 1976. *Multiculturalism and Ethnic Attitudes in Canada.* Ottawa: Minister of Supply and Services Canada.

Billingsley, B., and L. Muszynski. 1986. *No Discrimination Here.* Toronto: Social Planning Council of Metro Toronto and the Urban Alliance on Race Relations.

Bolaria, B. Singh, and Peter S. Li. 1988. *Racial Oppression in Canada,* 2nd edition. Toronto: Garamond Press.

Boldt, Menno, J. Anthony Long, and Leroy Little Bear. 1985. *The Quest for Justice: Aboriginal Peoples and Aboriginal Rights.* Toronto: University of Toronto Press.

Brym, Robert J., with Bonnie J. Fox. 1989. *From Culture to Power: The Sociology of English Canada.* Don Mills, Ontario: Oxford University Press Canada.

Darroch, Gordon A. 1979. "Another look at ethnicity, stratification and and mobility in Canada." *Canadian Journal of Sociology* 4(1): 1–25.

Driedger, Leo, and Jacob Peters. 1977. "Identity and social distance." *Canadian Review of Sociology and Anthropology* 14(2):158–173.

Filson, Glen. 1983. "Class and ethnic differences in Canadian's attitudes to native people's rights and immigrants." *Canadian Review of Sociology and Anthropology* 20(4):454–482.

Foschi, Martha, and Sari Buchan. 1990. "Ethnicity, gender, and perceptions of task competence." *Canadian Journal of Sociology* 15(1):1–18.

Frideres, James S. 1993. *Native Peoples in Canada: Contemporary Conflicts*, 4th edition. Scarborough, Ontario: Prentice-Hall.

Geschwender, James A. 1994. "Married women's waged labor and racial/ethnic sreatification in Canada." *Canadian Ethnic Studies* 26(3):53–73.

Globe and Mail. 1994. "Canadians showing signs of cultural insecurity." March 11, A6.

Henry, Francis. 1989. *Who Gets the Work in 1989?* Ottawa: Economic Council of Canada.

Henry, Francis, and Effie Ginsberg. 1985. *Who Gets the Work? A Test of Racial Discrimination in Employment.* Toronto: Social Planning Council of Metro Toronto and the Urban Alliance on Race Relations.

Henry, Francis, Carol Tator, Winston Mattis, and Tim Rees. 1995. *The Colour of Democracy: Racism in Canadian Society.* Toronto: Harcourt Brace & Company, Canada.

Lautard, Hugh, and Neil Guppy. 1990. "The vertical mosaic revisited: Occupational differentials among Canadian ethnic groups." In Peter S. Li, ed., *Race and Ethnic Relations in Canada,* pp. 189–208. Toronto: Oxford University Press.

Lautard, Hugh, and Donald J. Loree. 1984. "Ethnic stratification in Canada, 1931–1971." *Canadian Journal of Sociology* 9:333–343.

Li, Peter S. 1979. "Prejudice against Asians in a Canadian City." *Canadian Ethnic Studies* 11(2):70–77.

———. 1988. *Ehtnic Inequality in a Class Society.* Toronto: Thompson Educational.

———. 1990. "The emergence of the new middle class among Chinese in Canada." *Asian Culture* 14 (April):187–194.

———. 1992. "Race and gender as bases of class fractions and their effects on earnings." *Canadian Review of Sociology and Anthropology* 29(4):488–510.

———. 1995. "Racial supremacism under social democracy." *Canadian Ethnic Studies* 27(1):1–18.

———. 1998. *The Chinese in Canada,* 2nd edition. Toronto: Oxford University Press.

McDade, Kathryn. 1988. *Barriers to Recognition of the Credentials of Immigrants in Canada.* Ottawa: Institute for Research on Public Policy.

Midema, Baukje, and Nancy Nason-Clark. 1989. "Second-class status: An analysis of the lived experiences of immigrant women in Fredericton." *Canadian Ethnic Studies* 21(2):63–73.

Miles, Robert. 1989. *Racism.* London: Routledge.

Patterson, E. Palmer II. 1972. *The Canadian Indian: A History Since 1500.* New York: Collier-Macmillan of Canada Limited.

Pendakur, Krishna, and Ravi Pendakur. 1996. "Earnings differentials among ethnic groups in Canada." Ottawa: Strategic Research and Analysis, Department of Canadian Heritage.

Pineo, Peter. 1977. "The social standings of racial and ethnic groupings." *Canadian Review of Sociology and Anthropology* 14(2):147–157.

Porter, John. 1965. *The Vertical Mosaic: An Analysis of Social Class and Power in Canada.* Toronto: University of Toronto Press.

Rajagopal, Indhu. 1990. "The glass ceiling in the vertical mosaic: Indian immigrants to Canada." *Canadian Ethnic Studies* 22(1):96–105.

Reitz, Jeffery G., and Raymond Breton. 1994. *The Illusion of Difference: Realities of Ethnicity in Canada and the United States.* Toronto: C.D. Howe Institute.

Rex, John. 1983. *Race Relations in Sociological Theory.* London: Routledge.

Richmond, Anthony. 1974. *Aspects of Absorption and Adaptation of Immigrants.* Ottawa: Minister of Supply and Services Canada.

Roy, Patricia E. 1989. *A White Man's Province: British Columbia Politicians and Chinese and Japanese Immigrants, 1958–1914.* Vancouver: University of British Columbia Press.

Satzewich, Vic. 1989. "Racism and Canadian immigration policy: The government's view of Caribbean migration, 1962–1966." *Canadian Ethnic Studies* 21(1):77–97.

Satzewich, Vic, and Peter S. Li. 1987. "Immigrant labour in Canada: The cost and benefit of ethnic origin in the job market." *Canadian Journal of Sociology* 12:229–241.

Satzewich, Vic, and Terry Wotherspoon. 1993. *First Nations: Class, Race, and Gender Relations.* Scarborough, Ontario: Nelson Canada.

Scassa, Teresa. 1994. "Language standards, ethnicity, and discrimination." *Canadian Ethnic Studies* 26(3):105–121.

Statistics Canada. 1982. Statutes of Canada. *Charter of Rights and Freedom in Part I of the Constitution Act*, chapter 11.

———. 1986. *Employment Equity Act*, Chapter 31.

———. 1988. *Multiculturalism Act*, Chapter 31.

———. 1994a. *1991 Census of Canada. Public Use Microdata File on Individuals.* Ottawa: Minister of Industry, Science, and Technology.

———. 1994b. *Public Use Microdata File on Individuals, Final Edition.* Catalogue: 48-039E. Ottawa: Minister of Industry, Science, and Technology.

Zong, Li. 1994. "Structural and psychological dimensions of racism: Towards an alternative perspective." *Canadian Ethnic Studies* 26(3):122–134.

CHAPTER TWO

Representation of the Immigrant

Rose Baaba Folson

Migration is a key feature of contemporary times, which has led to fundamental changes in our understanding of culture and identity and our perception of the world. The key people involved in the processes of migration are migrants who become immigrants when they settle in nation-states. Immigrants[1] have been represented in various different ways, which have not always reflected realities of different migrant groups. For example, the picture of the "poor migrant" is a generalization that does not reflect the realities of the immigrant colonialist. This chapter explores some of the different perceptions and definitions of the immigrant, beginning from the nineteenth-century Marxist perception of the immigrant to that of Nikos Papastergiadis (2000).

WHO IS AN IMMIGRANT

Immigration is as old as history. However, the right to travel, or migrate, in search of work or a "better" life, has never been a universal right. The intensification of regulation of movement during the eighteenth and nineteenth centuries, paralleled by the remapping of geopolitical space on the basis of national boundaries and ethnicities, followed by the invention of the passport after World War I, had significant impact on migrant movements (Cohen 1996; Papastergiadis 2000). Citizenship and exile built the basis for inclusion and exclusion, and migrants increasingly found themselves at the hard end of the contradictions of nationalist ideologies (Cohen 1996; Papastergiadis 2000).

Although the most significant early large-scale migrant movement is supposed to have occurred in Asia (Lee Hanson 1961), every nation-state is believed to be the product of multiple overlapping generations of immigrants (Stalker 2001). Held et al. (1999) situate the movement of people/migrants in four historical periods of globalization; a "premodern" period, which covers an enormously long period beginning around nine to eleven thousand years ago and ending in 1500. The next period, the "early modern," ends in 1760 and is followed by the "modern" phase, which ushers in the "contemporary" phase, which begins at 1945 and is ongoing (1999:293–326). This historical categorization of migrant movements offers a framework to differentiate between the various forms of migration and different types of migrants.

Despite public conception of nations being "swamped" with immigrants (a notorious remark by a former British prime minister, Margaret Thatcher, in 1984, which was echoed and amplified a decade later by politicians across Europe), there are only about a hundred and fifty million people living outside the country of their birth (Stalker 2001), only 3 percent of the world population. Peter Stalker classifies migrants into roughly five categories:

- *Settlers*, who according to him, are migrants who intend to live permanently in their new country. About one and a half million people enter each year the main countries of settlement—the United States, Canada, Australia, and Aotearoa (10). There are numerous categories for migrants to qualify for settlement, the three significant ones being: 1) having skills, 2) having relatives in the country of settlement, and 3) having the ability and means to buy their way in as business investors. In Canada, the ability to invest around $250,000, in addition to having a minimum net worth of $500,000, will secure settlement rights for the potential immigrant, while the U.S. admits 55,000 potential immigrants each year through a visa lottery.

- *Contract workers* are admitted to other countries under the condition that their stay is of a temporary character. An example of this group of migrants are Polish seasonal workers moving to Germany, or sugar cane cutters moving from Mali to Ivory Coast. The Gulf countries accept the largest contingent of migrant contract workers and employ them for a year or more.

- *Professionals* include employees of transnational corporations, of which around 1 percent are expatriates. Work permits are issued to immigrant professionals.

- *Undocumented workers* are smuggled into a country or they overstay their tourist or student visas. The U.S. alone has around six million, Western Europe has around three million, and more than half of South Korea's quarter of a million foreign workers are believed to be undocumented.

- *Refugees and asylum seekers* are often suspected by immigration officials as claiming asylum because they would not qualify for admission as migrant workers. Since the 1990s, asylum seekers are referred to as refugees only when their claims are recognized by the receiving country (Stalker 2001:10–12).

It is important to note that these categories put forward by Stalker are not mutually exclusive; rather, most of them overlap.

A common definition of the term "migrant" is a person who comes to a country where they were not born to settle there on a temporary or permanent basis (Wordnet 2001, Princeton University). The Collins Dictionary of Sociology (2000) defines migration as "the movement of people from one country to another, who declare an intention to reside in the latter." Following the same line of thought, "emigrants" refers to people who move out of a country, and "immigrants" refers to those who move into a country. According to the same source,

> there is an international agreed definition of an immigrant as someone, who having lived outside the country for at least one year, declares an intention to live in the country for at least one year. An emigrant is defined in the opposite way. (397)

The public perception and scholarly constructions of the migrant are far more complex than is portrayed in the above definition. If migrants are defined as people who were born outside the country in which they reside, this suggests that not only are migrants a minority of the world's population, but it also raises questions about why the children, grandchildren, and great-grandchildren of migrants in Australia and Germany are referred to as second/third/fourth-generation "migrants."

There are no reliable records on the total number of illegal migrants or refugees. Furthermore, the official number of refugees is unreliable because it does not include displaced people within their own countries of birth. There are millions of such undocumented refugees in many countries in Africa, including Ethiopia, Kenya, Malawi, Burundi, Rwanda, Sierra Leone, and Liberia, and also in Iran, Afghanistan, Iraq, Turkey/Kurdistan, Palestine, and many others. Janet Abu-Lughod (1988) correctly remarks that there is "no concept to describe the phenomenon of 'exile' without moving" (62), or crossing international boarders. Obviously the strict definitions of immigrant or refugee we are presented with do not adequately address the complexity of the realities of international migration, the immigrant, or the refugee.

Given the political complexity in defining the migrant, Papastergiadis (2000) suggests a re-thinking of the sole representation of the migrant within "the sociological typology of the marginal man (*sic*) (55). He perceives the term "migrant" as having a "looming" presence. He points to the ambivalent association of the term as having both a positive image of cosmopolitanism and adventure, as well as issuing "a defensive reaction against the so-called 'dirty' foreigners and 'bogus' asylum-seekers." Papastergiadis contends that in the context of globalization such a display of hostility must inspire a critical re-thinking of the relationship between the stranger (the migrant) and the citizen. The fact that every nation is believed to be the product of overlapping generations of immigrants (Stalker 2001) does not appease Papastergiadis in any way, but rather prompts him to put the following questions: "If we are all, to some extent, the product of migration, then how do we distinguish between one story and another? Are we really equally displaced?"

Although scholars of migration studies do not agree on the total number of migrants and refugees, they do agree that there are different groups of migrants, whose movement in the world is regulated by a matrix of economic, political, sexual, and cultural factors (Cohen 1996; Held et al. 1999; Held and McGrew 2000; Sassen 1998, 1999, 2002; Stalker 2001; Papastergiadis 2000). These socio-economic and political flows and barriers define and determine migrant activities and identity formation to an unknown extent. There are "elite migrants," military conquerors, missionaries, merchants, bureaucrats, mass migrants of settling nomads, and peasant agrarians. In the contemporary phase of globalization and migration, migrant wives follow elite migrants, while migrant expatriates pursue labour and business opportunities in conquered and colonized regions of the world. Contemporary migration studies primarily concentrate on the movement of migrants from countries with less resources and infrastructure (often referred to as southern, developing, or Third World) to those with more resources and infrastructure (often referred to as northern, developed, or First World (Cohen 1996; Sassen 1998, 1999; Castles and Miller 1998). The spatial aspects of migration to the South and to the North, and the interaction with economic, political, sexual, and cultural factors in both spaces have not received adequate attention. Without attempting to minimize the impact of the differing social classes of these migrants, I focus on how the global hierarchy of nations constitutes spatial configurations that reflect the formations of identity and professional advancement of migrants. How do we account for neglecting basic questions like: A white male teacher moves from the North to the South and improves his career, while a professor from the South moves to the North and ends up being a taxi driver? Papastergiadis has argued:

> Space is neither a flat stage upon which subjects perform their historical tasks, nor a pre-defined volume through which they pass. Space is both a transformative force and a field that is transformed by the interactions that occur within it. (2000:52)

According to Doreen Massey (1993), the social and the spatial are inseparable. The spatial form of the social has causal effectiveness, whereby a particular space impacts the social life that takes place in it, which on the other hand transforms the spatial form. The system of global hierarchy of nations produces different bodies that transform national spaces along race, class, and gender lines. I contend that these transformations build the basis for professional advancement of migrants.

THE IMMIGRANT IN PUBLIC DEBATE

As stated before, contemporary globalization and international migration scholars observe that migrants primarily move from countries with less resources and infrastructure to those with more resources and infrastructure (Cohen 1996; Sassen 1998, 1999; Castles and Miller 1998). In the same line of thought, Koslowski (2000) describes migration from Eastern Europe to the West as a move towards a better life. Such arguments have led to the construction of the receiving countries of migrants as generous, kind, and honorable, while citing war, poverty, overpopulation, economic stagnation, and other unfavorable conditions in the sending country as the force driving migrants out. These public debates reflect the description of this phenomenon in the Penguin *Dictionary of Sociology* (1984):

> The "push" factors are the unemployment, poverty and underdevelopment of labour-exporting countries, which have high rates of population increase, high unemployment and low per capita incomes. (136)

Although the "push and pull" notion of migration has characterized the public conception of migration, there is no empirical evidence for this, as it is not the poorest who migrate but those with connections and networks (Portes 1995, 1999; Portes and Rumbaut 2001), and receiving countries have not been passive bystanders in the process (Sassen 1998, 1999). The linkage between macro developments and local settings plays an important role in migrant movements. It is international networks, activities of transnational corporations, militarization, the needs of the receiving nations—for example, the demand for cheap labour—that drive migrants. Jacques Derrida has a moral take on this. He argues that nation-states should extend hospitality to migrants without expectation of gains:

> But whilst I realize that what I have been saying about the event and the arrival is impracticable and unpolitical from the point of view of this concept of politics, I still want to claim that any politics which fails to sustain some relation to the principle of unconditional hospitality has completely lost its relation to justice. (1994:35)

The relationship between the migrant and the nation-state remains ambiguous. The tension between migrant contributions to the development of the nation-state, particularly national and global economies on one hand and allocation of citizenship rights on the other hand, is in a steady volcanic growth, since the differentiation between a citizen and a migrant is becoming increasingly absurd. Whilst public debates still posit the nation as benevolent in its relations to the burdensome migrant, scholarship on migrant contributions to national and global economies and cultures is increasing steadily (Portes 1995, 1999; Portes and Rumbaut 2001; Portes et al. 2002; Castles and Miller 1998; Sassen 2000, 2001, 2002). Also, policies increasingly favour labour migration, as is plainly demonstrated in the point system of the Canadian immigration policy (1969) and the draft German immigration policy (2001). There is an absolute consensus in the political arena that government immigration policies should exclusively reflect national economic interests and not ideals of morality and justice.

THEORIES OF MIGRATION

Research on migration is intrinsically interdisciplinary. There is no one theory that provides a comprehensive account of the complex and dynamic set of social, political, and economic interactions involved in the international movements of migrants. A full understanding of processes involved requires contributions from many different disciplines. The disciplines involved—sociology, political science, history, economics, geography, demography, psychology, law, anthropology—look at different aspects of migration from variety of approaches. All of these disciplines have developed theories of migration (Cohen 1996; Massey et al. 1994), but three of the most common approaches used since the last decade are: 1) neo-classical economic equilibrium theory, 2) the historical-structuralist approach, and 3) migration systems theory (Hugo 1993; Castles and Miller 1998).

The neo-classical economic equilibrium theory has its antecedents in the earliest systematic theory on migration by the nineteenth-century geographer Ravenstein (1885, 1889), who formulated statistical laws of migration, which were general statements unconnected with any actual migratory movement (Zolberg 1989). However, this tradition remains alive in the work of many demographers, geographers, and economists (for example, Jackson 1969). Such general theories emphasize tendencies of people to move from densely to sparsely populated areas or from low- to high-income areas, or link migration movements to fluctuations in the business cycle. These approaches are often known as "push-pull" theories, which perceive the causes of migration to lie in a combination of push factors, which impel people to leave their areas of origin, and pull factors, which attract them to certain receiving countries. Push factors are assumed to include demographic growth, low living standards, lack of economic opportunities, and political repression, while pull factors are supposed to include demand for labour, availability of land, good economic opportunities, and political freedoms.

Many migration scholars agree that this theory is essentialistic, individualistic, ahistorical, and "so far from historical reality that it has little explanatory value" (Castles and Miller 1998:62). It emphasizes the individual decision to migrate, based on rational comparison of the relative costs and benefits of remaining in the area of origin or moving to various alternative destinations. Constraining factors, such as government restrictions on emigration or immigration, are mainly perceived as distortions of the rational market. Zolberg (1989) suggests analyzing labour migration as a movement of workers propelled by the dynamics of the transnational capitalist economy, which simultaneously determines both the push and the pull. This implies that migrations are collective phenomena, which should be examined as sub-systems of an increasingly global economic and political system.

The historical-structuralist approach is an alternative explanation of international migration provided in the 1970s. With its intellectual roots in Marxism, it stresses the unequal distribution of economic and political power in the globalized economy as the principal driver of migration, which is seen mainly as a way of mobilizing cheap labour for capital (Cohen 1987; Castles and Kosack 1985; Sassen 1998). Such migration perpetuates uneven development, exploiting the resources of economically disadvantaged countries.

The historical-structuralist approach has also been criticized by many migration scholars (Zolberg 1989; Hugo 1993; Castles and Miller 1998; Kofman 1999). The main criticism is: If the logic of capital and the interests of states in the North were so dominant, how could the frequent breakdown of migration policies of different states be explained?

The migration systems theory emerged in the 1980s out of critiques of the previous two theories. Like the historical-structuralist approach, this theory emphasizes international relations, political economy, collective action, and institutional factors. A key tenet of this approach is the recognition that prior links between countries based on colonization, political influence, trade, investments, military activities, and cultural ties drive migrants. A migration system is constituted by two or more countries, which exchange migrations with each other. There is a tendency to analyze regional migration systems, such as the South Pacific, Caribbean/North America, or West Africa. However, distant regions may also be interlinked, such as the migration system embracing the Caribbean, Western Europe, and North America, or that linking North and West Africa with Europe. The migration systems approach means examining both ends of the flow and studying all the linkages between the places concerned. These linkages can be categorized as state-to-state relations and comparisons, mass culture connections and family, and social networks (Fawcett and Arnold 1987).

THE STRANGER/MIGRANT IN SOCIAL THEORY

Although Karl Marx was for the most part of his life a migrant and acknowledged the significance of migration, he failed to develop a theory of migratory forces of modern society. However, the significance of migration was explicitly addressed in the discussions of alienation, anomie, disenchantment, and estrangement in classical social theory by Karl Marx (1884), Georg Simmel (Wolff 1950), Emil Durkheim (1951, 1956), and Max Weber (1968). One of Karl Marx's most influential concepts was his representation of the vulnerabilities of migrant labour and its exploitation by industry in his "reserve army" thesis (Marx 1884). According to this thesis, the expansion of capital requires a flexible source of cheap labour, which capital can stretch and discard according to the cycle of production. This form of flexible exploitative labour can only be extracted from people with limited rights. Migrants, with limited social and political rights as well as economic limitations, serve a strategic role. They have provided this source of labour throughout history (Institute für Marxismus-Leninismus beim ZK der SED 1972).

In *The Division of Labour*, Emil Durkheim (1956) addressed the profound impact of migration on modern society. "His theorization of the shift from *traditional mechanical solidarity to modern organic solidarity* was underpinned by the assumption that society is always a negotiated balance between consensus and difference" (Papastergiadis 2000:63, emphasis added by Papastergiadis). With the focus of immigration policies on cheap labour and skills for exploitation and in the face of a growing tension between immigrant rights and citizenship rights, today's society is an anomaly compared to Durkheim's society as "always a negotiated balance between consensus and difference." The turbulence of today's society rather speeds up the process of plunging individuals, particularly immigrants, into a state of anomie (to borrow Durkheim's terminology).

Durkheim (1951) argued that suicide is an extreme case of the breakdown of social regulation and that the rate of suicide gives us insight into the individual's sense of moral disconnection. He proposed the term "anomie" to describe the conditions in which the connection of individual practices with broader social values breaks down, thus rendering the individual in a state of relative normlessness (250). Durkheim correctly concludes that liberation from traditional constraints not only provides a basis for freedom, but also creates a risk of falling into an anomic state. However, his generalized association of the migrant with rural-traditional societies and his notion of progress as associated with moving to modern urban freedom need to be rethought, as his analysis is limited to rural-urban migration. There is also a need for theorizing progress as it relates to "modernity" and "tradition" in this context, as, after all, the process towards modernity is not always a departure from cultural and traditional inferiority. Papastergiadis sums up:

> From Marx's economic and Durkheim's moral perspective, migrants were more exposed to the perils of modernity. Being separated from their original homeland, and having few ties to their place of arrival, they were placed in an ambiguous social position. This lack of allegiance to a local labour force and their exclusion from social networks and political institutions heightened their vulnerability. Their identity was as suspect as their tenure. They could be exploited without any protection from other political groups, just as they could switch allegiances to secure more profitable arrangements. Although migrants have historically been as willing as any other member of the working class to defend and extend the rights of labour, their loyalty to local political cultures has always been subjected to a racist "double scrutiny." (2000:63–64)

The most significant outcome of Max Weber's exploration of processes of modernization is "disenchantment," which he perceived as "a new spirit for self-invention and social reform" (Papastergiadis 2000:64). Weber's assertion of a "complex affinity" between migration and capitalism reflects strongly the focus of immigration policies of nation-states in the twentieth century, and disenchantment could be a much needed opening in the social and professional advancement of immigrants (Cohen 1996). Georg Simmel's (1950) works, *The Metropolis and Mental Life* and *The Stranger,* offer more complex insights into the ambiguous character of modernity. He did not only see the stranger as an emblematic figure in modernity, but also focused on the differing levels of displacement, which shed light on the dialectical patterns that shape the forms of inner experience and social interaction. Papastergiadis interprets Simmel's conception of the stranger as:

> someone who has come from elsewhere, whose language and practices are foreign, whose sense of attachment is partial, whose historical presence challenges the basis for social integration, and whose "contrary" perceptions offer a different perspective from which to establish critical judgements. (2000:65)

Also he sees Simmel's image of the stranger as not "just a social type" nor as an "empirical study of a solitary figure," but "the identity of the stranger is highlighted to illuminate the subjective experience of ambivalence" (65). However, I read Simmel's perception of the stranger as assuming difference and neglecting similarities. He defines the migrant in opposition to the citizen. Perhaps many scholars of migration studies might agree that:

While the structural forms of change in everyday life were carefully mapped by classical theorists, the actual experiences of displacement were not examined in any detail. Their attempts to understand the dynamics of complex societies were confined to the dominant institutional forms like the bureaucracy, normative structures and patterns of ownership. Hence while Marx, Durkheim and Weber charted the transformations in the spheres of ecomomic production, institutional cohesion and bureaucratic organization, and although their critiques were firmly guided by their conceptualization of alienation, anomie and disenchantment, the complex links and ruptures between the substantive social changes and the personal experiences of displacement in modernity have been often left underexamined. (Papastergiadis 2000:64)

THE CONSTRUCTION OF THE IMMIGRANT WOMAN

The Collins *Dictionary of Sociology* (1991) states:

There have been a number of *moral panics* about immigration since 1945, focusing on the immigration of black people, and it is therefore important to distinguish between immigrants and black people; it is wrong to assume that an immigrant is black, and it is equally wrong to assume that a black person is an immigrant. (113)

Nevertheless, many countries, including Australia, Canada, Germany, and the U.K., during a phase of their history, undertook an attempt to build a "white" nation-state by encouraging only white migrants to settle. These countries still hold a constructed image as being exclusively white nations, despite the presence of a large number of non-white citizens. White immigrants are often constructed as citizens, whilst non-white citizens are constructed as immigrants.

This section seeks to shed light on how a specific category—immigrant women—is constructed. According to Roxana Ng, "in everyday life … women who are white, educated, and English-speaking are rarely considered to be immigrant women" (1996:116). A common notion of an immigrant is a non-white person, who is professionally challenged and speaks with an accent. Many researchers find these women concentrated at the top and bottom of the occupational hierarchy (Boyd 1975, 1986; Arnopoulos 1979; Ng 1996; Folson 1999, 2002).

Ng defines the term "immigrant women," in the Canadian context, to mean women who are landed immigrants of Canada—"landed" being the term for permanent residency. But Ng argues that immigrant woman is a socially constructed category that goes beyond the legal definition. It is used to indicate a woman with a particular labour- market location, who does not speak the declared *lingua franca* of Canada. According to Ng, women who are considered to be immigrants today in Canada have not always been perceived as such; they become immigrant women when they enter certain positions in the labour market. "Thus, when we call someone an 'immigrant woman' we are in fact naming a process whereby the individual comes to be identified as an immigrant woman" (Ng 1996:16). This process reflects the notion of space as both a transformative force and a field that is transformed by the interactions that occur within it (Massey 1993; Goldberg 1993). In her attempt to map a trajectory of historical relationship between capitalist development and the labour of immigrant women, Ng uses documentation of employment counsellors and agencies. Relying on the analysis of Sassen-Koob (1981), Ng contends that immigrant women become a social entity after a rise in immigration, which in turn controls the dynamics of processes whereby the location of a different labour supply in the global economy is determined.

Ng contends that immigrant women become a visible social category when female labour is employed in large numbers. She cites examples from the latter half of the nineteenth century, when large numbers of British women were sent to the colonies to meet the need for British female labour, including being wives to the colonialists. Another example of constructing immigrant women as a visible social category occurred during the period when male immigrants were permitted to bring their families to Canada. She argues that the downturn of the Canadian economy in the 1970s led to the downsizing of the quota for the "independent" immigrants; rather, Canadian immigration policy focused on "family reunification." Ng's argument is thus: the focus on family reunification led to a large number of women migrating to Canada at a particular time. These sponsored immigrants are not entitled to public assistance for between five and ten years (Ng 1996:18). Thus, systematically a migrant woman is constructed who is dependent on a spouse or other sponsor and has no access to language schools or to professional advancement institutions. This process is a sure path to the creation of a "type" of woman who becomes part of an unskilled, cheap, exploitable labour force—the construction of the immigrant woman is completed.

Different struggles have developed around the construction of the immigrant in general and the categorization of the immigrant woman in particular. Some examples are portrayed in the conceptualization of Black British feminisms (Walby 1994; Yuval-Davis 1997; Indra 1999; Kempadoo and Doezema 1998), Marxist struggles within trade unions (Gilroy 1987), feminist analyses of the status of Muslim women in Britain and Europe (Brah and Minhas 1986), and worldwide struggles around exploitation of "expendable" women in the areas of entertainment and domestic labour (Thobani 2001).

CONCLUSION

Defining migration, international migration, and the immigrant is a deeply complex matter because the processes and people involved keep changing with time. The changes in the migration processes affect the geopolitical landscape, which in turn change migration processes. And all these processes are being strongly affected by the interaction of dynamic economic political, sexual, and cultural factors. Also family structures, notions, and definitions of home, sense of belonging, the nature of community and national affiliation, and processes of identity formation will continue to undergo significant modifications and reinventions in migratory processes. An addendum of all these processes will give future directions to understanding and describing the immigrant, as well as the citizen, in ways that will be acceptable for all members of a society. For the meantime, social scientists are compelled to re-think their conceptual frameworks.

ENDNOTE

1. The difference between a migrant and an immigrant is a huge one. The migrant is in a process of migration, whilst the immigrant has somehow completed an immigration process guided by immigration policy of any particular nation-state. There are nation-states that do not have migration policies in place because they do not refer to themselves as immigration states (i.e., Germany). In migration logic/history/writings, particularly in North America, both groups

are referred to as immigrants. I think it's about time we took this difference seriously because, to my mind, it has serious implications for all aspects of social and political life, including human rights.

REFERENCES

Abu-Lughod, J. 1988. "Palestinians: Exiles at Home and Abroad." *Current Sociology*, 32, 2.

Arnopoulos, S. 1979. *Problems of Immigrant Women in the Canadian Labour Force*. Ottawa: Advisory Council on the Status of Women.

Boyd, Monica 1975. "The Status of Immigrant Women in Canada." *Canadian Review of Sociology and Anthropology*, 12.

———. 1986. "Immigrant Women in Canada." In R.J. Simon and C.B. Brettell (eds.), *International Migration: The Female Experience*. Totowa, NJ: Rowman and Allanheld.

Brah, A., and R. Minhas. 1986. "Structural Racism or Cultural Difference? Schooling for Asian Girls." In G. Weiner (ed.), *Just a Bunch of Girls*. Milton Keynes: Open University Press.

Castles, S., and G. Kosack. 1985. *Immigrant Workers and Class Structure in Western Europe*. Oxford: Oxford University Press.

Castles, S., and M.J. Miller. 1998. *The Age of Migration: International Population Movements in the Modern World*. Second edition. New York: Guilford.

Cohen, Robin. 1987. *The New Helots: Migrants in the International Division of Labour*. Avebury: Aldershot.

———. 1996. "Introduction." In Robin Cohen (ed.), *The Sociology of Migration*. Cheltenham: Elgar.

Derrida, J. 1994. *Spectres of Marx: The State of the Debt, the Work of Mourning, and the New International*. New York: Routledge.

Durkheim, E. 1951. *Suicide*. New York: Free Press.

———. 1956. *The Division of Labour in Society*. New York: Free Press.

Fawcett, J.T., and F. Arnold. 1987. "Explaining Diversity: Asian and Pacific Immigration Systems." In J.T. Fawcett and B.V. Carino (eds.), *Pacific Bridges: The New Immigration from Asia and the Pacific Islands*. New York: Center for Migration Studies.

Folson, R.B. 1995. *The Contribution of Formal Education to Economic Development and Economic Underdevelopment Ghana as Paradigm*. New York: Peter Lang.

———. 1999. "Bildunspotential—Kulturelle Enterwetung—Verlust an Potential: Afrikanische und Asiatische Migrantenfrauen in Deutschland." In Afrikanisch-Asiatische Studentenforderung e. V., Goettingen (eds.), *Wissen und Produktion*. Frankfurt/M: IKO.

———. 2002. "Institutionalisierte Abhaengigkeit und berufliche Chancen von Migrantinnen aus dem Sueden In Deutschland." In Afrikanisch-Asiatische Studentenforderunge. V. Goettingen (eds.), *Afrikaner und Asiaten in Deutschland—Multiplikatoren des Wissenschaftstransfers zwischen Sued und Nord*. Frankfurt/M: IKO.

Gilroy, P. 1987. *There Ain't No Black in the Union Jack*. London: Hutchinson.

Goldberg, D.T. 1993. *Racist Culture*. Cambridge, UK: Blackwell.

Held, D., A. McGrew, and D. Goldblatt. 1999. *Global Transformation: Politics, Economics, and Culture*. Oxford: Polity Press.

Held, D., and A. McGrew. 2000. *The Global Tranformations Reader: An Introduction to Globalization Debate*. Malden, MA: Polity Press.

Hugo, G. 1993. *The Economic Implications of Emigration from Australia*. Canberra: Australia Government Publishing Service.

Indra, D. (ed.). 1999. *Engendering Forced Migration: Theory and Practice*. New York: Berghahn Books.

Institut fur Msrxismus-Leninismus beim ZK der 9 (1972). *Rosa. Luxemburg. Band 1.1893–1905 Zwieiter Halbband Fesammelte Werke*. Berlin: Dietz Verlag.

Jackson, J.A. (ed.). (1969). *Migration*. Cambridge: Cambridge University Press.

Kempadoo, K., and J. Doezema (eds.). 1998. *Global Sex Workers: Rights Resistance and Redefinition*. New York and London: Routledge.

Kofman, E. 1999. "Whose City? Gender, Class, and Immigration in Globalizing European Cities." In R. Fincher and J. Jacobs (eds.), *Cities of Difference*. New York: Guilford Press.

Koslowski, R. 2000. *Migrants and Citizens*. Ithaca: Cornell University Press.

Lee Hanson, Marcus. 1961. *The Atlantic Emigration, 1607–1860*. New York: Harper.

Marx, K. 1884. *Das Kapital* 1. and 3. Band. Berlin: Dietz Verlag.

Massey, D. 1993. "Politics and Space/Time." In M. Keith and S. Pile (eds.), *Place and the Politics of Identity*. London: Routledge.

Massey, D., et al. 1994. "An Evaluation of International Migration Theory: The North American Case." *Population and Development Review*, 20.

Ng, R. 1996. *Politics of Community Services: Immigrant Women, Class, and State*. Halifax: Fernwood.

Papastergiadis, N. 2000. *The Turbulence of Migration*. Malden, MA: Polity Press.

Portes, A. 1995. *The Economic Sociology of Immigration: Essays on Networks, Ethnicity, and Entrepreneurship*. New York: Russell Sage Foundation.

———. 1999. "Towards a New World: The Origins and Effects of Transnational Activities." *Ethnic and Racial Studies*, 22, 2 (March).

Portes, A., and R.G. Rumbaut. 2001. *Legacies: The Story of Immigrant Second Generation*. Berkeley: University of California Press.

Portes, A., et al. 2002. "Transnational Entrepreneurs: An Alternative Form of Immigrant Economic Adaptation." *American Sociological Review*, 67, 2 (Apr.).

Ravenstein, E.G. 1885. "The Laws of Migration." *Journal of Statistical Society*, 48.

———. 1889. "The Laws of Migration." *Journal of Statistical Society*, 52.

Sassen, S. 1988. *The Mobility of Labour and Capital*. Cambridge: Cambridge University Press.

———. 1998. *Globalization and Its Discontents*. New York: The New Press.

———. 1999. *Guests and Aliens*. New York: The New Press.

———. 2000. *Cities in a World Economy*. Thousand Oaks, CA: Pine Forge Press.

———. 2001. *The Global City: New York, London, Tokyo*, 2nd ed. Princeton, NJ: Princeton University Press.

———. 2002. "Towards a Sociology of Information Technology." *Current Sociology*, 50, 3 (May).

Sassen-Koob, S. 1981. "Toward a Conceptualization of Immigrant Labour." *Social Problems*, 29, 1.

Simmel, G. 1950. *The Sociology of Georg Simmel*, comp. and trans. Kurt Wolff. Glencoe, IL: Free Press.

Stalker, P. 2001. *No-Nonsense Guide to International Migration*. London: Verso.

Thobani, S. 2001. "Benevolent State, Law-Breaking Smugglers, and Deportable and Expendable Women: An Analysis of the Canadian State's Strategy to Address Trafficking in Women." *Refuge*, 19, 4.

Walby, S. 1994. "Is Citizenship Gendered?" *Sociology*, 28, 2.

Weber, M. 1968. *Economy and Society*. G. Roth and C. Wittich (eds.). New York: Bedminister Press.

Wolff, K. (ed.). 1950. *The Sociology of Georg Simmel*. New York: Free Press.

Yuval-Davis, A. 1997. *Gender and Nation*. London: Sage.

Zolberg, A.R. 1989. *Escape from Violence*. New York: Oxford University Press.

CHAPTER THREE

Selling (out) Diversity in an Age of Globalization

Yasmeen Abu-Laban and Christina Gabriel

In this chapter we summarize our major findings on the historical and contemporary evolution of immigration, multiculturalism, and employment equity policies in Canada and outline the implications of our findings. Finally and certainly not least, we turn our attention away from the empirical facts ("what is") and instead consider the grand normative question of "what ought to be." Specifically, we advocate the need for a new discourse on globalization that does not assume that there are global economic "imperatives," which necessitate neo-liberal policy rationales. A new framework and perspective on globalization might allow Canadians (and Canadian policy-makers) the room to really think about what kind of political community Canadians want in the future. A new perspective on globalization might allow the space to consider alternatives to neo-liberalism and political agendas that might really foster substantive equality for diverse groups in Canada and even globally.

SUMMARY OF FINDINGS

Globalization has become one of the most frequently invoked ideas of our time. We suggested that a useful understanding of contemporary globalization processes would see these processes as not necessarily new, but nonetheless distinct. As such, there is an intensification of economic, political, and cultural processes that transcend, but do not necessarily completely supercede, the state or its sovereignty. In terms of Canadian public policy specifically, we argued that instead of only engaging in abstract scholarly debates, it was useful to examine if and how state actors make use of a discourse of globalization and the extent to which policy ideas and rationales were "imported" to Canada or "exported" from Canada.

In terms of understanding contemporary public policy in Canada, our findings suggest that internationalization might go in different directions (both to and from Canada) depending on the policy. We demonstrated that recent policy changes and debates in the interrelated policy domains of immigration, multiculturalism, and employment equity have been underpinned by a particular reading of globalization that stresses measures informed by neo-liberal ideals. Together, each of these policy areas was (and is) implicated in the funding, framing, and managing of Canadian ethnocultural and racial relations, as well as other forms of diversity—including those relating to class and gender. In the contemporary moment, the policies of immigration, employment equity, and multiculturalism are all being rewritten in new directions.

Each new policy script epitomizes how "diversity" has been constructed—albeit in a number of shifting ways—in a manner that is often congruent with various neo-liberal ideals.

These neo-liberal ideals include the valuing of a smaller welfare state, whereby governments do less, and individuals, families, and volunteers undertake to do more in the area of social services. Neo-liberal ideals also stress the commodification of social goods (e.g., health care, education, and welfare services). In this process, Canadians are treated less as "citizens" and more as "individuals," "clients," or "customers." Not least, neo-liberal ideals emphasize and privilege the "free" market, economic efficiency, and unfettered competition. Thus, neo-liberal ideals carry a new understanding of what is "public" and what is "private," and many services that were considered public with the Keynesian welfare state are under threat of being wholly or partially privatized.

Over the contemporary period under examination (1993 to 2001) neo-liberal values have been stressed by state actors, and in the process the demands of groups that were viewed as disadvantaged during the rapid expansion of the welfare state during the 1960s and 1970s have been subject to a radical shift. Thus groups such as women, racial and ethnic minorities, Aboriginal people, people with disabilities, and the poor have increasingly been represented as "special interests" and different from so called "ordinary Canadians."[1] In this context, the demands of these groups for social justice and equality have sometimes even been transformed in popular and partisan debates into a threat to the cohesion and unity of the Canadian polity.

In the case of ethnic and racial minorities, their concerns for equality *via* the policies of immigration, multiculturalism, and employment equity have been repositioned by state actors as valuable to the Canadian polity insofar as these demands conform to a discourse on globalization that stresses neo-liberal ideals. However, the stress on attracting immigrants with skills and other human capital characteristics, or on the idea that workforce diversity or societal diversity can enhance national and global competitiveness and foster trade links abroad is not without consequences, as this book has detailed. Like neo-liberal repositionings of what is "public" and what is "private," such developments may threaten the possibility of those marginalized by virtue of their gender, race/ethnicity, and class for achieving greater substantive equality.

Immigration

The state has always played a key role in the selection of immigrants—that is, prospective citizens. The Canadian case demonstrates that this selection has always been premised on the perceived needs of the Canadian economy. The current period is marked by contradictory tendencies. Policy directions suggest Canada is opening its doors to individuals with human capital, those people who are highly skilled, well educated, and perceived as self-sufficient. Simultaneously, state power is being used to enact tougher border control through the adoption of stricter selection criteria for those deemed less desirable, especially members of the family class and refugees, erroneously constructed as "dependent" non-contributors. This dichotomy is very much premised on the need to attract immigrants/prospective citizens with the "right stuff" who will enhance Canada's competitive position in a global economy, but it has a differential impact on women and the poor. As a whole, the area of immigration reveals a powerful way in which the nation-state continues to exercise power in the contemporary era of globalization, which is certainly not "shrinking" as a result of neo-liberalism. Recent policy moves, such as the Metropolis project, suggest that Canadian policy-makers are eager both to share its own experiences and learn from the experiences of other countries (especially the wealthy countries belonging to the Organization for Economic Cooperation and Development/OECD).

Multiculturalism

We suggest that supposed economic imperatives also inform recent directions in Canadian multiculturalism policy. Where immigration policy may be seen as the source of Canada's increasing ethnocultural and racial diversity, multiculturalism policy addresses the value of this diversity for the Canadian nation. Thus, the emergence of multiculturalism policy in the 1970s signaled an important reconfiguring of Canada's symbolic order to include recognition of those groups that were not French, not British, and not Aboriginal in origin. The rearticulation of Canadian identity marked some departure from the implicit and explicit privileging of Anglo-conformity that framed Canadian national identity and nation-building historically. This rearticulation also provided the basis for subsequent—although limited—policy initiatives that attempted to address systemic racism. However, starting in the 1990s, these fragile initiatives have been challenged by a new debate (particularly in Canada outside Quebec), which has brought forward the idea that the state has no business in the area of culture and cultural maintenance, which should be left to the "private" sphere of the home and family. At a policy level, multiculturalism has been challenged by a new emphasis on diversity as a competitive lever. Under the initial call in 1986 that "multiculturalism means business," the policy focus since the 1990s especially emphasized the economic exploitation of Canada's racial and ethnic diversity to capture markets at home and abroad at the probable expense of gender equality and other equality initiatives. Multiculturalism has also been increasingly positioned as an area where Canada can "export" policy ideas to other countries.

Employment Equity

Our assessment of legislated employment equity programs at the federal level and in Ontario leads to some similar findings. Employment equity emerged as a social justice measure designed to address substantive inequality in the labour market. The federal government has pursued employment equity within the federally regulated sector with a record of limited success. The more ambitious experiment of the NDP government in Ontario sank under the weight of its own contradictions, partisan attack, employer opposition to government intervention in the "private sphere," and a virulent backlash against disadvantaged groups. What has come to the fore, in Ontario especially, are "managing diversity" measures often mistakenly presented as "employment equity." Such "managing diversity" measures construct diversity of any kind—gender, race, disability, age, or sexuality—as a means to enhance the bottom line. The managing diversity model has been a particular idea "imported" from recent American developments. Thus, a workforce is constructed in terms of comparative advantage, as a bridge to new markets (both at home and globally), and as a source of product innovation. This market-orientated emphasis effectively sidelines issues of systemic discrimination and inequality that employment equity was intended to address.

THE IMPLICATIONS OF THE RESEARCH FINDINGS

We would suggest that the trends in the policy areas of immigration, multiculturalism, and employment equity—trends which we call "selling diversity"—are premised on a particular reading of globalization by Canadian policy-makers. In no case has this meant that all the earlier incarnations and emphases in policies have been abandoned. This may be related to the continued importance of Canadian historical traditions and the kinds of connections that developed between state institutions and subordinate groups in Canada during the post-war period when Keynesian-inspired ideas created a rationale for the state to fund the activities of such groups as women and minorities. Not least there are international pressures and ideas that affect the Canadian state, like the salience of international human rights and the United Nations protocol regarding the protection of refugees. Nonetheless, the understanding of globalization taken by Canadian policy-makers has profound implications for the future of the role of the state, substantive equality, identity, and diversity in Canada.

The economic advantage to be gleaned from "selling diversity" seems to underwrite many of the recent policy changes within immigration, multiculturalism, and employment equity. Thus immigration changes are predicated on easing the entry of high-skilled workers and investors who can "contribute" to the Canadian economy. Similarly, multiculturalism and employment equity have been presented as areas in which to maximize comparative advantage in order to secure markets. This logic is premised on the assumption that a strategic alliance between economic competitiveness and equity commitment can peacefully co-exist with the equity commitments enshrined in the post-war incarnation of each policy. Whereas in the past competitiveness and equity may have been viewed as antithetical, the rationale behind selling diversity is that it is possible and desirable to have the best of both worlds. The implication of this is that there would be a new relationship between states, citizens, and markets. Increasingly, market ideals and private sector initiatives are constructed as the driving forces of change and dynamism. Presumably, such initiatives have the potential to provide equal opportunity to all individuals within a framework of formal equal rights. Within this refashioning, the state is to play a very different role compared to that of the post-war redistributive Keynesian welfare state.

The recent invocation of the "marketing and selling of diversity," we suggest, represents a distancing from the post-war ideal that was captured to some extent in Prime Minister Pierre Trudeau's vision of a "just society." This vision was articulated in the following manner:

> Now Canada seems to me a land blessed by the gods to pursue a policy of the greatest equality of opportunity. A young country, a rich country, a country with two languages, a pluralist country with its ethnicities and its religions, an immense country with varied geographic regions, a federalist country. Canada had, besides, a political tradition that was neither completely libertarian nor completely state dominated, but was based, rather, on the collaboration necessary between government and the private sector and on direct action of the State to protect the weak against the strong, the needy against the wealthy.[2]

The "just society" emphasized a pan-Canadian identity and a national set of institutions. It was a vision of the political community marked by the post-war ideals of social solidarity and collective values. Consequently, through the 1960s and 1970s the state consolidated a number of welfare provisions and labour market regulations, and equally importantly recognized the collective needs and demands of groups such as women, francophones, linguistic minorities, and ethnocultural minority groups. Thus, for example, through the Secretary of State, many advocacy organizations representing these groups received state funding. In the 1970s the state also established structures of representation within the bureaucracy, such as Status of Women Canada and a Multiculturalism Directorate. Other para-public bodies such as the Canadian Advisory Council on the Status of Women (CSCSW) also played a role in generating research and policy advice on behalf of women.

Through these measures, the state recognized the collective needs and demands of groups, including women, linguistic minorities, and multicultural groups. This recognition contributed to a broader policy agenda that was underwritten by ideals of fairness, solidarity, equity, and social justice. These found expression to some extent in immigration reform and the removal of overt criteria relating to race/ethnicity from the criteria for entry and through the attempt to balance, somewhat, humanitarian considerations with the points system (refugees, the family class). The emergence of multiculturalism and its subsequent legislative basis also signaled a commitment to these ideals. Legislated employment equity at the federal level is perhaps the most concrete expression of equity concerns. The recent emergence of the "marketing and selling of diversity" within these three areas marks a clear retreat from the post-war ideal of a "just society." This emergence comes alongside increasing inequality and polarization as well as a virulent backlash against marginalized groups who are often cast as the architects of their own misfortune.

In different ways each of these policy areas also plays a role in structuring the symbolic aspects of Canadian national identity. Canadians and Canadian policy-makers often take pride in the UN Human Development Index that places Canada as the best (or nearly best) country in which to live. Canadians often emphasize that we are a nation of immigrants and laud Canada's "multicultural" and "tolerant" face. Canadian social programs are held up as evidence of our more caring and compassionate nature, especially in comparison to the United States. This is the public persona that Canadian officials also like to present to the world community.

Paradoxically, this image may prove more difficult to sustain at the current moment, when the discursive construction of "diversity" portrays the ideal/model citizens as self-sufficient, self-reliant individuals. In the process, equity-seeking groups—women, people of colour, people with disabilities—have been cast as "special interests" whose demands are outside the norm of the "ideal citizen." Thus, state funding that was designed to improve representation and access to decision-making bodies is now often depicted as a "handout." Struggles for equality and inclusion within the Canadian nation are portrayed as divisive. As well, attempts to address labour market inequality have been attacked as "reverse discrimination." The very social programs that addressed issues of equality and inclusion and infused the content of the Canadian nation and Canadian identity are being eroded. Increasingly neo-liberal visions articulated through a particular reading of globalization dominate the public agenda and these are at odds with the promise of a "just society."

Under the guise of responding to a globalizing economy, state actors have emphasized neo-liberal values to guide new policy directions in immigration, multiculturalism, and employment equity. Central to these new directions is a re-conceptualization of the role of the state, for it coincides with various redrawings of the boundaries between "the public" and "the private." Increasingly, there has been a shift from a strong interventionist state that actively attempts to manage the economy and is focused on redistributive concerns and equity, to a decentralized, less interventionist state that tends to prioritize market-driven prescriptions and emphasize cost savings. Within this shift, the policy infrastructure of immigration, employment equity, and multiculturalism has not been completely torn down, but neither has it been consolidated or strengthened. New policy directions have weakened the value of equality that was found in some measure within each policy area during the 1980s.

Additionally, responses in these policy areas to the perceived exigencies of a global economy are almost solely couched in terms of economic processes (and supposed economic imperatives) associated with globalization. In this respect the purported needs of the economy are prioritized. Thus, there have been initiatives to secure border-free economies through the removal of trade barriers; to attract and foster a flexible, highly skilled workforce; and to encourage freer, more open markets through de-regulation and privatization. Yet [...] globalization also involves other crucial dimensions, including global cultural flows of people, images, and ideas. Policy-makers, in the three areas of immigration, multiculturalism, and employment equity, appear to have paid little attention to global cultural flows or their implications. Consequently, as the nation becomes more demographically diverse there is relatively less discussion of measures required to ensure belonging to Canadian society or the articulations of more inclusive variants of Canadian identity. Clearly, the populations in Canada's three major cities (Montreal, Toronto, and Vancouver) in the twenty-first century will be profoundly different than in the twentieth century, but existing measures to ensure the full integration of immigrants and minorities are being scaled back, and new initiatives to meaningfully accomplish this do not appear to be on the agenda.

A key implication of our assessment of the three policy areas is that people with certain characteristics and attributes are particularly valued. Increasingly, immigration policy is emphasizing the human capital strengths of independent applicants. People who are highly skilled, well educated, have job experience, and can speak one of the official languages are sought. As a country Canada has embarked on a project of trying to attract wealthy investors and entrepreneurs who will create jobs. Similarly, within multiculturalism policy the emphasis is placed on minority ethnic business leaders who have the potential to act as bridges to new markets. These class-advantaged people embody the very spirit of neo-liberalism—they are independent, self-reliant, active, and entrepreneurial. Within the "managing diversity model" workers of a firm or sector or even the entire workforce itself is constructed as a lever of global competition. Within these varying constructions of "diversity" there is a growing emphasis on the economic or potential economic contribution of individuals as the sum worth of a person. We suggest that constructing people as trade-enhancing commodities is a particularly superficial and narrow reading of diversity.

This is why the conceptualization of "diversity" within each policy area warrants further interrogation. In terms of immigration new directions emphasize diversity only within certain bounds. To the extent that new directions celebrate human capital characteristics and prize entrepreneurial and business activity there is a celebration of class advantage. Along with relations of class going unchallenged, there is silence on the consequences for other groups (such as women). As we noted, current immigration changes render most women, the poor, and other marginalized groups as not "desirable." They are not particularly valued as potential citizens. Additionally, multiculturalism policy, initially constructed as a reordering of Canada's symbolic identity to address increasing diversity, has become increasingly implicated in consumer culture. "Diversity" here is little more than something that can be consumed (products of "ethnic culture") or a feature to be capitalized upon and marketed. The diversity within the "managing diversity" model that has supplanted employment equity in important ways suggests that all individual differences are important and that firms and sectors that fail to acknowledge this will not be able to compete effectively in a global market. This reading of diversity is also narrow insofar as it fails to problematize structural inequalities that exist between groups of people. In each of the policy areas—immigration, multiculturalism, and employment equity—the focus on economic rationalism has rendered a profoundly narrow vision of diversity, which is basically a selling-out of an agenda based on pursuing substantive equality for those marginalized by race/ethnicity, gender, and class.

THE CANADIAN POLITICAL COMMUNITY IN THE TWENTY-FIRST CENTURY

In many ways our analysis suggests that the Canadian polity—at least as it was presented and discussed by policy-makers since the 1990s—defines the ideal citizen as someone who is economically productive and can contribute to Canada's national and global competitiveness. In this context, a narrow notion of "diversity" may be acceptable only to the extent that it does not conflict with the values underpinning the twenty-first-century "ideal citizen." Yet, in reality, diversity in Canada is extremely broad. Canadian men and women live in a society that is increasing multicultural, multiethnic, multi-religious, and multi-racial.

In the final analysis, our critique of "selling diversity" raises the very question of what we, as Canadians, actually want to value. Should economic productiveness be the basic measurement of membership in the Canadian polity? Should entrepreneurship be imperative to our definition of national belonging? Should economic efficiency be the rationale behind measures aimed at increasing the numeric representation of historically under-represented groups in the Canadian labour market and promoting social justice? Indeed, there are potentially a host of ways in which membership, belonging, and social justice may be approached, which look at indicators of worth other than the standard economic measures associated with productivity. These might include things like care-giving to children or the elderly; sense of family, community, or global responsibility; respect for the environment; respect for a wide range of cultures and languages; the desire to create a more egalitarian society and world by engaging in social action; or simply a shared sense of destiny. Answering the questions of how membership, belonging, and social justice should be approached in Canada requires entering the realm of the normative—the realm of what ought to be.

As noted, all three public policy areas—immigration, multiculturalism, and employment equity—have been, since the 1990s, the subjects of partisan media and popular debate and attack. Yet in these debates the increasing emphasis on "selling diversity" and "productivity," influenced by neo-liberal ideals, has seldom been noted. As well, the implications of these directions that we have outlined have seldom been noted, namely, that the commitment to enhance gender equality, ethnic and racial equality, and class equality has been watered down in the last decade. As a result, there has really not been a full and complete consideration given to the normative questions concerning how we may better define membership, national belonging, and social justice in the Canadian polity. However, by explicitly considering both the direction charted in policy areas related to diversity over the last decade and normative questions about the future of the Canadian polity, Canadians would be given an opportunity to engage in deeper thinking and rethinking about the kind of community they want to live in.

These sorts of normative questions also require thinking through whether or not there are alternatives to the direction public policy initiatives have taken in Canada over the course of the 1990s. We believe that there are indeed options which Canadian policy-makers and Canadian citizens have in the twenty-first century.

In many ways, the reading of globalization given by Canadian policy-makers rests on the idea that there is no other alternative to neo-liberalism. If there is no other alternative, then the stress on the free market, the individual, and competitiveness is seemingly inevitable. It is true that a return to the "welfare state model" prevalent in the 1960s and 1970s may not realistically happen. Indeed, through the 1980s and 1990s politicians across the political spectrum in Western industrialized countries, including Canada, faulted this model for the creation of public deficits. While it may be argued that the ideas of Keynes (especially those relating to saving during better economic periods) were never really followed by policy-makers, there are other alternatives to neo-liberal values even within a capitalist system.

For example, there is so-called "progressive competitiveness" whereby the economy is restructured, but measures are taken to make sure that there are provisions for adjustment, such as training allowances, job placement assistance, or income security.[3] Such ideas do have a practical example, if we consider developments in Great Britain under Labour Prime Minister Tony Blair, who has advocated a "Third Way" between the Keynesian welfare state and neo-liberalism. Blair's agenda has been influential with other current social democratic governments in Europe (e.g., Germany).

The Third Way has its detractors. It has been criticized by those on the left for not going far enough in challenging neo-liberal values and creating equality,[4] and those on the right for being too tied to state intervention and thus being a kind of "ill-disguised Second Way."[5] We view the discussion surrounding the Third Way as important primarily because it signals the possibility of options that do not simply rest on the ideals of neo-liberalism—and so opens up political space.

However, we do not find the Third Way an entirely satisfactory response in that aspects of it are still rooted in a sense of inevitability. This is exemplified in the thinking of the leading intellectual figure behind Tony Blair's Third Way, British sociologist Anthony Giddens. In a recent article Giddens suggests that globalization is a dominant influence that requires inevitable political responses. Hence,

> All center-left governments of Europe have given up their traditional hostility to ma rkets while, at the same time, embracing the idea that there must be new regulations on international currency flows and global companies. All the social democratic leaders of Europe have a similar interest in forging a new model of responsible capitalism because they know there is no alternative to a global market economy.[6]

This kind of discussion around globalization borders on some of the criticisms we have had of Canadian policy-makers insofar as it treats globalization as producing a certain inevitable logic that should lead to certain inevitable policies. In the British context, Hay and Watson have criticized the work of Giddens as insensitive to the diverse and uneven impacts globalization processes may have on different states and for narrowing a sense of political options for a host of actors, including policy-makers. As they put it:

> While such a conception remains relatively unchallenged, the greatest threat to democratic political choice is not the "harsh economic reality" of globalization as much as the convenient alibi it appears to provide in the view of many centre-left thinkers. If politicians continue to internalize the radical globalization orthodoxy, there may well be no alternative to processes of economic convergence which increasingly bypass national democratic structures. However, if they choose to resist such a position, then the parameters of the possible are both less economically restrictive and less democratically debilitating. The choice is stark; its consequences could scarcely be more significant.[7]

Our understanding of the case of Canada would lead us to a similar position as that articulated by Hay and Watson.

The reading of globalization advanced by Canadian policy-makers, which rests on neo-liberalism, comes with possible alternatives, which might place more emphasis on issues of equity. In the current period, Canadians still have an opportunity to conceive of ways of achieving greater equality between men and women, between ethnic and racial groups, and between classes. At the federal level, the Chrétien Liberals began the process of "post-deficit" budgeting in 2000. This leaves open the possibility of more money being directed into areas of social spending than was the case in the 1990s. It remains an open question whether the groups maligned and scapegoated as "special interests" and subjected to severe cutbacks in recent years (e.g., groups representing women or minorities) will have the strength to mobilize and successfully lobby for an alternative agenda. However, this budgetary development at least raises the possibility that understandings based on the emphasis on the "free market" so prevalent through the 1990s may be challenged.

Moreover, there are alternative readings of globalization that might be given to the contemporary order, for it is not only economic processes, global competitiveness, and a corporate agenda that could be considered. For example, Richard Falk has talked about the possibility of a "globalization from below." Thus, whereas "globalization from above" revolves around the political elites of core states and the agents of transnational capital, a "globalization from below," is driven by transnational social forces concerned variously with the future of the environment, improving human rights, and ending patriarchy, poverty, and oppression.[8] The emergence of a Hemispheric Social Alliance to address free trade issues in the Americas offers a case in point. Among its many activities during the April 2001 Quebec meetings on the Free Trade Areas of the Americas was an alterative "People's Summit." The Summit's workshops, discussions, and panels offered alternatives to neo-liberal strategies and provided a forum for the development of "people-centred alternatives."[9] These are premised on the idea that governments are responsible to the concerns of their populations and do not have to cede all control to corporations or be driven by a corporate agenda.

In addition to providing a different reading of globalization, the discussion of Richard Falk on globalization from below directly raises the possibility of a new form of citizenship—namely, a global citizenship. The idea of global citizenship (like that of global civil society) is highly debated and contested.[10] The notion of global citizenship "encompasses rights and obligations and/or forms of political participation and belonging which are de-territorialized and take on transnational and/or global forms."[11] In a world where there continues to be gross economic inequality between states, and where states continue to guard their borders from would-be immigrants (particularly Western states *vis à vis* migrants coming from the South), it is difficult to imagine a truly global citizenship easily emerging.[12] Nonetheless, a discourse on globalization from below and on global citizenship offers a very different reading of globalization, and thus offers a form (or even forms) of possible political engagement.

In fact, resistance to the neo-liberal reading of globalization has been a rallying point in transnational mobilization, as demonstrated by the wave of popular protests dubbed "anti-capitalist" or "anti-globalization" that accompanied the World Trade Organization meeting in Seattle in 1999, the meeting of the World Bank and the International Monetary Fund in Prague in 2000, and the summit for a proposed Free Trade Agreement of the Americas in Quebec City in 2001. Moreover, the fact that, as a result of popular protests, OECD countries (which include Canada) abandoned the proposed Multilateral Agreement on Investment in 1998 also highlights that nothing is inevitable when it comes to the neo-liberal reading of globalization.[13]

A reading of globalization that replaces neo-liberalism with a stress on transnational solidarity in struggles for equality opens the door to different kinds of concerns. For example, proponents of cosmopolitanism suggest that democratization in an era of globalization requires a greater transfer of power from the state to regional (e.g., continental) and especially global levels.[14] Instead of a corporate agenda driving the neo-liberal understanding of globalization, this understanding of globalization is driven by ways of improving the rights and sense of connectedness between peoples across the globe.

Such an understanding of globalization may be used to view Canadian citizenship in a different light as well. Cultural diversity, and ways to understand cultural diversity (e.g., through immigration, international travel, and new communications technologies like the World Wide Web) could become something that increases understanding between peoples of the world as a good in its own right, rather than as a mere means to achieve greater trade links and national prosperity as measured in Gross National Product or Gross Domestic Product indicators.

In addition, forms of globalization which impact culture—including the movement of people, the movement of ideas, the movement of images, and the movement of information—allow Canadians to engage in the wider world in ways that may be very different from that of the not-so-distant past. As a result, the possibility of being linked to peoples and struggles in other parts of the world can add a new dimension to the sense of citizenship rights, belonging, identity, and social justice than has been previously marshaled in the name of equality. Such possibilities give new life-force to the potential of respect for a wide range of diversity (ethnic, cultural, gender, and so on) in an era of globalization, and illuminate the fact that "selling-diversity" is but one approach to chart in the twenty-first century.

ENDNOTES

1. See Jane Jenson and Susan Phillips, "Regime Shift: New Citizenship Practices in Canada," *International Journal of Canadian Studies* 14 (Autumn 1996): 111–35.

2. "The Values of a Just Society," *Towards a Just Society, The Trudeau Years* (Markham: Viking, 1990), 358–59; cited in Claude Couture, *Paddling with the Current: Pierre Trudeau, Etienne Parent, Liberalism, and Nationalism in Canada* (Edmonton: University of Alberta Press, 1996) 89–90.

3. For a discussion of progressive competitiveness, see Stephen McBride, "Policy from What?," *Restructuring and Resistance,* ed. Mike Burke, Colin Mooers, John Sheilds (Halifax: Fernwood, 2000) 162–65. Also, on socialist economic policy, see Gregory Albo, "A World Market of Opportunities? Capitalist Obstacles and Left Economic Policy," *Socialist Register,* ed. Leo Panitch (London: Merlin, 1997).

4. John Westergaard, "Where Does the Third Way Lead?," *New Political Economy* 4.3 (November 1999): 429–36. *Academic Search Elite,* University of Alberta Library System, April 10, 2001: 3.

5. Robert Higgs, "The So-Called Third Way," *Independent Review* 4.4 (Spring 2000): 625–30. *Academic Search Elite,* University of Alberta Library System, April 10, 2001: 5.

6. Anthony Giddens, "Still a Third Way for Europe," *New Perspectives Quarterly* 17.1 (Winter 2000): 50–52. *Academic Search Elite,* University of Alberta Library System, April 10, 2001: 2.

7. Colin Hay and Matthew Watson, "Globalization: 'Sceptical' Notes on the 1999 Reith Lecture," *Political Quarterly* 70.4 (Oct–Dec 1999): 418–25. *Academic Search Elite,* University of Alberta Library System, April 10, 2001: 7.

8. Richard Falk, "The Making of Global Citizenship," *Global Visions: Beyond the New World Order*, ed. Jeremy Brecher, John Brown Childs, and Jill Cutler (Montreal: Black Rose Books, 1993) 39–40.

9. See: Action Alert: "Join Thousands protesting the proposed FTAA, April 20–21," www.corp watch.org/action/2001/007.html and "Building a Hemispheric Social Alliance to Confront Free Trade," www.igc.org/trac/feature/humanrts/resistance/hemispheric.html.

10. Yasmeen Abu-Laban, "Reconstructing an Inclusive Citizenship for a New Millennium: Globalization. Migration, and Difference," *International Politics* 37.4 (December 2000): 517–19.

11. Abu-Laban, "Reconstructing an Inclusive Citizenship" 517.

12. Abu-Laban, "Reconstructing an Inclusive Citizenship" 518–22.

13. Yasmeen Abu-Laban, "The Future and the Legacy: The Impact of Globalization on the Canadian Settler-State," *Journal of Canadian Studies* 35.4 (Winter 2000–2001): 262–76.

14. David Held, "Democracy and Globalization," *Re-imagining Political Community: Studies in Cosmopolitan Democracy*, ed. Daniele Archibugi, David Held, and Martin Kohler (Stanford: Stanford University Press, 1998) 180.

CHAPTER FOUR

Regulating Native Identity by Gender

Bonita Lawrence

For many Native people today, the common-sense nature of identity legislation may appear to be relatively innocuous. If they are band members (in Canada) whose Indian status has been threatened with removal, or if they (and their children) have sufficient blood quantum or in other ways qualify for tribal membership in the United States, identity legislation can even appear to be serving a necessary function in protecting their communities from mixed-blood or Bill C-31 "outsiders." Identity legislation, like all Indian legislation, has set the terms under which Aboriginal peoples must organize their lives and, in a sense, the terms that people must use to resist domination. Native people have adapted accordingly.

It is primarily those who are mixed-blood, as well as others who have been removed from their communities by any number of colonialist policies, who often find themselves caught on the "wrong side" of identity legislation. It is for these individuals that identity legislation is rendered highly problematic due to the arbitrariness of the various regulations, their utter indifference to traditionally Indigenous ways of evaluating who was a member/citizen of the nation and who wasn't (which was precisely their purpose, in terms of reshaping Indigenous identities), and the inherent dehumanization of having one's identity regulated by (largely biological) standards of "Indianness." However, because of the individual nature of each set of circumstances, it inevitably appears as if "the problem" resides solely with mixed-bloodedness or urbanity, not with dehumanizing identity legislation. The role that identity legislation has played in *creating* mixed-bloodedness (and urbanity) as problems for one's Indianness falls out of the picture—as well as the role such laws have played in controlling and therefore, in a sense, creating on-reserve/tribal/full-blood identities.

In Canada a history of gender discrimination in the Indian Act has created an ongoing conflict within Native organizations and reserve communities around notions of individual and collective rights organized along lines of gender. It is crucially important, then, to understand the central role that the subordination of Native women has played in the colonization process, in order to begin to see the violation of Native women's rights through loss of Indian status, not as the problems faced by individuals, but as a *collective* sovereignty issue.

GENDERING INDIANNESS IN THE COLONIAL ENCOUNTER

The nation-building process in Canada began to accelerate between 1781 and 1830, in what is now Southern Ontario, when the British began to realize the necessity of bringing in settlers on the lands where previously they had engaged in the fur trade to secure the territory they claimed against the threat of American expansion. Settlement of the area was only made possible as individual Anishinaabe (Ojibway) bands were gradually induced to cede, in small packages, the land immediately north of Lake Ontario and Lake Erie to the British. Many of these land surrenders were framed as peace treaties to ensure that the British would be allies to the Ojibway against the possible northern encroachment of American settler violence; on this basis, only male leaders or representatives were asked to participate in treaty negotiation and the signing away of land (Schmalz 1991, 120–22).

In negotiating only with men, the British deliberately cut out the stabilizing presence of older women and the general authority that was given to their voices in major decision concerning the land. As Kim Anderson has written, traditional Native societies were often matrilineal in very balanced ways (2000, 66–68). Even in societies where men made the decisions about which land to hunt on each year, clans organized along the female line frequently controlled land inheritance. To bypass older women in traditional societies effectively removed from the treaty process the people centrally responsible for regulating land access.

Moreover the British were confident in their knowledge that, as Major Gladwin articulated, "The free sale of rum will destroy them more effectively than fire and sword" (Schmalz 1991, 82). The "chemical warfare" of alcohol, deliberately introduced north of the Great Lakes after the Pontiac uprising of 1763, had an immediate and devastating effect on Ojibway communities in the Toronto and southwestern Ontario region, whose social disintegration and their resulting dependency on the British was devastating (Schmalz 1991, 87). In such circumstances, as the abilities of the men to make good choices for the future were increasingly destabilized by alcohol, it was frequently the women whose decision-making capabilities became crucial for the survival of the society as a whole. The fact that the women invariably spoke with the future of the children always in mind meant that "choices" being forced on the men, such as surrendering the lands they could no longer hunt or trap on in exchange for the promise of assistance in the transition to farming (or later, of jobs in resource development), were most strenuously resisted by the women, who saw holding on to the land base as the only way in which the social fabric of the society to nurture the next generation would survive at all.

Finally, as Kathleen Jamieson has noted, most of the early land treaties and Indian legislation were premised on the Indigenous peoples the English were most familiar with—the Anishinaabe (Ojibway) and Haudenosaunee (Iroquois) peoples. Especially in Haudenosaunee society, female-led clans held the collective land base for all of the nations of the confederacy. Removing women, then, was the key to privatizing the land base. For all of these reasons, a central aspect of the colonization process in Canada would be to break the power of Indigenous women within their nations (Jamieson 1978, 13).

It is also important to take into account not only the concerns of British colonial administrators, for whom Indian administration was but another post of the empire, but the fears of the growing body of white settlers, where colonial anxieties about white identity and who would control settler societies were rampant. As Ann Stoler has noted, the European settlements that developed on other people's lands have generally been obsessed with ways of maintaining colonial control and of rigidly asserting differences between Europeans and Native peoples to maintain white social solidarity and cohesion (Stoler 1991, 53). Colonial societies have had to invent themselves as new groupings of individuals with no organic link to one another, in settings that are often radically different from their places of origin. They have had to invent the social institutions that will then define them as a society—and they have to be capable of rationalizing or justifying their existence on other people's lands and the brutality through which their presence is maintained. The very existence of white settler societies is therefore predicated on maintaining racial apartheid, on emphasizing racial difference, both white superiority and Native inferiority.

This flies in the face of the actual origins of many white settlements in Canada—which frequently began with displaced and often marginal white men, whose success with the fur trade or settlement, and often their very survival, depended on their ability to insinuate themselves into Indigenous societies through intermarriage. The early days of European-Native contact frequently involved negotiated alliances with local Indigenous communities, often cemented through marriage. This was particularly the case in French Canada, where early policy, particularly in the Maritimes, hinged on the notion of creating "one French race" in North America through the marriage of French men with Native women. While "frankifying" Native women may have been the goal of the French regime at the time, actual practices suggest that Acadian colonists, marginal men within Europe with relatively few loyalties to empire, tended to adapt to Native realities, as being much more suitable than European ways of living in the new land. In 1753 one French missionary predicted that within fifty years the Acadian colonists would be indistinguishable from Mi'kmaq and Maliseet communities (Dickason 1985, 21–26). Perhaps in response to this apparent cultural ambiguity on the part of the Acadians that troubled colonial authorities, racial categories began to be hardened by legislation throughout French Canada, particularly in Quebec.[1]

Meanwhile the entire structure of the fur trade, in both eastern and western Canada, involved "country marriages" between European men and the Native women that the traders depended on so heavily for their survival—and a growing reliance on the mixed-blood children of these marriages to fill specific niches in the fur trade—which meant that, as time went on, the boundaries between who should be considered European and who should be considered Native (and by what means) have not always been clear. By the mid-nineteenth century, the presence of numerous mixed-blood communities in the Great Lake area made it difficult for Anglo settlers to maintain clear boundaries between colonizers and colonized.[2] Social control was predicated on legally identifying who was white, who was Indian, and which children were legitimate progeny—citizens rather than subjugated Natives (Stoler 1991, 53). To render this issue even more complicated was the precedent set by the case of *Johnstone et al. v Connolly*, which upheld the rights of a customary marriage between a fur trader and a Native woman over a later church marriage between this same individual and a wealthy white Montreal woman.[3]

Moreover fur trade society in western Canada, in the years before the 1885 Rebellion, was in many respects highly bicultural. Many settlements consisted primarily of white men married to Cree women, raising Cree families. While the language spoken in public was English, the language spoken in many of the homes was Cree. Clearly, if a white settler society modeled on British values was to be established, white women had to take the place of Native women, and Native women had to be driven out of the place they had occupied in fur trade society, a process that would continue through successive waves of white settlement from the Great Lakes westward across the continent. The displacement of Native women from white society, and the replacement of the bicultural white society that their marriages to white men created to an openly white supremacist society populated by all-white families, was accomplished largely through the introduction of punitive laws in the Indian Act concerning prostitution and intoxication off-reserve. These laws targeted Aboriginal women as responsible for the spread of venereal disease among the police and officials in western Canada and therefore increasingly classified urban Aboriginal women as prostitutes within the criminal code after 1892 (Carter 1997, 187).

The growing devaluation of mixed marriages in western Canada in the 1880s was sharply highlighted by *Jones v Fraser* in 1886, wherein the judge ruled that the court would not accept that "the cohabitation of a civilized man and a savage woman, even for a long period of time, gives rise to the presumption that they consented to be married in our sense of marriage" (Carter 1997, 191). Mixed-blood children were also targeted for removal from white society, often through court decisions that made it impossible for them to inherit their fathers' property.[4] Sarah Carter suggests, in fact, that forcing Native wives out of settler society could only truly be effected by restricting the rights of all wives in western Canada.[5] Therefore, in the process of driving Native women out of white settlements, serious restrictions were placed on the rights of white women.

GENDER DISCRIMINATION IN THE INDIAN ACT

Many of the legal disabilities for women in the Indian Act have existed as much by omission as by explicit statement, through the use of the constant masculine term in the legislation, even though a separate legal regime has existed for Indian women, with respect to marriage, childbirth, regulation of sexual conduct, exclusion from the right to vote or otherwise partake in band business, and rights to inherit and for a widow to administer her husband's estate. Because of the constant use of the masculine pronoun, confusion has existed at times in various communities as to whether Native women actually have any of the rights pertaining to men in much of the Indian Act legislation (Jamieson 1978, 56). Finally, definitions of Indianness have been asserted in such a patriarchal manner as to be fraught with discriminatory consequences for Indian women.

[...] [L]egislation in 1850 first defined Indianness in gendered terms, so that Indian status depended either on Indian descent or marriage to a male Indian. With the Gradual Enfranchisement Act of 1869, not only were wives removed from inheritance rights and automatically enfranchised with their husbands, but Section 6 began a process of escalating gender discrimination that would not be definitively changed until 1985. With this section, for the first time, Indian women were declared "no longer Indian" if they married anybody who lacked Indian status. On marrying an Indian from another "tribe, band, or body," she and her children now belonged to her husband's tribe only (Jamieson 1978, 29–30).

Prior to 1951 some recognition on a local basis was given to the needs of Indian women who were deserted or widowed. Indian women who lost their status were no longer legally Indian and no longer formal band members, but they were not considered to have the full rights that enfranchised women had. These women were often issued informal identity cards, known as "red tickets," which identified them as entitled to shares in treaty monies and recognized on an informal basis their band membership, to the extent that some of them were even able to live on the reserve. It was not until 1951 that women who lost their Indian status were also compulsorily enfranchised. This meant that they not only lost band membership, reserve residency, or any property they might have held on the reserve, but also access to any treaty monies or band assets (RCAP 1996, 19:301–02).

Section 6, governing loss of status, was only one of the many aspects of the 1869 legislation that limited the power of Native women in their societies. Particularly in the context of matrilineal practices, this act ripped huge holes in the fabric of Native life. The clan system of the Iroquois was disrupted in particularly cruel ways. Not only was the matrilineal basis of the society (and therefore its framework of land tenure) threatened by legislation that forced Native women to become members of their husbands' communities, but the manner in which white women received the Indian status of their husbands resulted in the births of generations of clanless individuals within reserve communities, since clan inheritance passed through the mother. Finally, in addition to these processes, which subverted and bypassed the power of Native women in matrilineal societies and opened up their lands for privatization, Native women were formally denied any political role in the governance of their societies. For example when the 1869 legislation divided reserves into individual lots, married women could not inherit any portion of their husband's lots, and they lost their own allocations if they married non-Natives. After 1884 widows were allowed to inherit one-third of their husband's lot—if a widow was living with her husband at his time of death and was determined by the Indian agent to be "of good moral character" (RCAP 1996, 4:28–29). Meanwhile, in 1876, the Indian Act prevented Native women from voting in any decisions about surrender of reserve lands. The many ways in which Native women were rendered marginal in their communities by patriarchal colonial laws not only made it more difficult for them to challenge the tremendous disempowerment that loss of status represented, it made land theft much easier.

From the perspective of the colonial administration, the 1869 legislation had two primary goals—to remove as many individuals as possible from Indianness and, as part of this process, to enforce Indianness as being solely a state of "racial purity" by removing those children designated as "half-breed" from Indian communities. At the same time, however, if reserve residents were to grow increasingly mixed-blooded, it would facilitate their enfranchisement as individuals who were "too civilized" to be Indians. In the respect it is, of course, important to note that when white women married Native men, they also produced "half-breed" children, who nevertheless were allowed to stay in Native communities as Indians. Because of patriarchal notions that children were solely the products of their fathers, these children were not recognized by colonial administrators as half-breed. However, communities where there was a great deal of such intermarriage were often reported of approvingly, as when glowing comments were made about Caughnawaga (Kahnawake) in the 1830s that "there is scarcely a pure blooded Indian in the settlement" (Jamieson 1978, 23).

It is clear from the government debates at the time that this legislation was also aimed at undermining the collective nature of Native societies, where lands, monies, and other resources were shared in common. By restricting reserves only to those who were granted location tickets, by externalizing the Indian women who married white men and their children, and by forcing exogamy on Native women (where the custom in many communities was that Native men would join their wives' extended family, who controlled the land along clan lines), most of the collective aspects of Native society were to be subverted or suppressed.

In 1874, legislation altered and elaborated upon the definition of the term *Indian*, making Indian descent solely flowing from the male line. With this act, the status of the illegitimate children of Native women was also continuously subject to changing standards at the whim of the superintendent of Indian Affairs, depending on whether the father was known to be Native or not. The superintendent was also given the power to stop the payment of annuities and interest to any women having no children, who deserted her husband, and "lived immorally with another man" (Jamieson 1978, 45). Other legislation criminalized Indian women further, targeting them as prostitutes and providing them with penalties of one hundred dollars and up to six months in jail. It should be noted that being externalized from Indianness through loss of status, and being therefore forced to leave their communities, did not free Native women from being subject to criminal restrictions under the Indian Act when they were off-reserve. Such criminalization continued because of the much looser definitions of Indianness created expressly for the liquor section of the act, and because of the custom followed by many judges at the time of punishing nonstatus Native women according to Indian Act stipulations.

The 1920s legislation that evicted or jailed Native "squatters" on band lands had severe implications for women who lost their status and were increasingly rendered homeless, especially if their husbands were not white but were, rather, nonstatus Indians or Métis, or if their marriages to white men failed, or they were widowed (Jamieson 1978, 51). Indeed throughout the 1930s, an ongoing issue for the Department of Indian Affairs involved the numbers of Native women who had lost their status through marriage and were still receiving annuities and who either continued to live on the reserve or squatted on its fringes with nonstatus Native husbands. Indian agents were given the authority to evict these families with impunity (Jamieson 1978, 53). While cutting down on welfare and medical expenses to Indians was continuously effected throughout the 1930s, one duty that was never neglected, regardless of the cost, was the relentless tracking down of the fathers of "illegitimate" children of Native women, which often involved having Indian agents travel across the country to find them. These fathers, whether Indians or white, were then asked to sign forms affirming paternity of the child (Jamieson 1978, 54).

While the 1951 Indian Act represents a lessening of colonial control for Indian men, it actually heightened colonial regulation for Indian women in general and especially for those women who married non-Natives. The membership section became even more elaborate, couched in almost unreadable bureaucratic language, which spelled out not only who was entitled to be registered as an Indian but who was not. The male line of descent was further emphasized as the major criterion of inclusion—in fact, mention of "Indian blood" was altogether removed. The areas of the act that dictated who was not an Indian included Section 12(1)(b), which removed the status of any women who married a non-Indian (which included American Indians and nonstatus Native men from Canada), and Section 12(1)(a)(iv), also known as the "double-mother" clause, which removed the status of any individual whose mother *and* paternal grandmother lacked Indian status prior to their marriages to Indian men. Section 12(2) also enabled the "illegitimate" child of an Indian woman to lose status if the father was known not to have Indian status. All band lists now had to be publicly posted, and an appeal process was put into place, so that the child's Indian status could be "protested" by the band within twelve months of the child's name being added to the band list, if the father's Indian status was in question. Because of this, large numbers of so-called illegitimate Indian children, in many cases with two Native parents (but with the father being nonstatus), were denied Indian status.

The major change for Native women who "married out" was that from the date of their marriages they were not only automatically deprived of their Indian status and band rights, but by order of the governor-in council they were declared enfranchised. Enfranchisement for these Indian women, however, did not involve the same conditions as those that had been experienced by Indian men and their families either through voluntary or involuntary enfranchisement. Individuals who enfranchised, voluntarily or involuntarily, had to have sufficient resources to survive off-reserve. No such condition was considered necessary for Indian women compulsorily enfranchised since they were assumed to be, effectively, "wards" of their husband. Their prior children were erroneously enfranchised with them until 1955; in 1967 these children were reinstated—when they could be traced. A federal government position of registrar was created to oversee the complex matter of who would be maintained on band lists and who would be struck off. In case Indian women attempted to hide their marriages to non-Indians by marrying in an urban center, at least some arrangements were effected between Statistics Canada and the Department of Indian Affairs in an effort to ensure that most, if not all, marriages of status Indians were eventually reported (Jamieson 1978, 65).

The financial losses experienced by Native women due to loss of status have been considerable. When enfranchised, the women were entitled to receive a per capita share of band capital and revenue, as well as the equivalent of twenty years' treaty money. Since the treaty money is either four or five dollars a year, depending on the treaty, the women were therefore entitled to receive either eighty or one hundred dollars. However, during the interval when large numbers of women were being enfranchised and "paid off," most Native communities had relatively few assets and revenue available to provide meaningful shares to the women. Many of those bands subsequently received significant monies from resource development, to which the enfranchised women and their children never had access.

Another series of financial losses that Native women experienced when they lost their Indian status included the lack of access to postsecondary-education funding, free day-care provisions in some communities, funding for school supplies and special schooling programs, housing policies that enabled on-reserve Indians to buy houses with assistance from the Central Mortgage and Housing Corporation and Indian Affairs, loans and grants from the Indian Economic Development Fund, health benefits, exemption from taxation and from provincial sales tax, hunting, fishing, animal grazing and trapping rights, cash distributions from sales of band assets, and ability to be employed in the United States without a visa and to cross the border without restrictions (Jamieson 1978, 70–71). Finally, Indian women were generally denied access to personal property willed to them, evicted from their homes, often with small children and no money (especially when widowed or separated), and generally faced hostile band councils and indifferent Indian Affairs bureaucrats (Jamieson 1978, 72).

However, it is the personal and cultural losses of losing status that Indian women have most frequently spoken about. Some of the costs have included being unable to participate with family and relatives in the life of their former communities, being rejected by their communities, being culturally different and often socially rejected within white society, being unable to access cultural programs for their children, and finally not even being able to be buried with other family members on the reserve. The extent of penalties and lack of compensation for losses suffered has made the forcible enfranchisement of Indian women "retribution, not restitution"; what Justice Bora Laskin, in his dissenting opinion in *Lavell and Bedard*, termed "statutory banishment" (Jamieson 1978, 72).

Finally, in terms of Native empowerment generally, it is important to note that this "bleeding off" of Native women and their children from their communities was in place for 116 years from 1869 until 1985. The phenomenal cultural implication hidden in this legislation is the sheer numbers of Native people lost to their communities. Some sources have estimated that by far the majority of the twenty-five thousand Indians who lost status and were externalized from their communities between 1876 and 1985 (Holmes 1987, 8) did so because of ongoing gender discrimination in the Indian Act.[6] But it is not simply a matter of twenty-five thousand individuals. If one takes into account the fact that for every individual who lost status and had to leave her community, all of her descendants (many of them the products of nonstatus Indian fathers and Indian mothers) also lost status and for the most part were permanently alienated from Native culture, the numbers of individuals who ultimately were removed from Indian status and lost to their nations may, at the most conservative estimates, number between one and two million.

By comparison, in1985, when Bill C-31 was passed, there were only 350,000 status Indians still listed on the Department of Indian Affairs' Indian register (Holmes 1987, 54). In comparing the potential numbers of people lost to their Native communities because of loss of status with the numbers of individuals still considered Indian in 1985, the scale of cultural genocide caused by gender discrimination becomes visible. Because Bill C-31 allowed the most recent generation of individuals who had lost status to regain it, along with their children, approximately one hundred thousand individuals had regained their status by 1995 (Switzer 1997, 2). But the damage caused, demographically and culturally, by the loss of status of so many Native women for a century prior to 1985, whose grandchildren and great-grandchildren are now no longer recognized—and in many cases no longer identify—as Indian, remain incalculable.

THE STRUGGLE TO CHANGE THE INDIAN ACT

Given the accelerating gender discrimination in the Indian Act created by the modifications of 1951, Mohawk women in the 1960s created an organization known as Indian Rights for Indian Women, which attempted to address the disempowerment of Indian women, particularly with respect to loss of status. In 1971 Jeannette Corbiere Lavell and Yvonne Bedard, two Indian women who had lost status through their marriages, challenged the discriminatory sections of the Indian Act in the Canadian courts. In doing so they relied on a precedent set in 1969 in *R. v Drybones*, where an Indian man named Drybones, who had been convicted of being intoxicated off-reserve under Section 94(b) of the Indian Act, appealed his conviction to the Supreme Court on the basis that this section was in violation of the equality guarantee against racial discrimination set out in Section 1(b) of the Canadian Bill of Rights.[7]

With the success of *Drybones*, Lavell challenged the deletion of her name from her band list, while Bedard, in a separate case, challenged the fact that her reserve was evicting her and her children from the house which her mother had willed to her, even though she was no longer married to her husband. Both women lost at the federal court level, but were successful at winning appeals, and their cases were heard together in the Supreme Court. Their argument was based on the fact that the Indian Act discriminated against them on the basis of race and sex, and that the Bill of Rights should therefore override the discriminatory sections of the Indian Act with respect to membership, as *Drybones* had with Section 94(b).

In 1973 the Supreme Court, by a five to four decision, ruled against Lavell and Bedard. Among other reasons, the decision noted that since not all Indians were discriminated against, only Indian women who married non-Indians, then racial discrimination could not be said to exist; and since enfranchised Indian women gained the citizenship rights that made them equal (in law) to white women, then gender discrimination could not be said to exist. While this judgment clarified none of the issues, it did assert that the Bill of Rights could not take precedence over the Indian Act. Because of the decision, the Indian Act was exempt from the application of the Canadian Human Rights Act in 1977 (Holmes 1987, 5).

The Maliseet community of Tobique was the next focus of resistance. The women at Tobique began their struggle over the issue of homelessness—the manner in which their band council interpreted Indian Act legislation to suggest that Indian women had no right to own property on the reserve. As the women addressed the problems they faced, their struggle slowly broadened until their primary goal became changing the Indian Act (Silman 1987, 119–72). Since the decision in *Lavell and Bedard* had foreclosed any possibility of justice within Canada, the Tobique women decided to support Sandra Lovelace in an appeal to the United Nations Human Rights Committee. Lovelace argued that Section 12(1)(b) of the Indian Act was in violation of Article 27 of the International Covenant on Civil and Political Rights, which provides for the rights of individuals who belong to minorities to enjoy their culture, practice their religion, and use their language in community with others from the group (Beyefsky 1982, 244–66). In1981 the United Nations determined that Sandra Lovelace had been denied her cultural rights under Article 27 because she was barred from living in her community. Canada, embarrassed at the international level, at this point stated its intention to amend the discriminatory sections of the Indian Act. After some degree of consultation and proposed changes, Bill C-31, An Act to amend the Indian Act, was passed in 1985.[8]

The violence and resistance that Native women struggling for their rights faced from male-dominated band councils and political organizations during this interval cannot be ignored.[9] For example, when Mary Two-Axe Earley and sixty other Native women from Kahnawake (then known as the Caughnawaga band) chose to focus international attention on their plight by bringing their organization, Indian Rights for Indian Women, to the International Women's Year conference in Mexico City in 1975, they were all served with eviction notices in their absence by their band council (Jamieson 1979, 170). Meanwhile when the Tobique women, protesting homelessness in their communities, occupied the band office in order to have a roof over their heads and draw attention to their plight, they were threatened with arrest by the band administration, physically beaten up in the streets, and had to endure numerous threats against their families from other community members.[10]

It was with *Lavell and Bedard*, however, that the polarization between nonstatus women demanding their rights as Indians and status Indian organizations such as the National Indian Brotherhood (now the Assembly of First Nations) and the Association of Iroquois and Allied Indians came to a head. For example, the National Indian Brotherhood, which intervened *against* Lavell and Bedard, supported the argument that gender discrimination against Native women had been instituted in the 1869 legislation (and enshrined in every Indian Act since then) as a benevolent process to protect Indians from the white men who married Indian women.[11] And a position paper of the Association of Iroquois and Allied Indians (AIAI), which had asked the government to intervene in the Supreme Court, concurred with the Supreme Court that Section 12(1)(b) was "merely a legislative embodiment of Indian custom" (Jamieson 1978, 83).

More damningly, the widespread discrimination against Native women first introduced in 1869 continues to be upheld by some individuals as legislation designed to "protect" Native communities from the white husbands of Native women. The most recent example of this argument, which continues to be raised whenever it is politically expedient, is demonstrated by Taiaiake Alfred in *Windspeaker* (February 2000). Alfred, in comments that are curiously suggestive of a belief in the benevolence of the Canadian government toward its colonized subjects, states that gender discrimination in the Indian Act was put there to oblige Native people because "the Indian complained" about what would happen if white men were allowed to marry Native women and live in their communities. Alfred also asserts that gender discrimination was traditionally practiced in Native communities but that it should not be *seen* as gender discrimination, simply because, culturally, women had to bear a stronger responsibility for who they married than men did, as mothers of the nation. Because of this, the virtual banishment of these women and their children from Native communities for marrying nonstatus individuals has been justifiable and certainly does not require redress (Alfred, in Barnsley 2000, 6–7).

Kathleen Jamieson has demonstrated, however, that the various government debates that attended the passing of this legislation make clear that the intent of the act was *not* to prevent white men from living on the reserve—it was to prevent their mixed-blood children from having any rights to community assets and to limit the abilities of community residents to support nonband-member relatives and others who would normally be welcome to share whatever resources the community had.[12] Other individuals in recent years have claimed that it was acceptable for the Indian Act to discriminate against Native women because "it was traditional" within Native societies. Jamieson refutes these arguments as well by documenting some of the objections raised by Native communities to this legislation at the time that it was passed.[13]

The federal government, moreover, with *Lavell and Bedard*, took the position that it could not alter any of the membership sections of the Indian Act until the entire act was revised, thus feeding status Indian fears created by the White Paper. In 1969, in a document known as the White Paper, the federal government proposed to unilaterally terminate Indian status, thereby terminating its fiduciary responsibility and the various rights and exemptions accruing to individuals of Indian status, including reserve land holdings. This preemptive move, if successful, would not only have enabled remaining Indian reserves to be privatized and lost to Native people but it would have removed any legal framework for redress of lost land. It would have removed Native control over education and thereby invalidated efforts to address the massive loss of language brought about by residential schools. Finally, the massive poverty and social problems of Native people—a result not only of loss of access to a resource base and tremendous structural racism within Canadian society but also through years of being denied, as Indians, the basic financial benefits accruing to Canadians and of having generations of Native people "imprisoned" in residential schools—would have become each individual's "fault," and it would have been up to the individual Native person to rectify the situation as best they could. Assimilation, rather than nation-building, would gradually become the only realistic or viable goal for Native people.

The response to the White Paper was immediate. A massive mobilization of Native people across Canada proceeded until the paper was shelved. There are repercussions, however, which have lasted until this day. First of all, the Canadian government continues to propose bills that reintroduce aspects of the White Paper in a more piecemeal fashion. Canada has, however, become far more expert at dividing opposition among status Indians in the process. Secondly, the emphasis that status Indian organizations now place on resisting changes to the Indian Act has effectively divided them from nonstatus Native people. Prior to the White Paper, throughout the 1960s, Native people across Canada were resisting their ongoing colonization in a relatively unified manner. After the White Paper, status Indian organizations became much more focused on protecting status Indian rights, while Native people who lacked Indian status were forced to begin to organize alone to acquire some rights as Native people.

Because of these many layers of fear engendered by the White Paper, and because Indian activists had already begun to see the Indian Act as a lever that could potentially embarrass Canada at the International level (as the Maliseet women in fact succeeded in doing in the Lovelace case) and that could therefore be a bargaining tool, many of the status Indian organizations supported the position of the federal government in refusing to alter any of the membership sections of the Indian Act without amending the act as a whole. Kathleen Jamieson has suggested that this was based on the erroneous assumption that the Canadian government was not also continuing to use the Indian Act as a lever against Native people, as it had been doing for a century already. She has also noted how, during the struggles over the White Paper and *Lavell and Bedard*, the Indian Act was somehow transformed from the legal instrument of oppression that it had been since its inception to "a repository of sacred rights for Indians"

(Jamieson 1978, 2). And yet despite the extreme positions taken by some of the activists at the time (and since), other individuals clearly saw the gender discrimination in the Indian Act as deeply problematic, and so there was no consensus within the National Indian Brotherhood initially over *Lavell and Bedard*.

In 1980, perhaps in anticipation of the upcoming Lovelace decision, Canada created an interim policy that allowed Indian bands to request suspension of Section 12(1)(b) and 12(1)(a)(iv). Fifty-three percent of all bands requested suspension of the "double-mother" clause (which affects adult Native men and women who live on reserves) while only nineteen percent chose to suspend Section 12(1)(b), which affects only Native women and their off-reserve male and female descendants. This tremendous discrepancy suggests that band governments in general at that point did not regard the rights of Indian women (and their off-reserve children) as important (Holmes 1987, 6). Indeed the multiple legacies for Native communities of having patriarchal relations enforced for over a century by the Indian Act continue to resonate throughout Indian Country.

After over a century of gender discrimination in the Indian Act, the idea that Native women should lose status for marrying nonstatus or non-Native men has become a normalized assumption in many communities. As a result, our basic understanding of who is mixed-blood and who is not is highly shaped by gender. The family histories of on-reserve Native people have routinely included the presence of white women married to Native men, as well as (in some cases) the children of Native women who had babies by white men but were not married to them, and whose status was not protested. These experiences have not been seen, or theorized, as mixed-blood experiences. These mixed-blood children have been allowed to have Indian status, they have been considered to be Indian, and have never had to leave their communities. Indian reserves, particularly those adjacent to white settlements, may have grown progressively mixed-blooded under these circumstances—but they have not been *called* mixed-blooded communities, and on-reserve mixed-blooded families have therefore not been externalized *as* mixed-blood people.

It has been the children of Native mothers and white, nonstatus Indian, or Métis fathers who have been forced to become urban Indians and who, in their Native communities of origin, are currently being regarded as outsiders because they *have* been labeled as "not Indian." Gender has thus been crucial in determining not only who has been able to stay in Native communities but who has been called mixed-blood and externalized as such. In this respect, gender discrimination in the Indian Act has shaped what we think about who is Native, who is mixed-blood, and who is entitled to access to Indian land. These beliefs are only rendered more powerful by the strongly protectionist attitudes toward preserving Native culture as it is lived on reserves at present, where outsiders may be seen as profoundly threatening to community identity.

This history has even deeper repercussions, however, for Native communities today. Because the subordination of Indigenous women has been a central nexus though which colonizers have sought to destroy Indigenous societies, contemporary gender divisions created by the colonizer continue to subvert sovereignty struggles in crucial ways. And yet almost inevitably, when issues of particular concern to Native women arise, they are framed as "individual rights," while in many cases, those who oppose Native women's rights are held to represent "the collective." In a context where a return to traditional collective ways is viewed as essential to surviving the ravages of colonization, Native women are routinely asked to separate their womanness from their Nativeness, as if violations of Native women's rights are not violations of Native rights.

Even the American court decision most often cited as a positive example for Aboriginal governments in terms of exercising the right to control their own membership, *Santa Clara Pueblo v Martinez*, involved upholding the sovereign right of a tribal government to deny membership rights to the children of a female tribal member, as part of resisting the imposition of federal rights legislation within tribal territories. *Santa Clara Pueblo v Martinez* involved the case of Julia Martinez, a member of Santa Clara Pueblo, who married a Navajo Indian two years after a tribal ordinance passed that clearly outlined that membership in the tribe was patrilineal, that nonmember husbands could not be adopted into the tribe while nonmember wives could. Martinez's children, who grew up at Santa Clara Pueblo and who are Tewa-speaking and culturally fully members of their community, could reside in the community only until the death of their mother and could not inherit her property.

Julia Martinez and her daughter Audrey therefore brought suit in federal court against the tribe and its governor, claiming that this membership rule discriminates on the basis of both sex and ancestry in violation of Title 1 of the Indian Civil Rights Act. This act, passed in 1968 with the goal of allowing the federal government to "protect Indians from their own governments" (as if the federal government is some neutral third party), was the first major federal legislation addressing the operation of tribal governments since the Indian Reorganization Act of 1934. Immediately after its enactment, the federal court began to take jurisdiction in cases challenging the decisions of tribal courts and councils, assuming that the Indian Civil Rights Act waived tribal sovereign immunity from suit. In *Santa Clara Pueblo v Martinez*, however, it was held that without congressional authorization, tribes are exempt from suit and that waivers of sovereign immunity cannot be implied but must be expressed. Julian Martinez was therefore barred by Santa Clara Pueblo's immunity from suit from taking the tribe to court (Clinton et al. 1973, 384–89). For women such as Julia Martinez, then, her tribe's victory meant her children's disenfranchisement.

ENDNOTES

1. A number of European French families attempted to challenge the inheritance of Quebec fortunes by Native wives and children, and some were successful. Meanwhile, in 1735, an edict was passed that required the consent of the governor or commanding officer for all mixed marriages in New France to be considered legal, while another edict restricted the rights of Native women to inherit their French husband's property (Dickason 1985, 28).

2. Recent research has documented the presence of mixed-blood communities at no fewer that fifty-three locations in the Great Lakes region between 1763 and 1830 (RCAP 1996, 1:150).

3. In 1803 John Connolly began a customary marriage, *à la façon du pays,* with a Native woman known only as Suzanne. In 1832 he married a wealthy white Montreal woman, Julia Woolrich, while his Native wife Suzanne was still alive. In the court case that followed, several fur traders gave testimony that customary marriages were usually monogamous, undertaken freely by both parties, and of long duration. The court at that point upheld the rights of the customary marriage over the church marriage (*Johnstone et al. v. Connolly,* Court of Appeal, 7 December 1869, cited in *La revue légale* 1:235–400).

4. For example, in 1899, the Supreme Court of the Northwest Territories ruled that the two sons of Awatoyakew, also known as Mary Brown, a Peigan woman, and Nicholas Sheran, the founder of a lucrative coal mine in the Lethbridge area, were not entitled to a share of

their father's estate. On Sheran's death, his sister took the children, placed them in a St. Albert orphanage, and paid a hundred dollars a year each for their care; neither child, however, ever received any direct returns from their father's mine (Carter, 1997,191–92).

5. In the Northwest Territories, the Real Property Act of 1886 abolished the right of a wife to dower (a lifetime interest in one-third of her husband's property upon widowhood). A further Disability Act was passed in the early years of the twentieth century that removed the rights of wives to any share of their husband's estate (Carter 1997, 193).

6. These figures include both those individuals who were enfranchised and those who lost their status because of gender discrimination in the Indian Act. However, the numbers of individuals who lost status due to enfranchisement only reached significant levels for a few years during the 1920s and 1930s, and the policy was ended for everybody but women marrying non-Natives in 1951. By comparison, for over a century, the majority of individuals who lost status were Indian women who married out.

7. *R. v Drybones*, 6 CNOR 273 SCC (1960).

8. In April 1985 the Charter of Rights and Freedoms came into effect. The identity legislation within the 1951 Indian Act was in violation of Section 15(1), which prohibited discrimination on the basis of race and gender, as well as other particularities. Because of this, when Bill C-31 came into effect on 28 June 1985, its amendments to the 1951 act came into legal effect retroactively back to 17 April 1985, the date that the charter came into effect (Gilbert 1996, 129).

9. At the time of *Lavell and Bedard*, there were no women on the National Indian Brotherhood executive council, and the Association of Iroquois and Allied Indians, who first enlisted the help of the solicitor general and turned the tide against Lavell, represented twenty thousand Indian men (Jamieson 1978, 91).

10. The American Indian Movement, with long experience in defending traditional and grassroots Native people against "puppet" Indian governments, offered their assistance to the Tobique women. The women declined, however, for fear that the situation would escalate still further if AIM entered the reserve to support them (Silman 1987, 129–30).

11. Factum of Isaac et al., 58–67, 74, in *Lavell and Bedard*.

12. According to Jamieson, the government debate about this legislation focused on fears raised by white men, for example, citizens of Chateauguay who resided on the Caughnawa reserve (Kahnawake), that they would be forced to leave the community. The repeated response of administrators was that the only white men who would be forced to leave Native communities were those found to be selling liquor or robbing the Indians of their timber. Those white men already resided at Kahnawake—twenty-eight at the time of the legislation—were permitted to stay there and in fact received licenses to do so (Jamieson 1978, 32).

13. In 1872 the Grand Council of Ontario and Quebec Indians sent a strong letter to the minister at Ottawa, protesting Section 6 of the 1869 Act, noting that Native women should have the privilege of marrying whom they pleased without suffering exclusion or expulsion from their tribe and consequent loss of property and rights. Other protests from the Six Nations and from Caughnawaga band (Kahnawake) also challenged the notion that Indian women should be externalized for marrying non-Indians (Jamieson 1978, 36).

BIBLIOGRAPHY

Anderson, Kim. 2000. *A Recognition of Being: Reconstructing Native Womanhood.* Toronto: Second Story Press.

Barnsley, Paul. 2000. Membership Issues Illustrate Cultural Differences. *Windspeaker* (February): 6–7.

Beyefsky, Anne F. 1982. The Human Rights Committee and the Case of Sandra Lovelace. In *The Canadian Yearbook of International Law.* Vol. 20.

Bill C-31: The Challenge. 1996. Classroom Edition. *Windspeaker* (March): 7.

Carter, Sarah. 1997. *Capturing Women: The Manipulation of Cultural Imagery in Canada's Prairie West.* Kingston and Montreal: McGill-Queen's University Press.

Clinton, Robert N., Nell Jessup Newton, and Monroe E. Price. 1973. *American Indian Law: Cases and Materials.* 3d ed. Charlottesville, VA: Michie Company.

Dickason, Olive Patricia. 1985. From "One Nation" in the Northeast to "New Nation" in the Northwest: A Look at the Emergence of the Métis. In *The New Peoples: Being and Becoming Métis in North America,* edited by Jacqueline Peterson and Jennifer S.H. Brown. Winnipeg: University of Manitoba Press.

Gilbert, Larry. 1996. *Entitlement to Indian Status and Membership Codes in Canada.* Toronto: Thompson Canada Ltd.

Holmes, Joan. 1987. *Bill C-31—Equality or Disparity? The Effects of the New Indian Act on Native Women.* Background Paper. Canadian Advisory Council on the Status of Women.

Jamieson, Kathleen. 1978. *Indian Women and the Law in Canada: Citizen Minus.* Canadian Advisory Council on the Status of Women and Indian Rights for Indian Women.

———. 1979. Multiple Jeopardy: The Evolution of a Native Women's Movement. *Atlantis 4,* no. 2:157–76.

Royal Commission on Aboriginal Peoples (RCAP). 1996. *For Seven Generations: Report of the Royal Commission on Aboriginal Peoples.* Vols. 1–5. Ottawa: Government of Canada.

Schmalz, Peter S. 1991. *The Ojibwa of Southern Ontario.* Toronto: University of Toronto Press.

Silman, Janet. 1987. *Enough Is Enough: Aboriginal Women Speak out,* as told to Janet Silman. Toronto: The Women's Press.

Stoler, Ann. 1991. Carnal Knowledge and Imperial Power: Gender, Race, and Mortality in Colonial Asia. In *Gender at the Crossroads: Feminist Anthropology in the Post-Modern Era,* edited by Micaela di Leonardo. Berkeley: University of California Press.

Switzer, Maurice. 1997. Time to Stand up and Be Counted. *The First Perspective* (December): 2.

CHAPTER ONE, *Peter Li*

Further Reading

Fleras, A., and J.L. Elliott. (2007). *Unequal Relations: An Introduction to Race, Ethnic, and Aboriginal Dynamics in Canada*, 5th ed. Toronto: Pearson Prentice Hall.

This book has comprehensive coverage of racism, multiculturalism, and diversity. It has a critical approach, combined with a strong balance of research, application, and attention to key current issues.

Pendakur, K., and R. Pendakur. (2002). "Colour My World: Has the Minority-Majority Earnings Gaps Changed over Time?" *Canadian Public Policy* 28 (4), 489–513.

Using the Census main bases from 1971 through 1996, the article estimates earnings equations for Canadian-born female and male workers to assess the size of White, Aboriginal, and White visible minority earnings differentials in Canada. These databases allow researchers to focus on the small populations of Canadian-born visible minority and Aboriginal workers in Canada and on eight large Canadian metropolitan areas. Authors of the article find that differentials narrowed through the 1970s, were stable through the 1980s, and grew between 1991 and 1996.

Stelcner, M. (2000). "Earnings Differentials among Ethnic Groups in Canada: A Review of the Research." *Review of Social Economy* 58 (3), 295–317.

Canada has a large foreign-born population with an increasingly diverse ethnic profile. The 1986 Employment Equity Act designated "visible minorities," Aboriginal peoples, women, and disabled people as facing labour market disadvantages. This review of a growing body of research on ethnic earning differentials shows that the sizeable earnings shortfall of Aboriginal peoples could be "explained" by their lesser endowments of work-related characteristics. The high variance in discrimination estimates among men can be traced to the treatment of immigration effects, aggregation of diverse ethnic groups, and the choice of the non-discriminatory earnings norm.

Related Web Sites

Metropolis Project
canada.metropolis.net

The Metropolis Project is an international co-operative research project designed to stimulate multidisciplinary research on the effects of international migration on cities in Canada.

Policy Research Initiative (PRI)
www.policyresearch.gc.ca

This site is for the Policy Research Data Group (PRDG), which is an interdepartmental forum for the identification of data gaps and for collaboration in the development of new data products for research in priority horizontal policy areas in Canada. The PRDG was formed in early 1998 as part of the PRI. Its membership was made up of approximately 30 senior managers drawn from departmental research policy branches in the federal government, as well as from the Privy Council Office, the Department of Finance, and the Treasury Board Secretariat.

Statistics Canada: Population and Demography
www40.statcan.ca/l01/cst01/popula.htm

This site contains official statistics of the population and demographics of Canada.

CHAPTER TWO, *Rose Baaba Folson*

Further Reading

Epp, M., F. Iacovetta, and F. Swyripa. (2004). *Sisters or Strangers?: Immigrant, Ethnic, and Racialized Women in Canadian History.* Toronto: University of Toronto Press.

This book discusses race in the context of nation-building, encounters with the state and public institutions, symbolic and media representations of women, familial relations, domestic violence and racism, and analyses of history and memory. In different ways, the authors question whether the historical experience of women in Canada represents a "sisterhood" of challenge and opportunity, or if the racial, class, or marginalized identity of the immigrant and minority women made them in fact "strangers" in a country where privilege and opportunity fall according to criteria of exclusion.

Granatstein, J.L., and N. Hillmer. (2006). *The Land Newly Found: Eyewitness Accounts of the Canadian Immigrant Experience.* Toronto: Thomas Allen Publishers.

This book is a collection of first-hand accounts from the frontiers of Canadian immigration history. Drawn from letters, newspapers, and reportage, these vivid accounts range from the 18th century to the present day, and provide an insightful look into the lives and minds of newly arrived immigrants to Canada as well as the politicians, policy makers, and public who witnessed their arrival. This book not only explores the personal stories of those who choose to make Canada their new home, but provides keen insight into the policies and political struggles of a budding multicultural nation.

Zaman, H. (2006). *Breaking the Iron Wall: Decommodification and Immigrant Women's Labor in Canada.* Toronto: Rowman & Littlefield.

By providing empirical as well as historical evidence, the author undertakes a rigorous analysis of immigrant women's commodification and the possibility of their decommodification in Canada.

Related Web Sites

Affiliation of Multicultural Societies and Service Agencies of British Columbia (AMSSA)
www.amssa.org/

This site contains information and resources for new immigrants in British Columbia in the areas of health promotion and anti-racism.

Canadian Ethnocultural Council (CEC)
www.ethnocultural.ca/about_cec.html

> This site is from a non-profit, non-partisan coalition of national ethnocultural umbrella organizations that, in turn, represent a cross-section of ethnocultural groups across Canada. It provides publications and reports in a variety of areas, including immigration, multiculturalism, and employment for new immigrants.

National Anti-racism Council of Canada (NARCC)
www.narcc.ca//index.html

> This site provides information on racism, racialization, and all other forms of related discrimination in Canada. It also includes research reports and publications in these areas.

CHAPTER THREE, *Yasmeen Abu-Laban and Christina Gabriel*

Further Reading

Abu-Laban, Y. (2000–2001). "The Future and the Legacy: The Impact of Globalization on the Canadian Settler-State." *Journal of Canadian Studies* 35 (4), 262–276.

> This article examines the impact of globalization as a discourse and as a process affecting the politics of the 21st century in light of Canada's foundation as a "White settler-colony." By the end of the 20th century, identity politics—the collective demands for inclusion and equity by minoritized groups, including women, ethnic minorities, Aboriginal peoples, the Quebecois, and other French-Canadians—sat uneasily with Ottawa's neo-liberal reading of globalization, which tends to give value to the individual as a taxpayer. Canada's yet-to-be publicly acknowledged historical legacy of colonialism and ethnic and racial inequality ensure that Canadian national symbols and institutions continue to be key targets of minoritized groups demanding fairness and inclusion. Given this, the starting point for institutional change is the recognition and redressing of the inequities of past state practices and the creation of a new dialogue among equals.

Burke, Mike, C. Mooers, and J. Shields. (eds.). (2000). *Restructuring and Resistance: Canadian Public Policy in an Age of Global Capitalism.* Halifax: Fernwood.

> Examining the political meaning and social implications of neo-liberal restructuring in Canada, surveying examples of such restructuring within major policy fields, and theoretically placing it within the broader context of globalizing capitalism, this book contributes to the understanding of Canadian public policy in the contemporary context. The book also presents an interesting and informative overview of the state of debates on the left regarding strategies of resistance to neo-liberal restructuring.

Held, D. (1998). "Democracy and Globalization." In Daniele Archibugi, David Held, and Martin Kohler (eds.), *Re-imagining Political Community: Studies in Cosmopolitan Democracy*, pp. 11–27. Stanford: Stanford University Press.

> This book explores the changing meaning of political community in a world of regional and global social and economic relations. The authors, who reflect a variety of academic disciplines, reconsider some of the key terms of political association, such as legitimacy, sovereignty, identity,

and citizenship. Their common approach is to generate an innovative account of what democracy means today and how it can be reconceptualized to include subnational as well as transnational levels of political organization.

Related Web Sites

CCPA—Canadian Centre for Policy Alternatives
www.policyalternatives.ca

> The CCPA is an independent, non-partisan research institute concerned with issues of social and economic justice. Their research and analysis show that there are workable solutions to the policy questions facing Canadians today.

National Organization of Immigrant and Visible Minority Women of Canada
www.noivmwoc.org

> The National Organization of Immigrant and Visible Minority Women of Canada exists to ensure equality for immigrant and visible minority women within an officially bilingual and multicultural Canada.

Polaris Institute
www.polarisinstitute.org

> This is a Canadian-based NGO designed to enable citizen movements to re-skill and re-tool themselves to fight for democratic social change in an age of corporate-driven globalization.

CHAPTER FOUR, *Bonita Lawrence*

Further Reading

Anderson, K. (2000). *A Recognition of Being: Reconstructing Native Womanhood*. Toronto: Second Story Press.

> The author has written a critical and inspiring history of Native womanhood. She traces the construction of the negative female stereotypes forced on Native women during colonization. Through interviews with 40 contemporary Native women across Canada, she explores the issues shaping their lives and the many ways they are reclaiming positive and powerful images of themselves.

Lawrence, B. (2004). *"Real" Indians and Others: "Mixed-Blood Urban Native Peoples and Indigenous Nationhood*. Vancouver: UBC Press.

> This book is exceptional in providing readers with considerable detail and analysis revealing that urban mixed-blood Native peoples are not extraneous to indigenous communities; instead, they represent the other half of the history of colonization, the descendants of those displaced as a result of residential schooling, enfranchisement, the abduction of Native children into the child welfare system, and a century of removing Indian status from Native women and their descendants. The question of "Who is an Indian?" is thus highlighted as one impregnated with the history of colonial genocide.

Silman, J. (1987). *Enough Is Enough: Aboriginal Women Speak Out.* Toronto: Women's Press.

> This book offers a candid story of a group of women from Tobique Reserve in New Brunswick who were at the forefront of the struggle by Native women to amend the Indian Act and regain their full Native status, rights, and identity.

Related Web Sites

Native Women's Association of Canada
www.nwac-hq.org

> The Native Women's Association of Canada (NWAC) is founded on the collective goal of enhancing, promoting, and fostering the social, economic, cultural, and political well-being of First Nations and Métis women within First Nations and Canadian societies.

Métis National Council of Women
www.metiswomen.ca

> The Métis National Council of Women is mandated to improve the lives of Métis women.

Assembly of First Nations (AFN)
www.afn.ca

> The Assembly of First Nations (AFN) is the national organization representing First Nations citizens in Canada. The AFN represents all citizens regardless of age, gender, or place of residence.

PART TWO

Economic Inequality and Social Exclusion

OBJECTIVES

To comprehend concepts of social exclusion, structural inequalities, and economic apartheid

To understand the connections between the global economy and Canada's garment industry

To analyze how race and gender assumptions underlie strategies of restructuring, privatization, downsizing, and deregulation in Canada

To understand how national borders are an integral way in which power and relations of ruling are exercised

To critically analyze how the underutilization of foreign-trained immigrants affects the Canadian economy both positively and negatively

To comprehend precarious employment as the result of globalization and systemic discrimination, and to see it as a highly gendered and racialized phenomena

INTRODUCTION

The social construction of "race" and its subsequent devaluation and marginalization have several consequences for racialized individuals, especially racialized women. In this second part, we will examine the economic consequences of "race" and gender.

In Chapter 5, Grace-Edward Galabuzi focuses on *social exclusion*, which refers to the inability of certain groups or individuals, due to structural inequality relating to race, class, gender, disability, and sexual orientation, to participate fully in Canadian life, and to access Canada's social, economic, political, and cultural resources. Using Census data, he highlights the *racialization of poverty*, and documents the vertical mosaic in Canada by showing the socio-economic crisis among racialized groups and Aboriginal peoples. This experience of economic apartheid challenges Canada's definition of itself as a liberal democratic state.

In Chapters 6 and 7, Roxana Ng and Jo-Ann Lee, respectively, focus on racialized women and their experiences in the Canadian labour force. In Chapter 6, Roxana Ng examines homeworking in a study to analyze the wages and working conditions of garment workers. Low hourly rates and violations of the Employment Standards Act are routine in the sector. This economic exploitation of racialized women provides the scaffolding of a globalized economy.

In Chapter 7, Jo-Ann Lee examines the working conditions of racialized minority women as workers in Canada's immigrant settlement and integration services sector. According to Lee, the state has used gender and race assumptions to structurally organize the immigrant integration sector as a separate, parallel, and marginalized sector of publically funded social services. Racialized women in this sector experience occupational segregation, low wages, burnout, isolation, and marginalization. This racialized and feminized immigrant services sector is the specific, local consequences of globalization and neo-liberalism. Jo-Ann Lee concludes that "under restructuring, the financial costs of providing even these narrow and truncated welfare rights of democratic citizenship to newly-arrived Canadians are transferred onto immigrant communities themselves, and within these communities, to women."

In Chapters 8, 9, and 10, Nandita Sharma, Lorne Foster, and Tania Das Gupta examine some of the structural conditions of racialized poverty. In Chapter 8, Nandita Sharma analyzes the way migrant workers help define practices of nationalism and citizenship. These "foreign workers" are thereby defined as unfree temporary labour with severe restrictions on their mobility, rights, and entitlements. These social and legal differentiations of labour both impoverish and render homeless temporary, migrant workers in Canada.

In Chapter 9, Lorne Foster shows how even permanent residents face barriers in employment. He examines specifically the barriers that foreign-trained immigrants—permanent residents—face in having their skills and credentials recognized. These barriers include the various rules, regulations, and requirements of provincial regulatory bodies; the requirements of education institutions; and the subjective and often discriminatory hiring and promotion rules of employers. The underutilization of immigrants' skills, and their use as reserve labour in low-paying employment, Foster argues, must be addressed as both "human capital" and "human rights" needs.

In Chapter 10, the last article in this part, Tania Das Gupta writes that precarious employment is a highly gendered and racialized phenomenon. In Canada, the precarious employment situation that characterizes the work of immigrants, people of colour, and Aboriginal workers is produced by both globalization and their precarious citizenship status in Canada. Unions, predominately White, also play a role in reproducing a racially segregated labour market. All of the above levels of policies, procedures, and practices amount to systemic racism as they disproportionately disadvantage people of colour. Tania Das Gupta concludes that the structural changes and union democracy desired by equity-seeking groups within the labour movement are the same changes that workers in precarious employment require to participate fully in the labour movement.

All of the above articles demonstrate the deepening racialization and feminization of poverty in Canada. In the following sections we will show how economic location affects racialized people's, especially women's, quality of life in Canada.

CHAPTER FIVE

Social Exclusion: Socio-economic and Political Implications of the Racialized Gap

Grace-Edward Galabuzi

INTRODUCTION

In this chapter, we tackle the experience of exclusion and one of its most profound manifestations, racialized poverty. Social exclusion describes the structures and processes of inequality and unequal outcomes among groups in society. In industrialized societies, social exclusion arises from uneven access to the processes of production, wealth creation, and power. In the Canadian context, social exclusion refers to the inability of certain groups or individuals to participate fully in Canadian life due to structural inequalities in access to social, economic, political, and cultural resources arising out of the often intersecting experiences of oppression relating to race, class, gender, disability, sexual orientation, and immigrant status. Social exclusion is a form of alienation and denial of full citizenship experienced by particular groups of individuals and communities; among its characteristics are high levels of poverty, uneven access to employment and employment income, segregated neighbourhood selection leading to racialized enclaves, disproportionate contact with the criminal justice system, and low health status.

Social exclusion is both process and outcome. In the late 20th and early 21st centuries, social exclusion is a by-product of a form of unbridled accumulation whose processes commodify social relations, and validate and intensify inequality along racial and gender lines (Byrne, 1999; Madanipour et al., 1998). Processes of social exclusion intensified in the late 20th and early 21st centuries. This intensification can be traced to the restructuring of the global and national economies, which emphasized deregulation and re-regulation of markets, the decline of the welfare state, the commodification of public goods, demographic shifts leading to increased global South-North migrations, changes in work arrangements toward flexible deployment and intensification of labour through longer hours, work fragmentation, multiple jobs, and increasing non-standard forms of work. Not only have these developments intensified exploitation in the labour market, but they have also engendered urban spatial segregation processes, including the gendered and racialized spatial concentrations of poverty.

* * * * *

In Canada, four groups have been identified as particularly at risk for processes of exclusion: women, new immigrants, racialized group members, and Aboriginal peoples (CIHR, 2002). In this chapter, we use the social-exclusion framework to shift the focus back to the structural inequalities that determine the intensity and extensiveness of marginalization in early 21st society, and also focus on some of the groups highly vulnerable to the processes of social exclusion. The conceptual shift moves the burden of social inequality from the individual back to society, recognizing it as an outcome of social relations and raising the possibility of the reassertion of welfare state-type social rights based on the concept of social protection as the responsibility of society. The liberal conception of social inclusion, as presently constituted in policy discourse, promises equal opportunity for all without a commitment to dismantling the historical structures of exclusion; in contrast, the discourse of social exclusion seeks to unravel the structures and processes of marginalization and alienation.

In this book, we acknowledge the intellectual debt owed to the Europeans for developing the discourses and framework of social exclusion based on poverty as the primary form of alienation and exclusion. However, we see the need to broaden the concept to allow for an exploration of the other dimensions of exclusion relating to multiple forms of oppression. In a very vivid way, racism, sexism, and poverty intersect to create specific forms of exclusion in Canada today. Here we will discuss the racialization of poverty as a specific expression of social exclusion in the early 21st century. The racialization of poverty refers to the dispro-portionate and persistent experience of low income among racialized groups in Canada. We embrace the now fairly well-established holistic view of poverty as encompassing not only low income and consumption but also low achievement in education, health, nutrition, and other forms of human deprivation. Among others, the experience of poverty includes powerlessness, marginalization, voicelessness, vulnerability, and insecurity. This understanding of poverty and its causes suggests that the different dimensions of the experience of poverty interact in important ways. Anti-poverty strategies must therefore target poverty in all its various dimen-sions. It is this idea and the approach that can be effectively articulated using the discourse and framework of *social exclusion.*

Social exclusion as a framework is increasingly used by social justice advocates as well as decision-makers because it gets at the root causes of the structural disadvantages experienced by racialized groups and other marginalized groups in society. It also puts the burden of addressing marginalization on the society and not the individuals who are its victims. By so doing, it represents a critique of the neo-liberal notion that the market should be the primary organizing principle of society. It also suggests possibilities for the transformation of the condi-tions of exclusion that have come to define the experience of racialized groups in Canada.

DISTINGUISHING SOCIAL EXCLUSION FROM SOCIAL INCLUSION DISCOURSES

Social exclusion as an idea and discourse has often been confused with *social inclusion,* because it is assumed that, in a linear thought process, the remedy to exclusion is inclusion. However, social inclusion has its own meaning and application as well as ideological foundation, which don't necessarily connect to social exclusion. There is no continuum of experience that runs from exclusion to inclusion in a linear fashion. There are weak and strong versions of the social inclusion discourse. Much of the official policy discourse is of the weak variety, advocating a process similar to assimilation. The focus is on reconciling the "excluded" and the "included," on the terms of those who are included, by changing the excluded and integrating them into the predetermined structures of society. Social inclusion essentially means bringing the excluded into the tent, but likely allowing the persistence of the processes and structures of exclusion and so damning them to the periphery or the margins of the tent. However, there are strong versions that suggest a structural approach, acknowledging the historical processes that continually reproduce oppression, discrimination, and exclusion.[1] But they still don't commit to the need for transformative action, choosing instead to focus on addressing the unequal outcomes.

* * * * *

There is some growing concern among Canadian policy-makers and advocates about the emergence of differentiated experiences of social exclusion. But while they acknowledge that marginal subgroups pose a threat to social cohesion in industrial societies, they still see the discourse of social inclusion and resultant policy framework as an appropriate response.[2]

DEFINING SOCIAL EXCLUSION

Social exclusion is used broadly to describe both the structures and the dynamic processes of inequality among groups in society that, over time, structure access to critical resources that determine the quality of membership in society and ultimately produce and reproduce a complex of unequal outcomes (Room, 1995; Byrne, 1999; Littlewood, 1999; Madanipour et al., 1998). Social exclusion is both process and outcome. The idea of social exclusion has attracted the attention of scholars as well as of mainstream policy-makers concerned about the emergence of marginal subgroups who may pose a threat to social cohesion in industrial societies. Madanipour et al. (1998) have suggested that social exclusion in industrialized countries such as Canada is a by-product of a form of unbridled accumulation whose processes commodify social relations, and validate and intensify inequality along racial and gender lines (Madanipour et al., 1998).[3]

According to White (1998) there are four aspects of social exclusion:

1. Social exclusion from civil society through legal sanction or other institutional mechanisms, as often experienced by status and non-status migrants. This conception may include substantive disconnection from civil society and political participation because of material and social isolation, created through systemic forms of discrimination based on race, ethnicity, gender, disability, sexual orientation, and religion. In the post-September 11 era, racial profiling and new notions of national security have exacerbated the experience of this form of social exclusion.

2. Social exclusion refers to the failure to provide for the needs of particular groups—the society's denial of (or exclusion from) social goods to particular groups such as accommodation for persons with disability, income security, housing for the homeless, language services, sanctions to deter discrimination.

3. Exclusion from social production, a denial of opportunity to contribute to or participate actively in society's social, cultural activities.

4. Economic exclusion [...]. The experiences of structures and processes of exclusion that condition access to economic resources and opportunities represent a form of economic exclusion from social consumption and ultimately unequal access to normal forms of livelihood and economy.

* * * * *

SOCIAL EXCLUSION AND CITIZENSHIP

In order for the social exclusion framework to be effective, it assumes a community or a society from which the process of exclusion is affected. The multiple dimensions of exclusion may suggest different ways of drawing the boundaries, and here the discourse on citizenship is helpful in demarcating the boundaries of the community or polity that provides the context within which the discussion on social exclusion takes place. The primary assumption is that the boundaries are along nation-state lines and represent the assertion of claims of belonging to a collective on the basis of agreed-upon notions of citizenship, first on the national scale, but potentially on the local or global scales. Citizenship is understood here as a:

> Relationship between the individual and the state as well as among individuals, it is the concrete expression of the fundamental principle of equality among members of the political community. (Jenson and Papillon, 2001)

This notion of citizenship invokes the state as guarantor of the principle of equality among members. Citizenship and equality are time and space-specific concepts. Kymlicka and Norman (1995) have argued that the "return of the citizen" in popular political and academic discourse is the result of major transformations in modern polities and political economies brought about by neo-liberal globalization. It is both a signal and a symptom of profound changes in industrial societies. This follows a trajectory of liberal democratic conceptions of citizenship that began with the connection between civic participation and access to political power, an idea of nationhood and popular citizenship that led to the replacement of divine authority with the secular institutions of self-government following the Treaty of Westphalia in 1648.

* * * * *

In the late 20th and early 21st centuries, social justice advocates and other political actors are increasingly using inclusive notions of citizenship to resist exclusion. In Europe, for instance, where the concept of social exclusion has its roots, France's *Le movement social*, a broad-based aggregation of associations and actors seeking to address social inequalities and exclusion, has been making claims for inclusion on the basis of equal citizenship (Helly, 1998).

CANADA AND THE EXPERIENCE OF SOCIAL EXCLUSION

Historically in Canada, structural inequalities in access to social, economic, political, and cultural resources have arisen out of the often intersecting experiences of oppression relating to race, class, gender, disability, sexual orientation, and immigrant status; these inequalities have defined social exclusion. More recently, the demands for labour-market flexibility in the urban "globalized" economy have disproportionately exposed racialized groups to precarious employment and higher levels of poverty than other Canadians. So, for the historically vulnerable groups in the labour market, globalization exacerbates the impact of racial and gender discrimination in employment. Economic restructuring has not only polarized the labour market through labour-market segmentation, but also created employment structures that have altered the traditional workplace relationships and intensified the working experience of racialized communities through longer working hours and multiple part-time or contract jobs. The characteristics of the various forms of precarious work on offer are low pay, no job security, poor and often unsafe working conditions, intensive labour, excessive hours, and low or no benefits. Social exclusion defines the inability of certain subgroups to participate fully in Canadian life. Along with the socio-economic and political inequalities, social exclusion is also characterized by processes of group or individual isolation within and from such key Canadian societal institutions as the school system, criminal justice system, and health care system. Spatial isolation or neighbourhood segregation also characterize social exclusion.

These various forms of exclusion and isolation engender experiences of social and economic vulnerability, powerlessness, voicelessness, a lack of recognition and sense of belonging, limited options, diminished life chances, despair, opting out, suicidal tendencies, and increasing community or neighbourhood violence. Aside from numerous health implications, the emergence of the institutional breakdown and normlessness characterized by such phenomena as the resort to the informal economy and community violence represents a threat to social cohesion and economic prosperity.

BOX 5.1

Social Exclusion in the Canadian Context

- Historically, Canada was conceived as a White-settler colony.

- The colonization of Aboriginal peoples and marginalization of non-European groups contributed to their social exclusion.

- Social exclusion is manifested through structural inequalities in access to social, economic, political, and cultural resources.

- Structural inequities persist on the basis of race, gender, disability, sexual orientation, immigrant status, etc.

BOX 5.2

Recent Patterns of Exclusion

- Post-September 11 legislative and administrative measures have limited the freedom of movement of racialized groups—such as members of Muslim, Arab, and Asian communities targeted

- Canadian citizenship increasingly defined by place of origin

- Lack of representation in political institutions

- Contact with the criminal justice system

- Neighbourhood selection

- Exposure to various forms of violence

- Poor health status

- Racialization of poverty

---

* * * * *

The experience of racialized groups is that certain forms of economic, political, social, and cultural privilege occur at the expense of those lower in the hierarchy of power. This is especially true in a market-regulated society where the impetus for state intervention to reduce the reproduction of inequality is minimal, as is increasingly the case under the neo-liberal regime. [...] Important aspects of social exclusion are manifested in the economy, in the experience of poverty, in the contact with the criminal justice system, in health status, in education, in housing and neighbourhood selection, in the way major, cultural institutions such as the mainstream media depict the group, and in access to political processes. Below, we briefly outline some of the representative experiences in the Canadian context as they relate to racialized groups beginning with the racialization of poverty.

BOX 5.3

Racialized Groups and New Immigrants Experience Differential Life Chances

Characteristics include:

- A double-digit racialized income gap

- Deepening levels of poverty

- Differential access to housing and neighbourhood segregation

- Disproportionate contact with the criminal justice system

- Higher health risks

"POVERTY IS NOT KNOWING WHERE YOUR NEXT MEAL IS GOING TO COME FROM, AND ALWAYS WONDERING WHEN THE LANDLORD IS GOING TO PUT YOUR FURNITURE OUT"

"Poverty is always praying that your husband must not lose his job. To me that's poverty"
—participant at an anti-poverty forum, Toronto 2002

A most significant development in the last two decades is the *racialization of poverty*. The term refers to the emergence of structural features that pre-determine the disproportionate incidence of poverty among racialized group members. These trends are due to structural changes in the Canadian economy that conspire with historical forms of racial discrimination in the Canadian labour market to create social and economic marginalization, the result of which is the disproportionate vulnerability to poverty of racialized group communities. Racialized groups are often immigrant communities, and also suffer the impact of the immigration effect. However, current trends indicate that the economic inequality between immigrants and native-born Canadians is becoming greater and more permanent. That was not always the case. In fact, according to the historical trajectories of immigration settlement, immigrants tended to outperform native-born Canadians because of their high educational levels and age advantage.

The racialization of poverty is linked to the deepening oppression and social exclusion of racialized and immigrant communities on one hand, and to the entrenchment of privileged access to economic opportunity for an elite section of the majority population on the other. Economic exclusion takes the form of labour-market segregation, unequal access to employment, employment discrimination, disproportionate vulnerability to unemployment, and underemployment. These are both characteristics and causes of social exclusion. Attachment to the labour market is essential to both livelihood and the production of identity in society. It determines not only the ability to meet material needs, but also a sense of belonging, dignity, and self-esteem. Labour market-related social exclusion involves income inequality as well as poor working conditions, lack of or limited mobility in workplaces, intensive work assignments, often requiring multiple shifts or multiple jobs and long hours, unequal distribution of opportunities, failure to utilize acquired skills, all of which contribute to the intensification of poverty among racialized groups.

The neo-liberal restructuring of Canada's economy and labour market towards flexible labour markets has increasingly stratified labour markets along racial lines, with the disproportionate representation of racialized group members in low-income sectors and low-end occupations, and underrepresentation in high-income sectors and occupations. It is these broader labour market processes that are responsible for the emergence of the phenomenon of the racialization of poverty in the late 20th century. Its dimensions are identifiable by such indicators as disproportionate levels of low income and racialized spatial concentration of poverty in key neighbourhoods.

The concentration of economic, social, and political power that has emerged as the market has become more prominent in social regulation in Canada helps explain the growing gap between rich and poor as well as the racialization of that gap (Yalnizyan, 1998; Kunz et al., 2001; Galabuzi, 2001; Lee, 2000; Dibbs and Leesti, 1995; Jackson, 2001). Racialized groups and Aboriginal peoples are twice as likely to be poor as other Canadians because of the social and economic exploitation they suffer. Members of these communities have had to endure historical racial and gender inequalities accentuated by the restructuring of the Canadian economy, and more recently by racial profiling. In the midst of the socio-economic crisis that has resulted, the different levels of government have responded by retreating from anti-racism programs and policies that would have removed the barriers to economic equity. The resulting powerlessness and loss of voice have compounded the groups' inability to put issues of social inequality, and particularly the racialization of poverty, on the political agenda.

RACIALIZED GROUP MEMBERS TWICE AS LIKELY AS OTHER CANADIANS TO LIVE IN POVERTY

In 1995, 35.6% members of racialized groups lived under the low income cut-off (poverty line) compared with 17.6% in the general Canadian population. The numbers that year were comparable in urban areas—38% for racialized groups and 20% the rest of the population, a rate twice as high (Lee, 2000). In 1996, while racialized groups members accounted for 21.6% of the urban population, they accounted for 33% of the urban poor. That same year, 36.8% of women and 35% of men in racialized communities were low-income earners, compared to 19.2% of other women and 16% of other men. In 1995, the rate for children under six living in low-income families was an astounding 45%—almost twice the overall figure of 26% for all children living in Canada. The improvements in the economy have not dented the double-digit gap in poverty rates. Family poverty rates were similar—in 1998, the rate for racialized groups was 19% and 10.4% for other Canadian families (Lee, 2000; Jackson, 2002).

According to 1996 data, racialized group members experienced higher rates of poverty than other Canadians, with a rate in 1995 twice that of other Canadians (35.9% compared to 17.6%). While poverty among racialized communities varies from province to province—ranging from 24.3% in Newfoundland to a high of 52.2% in Quebec—these groups consistently face higher average rates of poverty than other Canadians in all provinces. In the three provinces with the highest concentration of racialized group members, the situation was as follows: In Ontario, with the highest population of racialized communities, the rate was 34.3% compared to 14.6%; in British Columbia, it was 32% compared to 16.9%; while in Quebec, it was 52.2% compared to 21.5% in the rest of the population.

Looking at the social economic status of racialized groups in the city of Toronto, Ornstein (2000) revealed that high rates of poverty are concentrated among certain groups such as Latin Americans, African Blacks and Caribbeans, and Arabs and West Asians—with rates at 40% and higher in 1996, or roughly three times the Toronto rate. This research is confirmed by accounts in the popular press, which reveal a dramatic increase in the use of food banks by highly educated newcomers (Quinn, 2002).

A United Way of Greater Toronto (2004) study looking at the geography of neighbourhood poverty between 1981–2001 found that poverty had increased dramatically, especially in neighbourhoods dominated by racialized people and immigrants.[4]

RACIALIZATION OF POVERTY AMONG IMMIGRANTS

Another way to look at the experience of poverty among racialized groups is to look at the incidence of poverty among recent immigrants. As documented above, racialized groups compose the disproportionate number of recent immigrants (post-1970s). According to 1996 data, two-thirds of racialized group members were immigrants (68%). The data also showed that both racialized group members and immigrants earned less than their counterparts.[5] Immigrants were more likely to be poor than Canadian-born—on average 30% living in poverty as opposed to 21% of Canadian-born. The population of immigrants that arrived in the last 25 years, 1980 to present, are particularly vulnerable to high rates of poverty. This population is a highly racialized population group. Studies of urban areas where this group is concentrated show both the incidence of racialized group's immigration to Canada's cities and their experience with poverty rising.[6]

Immigration studies show that former waves of immigrants (pre-1970s) were subject to a short-term "immigration factor," which over time—not longer than 10 years for the unskilled and as low as two years for the skilled—they were able to overcome and either catch up to their Canadian-born counterparts or even surpass them in their performance in the economy. Their employment participation rates were as high or higher than the Canadian-born, and their wages and salaries rose gradually to the level of the Canadian-born. Today, 10 years after arriving, the average immigrant earns on average 80% of what a Canadian-born worker takes home, and recent immigrants—those living in Canada for less than five years—are much more likely to be unemployed than the Canadian-born.

While immigrant men are arriving with much more education than their predecessors, their inflation-adjusted earnings fell an average of 7% between 1980 and 2000. Male recent immigrant full-time employment earnings fell 7% between 1980 and 2000. This decline was evidently not the product of a poor economy since the earnings of Canadian-born men improved by 7% during the same time.

Research also shows low-income rates have been rising steadily among immigrants during the past two decades while falling among the Canadian-born. The trend is most pronounced in Canada's largest cities where over 76% of immigrants live (Toronto, Vancouver, and Montreal).

Kevin Lee's CCSD study (2000) documented the prevalence of poverty among immigrants, newcomers, and refugees. While the most recent arrivals were most disadvantaged, suffering 52.1% poverty, the rate for those in the country for 15 years was also high, at 35%, compared to a Canadian-born rate of 21%. The rate for immigrant populations arriving before 1986 is slightly lower than that of the Canadian-born group.[7]

Lee's study has been updated by M. Frenette and R. Morissette's study looking at low-income among immigrants between 1980 to 2000 (Frenette and Morissette, 2003). Their analysis shows that post-1980s immigrants experienced some of the highest increases in low-income rates in Canada in the last two decades. Low-income rates among successive groups of immigrants almost doubled between 1980 and 1995, peaking at 47.0% before easing up in the late 1990s. In 1980, 24.6% of immigrants who had arrived during the previous five-year period lived below the poverty line. By 1990, the low-income rate among recent immigrants had increased to 31.3%. It rose further to 47% in 1995 but fell back somewhat to 35.8% in 2000 (Frenette and Morissette, 2003).

In 1998, the annual wages of racialized immigrants were up to one-third less those of other Canadians, partly explaining why the poverty rate for racialized immigrants arriving after 1986 ranged between 36% and 50% (Jackson, 2001). This was happening at a time when average poverty rates had generally been falling in the Canadian population. Among the university-educated the drop was deeper (13%). Earnings rose for female recent immigrant full-time employment, but by less than other female full-time. More alarming are the low-income trends among highly educated immigrants. While low-income rates among recent immigrants with less than high school graduation increased by 24% from 1980 to 2000, low income rates increased by 50% among high school graduates and a whopping 66% among university-educated immigrants (Frenette and Morissette, 2003).[8]

Recent immigrants' rates of employment declined markedly between 1986 and 1996. The result is that Canada's immigrants exhibit a higher incidence of poverty and greater dependence on social assistance than their predecessors, in spite of the fact that the percentage of university graduates among them is higher in all categories of immigrants, including family class and refugees as well as economic immigrants, than it is for the Canadian-born (CIC, 2002).

This raises the question of whether it is simply the period of stay that is responsible for the differences in levels of poverty. Arguably, it is to some extent; however, the racial composition of the immigration pool has changed dramatically over the last 25 years, and even more intensely over the last 15 years. Given the previous patterns that documented income parity and in many cases advantages for immigrants during the pre-1980s period, period of stay cannot be the only explanation. Another possible explanation is educational attainment differentials. However, most of the immigrants in the post-1991 group gained entry through a strictly enforced point system, which favoured those in the economic class.

However, as we have indicated throughout this chapter, in the post-1980s period, there are persistent and growing difficulties in the labour-market integration of immigrants, especially recent immigrants. Rates of unemployment and underemployment are increasing for individual immigrants, as are rates of poverty for immigrant families (Gabaluzi, 2001; Ornstein, 2000; Pendakur, 2000; Reitz, 1988; Shields, 2002). The traditional trajectory that saw immigrants catch up with other Canadians over time seems to have been reversed in the case of racialized immigrants. The irony is that over that period of time, the level of education, usually an indicator of economic success, has been growing.

* * * * *

TABLE 5.1

Poverty Rate by Racialized Group Status, by Province, 1995

	POVERTY RATE	
PROVINCE	RACIALIZED GROUPS	MEMBERS OF OTHER GROUPS
Newfoundland	24.3%	21.3%
P.E.I.	28.0%	15.1%
Nova Scotia	37.9%	18.1%
New Brunswick	34.2%	18.9%
Quebec	52.2%	21.5%
Ontario	34.3%	14.6%
Manitoba	31.3%	19.7%
Saskatchewan	29.9%	18.0%
Alberta	31.9%	16.9%
British Columbia	32.0%	16.9%
Canada	35.9%	17.6%

CONCLUSION

Social exclusion describes the structures and processes of inequality and unequal outcomes among groups in society. In industrialized societies such as Canada, social exclusion arises from uneven access to the processes of production, wealth creation, and power. It represents a form of alienation and denial of full citizenship experienced by racialized groups or individuals. Its characteristics occur in multiple dimensions, with racialization being a major one in early 21st-century Canada. Manifestations of social exclusion include high levels of poverty, uneven access to employment and employment income, segregated neighbourhood selection leading to racialized enclaves, disproportionate contact with the criminal justice system, and low health status. Social exclusion is different from social inclusion because the former seeks to identify and transform the root causes of exclusion, while the latter in practice seeks to reconcile the excluded to the existing societal institutions without changing them.

Of particular concern is the racialization of poverty as an expression of social exclusion. The racialization of poverty refers to the emergence of disproportionate incidence of poverty among racialized group members on a structural level. It tends to compound the dimensions of exclusion; it creates further alienation and detachment from the body politic, ultimately leading to actions that engender social instability. Some of those we have detailed above, while others will inevitably intensify if these processes of economic exclusion, exclusion from civil society, exclusion from social goods, and exclusion from social production are not addressed. The exclusions manifested in declining health status, differential access to education, neighbourhood selection, social services, differential experiences with the criminal justice system, and the national security regime all contribute to a situation in which racialized groups increasingly live in the same cities with non-racialized Canadians, but lead separate existences. The experience of economic apartheid may move beyond the economy to the neighbourhoods and the institutions that define Canada as a liberal democratic state.

ENDNOTES

1. A. Saloojee, *Social Inclusion, Anti-racism, and Democratic Citizenship* (Toronto: Laidlaw Foundation, 2003); J. Veit-Wilson, *Setting Adequacy Standards* (Bristol: The Policy Press, 1998).

2. Recently the Laidlaw Foundation commissioned a series of papers on social inclusion (www. laidlawfdn.org): P. Barata, *Social Exclusion: A Review of the Literature* (Toronto: Laidlaw Foundation, 2000); Saloojee (2003); R. Omidvar and T. Richmond, *Immigrant Settlement and Social Inclusion in Canada* (Toronto: Laidlaw Foundation, 2003); Z. Hajnal, "The Nature of Concentrated Urban Poverty in Canada and the United States," *Canadian Journal of Sociology* 20 (1995): 497–528; B. Baklid, *The Voices of Visible Minorities—Speaking out on Breaking down Barriers* (Ottawa: Conference Board of Canada, 2004); J. Guildford, *Making the Case for Economic and Social Inclusion* (Ottawa: Health Canada, 2000).

3. For a further discussion of social exclusion and racialized groups, see G. Galabuzi, "Social Exclusion," in *Social Determinants of Health: Canadian Perspectives*, 233–251, edited by D. Raphael (Toronto: Canadian Scholars' Press, 2004).

4. While in 1981, Toronto's rate of poverty equalled that of Canada at 13% and 13.3% respectively, by 2001 Toronto's was at 19.4% compared to 12.8% for Canada. A key contributing factor was poverty increases among highly racialized low-income neighbourhoods where poverty rose from 17.8% in 1981 to 43.1% in 2001. These findings are also supported by a study Khosla (2003) on low-income women in Toronto, which found that racialized single families led by women experienced over 60% rates of low income. United Way of Greater Toronto, *Poverty by Postal Code: The Geography of Neighbourhood Poverty 1981–2001* (Toronto: UWGT/ CCSD, 2004); P. Khosla, *If Low-Income Women of Colour Counted in Toronto: Breaking Isolation, Getting Involved* (Toronto: Community Social Planning Council, 2003).

5. Statistics Canada, "1996 Census: Ethnic Origin, Visible Minorities," *The Daily* (February 17, 1998).

6. A study by M. Ornstein, *Ethno-racial Inequality in Toronto: Analysis of the 1996 Census* (Toronto: City of Toronto, 2000) documents poverty levels for racialized groups that are three times those for non-racialized groups. It also points to deep pockets of poverty among among segments of the racialized communities as high as 70%, with single women and children especially affected.

7. K. Lee, *Urban Poverty in Canada: A Statistical Profile* (Ottawa: Canadian Council on Social Development, 2000).

8. M. Frenette and R. Morisette, *Will They Ever Converge? Earnings of Immigrants and Canadian-Born Workers over the Last Two Decades*, Analytical Studies Paper No. 215 (Ottawa: Statistics Canada: 2003); F. Hou and G. Picot, *The Rise in Low-Income Rates among Immigrants in Canada*, Catalogue no. 11F0019M1E-No. 198 (Ottawa: Statistics Canada, 2003); G. Schellenberg, *Immigrants in Canada's Census Metropolitan Areas*, Catalogue no. 89-613-MIE-No. 003 (Ottawa: Statistics Canada 2004); E. Smith and A. Jackson, *Does a Rising Tide Lift All Boats? The Labour Market Experiences and Incomes of Recent Immigrants, 1995 to 1998* (Ottawa: CCSD, 2002).

BIBLIOGRAPHY

Byrne, D. *Social Exclusion*. Buckingham: Open University Press, 1999.

Canadian Institute of Health Research: *Charting the Course: Canadian Population Health Initiative—A Pan-Canadian Consultation on Population and Public Health Priorities*. Ottawa: Canadian Institute for Health Research, 2002.

Citizenship and Immigration Canada. *Facts and Figures 2001*. Ottawa: CIC, 2002.

Dibbs, R., and T. Leesti. *Survey of Labour and Income Dynamics: Visible Minorities and Aboriginal Peoples*. Ottawa: Statistics Canada, 1995.

Frenette, M., and R. Morissette. *Will They Ever Converge? Earnings of Immigrants and Canadian-Born Workers over the Last Two Decades*. Statistics Canada (2003). Analytical Studies paper No. 215. Ottawa: Statistics Canada, 2003.

Galabuzi, G. *Canada's Creeping Economic Apartheid: The Economic Segregation and Social Marginalization of Racialized Groups*. Toronto: CJS Foundation for Research and Education, 2001.

Helly, D. "An Injunction: Belong, Participate. The Return of Social Cohesion and the Good Citizen." *Lien Social et Politiques—RIAC 41*, no. 81 (Spring, 1998): 35–46.

Jackson, A. *"Poverty and Immigration." Perception* 24, no. 4 (Spring, 2001).

———. *Is Work Working for Workers of Colour?* Ottawa: Canadian Labour Congress, 2002.

Jenson, J., and M. Papillon. "The Changing Boundaries of Citizenship. A Review and a Research Agenda." Canadian Policy Research Networks (CPRN), 2001. www.cprn.org.

Kunz, J.L., A. Milan, and S. Schetagne. *Unequal Access: A Canadian Profile of Racial Differences in Education, Employment, and Income*. Toronto: Canadian Race Relations Foundation, 2001.

Kymlicka, W., and W. Norman. "Return of the Citizen: A Survey of Recent Work on Citizenship Theory," in *Theorizing Citizenship*, edited by Ronal Beiner, 283–322. Albany: State University of New York Press, 1995.

Lee, K. *Urban Poverty in Canada: A Statistical Profile*. Ottawa: Canadian Council on Social Development, 2000.

Littlewood, P. *Social Exclusion in Europe: Problems and Paradigms*. Aldershot: Ashgate, 1999.

Madanipour, A. "Social Exclusion and Space," in *Social Exclusion in European Cities*, edited by A. Madanipour, G. Cars, and J. Allen, 750–94. London: Jessica Kingley, 1998.

Madanipour, A., G. Cars, and J. Allen, eds. *Social Exclusion in European Cities*. London: Jessica Kingsley, 1998.

Ornstein, M. *Ethno-racial Inequality in the City of Toronto: An Analysis of the 1996 Census*. Toronto: City of Toronto, 2000. http:/ceris.metropolis.net.

Pendakur, R. *Immigrants and the Labour Force: Policy, Regulation, and Impact*. Montreal: McGill-Queen's University Press, 2000.

Quinn, J. "Food Bank Clients Often Well-Educated Immigrants." *The Toronto Star* (March 31, 2002): A12.

Reitz, J.G., "The Institutional Structure of Immigration as a Determinant of Inter-racial Competition: A Comparison of Britain and Canada." *International Migration Review* 22 (Spring, 1988): 117–46.

Room, G. "Conclusions" *in Beyond the Threshold: The Measurement and Analysis of Social Exclusion,* edited by G. Room. Bristol: The Polity Press, 1995.

Shields, J. "No Safe Haven: Markets, Welfare, and Migrants." Paper presented to the Canadian Sociology and Anthropology Association, Congress of the Social Sciences and Humanities, Toronto, June, 2002.

White, P. "Ideologies, Social Exclusion, and Spacial Segregation in Paris." In *Urban Segregation and the Welfare State: Inequality and Exclusion in Western Cities,* eds. S. Musterd and W. Ostendorf, 148–67. London: Routledge, 1998.

Yalnizyan, A. *The Growing Gap: A Report on Growing Inequality between the Rich and the Poor in Canada.* Toronto: Centre for Social Justice, 1998.

Homeworking: Dream Realized or Freedom Constrained? The Globalized Reality of Immigrant Garment Workers

Roxana Ng

In the 1990s, as employment patterns fluctuate and work place restructuring becomes the norm rather than the exception, homeworking—conducting one's paid employment from the privacy of one's domicile—is heralded as the viable and preferred alternative to a more structured work environment. By examining the working conditions of women who sew garments at home (heretofore homeworkers), this article reveals that this rosy and romantic picture of homeworking, painted by the media and encouraged by governments and employers, does not apply to everyone who does homework. Although homeworking seems to provide both the homeworker and the employer/client more flexibility, and certainly reduces overhead costs for the employer, specific conditions of homeworking vary across occupational sectors and from individual to individual. They are shaped by factors such as the occupational strata, education, class, gender, and above all family responsibilities of the homeworker. For example, the experience of a professional man who operates a consulting business from his residence is very different from that of garment workers, many of them immigrant women with low English language proficiency, who sew at home for subcontractors because they cannot afford daycare services.

This article focuses on the conditions of sewers who are homeworkers in the Greater Toronto Area. Through in-depth and telephone interviews with 30 homeworkers who are immigrant women from Asia (Hong Kong, China, and Vietnam), my study adds to present knowledge on the conditions of homeworkers in Toronto and raises questions about the popular image of homeworking as the desired alternative to full-time, stable, and office- or factory-based employment.

CHANGES IN THE GARMENT INDUSTRY

The city of Toronto has been a major centre of garment production in Canada since industrialization. As an industry that makes use of what are assumed to be women's skills, the garment trade has always been an employer of female immigrant workers, firstly from Europe and later from Asia. Historically, homeworking and sweatshop operation were an integral part of the garment trade. With the formation of the International Ladies Garment Workers' Union (ILGWU), firstly in the U.S. and later in Canada, garment workers became the few unionized female work force that enjoyed decent wages and employee benefits. They were protected by labour standard legislation and rights to collective bargaining.

From the early 1980s to 1990s, however, like many other industrial sectors, the garment industry had gone through drastic restructuring. This was the product of many forces: technological changes, changing tariff and trade protection by national governments due to global competition, and a shifting locus of control in the industry itself. Electronic data processing, for example, makes possible the communication of sales directly from retail stores to the factory, enabling manufacturers and retailers to cut down on stock. The opening up of labour markets in the so-called third world, especially the industrialization of the Asia Pacific Rim countries and the establishment of free trade zones there, has enabled much cheaper garment production. Trade agreements, such as the North American Free Trade Agreement (NAFTA), have made it possible for retailers to order garments from places like Mexico with cheaper labour costs. The shift of control from manufacturers to retailers such as the Hudson's Bay Company (which owns Zellers, Simpson's, Robinson's and Fields, and K Mart) has made it difficult for manufacturers to control the production process. So, many of them either retired or got out of the business altogether. Those who remained scaled down the factory, and became contractors for big retailers or subcontractors for large manufacturers.[1]

This story, recorded in Laura Johnson's classic, *The Seam Allowance*, describes this transition well:

> Seven years ago, James Morris owned a clothing factory in Toronto. The enormous increase in imported clothing affected his business and he began losing money. He laid off all but one of his 45 workers—a skilled cutter—and started over again, this time without the factory. He began to take bundles of ready-cut cloth to the women who used to sew for him in the factory. They sewed up the dresses and returned them to him for finishing and pressing. Today, Morris runs a highly successful, moderately sized dress manufacturing business. Says Morris: "Homework is the only way to go in Canada.... I won't replace homeworkers for a long time. I don't want another factory." Morris' workplace now employs only ten workers, who do the cutting, samples, finishing, pressing, and office work. He also uses three contractors who have their own factories and/or homeworkers. Morris does not concern himself with the employment condition of the women who make the dresses; he cares only that the finished product is made to his exacting specifications and delivered to him in the time agreed. James Morris finds that the homework system meets his needs. (19)

The effects of these changes were the downsizing of industrial plants and factory closures in Toronto (and elsewhere in Canada). They in turn led to massive lay-off and displacement of garment workers, many of whom are women from Asian countries such as Hong Kong, Vietnam, and India. This did not mean these immigrant women lost their jobs; it meant that they were now sewing garments at home for contractors and subcontractors. This is the context within which my study is situated.

WAGES AND WORKING CONDITIONS OF HOMEWORKERS

By the 1990s, sweatshops and homeworking are once again an integral part of the garment industry in Canada. This article reports on a study done in the spring of 1999, as part of a larger project I am doing in collaboration with the Home-workers' Association (HWA). The objective of the study was to see whether wages and working conditions of homeworkers have changed since the early 1990s, when the HWA did two surveys on homeworking in Toronto in an attempt to discover the work reality of increasing numbers of garment workers who had become homeworkers.[2]

My study found that the wages of sewing machine operators have not risen since the 1980s. Laura Johnson's 1982 study reported that the piece rate for skirts was $2. Today, workers also make $2 for a skirt. A shirt is around $3, and a dress pays $4 to $5. This is clothing that retails for up to $200. For section work (that is, sewing on pockets or collars), workers make between 20 to 50 cents per piece. Based on the piece rate and number of items completed per hour, we estimate the average hourly rate to be between $6 and $8.[3] The highest hourly rate reported is $17 per hour for evening gowns, and the lowest is $2 per hour.

What is more critical to note is that as homeworkers become skilled at what they are sewing, and begin to make more than minimum wage, the employers drop the piece rate so their earning is effectively reduced. For example, one woman reported that depending on the complexity of the design, she used to get $3 to $4 per skirt; now she is paid $2.80 to $3. This finding concurs with a larger study on the garment trade, which reported on a decline in the piece rate (Yanz).

Another strategy used by subcontractors is to not disclose the piece rate until the batch of garments is completed, as the following interview shows:

> The lowest salary I earned was about $3 per hour, with the same employers I'm now working. [I asked why she didn't complain about the low rate.] I didn't say anything at the beginning. I dared not. But now I start to talk to them about this. The kind of pocket-cover sewing I'm now doing also requires me to cut certain fabric before I can start sewing. But the employers don't count the cutting time. I told the employers about this. But they said that almost every homeworker asks them for a raise. But they get no raise from their contractor who gives them the fabric. I don't know other homeworkers who also work for them. It would be better if I know. Their factory is very small. They only have two workers in their factory, plus some part timers, and the two owners. The highest salary I earned was around $8 per hour. That was at the beginning when I first worked for these employers, when they let me know the piece rate before I sewed. But now they don't tell me the piece rate before I sew.
>
> Every time I ask them for the piece-rate, they always say they haven't had time to think about it yet. At the beginning they gave me the piece-rate before I sewed. But now they don't. They never tell me the piece-rate until I finish sewing the garments.

In other words, contrary to the common notion that as workers become more experienced and skilled, their wages increase accordingly, homeworkers are being punished for being more productive and skillful.

Most workers are paid by cheque every two weeks, and have little problem getting paid. Some receive cash payments occasionally. Several workers did not report on late payment or not being paid at all, as this woman told us:

> I don't have very serious problems with getting paid. What sometimes may happen is getting late payment. One time there was this employer who owed me about $500 to $600. He admitted to it and kept saying sorry. But I still haven't got any pay from him. It was six to seven years ago. He later referred me to another sub-contractor, who sent the fabric from Montreal to his place. So I would go to his place to pick up the fabric and my pay.

Another time, he asked me to lend him money. I did. And he has never paid me back. I still see him from time to time, but I do not work for him anymore.

According to the Employment Standard Act of Ontario, homeworkers are entitled to four percent vacation pay, which must be included in the paycheque. They are also entitled to overtime pay if they work more than 44 hours per week. In reality, they are treated by employers as if they were self-employed. My study found that only two workers receive vacation pay; none receive overtime pay. In other words, most, if not all, employers violate provincial labour standards legislation. In these situations, the women felt that their only recourse, after pursuing the employer repeatedly, was to discontinue work with a particular employer.

In order to be employed as homeworkers, women must own industrial-quality sewing machines. All the women we interviewed owned their sewing machines. A few also own a serger, which enables them to sew a larger variety of garments. The prices of their machines ranged from $300 to $2800, depending on when they purchased them and the type of machine purchased (for example whether it has auto-thread cutting). The woman who paid $300 for her machine purchased it in 1982 when she began working at home.

Although considered employees under the Ontario labour legislation, homeworkers are nevertheless responsible for the maintenance and upkeep of their machines. The woman who paid $300 for her machine said that she had been very lucky with hers, which needed very little upkeep until recently. She also had a very good and reasonable repair man, who did not charge a lot for house calls. Another woman, on the other hand, has purchased three sewing machines since she began working at home.

In addition, women pay for other overhead costs such as lighting and hydro. Some women have learned to deduct these expenses from their income tax claim, but others are either unaware that they can do so, or think that claiming expenses is too much work due to their lack of familiarity with English and dealing with bureaucratic procedures. Usually, threads for the garments are supplied by employers. However, one worker has to supply threads for the clothing she sews.

To be homeworkers, women have to have a designated area for their work. Most of the women in the study have a designated work space, usually in the basement of their homes. However, some women have to share spaces with other family members, such as occupying a corner of a family room. The women who live in apartments use part of the living or dining area for their home work.

Operating a sewing machine is repetitive work that requires attention to details. It is therefore not surprising that most women, like other workers who spend long hours doing something repeatedly, suffer from different kinds of repetitive strain syndrome. By far the greatest complaint is back pain, reported by 15 workers. Four reported on shoulder pain; three neck pain; one knee pain; four numbness in arms, hands, and fingers; and one eye strain. Another health issue concerning homeworkers is allergy due to the dust produced by the fabric in the sewing process. Nine out of the 30 workers reported fairly serious allergies, such as itchiness, rashes, and stuffiness resulting from fabric dust. These findings are consistent with the two surveys conducted by ILGWU in the early 1990s. Whereas allergic reactions were the chief complaints in the 1991 survey, both the 1993 and the present surveys found that back strain was a major concern.

Most women do not tell their employers work-related health problems because they don't think anything would result from complaining. Homeworkers are explicitly exempt from the

Workplace Safety and Insurance Act. This means that they cannot claim compensation from the government in work-related injuries.

The women interviewed use a combination of methods to help alleviate problems associated with their work, including medication, physiotherapy, exercise, and rest. To reduce fabric dust, women vacuum often and keep the work area as dust free as possible. One woman, whose work space is a closet in the basement, closes the door to her work space as much as she can so other family members are not as affected by the dust.

In addition to the physical problems, women talked about the psychological pressure generated by work and family demands. Again, this is consistent with previous studies, as well as studies on women's paid and unpaid work in general. One woman said she even dreamed about sewing when she had to meet a deadline.

WORKING HOURS: MERGING THE PUBLIC AND PRIVATE SPHERES

It is when we examine the working hours of homeworkers that the romantic myth of homeworking is completely shattered. Although women felt that they could make more money working in factories, especially in unionized plants, women know that this is not an option. Why?

The single most important reason given by women for homework is child care, or rather the lack of affordable child care. Since wages for garment workers are low, they cannot afford to put their children in daycare centres or to hire private care. From their point of view, homeworking is a reasonable compromise that enables them to combine paid work and child labour.

Closely related to child care is the fact that although women's paid work is central to sustaining the family income, they are also responsible for the lion's share of household duties and caregiving for their family. Thus, they must find ways to meet the multiple demands placed on them. It is in this context that homeworking becomes a viable, rather than desirable, alternative for women in the garment trade. The women in the study gave three reasons for preferring homework.

- homework is more flexible;

- no supervisor and more able to manage own time;

- able to combine paid work with child care.

However, women also express the internal pressure they feel from having to meet the multiple demands of the household, family, and employment. Although women are not supervised directly, they have to meet the deadline set by employers, or they may not be given more work. Almost half (13 or 30) women work ten- to twelve-hour days on their sewing. Seven work eight to nine hours. Seven work five to six hours. We do not have information on the remaining three workers. The narrative of this homeworker illustrates the pressure women felt combining paid employment and household responsibilities:

> I work eight to nine hours a day, six days a week. My daily schedule usually starts with getting my kids ready for school at about 8:00 a.m., preparing their breakfast. After washing their dishes, I eat something and start working at about 9:00 a.m. until 12:00 noon.

Then I eat something and go back down to work until the kids come back from school at about 3:00 p.m. I would make something for them to eat and get back to work after that until 6:00 p.m. Then I have to start preparing for dinner. If I do not have a rush job, I usually do not go back to the basement and work. But if it's in a rush, I would have to work again after dinner until 1:00 a.m. It's in fact quite often that we have to rush.

The major problem of homeworking is that it blurs the division between paid work and family life. Women tend to organize their sewing around the schedules of children and other family members, thus frequently sewing late into the night when they have to meet employer demands. Given a choice, some of the women said that they would prefer to work in a factory because there is a clear beginning and end to the work day. Some of the problems raised by the homeworkers interviewed are:

- irregular working hours and having to work all the time;

- less focused when sewing because of distraction by household chores and children;

- less stable income;

- feeling confined at home and lack of knowledge of outside world except through the radio.

One homeworker expressed her sentiments thus:

I do not like to work at home. Working outside, I can meet and know more people. I also learn different things. Working at home, I only see my family members. And you don't have much time concept working at home. Sometimes you go to sleep, or watch TV in-between. There is no work routine, I don't like it. When I was young, I liked to go out. I didn't like to hide and confine myself at home. I felt bored. And I felt that when I didn't have a chance to go out and meet more people, I felt out of touch with the society.

Contrary to the two earlier surveys by the ILGWU indicating that family members were frequently involved in helping with homework, most workers in this study do not involve family members in their work. Three workers said their husbands help with delivering the garments. Three have their children help turn clothes inside out. In fact, many said that family members help out minimally in other family duties as well. This means that women carry a double burden, taking almost total responsibility for waged and unwaged work.

In conclusion, whereas homework may be a dream come true for people in professional occupations and a solution for employers who want to downsize their operations, this work organization has a different impact on working-class immigrant women's lives. My study reveals very clearly that homeworking merges the public and private spheres, creating additional pressures for garment workers who have to juggle the demands of paid work and family responsibilities. They are an increasing number of women in both the first and third worlds, whose waged and unwaged labour provides the underpinning of a globalized economy with profit augmentation as its ultimate goal. The everyday reality of homeworkers in Canada and elsewhere is a poignant reminder that equality and quality of life for working people are never part of the corporate and state agenda for globalization.

ENDNOTES

1. For a fuller discussion, see Ng.

2. The Homeworkers' Association began as an affiliate of the International Ladies Garment Workers Union (ILGWU) in 1992. In 1995, the ILGWU merged with another union in the garment industry to form UNITE (Union of Needletrades, Industrial, and Textile Employees). The HWA remained an affiliate of the Ontario District Council of UNITE after the merger.

3. The two surveys are "Working Conditions of Chinese-Speaking Homeworkers in the Toronto Garment Industry: Summary of the Results of a Survey Conducted by the International Ladies Garment Workers Union" by Barbara Cameron (1991) and "ILGWU 1993 Homeworkers' Study: An Investigation into Wages and Working Conditions of Chinese-Speaking Homeworkers in Metropolitan Toronto" by Jan Borowy (1993).

4. The minimum wage in Ontario is $6.85 per hour. Legally, homeworkers should receive ten per cent more than this amount to cover overhead costs, bringing their minimum wage up to $7.54 per hour. As seen from this calculation, most homeworkers made less than minimum wage.

REFERENCES

Johnson, Laura, and Robert Johnson. *The Seam Allowance: Industrial Home Sewing in Canada.* Toronto: Women's Educational Press, 1982.

Ng, Roxana. "Work Restructuring and Recognizing Third World Women: An Example from the Garment Industry in Toronto." *Canadian Woman Studies* 18(1) (1998):21–25.

Yanz, Lynda, et al. *Policy Options to Improve Standards for Garment Workers in Canada and Internationally.* Ottawa: Status of Women Canada, 1999.

CHAPTER SEVEN

Immigrant Women Workers in the Immigrant Settlement Sector

Jo-Anne Lee

In the 1990s, governments at all levels reduced their involvement in the provision of basic welfare services. Strategies such as restructuring, privatization, downsizing, and deregulation have been initiated by the neo-liberal state to enhance global economic competitiveness by reducing the debt load on the state and the tax burden on corporations and capitalists (Bakker). In this essay, I examine one aspect of neo-liberal state restructuring in Canada that has received relatively little attention to date: the selective incorporation of immigrant women workers into the immigrant settlement and integration services sector.

Over the last 30 years, since the arrival of increasing numbers of immigrants from the developing third world, the state has organized and funded "immigrant integration and settlement services" as a sub-sector of the public social welfare system (Creese). As the name suggests, this sub-sector is directed at immigrants, refugees, and the new Canadians not yet able to access the "Canadian" social services system because they do not fit the normatively constructed model of the typical "Canadian" social services client. The state-supported and funded immigrant settlement service sector involves a number of not-for-profit, community-based, multi-ethnic, and ethno-specific organizations and groups, as well as branches and divisions of mainstream institutions such as schools and hospitals (Owen; Creese). In larger urban immigrant receiving centers like Vancouver, Toronto, and Montreal, there are several hundred organizations and groups involved in the delivery of a variety of human welfare services, including housing, English language training, individual counseling, parenting and youth services, employment training and social welfare assistance—core citizenship welfare benefits that most Canadians assume as their right. There is a tremendous range and variety of organizational providers of services in this sector. Groups and organizations offering immigrant and refugee-related services range from agencies with large multi-million dollar budgets to very small volunteer-based groups. Some are multi-service agencies serving all immigrants and refugees while others offer more specialized services to one or two minority ethnic communities.

Although there has been some recent research on the effects of neo-liberal state practices on women (Bakker), there has been little research directed at the immigrant integration sector, and even less research that has examined the effects on racialized minority women as workers and providers of welfare services, and not merely as needy consumers. Recently, however, some attention is being paid to the effects of political and economic restructuring on the immigrant settlement services sub-sector (Creese; Mwarigha; Owen; Richmond). This body of research has examined the effects of devolution and privatization on the organization of the immigrant settlement and integration sector. Agencies view the federal government's Settlement Renewal Plan as a major element in restructuring. Under the Settlement Renewal Program, federal responsibility has been devolved to provincial governments bringing with it major losses in funding and contraction in services (Mwarigha; Richmond; Creese). However, this emerging body of research has not yet examined the specific effects of restructuring on working conditions for female immigrant settlement workers who constitute the majority of workers in this field.

Through the testimony of immigrant women workers it becomes possible to shed light on how the state had used gender and race assumptions to structurally organize the immigrant integration/multiculturalism sector as a separate, parallel, and marginalized sector of publicly funded social services. Client advocates and researchers have observed the effects of streaming and separation of immigrant and refugee clients from "mainstream" clients and have highlighted the failure of mainstream social services organizations to meet the needs of immigrant and refugee clients (Tator). However, devolution and cutbacks are only part of the story of restructuring.

This essay draws on a study conducted on behalf of the British Columbia Ministry Responsible for Multiculturalism and Immigration (BCMRMI) during the winter of 1998–99 that examined the impact of funding programs on projects for immigrant women (Lee). Ten sponsoring organizations and their projects for immigrant women were selected on the basis of a number of criteria, and approximately 50 individuals were interviewed. It was not the purpose of the government-sponsored study to examine working conditions for immigrant women workers in the multicultural and immigrant serving sector. Nevertheless, in the process of conducting semi-structured interviews, immigrant women respondents talked openly about their experiences of working in the sector.

Immigrant women participants in the study generally expressed widespread dissatisfaction with their working experiences in the immigrant settlement sector, a finding that merits special discussion. The study found that racialized immigrant women workers almost unanimously expressed feelings of anger, bitterness, and frustration with the working conditions in immigrant settlement agencies. They felt exploited and ghettoized in part because working conditions for immigrant and visible minority women in this sector is characterized by part-time, low-waged, term-limited, and unstable employment.

OCCUPATIONAL SEGREGATION

Respondents perceive that agencies ignore and even promote occupational segregation by failing to challenge government funding policies for providing the framework that confines immigrant women to ethno-specific, front-line settlement, and counseling jobs. Although respectful of the dedication and commitment of their white Caucasian colleagues and superiors, respondents still felt that they worked within the same general "racial" hierarchy that exists in the wider society. In the largest of these agencies, known as the "big five" agencies, because of their large numbers of employees, the variety of services offered and their multi-million dollar budgets, with the exception of SUCCESS, a community-based agency primarily serving the Chinese-speaking community, senior management is almost entirely white and female.

A study conducted in the early 1990s for the British Columbia Settlement and Integration Workers Association (BCSIWA) found that in the settlement sector, women constitute and estimated 80 per cent of the labour force, 75 per cent are first-generation immigrants, and approximately 70 per cent are visible minority men and women. The majority of immigrant women are concentrated in front-line counseling and community outreach jobs (BCSIWA).

In contrast, English-as-a-second-language (ESL) instruction and employment training jobs, which are more stable and better paid, and funded by Human Resources Development Canada (HRDC), tend to be held by white and/or Canadian-born women.

Some individuals commented on the "institutional oppression" formed by different funding programs that establish a hierarchy and segregation of jobs in the agencies. This funding structure affects the total experience of work: from wages and benefits, to self-esteem, to the way work is organized and managed. Management has responded in different ways to the funding context. One agency has placed all workers, including senior management, on one- or two-year contracts while two agencies have unionized. But neither strategy has successfully addressed occupational segregation and inequality in wages and benefits. One respondent suggested that unionization may make it even more difficult to address wage and benefit inequality by locking workers into fixed labour contracts. Many respondents expressed a high level of critical self-awareness of their working conditions.

> If you look at job training programs, most of these (teaching) jobs are taken up by white women, there are some minorities, but most of them are white women. That sector gets paid a lot better than the settlement services sector. So even though workers might have equivalent education and training, the people who work in the training sector at ___ and _____ are a lot better paid and unfortunately most of those jobs are taken up by white women. The ones who work in the settlement sector, the ones who work for ten or fifteen years, are getting low pay. Those inequities are there. They are very apparent and at one point it created some conflict. I think ___ has taken some steps to address this. She has tried to level it out a little bit.
>
> The funding from employment will allow you to pay a decent wage, while funding from the settlement sector is always more restricted. The pay is very low. If you try to pay more money, the project officer will question you. So it is institutional oppression. It is created by government in the way that they give out funding. The immigrant settlement funding doesn't give out very much. (Source Card No. 6920)

The following excerpts illustrate how the context of settlement work, shaped by different funders who provide different levels of funding for similar jobs, affect immigrant women's experiences and perceptions of their work:

> (Staff are) isolated. And because we're being funded in a disconnected way, that's how we operate together. You are funded by HRDC, oh, that doesn't affect me, I'm funded by these settlement grants. You're funded by whatever, RAP [Refugee Assistance Program], that doesn't affect me because I'm funded by the HRDC. So we just all stay in our own programs. This is my funder category, I don't need to actually know what you do. All we need to know is whether people can come in and out of the program. So for me it is an open program, anyone can come, so I get to know everybody, but for some employment programs I don't get to know them because you can only go in if you have EI [Employment Insurance], or you can only go in if you're on welfare, or, what is it three years and under at settlement services? So there's all these, it's the only way that we get to know each other. There's no conscious getting to know each other here at the agency. (Source Card No. 15855)
>
> … you'll see a division of labour that is done in a particular way. And so, the people who are providing English, which is huge. And the people who are providing pre-employ-

ment programs, are white. The majority. Like if you leave here right now and go to the other office and just walk through all the ESL classes and then go to the sixth floor and walk through all the employment training programs, you will notice that it doesn't look like this. So the settlement services component is community-based. This is more the community part. This is why the agency started in the first place—to help and support and integrate immigrants and refugees. But now it's become Human Resources Development Canada. It [this government department] [is] commodifying labour, processing, making sure everyone has the same English level. So it is very different. The look, the feel of it is very different. So that's the other thing is that it's going to be.... I don't know if it's that way in other places, but I've seen that it's similar in terms of English teachers and the ESL teachers community and if you look at employment counsellors, that community, they're not necessarily diverse. (Source Card No. 81666)

... we have had discussions that every time a managerial role comes up, it is always someone who is imported from outside. They never give an opportunity to those who have been working there for a very long time because multicultural means that there must be whites there as well. That makes sense. But you start comparing what chances do we have of reaching out and getting someone to get onto the board (or senior position). (Source Card No. 37307)

I am actually the only full-time staff person, but there are seven of us in the office and several of those people work close to full-time, like 30 hours, 28 hours a week. Our program staff work very part-time: they might do five to nine hours a week. Some of them up to 15, if they're working in two programs. So it's very part-time for them, not only in terms of hours per week, but also weeks per year because we don't run programs in the summer. And our programs are very much based on not providing employment to people, although we do, but on the needs of the client group that we're serving. (Source Card No. 2493)

Although the prevailing conditions of work for immigrant women are largely externally determined, one smaller, women-centered agency, while still offering only pat-time, seasonal jobs, has refused to permit funders to dictate wages and benefits. This board has taken the position that all staff doing the same job will receive the same wage. Although even here, the question of wage inequality and how to address this problem has been an issue of ongoing debate at the board level.

VOLUNTEERISM

The line between paid and unpaid work is tenuous for immigrant women working in the settlement sector. Some respondents reported that they are often expected to volunteer without pay so that programs continue during times of transitional funding, or to volunteer to do community fundraising or community development and outreach work to their community on behalf of the agency:

... I am surprised that _____ does the amount of work it does. The people here do the amount of work that they do and I'm amazed at how those who run the program, the managers here, can make it work at all because clearly the funding is minimal. The amount of work done that's volunteer work, you wouldn't believe the amount of volunteer work.

Just about everything. As I say, coming from a different place, it is really shocking. (Source Card No. 65120)

In some ESL, life skills, and leadership training programs, immigrant and refugee women are often used as "assistants" to white Canadian facilitators. As one interviewee stated, the use of immigrant women as volunteers or "assistants" is a double-edged sword. On the one hand, they gain experience and confidence, but on the other hand, they are not able to earn a living wage. In addition, the present system screens out working-class women who cannot afford to work part-time. Women who need a full-time wage cannot avail themselves of these "opportunities."

> Some people are looking for part-time work, and it suits them well. Many women who may be are lucky enough to be in the position where they can afford to work part-time. So for those people, we're really offering them something that fits with their life, but of course many of the staff who work for us start with us and get experience and training and, eventually, they move on to full-time work because that's what they want and we're not able to provide it for them. They may work for us as well as another organization. And that can be difficult because you're pretty scattered, even if those jobs are similar in the kind of work you do, you spend more time getting to work. If you're going to work for eight hours, your travel time is less significant than if you're going to work for three or four. So there certainly are issues like that for our staff and we've lost some good people because they've needed to find full-time work. Somehow I feel not bad about that, because they're working for ____ for a year or two years, and that part-time position has helped them to get that full-time job, so I feel that, while we weren't able to offer a full-time job, we were able to offer an "in" to the labour market for those women. (Source Card No. 2493)

Clearly, many respondents see volunteering as a positive program outcome for individual immigrant and refugee women. But as stated earlier, volunteerism in the settlement sector has mixed effects. The negative outcomes are clearer when the immigrant settlement and orientation departments are compared to the ESL and employment training departments even in the same agency. Workers in training departments tend to receive higher compensation for their work, and in general, jobs are more permanent and full-time. There is little reliance on volunteer labour to keep employment training programs in operation in contrast to the settlement service sector.

BCMRMI funding for immigrant women support groups helps to institutionalize volunteerism in the sector. For example, the dominant program model of support groups for immigrant women is designed to recruit, train, and place immigrant women in volunteer positions within the sponsoring agency or in other community-based social service agencies. While these strategies offer opportunities to immigrant and refugee women to use their skills in the community, they also limit and channel these skills. Notwithstanding the benefits that individual women gain by volunteering, many skills gained through volunteering at agencies prepare immigrant women to work as front-line staff regardless of their qualifications and previous work experience. As one agency reported, immigrant women stuff envelopes, send faxes, type letters, and act as volunteer receptionists in order to have one line on their resume stating they have "Canadian" work experience.

While some do move on to take full-time work in the wider community, many respondents reported that immigrant and refugee women move out of volunteer positions into part-time paid positions either at the sponsoring agency or at the other community-based agencies. The present model, at best, provides opportunities for lateral movement, but very little formal support for upward or orthogonal movement out of the sector. The present volunteer training model offers the means for reproducing the volunteer base of settlement work in the sector. Immigrant women volunteerism is one of the key mechanisms for racializing and feminizing settlement work as low-paid and undervalued. It provides the structural underpinning to support the sector.

MARGINALIZATION, LACK OF VOICE, AND REPRESENTATION

Interviewees expressed dismay that within their own worker association, BCSIWA, the executive is dominated by white Canadian men and women, even though it was started by racialized workers. Racialized women settlement workers lack a voice and an organization to voice their concerns. Since immigrant women constitute the front-line staff, they do not have the time or the funding to allow them to participate in BCSIWA meetings. The meetings are attended by management staff, who are mainly mainstream, white Canadian-born men and women. The exclusion of front-line female staff from BCSIWA deliberations is not a consequence of any deliberate actions; rather, like other mechanisms of marginalization, it reflects the taken-for-granted practices and dominant assumptions prevailing in society.

Boards of agencies have contributed to the exploitation of the immigrant women staff by agreeing to provide services and by managing the agencies in a segmented way so that these discrepancies in wages and benefits are accepted as "normal" and unavoidable. The lack of representation of racialized women in decision-making positions in this sector contributes to feelings of low self-esteem and self-doubt. As one person put it, it leads to "internalized oppression":

> I've actually attended forums where people openly said, you look at the immigrant agencies, the five big agencies, including Victoria, all the Executive Directors are white people except for SUCCESS [an agency serving primarily Chinese-speaking immigrants]. Again it is a matter of leadership—of how much energy and effort are being put into leadership by minorities.
>
> When I became the first coordinator, I was the only coordinator of an immigrant background within a system that funded three people of Asian background. They were all Canadian born. So you always hear that you got the job because you can speak Chinese. I don't know whether it is internalized oppression or not, people are talking about it and see that you got the job because of your language, not because of your ability. So you need to get out of that situation. I don't know whether that is part of the self-fulfilling prophecy that maybe minority people who are very good may want to prove themselves elsewhere rather than inside the immigrant communities. But then on the other hand, they won't hire you because they don't think you are good enough to do the job. (Source Card No. 6920)

The lack of professional development and cross-skill training opportunities for front-line workers means that when the need for front-line counselling and settlement services declines for a particular ethno-linguistic group, workers who are seen to have only language and cultural skills are easily dismissed and replaced by new workers who have the language and cultural skills needed to work with newer immigrant groups. When immigration slows and their language skills are no longer in demand, such as the situation with Portuguese and Italian groups in Vancouver, these older workers find themselves without employment and without possibilities for equivalent employment elsewhere.

A high turnover rate in staff was reported in some projects funded by BCMRMI. In one program offering family support, there were seven different staff over a period of three years. Such a high rate of turnover obviously affects the quality of service provided. Different reasons were suggested for high job turnover in the immigrant settlement services sector. In addition to the conditions discussed above, some mentioned the isolation and marginalization that outreach workers experience in doing outreach work in community settings without the support of colleagues who are working on similar issues and with similar clients. Burnout and isolation were frequently mentioned causes:

> Some get better job opportunities, but I think it's burnout as well. It's about saying we don't want to work in this way and doing this kind of work because you really are struggling to stay above water because people don't know what you do and they don't know the level of intensity. When I worked at a rape crisis centre, you had everyone working on one issue, although there's other issues—child sexual abuse or battering or other issues— that women would bring in, but you had everyone working on the same issues and you'd get support and you were working in a kind of team on some level, or even in transition house, when I worked in transition houses there'd be still everyone working together. It's very specific and everyone's working on it. Whereas here you have people who are doing basic settlement, food, shelter, clothing, you have people doing ESL, LINC, pre-employment training, and then you have the family support program kind of out there. (Source Card No. 79171)

Feelings of isolation can also be felt by staff who may be working in an area not directly linked to settlement, or whose political stance on immigration and multiculturalism differs from the majority. If they speak up, they fear that they will not be rehired when their contract or project funding runs out. Yet there is also a sense of not being able to make any significant changes; consequently they express intense feelings of powerlessness.

Immigrant women respondents also feel caught in contradictory tensions. On the one hand, they feel loyalty to the agency, a commitment to the work and to helping their ethnic community, yet on the other hand, they feel unhappy that the core work of settlement services is being supported only by their willingness to work for low wages and unstable employment. Many immigrant women workers expressed profound ambivalence about their work. They are extremely dedicated, committed, and passionate, yet they also feel very isolated, exploited, and devalued.

> It is frustrating and yet it's privileged because I feel that because of my analysis and because I'm kind of defiant and ultimately I'm not scared of being fired and I don't have kids to support or a mortgage to pay, I'm not ... like I have a lot of privileges and when I speak about these issues and identify them—and a lot of times I end up being the person that other people who are scared to speak about the issues come to because they're really worried that they're never going to work somewhere else and I understand that and I don't have the same level of fear and I have a lot of reasons not to. I don't have those obligations, so a lot of times I'm in a place of speaking up, but it is very tiring. [I feel] ...

incredibly isolated, undersupported, targeted in terms of other people. I know now we are doing this focus on anti-racism and this is a new thing for this agency. This agency has been around for 25 years and this is a new thing to talk about anti-racism. (Source Card No. 81576)

As the above interview suggests, it is still difficult to address racism within an immigrant settlement agency. In part, this difficulty is due to the general impression, sometimes fostered by the agency's internal culture, that racism is something that occurs "out there" in the wider society and not "in here." A lack of space to talk about racism as a systemic issue that positions minority women and men in subordinate positions, that affects social relations between people, and that results in pain and hurt helps to keep many minority women silent and isolated in immigrant settlement agencies.

CONCLUSION

Globalization is a process that supports flexible capital accumulation that, in turn, requires flexible citizenship. It is through flexible citizenship that the nation-state maintains its sovereignty and its legitimacy by maintaining, strengthening, and intensifying national boundaries and citizenship categories. Using a race and gender-sensitive lens and attending to the voices of immigrant women workers, this essay demonstrates that state multiculturalism and immigrant integration policies have not yet resulted in the development of common institutions into which new Canadians and minorities integrate. Current practices and policies have created a separate racialized and feminized immigrant services sector wherein parallel proto-institutions deliver a limited set of welfare benefits of citizenship to immigrants and refugees. Under restructuring, the financial costs of providing even these narrow and truncated welfare rights of democratic citizenship to newly arrived Canadians are transferred onto immigrant communities themselves, and within these communities, to women. Devolution, privatization, cutbacks, and other strategies of neo-liberal restructuring have profound gender and race effects that, in turn, profoundly affect the ways that new immigrants and refugees are being integrated into Canadian society and ultimately the nature of Canadian society.

Without much notice, the existing and normalized multi-tiered social welfare system is already differentially subjectifying and embodying new immigrants as second-class subject-citizens on the basis of numerous social signifiers. Socially constructed signifiers associated with categories of citizenship such as "immigrant" and "refugee" position individuals onto different tracks. Although not fully determining of life chances, differential access to the social safety net affects life experiences that help to construct and reproduce differentially valued raced, classed, and gendered subject identities.

In the absence of public debate and recognition, globalization and its partner, neo-liberalism, has encroached into the life worlds of citizenship and democratic processes. Universal citizenship in Canada has been premised on equality of rights, responsibilities, and opportunities for all citizens to access common institutions of the nation. Whether the present phase represents a transition to more common institutions, as liberals such as Kymlicka hope, or, as I suspect, a reformulation and reorganization of institutional policies, procedures, and practices in ways that ultimately continue the institutionalized hegemony of the dominant cultural groups, is a question that remains to be determined.

What is clear is that as front-line settlement workers and volunteers, immigrant women provide the unpaid and low-paid labour that enables the state to resolve its need for legitimacy in several ways by:

- ensuring that immigrants do not threaten social cohesion by failing to integrate;

- enabling the dominant culture to continue to shape mainstream institutions with minimum disruption thereby reasserting the hegemony of the dominant groups; and

- allowing the state to provide the conditions necessary for global capital competitiveness through the availability of skilled low-cost labour while simultaneously ensuring that immigrant integration is achieved in structural selective ways without overburdening the neo-liberal state.

The impact of transferring the financial costs of immigrant integration through the mutually reinforcing dynamics of voluntarism, downloading, and privatization on immigrant settlement workers has remained invisible and hidden, in part, because the state is able to draw upon already existing assumptions of women's traditional role in providing care and support, and on assumptions around cultural "differences" in racialized ethnic minority communities' responses to their members' social welfare needs.

Due to lack of space, I have not discussed strategies of resistance and advocacy in this essay, yet a number of strategies of resistance are being employed to resist the negative effects of restructuring (Creese, Owen). Increased cooperation, reorganization of work, coalition advocacy, more critical analyses and research, better communication strategies are all being undertaken. Yet these strategies also need to be subjected to critical gender and race sensitive analyses, since these strategies are also traversed by societal assumptions and hegemonic practices. Nevertheless, the opening of a sub-sector of human welfare services that is primarily based on the labour of immigrant women has allowed a space where immigrant women are able to assert themselves as active citizens in civil society. Excluded from other spheres of public life, the space provided by immigrant integration and multiculturalism policies is, and continues to be, a space of possibility for affirmation and for broadening immigrant and refugee women's inclusion into the public sphere.

REFERENCES

Bakker, I., ed. *Rethinking Restructuring: Gender and Change in Canada*. Toronto: University of Toronto Press, 1996.

Creese, Gillian. "Government Restructuring and Immigrant/Refugee Settlement Work: Bringing Advocacy Back in." Vancouver Centre for Research on Immigration and Integration in the Metropolis (RIIM) Working Paper Series, 1998.

Kymlicka, W. *Finding Our Way: Rethinking Ethnocultural Relations in Canada*. Toronto: Oxford University Press, 1998.

Lee, J. "Immigrant Settlement and Multiculturalism Programs for Immigrant, Refugee, and Visible Minority Women: A Study of Outcomes, Best Practices, and Issues." A report submitted to British Columbia Ministry Responsible for Multiculturalism and Immigration, Vancouver, B.C., 1999.

Mwarigha, M.S. "Issues and Prospects. The Funding and Delivery of Immigrant Services in the Context of Cutbacks, Devolution, and Amalgamation." Paper presented at the Urban Forum on Immigration and Refugee Issues, Toronto, Sept. 29, 1997. http://ceris.metropolis.globalx. net/vl/other/Mwarigha29Sept97/html

Owen, T. "The View from Toronto: Settlement Services in the Late 1990s." Paper presented at the Vancouver Metropolis Conference, Jan. 13–16, 1999. http://ceris.metropolis.globalx.net/vl/community/owen1.html

Richmond, T. "Effects of Cutbacks on Immigrant Service Agencies." City of Toronto: Public Health Department, 1996. http://ceris.metropolis.net/vl/other/richmond2.html

Tator, C. "Anti-racism and the Human Service Delivery System" *Perspectives on Racism and the Human Services Sector. A Case for Change.* Ed. Carl E. James. Toronto: University of Toronto Press, 1996. 152–170.

CHAPTER EIGHT

Home(lessness) and the Naturalization of "Difference"

Nandita Sharma

National borders and their relationship to ideas of *home*, and in particular, how borders make many people *homeless* in the very places where their lives are lived is the topic of this book. By examining the social organization of one Canadian state category of entry, residency, and work, that of migrant workers, I discuss how it is the very construction of an always-limited sense of homeyness in the Canadian "nation," what Benedict Anderson (1991) calls "nation-ness," that makes migrant workers non-members of Canadianized society. A type of *home economics* is at play in this process of hierarchically organizing various groups of people through differential state categories of belonging. There is a materiality to the "differences" between "citizens," "immigrants" (i.e., permanent residents), and migrant workers; this materiality is based in the relationship between ideas of *nation* and those of *race, gender,* and *class.*

In this [...] chapter I discuss how the idea of home has been both occupied by national-ist practices and colonized by nationalized imaginations. Within such conceptualizations of home, those with national subject identities come to participate in what Dorothy E. Smith (1990) calls "relations of ruling." By making themselves at home in the nation, the national state relies on the complicity of those with national subjectivities to make common sense of the highly differential treatment accorded those classified as the nation's Others, particularly those placed in legal state categories, like migrant worker, that organize their foreign-ness within Canadian space.

* * * * *

OCCUPIED HOMES AND THE MAKING OF NATIONAL SUBJECTIVITIES

Home, and the ways it helps to organize ideas of family, household, ethnic community, and nation, is one of the most naturalized of concepts and therefore one of the most dangerous. Modernist ideas of home, in particular, help to organize and legitimate the differential treatment of those living within the same space: Differences between diverse indigenous people, citizens, immigrants, and migrant workers are organized through ideas of Canada being the home of some but not Others. With the overlaying of the idea of *home* onto that of *nation*, migrant workers are easily understood as foreigners labouring within a "foreign labour market" instead of being an integral component of Canadian society.

Home acts as a conceptual bridge between modern notions of family and nation, so much so that, as Anders Johansen (1997:171) notes, the nation is understood to be a "magnified version of the family and the circle of close friends." This is well captured by former British prime minister Margaret Thatcher, who characteristically proclaimed that "the family and its maintenance really is the most important thing, not only in your personal life, but in the life of any community, because this is the unit on which the whole nation is built" (in Rutherford, 1990:12).

As Philip Tabor (1998:218) puts it, "house identified with the self is called a home, a country identified with the self is called a 'homeland.'" "Its territory is our home; its people is marked by a common 'character,' much like the members of a family; its past is a 'heritage' passed down from our 'forefathers'" (Johansen, 1997:171). The ties between family, nation, and state are elaborated by Anne McLintock (1995:357), who observes that "the term nation derives from *natio*: to be born—we speak of nations as 'motherlands' and 'fatherlands.' Foreigners 'adopt' countries that are not their native homes and are nationalized in the 'national family.' We talk of the 'family of nations' of 'homelands' and 'native' lands. In Britain, immigration matters are dealt with at the Home Office; in the United States the president and his wife are called the First family."

Home, then, is an idea that masquerades as a place. Having a home within a nation, in particular, is not a geographical signpost but an ideological signifier. Yet, as David Morley (2000:8) notes, "if home is not necessarily a spatial concept, it is nonetheless often lived out as if it were such." Because of this, it profoundly shapes our consciousness of the relationship between place and "belonging." Its power rests in its ability to project modernist formulations of home back through human history so that our contemporary understandings of homelands come to be seen as merely the outcomes of some supposedly primordial need for rootedness.

* * * * *

Being at home in the land—just as *not* being at home—is based both on what Anjelika Bammer (1992:ix–x) calls "mythic narratives, stories the telling of which has the power to create the 'we' who are engaged in telling them' as well as constructing 'the discursive right to a space (a country, a neighbourhood, a place to live) that is due us … in the name of the 'we-ness' we have just constructed." Morley (2000:217) argues that such a discourse "allows us to imagine that we do not have to share our space with anyone else unless they are of exactly our own kind by virtue of consanguinity." What such a conflation allows is the identification of family cum nation as race. This has had a particularly damaging effect on migrants.

Historically, as ideologies of highly racialized nations as natural homelands became hegemonic, people's understanding of geographical movements profoundly shifted. Indeed, as borders became more fixed, migrants increasingly were portrayed as trespassers. In other words, as the nation became more homey to those seen as its members, migrants were made even more homeless. To be a migrant became tantamount to being a vagrant. Moreover the imposition of the idea that homelessness is akin to godlessness allowed vagrancy to be understood as a moral (and often a criminal) offence to the community of "honest residents." Migrants were thus strongly associated not only with losing their homes but also their moral standing.

* * * * *

Since "concepts of nation, people, and race are never very far apart," as Hardt and Negri note (2000:103), an examination of nationalist practices helps to explain why within the homeland "not all strangers are equally strange" (Peter Fitzpatrick, cited in Morley, 2000:249).

Nationalist practices are concerned with issues of spatial allocations of people and the suppos-edly "rightful" position of various differentiated people within national states in ways that rac-ist practices are not always. In this regard, Hage (2000:28) maintains that nationalist practices are those that "assume, first, an image of a national space; secondly, an image of the nationalist himself or herself as master of this national space and, thirdly, an image of the 'ethnic/racial other' as a mere object within this space." Members of the nation have a sense of "empowered spatiality" in relation to Others who do not, so that "in every [epithet of you] 'go home,' there is an 'I want to and am entitled to feel at home in my nation'" (ibid.:40).

There is, therefore, a particular kind of national subject that is important to construct and to maintain for power to be wielded within modern national states. Michel Foucault's (1991) discussion of self-regulation helps us to understand the crucial importance of the creation of a particular subjectivity to the realization of national state power. Thus, historically in Canada, "the entities being regulated were in the first instance the characters of individuals ... but the nation was also seen as held together by a common subjectivity, whose constant re-creation at the individual level ensured the continued survival of the collectivity. The collectivity thus orga-nized had very specific class, gender, and racial/ethnic characteristics" (Valverde, 1991:33).

National Self-regulation, then, is not only about constructing and regulating a proper national subject. Instead, having the nation stand in for various levels of homeyness—family, household, ethnic community, all of which are seen as discrete and secure sociogeographical environments—also requires the existence of a "threat" to create a secure sense of Self. In this regard, Hage (2000:37), using insights from Lacanian psychoanalysis of "fantasy spaces," maintains that nationalist discourses would fall apart if there were not Others against whom the nation could be defined. In the never-ending struggle to realize the nation, Hage (1993:99–100) notes that "in fact, the other is what allows the nationalist to believe in the possibility of that goal. It spares him the anxiety of having to face the fact that such a goal is impossible ... by the very fact of being posited as that which threatens it." Opposition to foreigners, thus, becomes a way for those Self-defined as being at home to argue for their own fuller integration into the nation.

Hence, Hage argues that nationalist practices are based on discourses of undesirability rather than on discourses of inferiority that underscore racism (2000:37). While discourses of inferiority do not necessarily necessitate Self-defence, discourses of undesirability motivate *action* towards the neutralization of whoever is presented as threatening the security of the homeland. Because the nation is presented as a community of similarity, threats always come to be defined as foreign, regardless of the actual location of the people so identified.

* * * * *

The ideology of the state acting in the "Common Good," often formulated as "democracy," shapes the legitimacy for the exclusion of Others not only from the space of the nation but from claims to the entitlements associated with membership in it. As Phil Cole (1998:137) notes, the "existence of a liberal polity made up of free and equal citizens rests upon the exis-tence of outsiders who are refused a share of [its] goods." This is not coincidental. Throughout the history of national states, the purported enemy or foreigner has never been limited to those *outside* of national space. In fact, the targeting of people represented as foreigners *within* the nation has often been more of a spur to nationalist activity than outside threats have been (see Hyslop, 1999:405).

Nancy Fraser (1993:8), in rejecting classical theories of national citizenship with their ideas of progressive inclusion of all in the nation, points out that the organization of civil society, or what has been called the public sphere of capitalist liberal democracies, is premised on many layers of separations and exclusions. There is both the separation of state from (civil) society, and the existence of separate spaces of belonging for various types of people classified according to deeply entrenched ideologies of separate races and gender roles and, perhaps most legitimately, by the belief that there are different territorial spaces for differently nationalized people. Full inclusion is not a possibility within the logic of national citizenship.

The notion of the nation as a homey place for all who live there (even as a potentiality), then, is ideological. It conceals the fact that the exclusions organized through it are integral— not tangential or merely contingent on historical—processes. In this respect, Avner Offer's (1989:235) argument that racist practices are *part of* the liberal "virtues of democracy, civic equality and solidarity" takes on greater relevance. So, too, does John Holloway's (1994:32) argument that, because the state is formed through assertions of national sovereignty that are constructed through the organization of racialized differences between Us and Them, "the very existence of the state is racist."

* * * * *

Concepts of citizenship are the ideological glue that bonds the nation to the state. Citizenship provides the legal framework through which the state performs its role as ruler *for* the nation. Together they legitimate the power of the state to subordinate foreigners. Denying the rights, entitlements, and protections that citizens have to those positioned as non-citizens is a crucial feature of how hegemonic conceptualizations of nations as homes operate within today's global capitalist economy. In this, citizenship and immigration policies are the key avenue through which nationalism is performed.

Immigration policies have historically played a significant part in organizing, materializing, and then regulating national differences. This is why it continues to be onto the bodies of (im)migrants that a foreign identity can most easily be grafted. In this period of increased mobility (of capital, goods, and people), it is the process of *differential inclusion*—not simply exclusion—that works to facilitate how people are seen and see themselves—as being at home or not in the spaces in which they find themselves.

NATIONAL HOMELESSNESS: THE MAKING OF NON-IMMIGRANT "MIGRANT WORKERS" IN CANADA

Being homeless in Canada is of particular significance for those categorized as temporary, foreign, migrant workers. The making of migrant workers allows us to clearly recognize how nationality operates as a legitimate mode of discrimination. For the last twenty-five or so years, most people (im)migrating to Canada arrive not as immigrants (those with "landed" or permanent, resident status) but as foreign migrant workers. The state category of *foreign worker* is a clear demonstration of how (im)migration controls are inextricably linked with the regulation of citizenship. Together they define who can be a member of the Canadian nation *and* who can legally make claims for protection or benefits from the Canadian national state. With the categorization of people as migrant workers, the state quietly borrows from the exclusionary practices organized through concepts of citizenship and its ideas of the fictive national society, in order to reposition migrant workers as part of a foreign workforce in Canada.

The categorization of certain (im)migrants as migrant workers is authorized through the regulatory framework of the Non-Immigrant Employment Authorization Program (NIEAP) introduced on 1 January 1973. Its broad parameters are entrenched within successive Canadian Immigration Acts. By law, a migrant worker is the "foreign worker" who upon arrival must have with her or him an official temporary employment authorization from the Canadian state. This foreign work visa, as it is commonly known, assigns her or him to a specified employer and stipulates her or his occupation, residence, length and terms of employment in Canada (Citizenship and Immigration Canada (CIC), 1994:1). Migrant workers must exit the country immediately after their labour contract expires. Written permission from immigration officials is required to alter any of the conditions of work. If the terms are changed without official permission, migrant workers are subject to immediate deportation.

As a result of these conditions, people admitted through the NIEAP are denied the freedoms of labour market and spatial mobility available to those existing within the legal designation of citizen or permanent resident. In fact, the NIEAP exists because it is unconstitutional for the state to restrict the mobility of citizens or immigrants. Such restrictions apply *only* for non-immigrants or "foreign visitors" who can *legally* be indentured to employers in Canada. The non-immigrant, or migrant worker, category, therefore, allows the social category of foreigner to be fully realized in Canadian law. Through it, the social organization of nationalized difference is materialized within the Canadian labour market and within Canadian society at large.

The NIEAP makes migrant workers available to employers concerned with securing a post-Fordist labour force: efficient, flexible, and globally competitive. Part of the flexibility and competitiveness of migrant workers is that they do not have access to many of the things that capitalist lobby groups complain make Canadian workers "too expensive": collective bargaining rights and access to social programs and protections (Swanson, 2001). Those categorized as migrant workers have little, or no, de facto claims to the minimum wage and labour standards and protections available to the citizenry (including, for the most part, permanent residents). Migrant workers are also usually made ineligible for certain social benefits, such as unemployment insurance or welfare payments even while they do pay taxes in the country.

Employers benefit in numerous ways as a result. Migrant workers can be paid much less than citizens or permanent residents and be made to work and live under conditions seen as "unattractive" to Canadians (Bolaria, 1992; Wall, 1992). Moreover, migrant workers are highly circumscribed from collectively organizing to realize the limited rights they do have access to or to agitate for more. This is mainly for two reasons. First, some migrant workers face severe isolation from other workers. For example, migrant domestic workers must live in the residence of their employer(s) as a condition of their temporary employment authorization. Second, because employers can end the labour contract at any time they are dissatisfied, and since such a termination often results in deportation, migrant workers are severely constrained by the system of patronage that develops (Wall, 1992). Such practices embolden employers and contribute to the substandard conditions found in jobs performed by migrant workers.

Unsurprisingly, then, since the introduction of the NIEAP in 1973, the Canadian state has successfully shifted immigration policy away from a policy of permanent immigrant settlement towards an increasing reliance upon unfree, temporary migrant workers. Such a shift is part of the overall neoliberal turn in state policy. For the majority of the years following its introduction, the number of people admitted to work in the labour market in Canada as immigrants (i.e., permanent residents) has declined both in proportion and in number relative to those recruited as migrant workers. From making up 57 per cent of the total number of those recruited for the Canadian labour market in 1973, only 30 per cent of the (im)migrant workforce received permanent resident status by 1993 (Sharma, 1995:122). By 2004 the proportion of (im)migrants admitted with permanent resident status was 35 per cent. By looking only at the numbers of people admitted as part of the independent class,[1] the shift is even greater: by 2004 only 22 per cent of all (im)migrants recruited for the Canadian labour market were given permanent resident status and rights while 76 per cent were recruited as migrant workers.

Yet, despite such dramatic changes in (im)migrants' status, there has been very little attention and even less outcry about the NIEAP. This is because the NIEAP does not work against but *through* hegemonic notions of Canadian nationness. The commonsensical understanding of migrant workers is that they are non-Whites from the global South who are lucky to work legally in Canada. The act of allowing Them into the country with a temporary employment authorization is seen as an act of charity extended by Canadians to foreign Others (Arat-Koc, 1992).

In conjunction with bounded ideas of national homes, creating conditions of work that are unacceptable, even illegal, for Canadians is easier to impose on those non-citizens who are also seen as racialized and/or cultural outsiders.[2] Hence, because migrant workers are not entering a "neutral ideological context" (Miles, 1982:165) when coming to Canada, the NIEAP needs to be located within the ideological organizaton of the Otherness of non-Whites both historically and during the time of its introduction. A look at Canadian parliamentary debates the five years prior to 1973 is illuminating in this regard.

As official discourses are an integral part of how the state constructs national society and its members, these debates not only articulate the agenda for specific state policy directions and provide a blueprint for policy implementation, they also shape the discursive framework of state practices. That is, they actively reshape, recreate, and redefine the "issues of the day" and, as such, constitute a site where a certain kind of discursive practice is put together around the framework of problems and their solutions. In doing so, such official discourses, because they are infused with societal norms and values help to construct subject—and object—identities (Doty, 1996). Part of the work done by such discourses, then, is to provide a particular frame for reading (and hearing) the debates whereby a certain kind of knowledge helpful to the accomplishment of ruling is produced (Smith, 1990).

Kari Dehli (1993:87) notes that such discursive state practices have "consequences beyond the contexts in which they are written and read." Parliamentary debates get entered into the work process of state apparatuses and by doing so help to construct categories of legally differentiated membership. These categories become what Lim Pui Huen and Diana Wong (2000) have called "discursive facts" that shape how people both know and interact with one another. State categories, thus, become cultural forms (Corrigan and Sayer, 1985:3).

Since parliamentary debates take place for the expressed purpose of governing society, they have great power not only in constructing but also legitimizing state categories. Parliamentary debates, in this sense, can be seen as a *technology* of liberal democratic forms of ruling that normalizes both the exercise of state power and the boundaries of those who belong—as well as those that do not—within national society (Foucault, 1991). A textual analysis of these debates, then, provides more than an interpretation of the utterances of parliamentarians. Rather, an analysis of them helps to uncover the social relations and social practices that allow these utterances to make common sense. This method of inquiry reveals that parliamentary debates, though not synonymous with ruling relations or state power, are a *form* of constructing knowledge through state practices, a form particularly attentive to the performance aspects of state authority and power.

In the context of Canada's liberal democracy the performance of parliamentary rituals is especially productive of notions of nationhood that legitimate the wielding of state power. This is most clearly evident in the daily Question Period where questions and answers between members of Parliament of different political parties are publicly conducted.[3] Adam Ashforth (1990:11) rightly points out that it would be more useful for us to interpret public performances of this type "less as instruments of 'policy' and 'intelligence' and more as symbolic rituals aiding in establishing and reproducing the power of modern states." Hage adds that debates on immigration in particular ought to be seen "in a more anthropological spirit, as rituals of *White empowerment*—seasonal festivals where White[s] … renew the belief in their possession of the power to talk and make decisions about Third World-looking people" (2000:241).

Significantly, the problem that the NIEAP is said to have solved is the problem of the *permanence* of non-Whites within Canadian society. Following the liberalization of Canadian immigration policy in 1967, non-Whites admitted as immigrants, that is, permanent residents, came to have (virtually) the same rights as White Canadians. Moreover, after 1967, a growing proportion of immigrants came from the global South, eventually becoming the majority of new permanent residents by 1974. In the five-year period surrounding the introduction of the NIEAP, a common conceptual practice within Parliament was to organize the discursive problem of there being "too many" non-Whites in the country and the resulting irreparable damage that was being done to the "character of Canadian society."

The NIEAP was one parliamentary solution to this problem. It legalized the resubordination of many non-Whites entering Canada by recategorizing them as temporary and foreign workers. Following the reversal of the liberal policies of the mid- to late 1960s, then, the racialized criteria of admittance in Canadian immigration policy was shifted from the pre-1967 categories of "preferred races and nationalities" onto the new category of non-immigrant (or migrant) worker. One trend towards the liberalization of racism was met by a counter-trend towards the greater restriction of the rights and entitlements of non-Whites.

Parliamentary discursive practices and the legislative changes they legitimate have, in this, the early part of the latest period of capitalist globalization, worked to reconstruct the idea of nations as homes for some but not Others. One result has been greater competition within the labour market in Canada. This has worked to reorganize national labour markets to become more competitive within global markets for both capital and labour. Parliamentarians, therefore, have contributed both materially and ideologically to processes of globalization. The construction of the NIEAP is, of course, an extension of past global practices that saw non-Whites brought to Canada as indentured workers while Whites were positioned as permanent settlers. Indeed, Hyslop (1999:405) shows that, historically, an imperial White working class made itself through a common ideology of homey racism that was, in part, designed to secure them access to key and relatively privileged parts of nationalized labour markets.

A significant aspect of White, male privilege was the claim to freedom from constraints on their mobility in the labour market. In making their claims to national subjecthood, it was the continuing unfreedom of negatively racialized and gendered Others that consolidated the view among White men that contractual servitude was involuntary labour. Consequently, those made to labour in unfree employment relationships, although integral to the production and reproduction of Canadian society, were constituted (in varying degrees) as foreigners to it. Such arguments came to form an integral part of nationalist practices of Othering. It can be said, therefore, that the freeing of White male workers *strengthened* racialized and gendered understandings of who could be a member of the nation.

Being rendered a foreign Other within Canadian society and working in unfree conditions within its nationalized labour market have, thus, often been historically coterminous. Organizing unfreedom for Others has operated as a technology of keeping these Others in their place, both spatially as well as keeping them as subordinated people within Canadian society. The contemporary practice of organizing a migrant labour force in Canada, many from the global South, demonstrates how racism and sexism continue to operate *through* nationalist practices. Because such practices are seen not only as legitimate but as *necessary* for the defence of the home(land), nationalist practices are able to accomplish racist and sexist aims in a social and policy environment where explicit racialized criteria in immigration selection have been mostly removed.

In this latest period of globalization, *nationalist* practices that produce feelings of both homeyness and of foreignness have become even more important. Because the state is widely seen to be legitimate in using its power against foreigners, the existence of people as migrant workers in Canada is predicated on naming those "embraced" by this category as *not* being at home. As in the past, the construction of subordinate categories of entry and work (slave or coolie labour and now migrant worker) shapes the competitiveness and profitability of contained and therefore competitive labour markets.

Thus, in contrast to John Holloway (1994:30), who argues that "the destruction of personal bondage was also the destruction of geographical constraint," it is clear that the existence of unfree labour is not predicated on people's spatial *immobility* but on exactly the opposite. Oftentimes (though not always) it is people's dependence on migration across nationalized boundaries that places them in situations where, having been categorized as foreigners, they are denied the same rights that citizens lay exclusive claim to. Immigration policies become the vehicle through which their unfreedom is organized precisely because they allow the national state to utilize its internationally recognized power to determine membership in the nation.

A critical examination of the migrant worker category, thus, reveals that border controls and immigration restrictions are thoroughly ideological. This is for two reasons. First, they do very little to actually control people's mobility across borders. Second, because they are imagined as natural, and as crucial manifestations of state sovereignty, their operation as an integral feature of the global expansion of capitalism is concealed. Thus, whether we talk about such border control spectacle, as the more than 2,000-mile long steel fence erected, patrolled, and armed by the U.S. Immigration and Naturalization Service across the border separating Mexico from the United States, or the spectacle of "Europe's new Berlin Wall": the eight-kilometre fence between the Spanish-claimed enclave of Melilla and the rest of Africa or the ever more restrictive immigration policies of virtually every national state in the global North, restrictions on who is legally able to enter with full status do very little to actually restrict migration itself. Nor would I argue are they intended to.

Restricting *immigration* is not tantamount to restricting people's mobility. In Canada, where there has been a steady closing down of avenues to obtain immigrant (or permanent resident) status over the last thirty years, there has been an increase in the numbers of people legally admitted to work in the country. The categorization of the majority of (im)migrants admitted to the country as migrant workers has meant that they encounter a differential regulation of their labour power and a differentiated position once within Canada than do immigrants. In short, constructing people as foreigners has not resulted in their exclusion from Canadian society. Limits to immigration, then, lay not so much in the ability of states to restrict people's geographical mobility but to restrict their freedom once they are *within* nationalized labour markets.

The greater policing of the purified boundaries of nationalized identities have therefore been beneficial to employers trying to gain advantages from the dramatic increase in people's displacement and subsequent migrations. The simultaneous presence of anti-immigration discourses evident in Canadian parliamentary debates and increases in the number of people entering Canada as non-citizens without permanent, full status are, therefore, not at all contradictory but are instead complementary processes. As Hage (2000:135) comments, "anti-immigration discourse, by continually constructing the immigrants as unwanted, works precisely at maintaining [their] economic viability to … employers. They are best wanted as 'unwanted.'"

Greater competition within national labour markets relies on the social organization of difference and the regulation of this differentiated inclusion through the disciplinary model of nationalism with its exclusionary inclusivity. In this regard, the rhetoric of border controls with its accompanying moral panics against those identified as (im)migrants helps to further the project of capitalist globalization. By first creating a group of foreigners and then presenting Them as the problem facing Us, the reality that the NIEAP, with its institutionalization of differentials in wages and standards, actually works against the interests of *all* workers becomes difficult to see.

Border controls enable national states to reorganize their nationalized labour markets to *include* a group of migrant workers who are made vulnerable to employers' demands through their lack of status. In the current historical juncture where both people's displacement and subsequent migration are occurring at a historically unprecedented level—the United Nations (2003) estimates that every year more than 175 million people migrate across national borders—nationalism, with its legitimization of differential treatment for foreigners and citizens, has become a motor force of capitalist globalization. It is the social organization of difference that regulates the space between national homes and global capitalist economics.

To better understand the significance of difference to such ruling projects, we need to problematize the existence of differences by clearly distinguishing between difference and diversity. Diversity is the tangible existence of heterogeneity and mutual reciprocity within nature and within that part of nature that is humanity. Differences, on the other hand, are socially organized inequalities between human beings and between humans and the rest of the planet. The social organization of difference is the effect of practices and beliefs founded upon hierarchies of differential value and worth.

When we say someone is different, we are not recognizing that person's singularity. Instead, we are setting her or him aside as a member of a group that does not meet normative or hegemonic standards for subjecthood, agency, and belonging. Difference, then, is mutually constitutive. It is relational. As Brah (1996:124) points out, "the proclamation of a specific collective identity is a political process [whereby] the commonality that is evoked can be rendered meaningful only in articulation with a discourse of difference." It is to this relational aspect of difference that Gregory Bateson (1979:78) refers when he says that "it takes at least two somethings to create difference … Clearly each alone is—for the mind and perception—a nonentity, a non-being … An unknowable, a *Ding an sich,* a sound from one hand clapping."

In the making of difference, however, the "two somethings" are quite unequal in their respective ability to affect both the relationship and the representation of themselves. The norms which are constructed through such binary oppositions always pivot on the experiences, desires, and power held by those in the dominant half of Self/Other codes. Frantz Fanon (1965:32) understands this well when he states, "it is the [colonial] settler who has brought the native into existence and who perpetuates his existence." Sardar et al. (1993:89) and that within such binaries, even the "the distinctiveness of a particular Other … [is] lost in the generality shared with all Others, that of being different ... from the West," so that one overarching category of Other is created as the definitive opposite of the Self.

The politics of constructing and maintaining negative dualities of worth in which one half of the binary equation is privileged both symbolically and materially is what constitutes the identity politics of rulers (see Bannerji, 1995). This is evident in everyday understandings of difference. People who are different are so identified because of the ways they are seen as standing apart from those with the power to define them. Their difference is organized by the ways they have been negatively racialized, gendered, sexualized, classed, and so on. The lines of difference drawn between Self and Other are related to narratives of belonging.

* * * * *

The central distinction between difference and diversity, then, is that unlike diversity, difference, perhaps ironically, has *homogeneity* as its architectural frame. The organization of difference is about ensuring conformity to hegemonic beliefs and practices in an attempt to shape the world in the image of dominant groups. Difference, then, is about universalizing a *particular* parochial interest. Vandana Shiva (1997:93) sees the process of taking diversity and filtering out of it any divergence from the norm the creation of a "monoculture of the mind."

What, then, are we to make of current attempts to validate and valorize *difference* within postmodern and post-structuralist theory with its rightful attention to the politics of representation and identity (Young, 1989:261)? [...] It is important to note only that such celebrations of difference have often conflated difference with diversity, and this leads to a serious lack of attention to how the organization of differences is a strategy of ruling.

The attempt to end oppressive and exploitative social relations, particularly those of racism, through an acknowledgment of *differences* has led to political solutions such as the official promotion of "tolerance" for different people. This kind of political practice has come to be called demonstrating a "respect for diversity." Of course, the stated aim of this respect is to secure the proper functioning of society as a singular body, again, in the image of Self-defined rulers. In such rhetoric, the nation is thought to be able to simply transcend conflict through a respect and celebration of difference without the eradication of any differentials in power and wealth and with no transformation at a systemic level.

This is, of course, the kind of diversity embraced by the state. It is one that enables those in positions of power over Others to tolerate people who have been differentiated. Yet, as Hage (2000) well notes, when those in positions of power are asked to be tolerant, their power to be intolerant is not taken away from them. It is, in fact, reasserted by the very request to have them not exercise it. In this regard, respect for diversity does not eclipse the social organization of difference but becomes a contemporary form of reproducing hierarchal social relations and recentring the White national subject. It legitimates the continued organization of difference in order to both organize and legitimate the subordination that the differentiated experience.

This kind of *official diversity* needs to [be] distinguished from the kind of diversity I have discussed earlier. Perhaps we need to rename that kind of diversity *radical diversity* since the former has been co-opted and has come to connote its exact opposite: the power of One (one law, one society, one People) over the Many, or what Deleuze and Guattari (1987) call the "multiplicity," and what Hardt and Negri (2000; 2004) refer to as the "multitude." Social systems based on radical diversity, unlike those founded on differences, are wholly dependent on maintaining heterogeneity while recognizing commonalities based on shared practice or experience for their continued survival and pleasure.

The social organization of difference is, therefore, a highly ideological practice and one linked to the material production of unjust social relations. In this regard, it is crucial to recognize that difference has its own materiality. Indeed, the entire history of the capitalist mode of production and its ever-expanding global reach has been organized through the structuring of difference. How one is identified shapes how one is positioned within global capitalism. The accumulation of capital continues to take place through the social and legal differentiation of labour (Lowe, 1996:159).

Within the conceptual carving out of differentiated zones of belonging lie concealed the interconnected relations and mutual constitutiveness between so-called local and global spaces, between the inside and the outside of nations. Indeed, the idea that there exist two supposedly discrete spaces—the national one in which Canadians exist and a global or foreign one that contains Others—has structured the sense of Canadian homeyness that legitimates the subordination of migrant workers within the space occupied by Canada. The social organization of difference, therefore, always works to create forms of separation, whereby discrimination is organized through exclusionary inclusion. Nationalized differences, in particular, are consequential to the emergence and further entrenchment of what Anthony Richmond (1994) has aptly identified as "global apartheid." He refers to the organization of an ever-widening differentiation between people in wealthy and impoverished national states through restrictive immigration policies that imprison impoverished people within zones of poverty.

ENDNOTES

1. The independent class of immigration recruits people as permanent residents through the "points system" that evaluates applicants according to their occupation, educational qualifications, and English and French language skills, as well as "adaptability" to Canadian society and then assesses applicants on their ability to meet a minimum number of "points" in these areas.

2. Remembering that it is the global system of nation-states that organizes people as either citizens or (im)migrants, it is important to note that the imposition of unfree conditions upon those constructed as (im)migrants is part of a long historical trajectory. For instance, Richard Plender's research shows that the first instance of permanent immigration control, England's Alien Law of 1793, included the ability of the King to limit the spatial mobility of (im)migrants who could be forced to live in a specified district (1972:43). These laws, Petras argues, "marked the decline of free movement and the establishment of the right of states to impose direct controls on alien immigration" (1980:166). It was during the earlier part of the twentieth century, however, that there was a marked increase in immigration legislation among nation-states. For instance, it was during this time that the international system of passports was first developed (Torpey, 2000).

3. Although traditional political science approaches see MPs of the governing party but not the opposition parties as part of the *government,* I believe it is more fruitful to view the MPs of all political parties as participating in state governance, especially in discursive activities concerned with legitimizing the existence of the state and its power.

REFERENCES

Anderson, Benedict. 1991. *Imagined Communities: Reflections on the Origin and Spread of Nationalism.* London: Verso.

Arat-Koc, Sedef. 1992. "Immigration Policies, Migrant Domestic Workers, and the Definition of Citizenship in Canada." In *Deconstructing a Nation: Immigration, Multiculturalism, and Racism in '90s Canada.* Ed. V. Satzewich. Halifax: Fernwood.

Ashforth, Adam. 1990. "Reckoning Schemes of Legitimation: On Commissions of Inquiry as Power/ Knowledge Forms." *Journal of Historical Sociology* 3:1, 1–22.

Bammer, Anjelika. 1992. "Editorial." *New Formations* 17.

Bannerji, Himani. 1995. *Thinking through: Essays on Feminism, Marxism, and Anti-racism.* Toronto: Women's Press.

Bateson, Gregory. 1979. *Mind and Nature: A Necessary Unity.* New York: Dutton.

Bird, John. 1995. "Dolce Domum." In *House.* Ed. J. Lingwood. London: Phaidon.

Bolaria, B. Singh. 1992. "From Immigrant Settlers to Migrant Transients: Foreign Professionals in Canada." In *Deconstructing a Nation: Immigration, Multiculturalism, and Racism in '90s Canada.* Ed. V. Satzewich. Halifax: Fernwood.

Brah, Avtar. 1996. *Cartographies of Diaspora: Contesting Identities.* London: Routledge.

Burton, Antoinette. 1997. "Who Needs the Nation? Interrogating 'British' History." *Journal of Historical Sociology* 10:3, 227–48.

Citizenship and Immigration Canada (CIC). 1994. *Hiring Foreign Workers: Facts for Canadian Employers.* Ottawa: Minister of Supply and Services.

Cohen, Philip. 1996. "Homing Devices." In *Re-situating Identities.* Ed. V. Amit-Talai and C. Knowles. Peterborough, ON: Broadview Press.

Cole, Phil. 1998. "A Game of Two Halves: 'English' Identity Fifty Years after the Windrush." *Soundings,* no. 10.

Corrigan, Philip, and Derek Sayer. 1985. *The Great Arch: English State Formation as Cultural Revolution.* Oxford: Blackwell.

Cresswell, Tim. 1996. *In Place/out of Place.* Minneapolis: University of Minnesota Press.

Dehli, Kari. 1993. "Subject to the New Global Economy: Power and Positioning in the Ontario Labour Market Policy Formation." *Studies in Political Economy* 41, 83–110.

Deleuze, Gilles, and Felix Guattari. 1987. *A Thousand Plateaus: Capitalism and Schizophrenia.* Trans. B. Massumi. Minneapolis: University of Minnesota Press.

Doty, Roxanne L. 1996. "The Double-Writing of Statecraft: Exploring State Responses to Illegal Immigration." *Alternatives* 21, 171–89.

Fanon, Frantz. 1965. *The Wretched of the Earth.* London: MacGibbon and Kee.

Foucault, Michel. 1991. "Questions of Method." In *The Foucault Effect: Studies in Governmentality.* Ed. G. Burchell, C. Gordon, and P. Miller. Chicago: University of Chicago Press.

Fraser, Nancy. 1993. "Rethinking the Public Sphere." In *The Phantom Public Sphere.* Ed. B. Robbins. Minneapolis: University of Minnesota Press.

Goldberg, David Theo. 1992. "The Semantics of Race." *Ethnic and Racial Studies* 15:4, 543–65.

Gordon, Colin. 1991. "Government Rationality: An Introduction." In *The Foucault Effect: Studies in Governmentality.* Ed. G. Burchell, C. Gordon, and P. Miller. Chicago: University of Chicago Press.

Guillaumin, Colette. 1995. *Racism, Sexism, Power and Ideology.* London: Routledge.

Hage, Ghassan. 1993. "Nation-Building-Dwelling-Being," *Communal/Plural* 1, 73–103.

———. 2000. *White Nation: Fantasies of White Supremacy in a Multicultural Society.* New York, and Annandale, NSW, Australia: Routledge and Pluto Press.

Hardt, Michael, and Antonio Negri. 2000. *Empire.* Cambridge: Harvard University Press.

———. 2004. *Multitude: War and Democracy in the Age of Empire.* New York: Penguin.

Hebdige, Dick. 1995. "On Tumbleweed and Bodybags: Remembering America." In *Longing and Belonging: From the Faraway Nearby.* Ed. B.W. Ferguson. New York: Distributed Art Publishers.

Hobsbawm, Eric. 1990. *Nations and Nationalism since 1780.* New York: Cambridge University Press.

Holloway, John. 1994. "Global Capital and the National State." *Capital and Class* 52 (Spring), 23–50.

Hyslop, Jonathan. 1999. "The Imperial Working Class Makes Itself 'White': White Labourism in Britain, Australia, and South Africa before the First World War." *Journal of Historical Sociology* 12:4, 398–421.

Johansen, A. 1997. "Fellowmen, Compatriots, Contemporaries." In *Cultural Politics and Political Culture in Postmodern Europe.* Ed. J. Peter Burgess. Amsterdam: Editions Rodopi.

Keith, Michael, and Steven Pile. 1993. "The Politics of Place." In *Place and the Politics of Identity.* Ed. M. Keith and S. Pile. London: Routledge.

Kumar, Krishan. 1994. "Home: The Nature of Private Life at the End of the Twentieth Century." In *Private and Public in Thought and Practice.* Ed. J. Wintraub and K. Kumar. Chicago: University of Chicago Press.

Lowe, L. 1996. *Immigrant Acts: On Asian American Cultural Politics.* Durham, NC: Duke University Press.

Mackay, H. (ed.). 1997. *Consumption and Everyday Life.* Milton Keynes: Open University Press.

Malkki, Lisa. 1997. "National Geographic." In *Culture, Power, Place.* Ed. A. Gupta and J. Ferguson. Durham, NC: Duke University Press.

Marx, Karl, and Frederick Engels. 1969. "Feuerbach. Opposition of the Materialistic and Idealistic Outlook (Chapter 1 of *The German Ideology*)." In *Selected Works,* Vol. 1. Moscow: Progress.

Massey, Doreen. 1994. *Space, Place, and Gender.* Cambridge: Polity.

McLintock, Anne. 1995. *Imperial Leather.* London: Routledge.

Mercer, Kobena. 1994. *Welcome to the Jungle: New Positions in Black Cultural Studies.* New York: Routledge.

Michaels, Anne. 1996. *Fugitive Pieces.* Toronto: McClelland & Stewart.

Miles, Robert. 1982. *Racism and Migrant Labour: A Critical Text.* London: Routledge and Kegan Paul.

———. 1993. *Racism after "Race Relations."* London and New York: Routledge.

Morley, David. 2000. *Home Territories: Media, Mobility, and Identity.* London and New York: Routledge.

Offer, Avner. 1989. *The First World War: An Agrarian Interpretation.* New York: Oxford University Press.

Petras, Elizabeth McLean. 1992. "The Shirt on Your Back: Immigrant Workers and the Reorganization of the Garment Industry." *Social Justice* 19:1, 76–114.

Plender, R. 1972. *International Migration Law.* Leiden: A.W. Sijthoff.

Poulantzas, Nicos. 1973. *Political Power and Social Classes.* London: New Left Books.

Rathzel, Nora. 1994. "Harmonious Heimat and Disturbing Auslander." In *Shifting Identities and Shifting Racisms.* Ed. K.K. Bhavani and A. Phoenix. London: Sage.

Richmond, Anthony H. 1994. *Global Apartheid: Refugees, Racism, and the New World Order.* Don Mills, ON: Oxford University Press.

Rutherford, J. (ed.). 1990. *Identity: Community, Culture, Difference.* London: Lawrence and Wishart.

Sardar Zianddin, Ashis Namdy, Claude Alvarez, and Merryl Wyn Davies. 1993. *Barbaric Others: A Manifesto on Western Racism.* London/Boulder, CO: Pluto Press.

Sassen, Saskia. 1999. *Guests and Aliens.* New York: New Press.

Sharma, Nandita. 1995. "The True North Strong and Unfree: Capitalist Restructuring and Non-immigrant Employment in Canada, 1973–1993." Master's thesis, Simon Fraser University.

———. 2001. "On Being Not Canadian: The Social Organization of 'Migrant Workers' in Canada." *Canadian Review of Sociology and Anthropology* 38:4, 415–439.

Shiva, Vandana. 1997. *Biopiracy: The Plunder of Nature and Knowledge.* Toronto: Between the Lines.

Smith, Dorothy E. 1990. *The Conceptual Practices of Power: A Feminist Sociology of Knowledge.* Toronto: University of Toronto Press.

Stallybrass, Peter, and Allon White. 1986. *The Politics and Poetics of Transgression.* London: Methuen.

Stolcke, Verena. 1995. "Talking Culture: New Boundaries, New Rhetorics of Exclusion." *Current Anthropology* 36:1.

Sutcliffe, Bob. 2001. "Migration and Citizenship: Why Can Birds, Whales, Butterflies, and Ants Cross International Frontiers More Easily Than Cows, Dogs, and Human Beings?" In *Migration and Mobility: The European Context.* Ed. Subrata Ghatak and Anne Showstack Sassoon. New York: Palgrave.

Swanson, Jean. 2001. *Poor-Bashing: The Politics of Exclusion.* Toronto: Between the Lines.

Tabor, Philip. 1998. "Striking Home—the Telematic Assault on Identity." In *Occupying Architecture:* Ed. J. Hill. London: Routledge.

Torpey, John. 2000. *The Invention of the Passport: Surveillance, Citizenship, and State.* Cambridge and New York: Cambridge University Press.

United Nations Population Fund. 2003. *The State of World Population.* New York: United Nations.

Urry, John. 1989. "The End of Organized Capitalism." In *New Times.* Ed. S. Hall and M. Jacques. London: Lawrence and Wishart.

Valverde, Mariana, 1991. *The Age of Light, Soap, and Water: Moral Reform in English Canada, 1885–1925*. Toronto: McClelland & Stewart.

Vancouver Sun. 1998. "If You Feel Worse Off—You Probably Are." 13 May.

Wall, Ellen. 1992. "Personal Labour Relations and Ethnicity in Ontario Agriculture." In *Deconstructing a Nation: Immigration, Multiculturalism, and Racism in '90s Canada*. Ed. V. Satzewich. Halifax: Fernwood.

Young, Iris Marion. 1989. "Polity and Group Difference." *Ethics* 99:2.

CHAPTER NINE

Foreign Credentials in Canada's Multicultural Society

Lorne Foster

* * * * *

In this chapter, I will begin to explore the social problem of foreign accreditation barriers and the social consequences of this process in the context of Canadian immigration policy and the knowledge-based political economy. In particular, I will explore Canadian immigration policy and the discounting of foreign credentials as an illustration of the link between immigration and political economy in the context of a colour-coded national and international division of labour. The main objective of this chapter is to examine the hierarchical relationship between racialized individuals and groups as the new recurring theme in Canada's vertical mosaic, and the postindustrial base for class and power. This, of course, is a very large topic and so my treatment of it will be limited. Stated generally and briefly, I argue that race is the new foundation for the social construction of twenty-first-century global reality.

* * * * *

In postindustrial societies, there is evidence to suggest that the relationship between dominant and sub-dominant groups does not usually extend over diverse ethnoracial relationships in a way that reinforces institutional realms across the society. On the contrary, everyday life does not reflect a "back of the bus" formal segregation and hierarchy, and there are no public spaces designated "Whites Only" or "Coloureds Only." This pattern in social institutions gives contemporary pluralism a non-caste-like public image in which society looks as though it is not resistant to change or to the social mobility of people of colour. Instead, visible minority progress from accommodation to assimilation appears to be, and is presented as, a straight-forward "first come, first serve queue" and "point system" proposition—a matter of individual merit and personal initiative. However, the fluidity of social institutions does not necessarily correspond to, or interface with, the political economy where the subtlety of racial domination and discrimination in the workplace is negated by the informality of unassuming policies and practices that are woven into the framework of economic institutions.

Canadian immigration policy is an example of an institution that features specific racial-ized biases. Like many other social problems, racialized immigration signals a discrepancy between the ideals and realities of Canadian society. While equality of opportunity and free-dom for all—regardless of country of origin, body colour, creed, or language—are stated Canadian ideals, many subordinate minority group members experience discrimination on the basis of racializing factors. Although passage of employment equity legislation, human rights legislation, official promotion of multiculturalism, and the introduction of universality in Canada's immigration system are aimed at eliminating overt institutional discrimination in and by Canadian society, people of colour, particularly visible immigrants, are often marginalized (Foster 2002). Accordingly, in the contemporary workplace, while there are variations in income levels between visible minority groups, research has consistently found that earnings disadvantages are particularly significant for immigrants from non-European backgrounds (Reitz and Sklar 1977).

* * * * *

Sociological research has recognized the "social fact" that contemporary immigration to Canada is both urbanized and racially segmented (Durkheim [1895] 1964). That is, a large number of foreign-trained professional immigrants have experienced downward social mobility after immigrating to Canada, and the significant human capital belonging to this immigrant population has been underutilized. Further, it is a well-established social fact that the economic returns on human capital appear to be lower for immigrants who belong to visible minority groups (Baker and Benjamin 1994). Further, Richmond (1984: 253) found that despite high levels of education, visible minority immigrants from "Third World" countries appear to be particularly vulnerable in the Canadian labour market. Subsequently, immigrant skills are significantly discounted in Canada, and the groups affected by this process are primarily composed of racial minorities (Reitz 2005).

* * * * *

The First Research Theme Stresses Individual Factors: In an open society that sanctions achievement and merit in the form of education-based skills, how do we account for occupational disadvantages across colour lines? Much research suggests that the idea that racial minorities experience greater problems of skill underutilization is not conclusive or unproblematic evidence of racial discrimination. Some would argue, particularly in the context of diverse multicultural and multiracial society, that the influences of confounding factors on income differences are complicated. Therefore, without careful controls of demographic and motivational influences, structural factors (ethnicity and race) in income differences and discrimination may be exaggerated. Different rates of occupational return may relate more to personal qualifications than to blocked mobility. It is argued that multivariate analysis is essential in adjusting the effects of other influential factors, including schooling, age, sex, nativity, language, occupation, and labour-force activity (Boyd 1992).

One general finding in the literature is that after controlling for various factors that affect earnings, including years of education and labour market experience, immigrants appear to start at a significant disadvantage relative to native-born Canadians, but catch up over time. This phenomenon is known as the "years since immigration" effect. Virtually all ethnic groups have experienced overall improvement in educational attainment over the last three decades (Herberg 1990; Shamai 1992). The implication of this is that at some point, the immigrant gap could be eliminated. The expectation of better prospects for second-generation immigrant children is based, in part, on the importance attached to education by highly educated immigrants, which they often pass on to their children. Also employers are more likely to accept this second generation, because their education, unlike that of their parents, will be acquired in Canada. Previous studies on the offspring of immigrants generally confirm this optimism (Boyd 1992). However, there seems to be general agreement that for non-White immigrants who arrived in Canada since the 1980s, the initial earnings gap has widened and the catch-up rate has slowed (Baker and Benjamin 1994). Black men of Caribbean origin, for example, seem to carry a long-term disadvantage and may never reach the wage level that one might expect (Simmons and Plaza 1995).

Alboim, Finnie, and Ming (2005) found evidence that minorities who hold at least one degree from Canada and one from abroad achieve very high levels of income, even in comparison to White immigrants with similar credentials. Further, minority immigrants with multiple degrees do exceptionally well in the labour force, and immigrants of colour with only one foreign degree do very poorly. This is in comparison to similarly educated White immigrants who consistently earn substantial returns for their schooling. There is very little difference between White and visible minority immigrants who obtain their university degrees in Canada, and there is little difference in the returns for a Canadian degree when comparing White and non-White native-born Canadians. That is to say, both immigrants and native-born Canadians with Canadian degrees—visible minority or White—receive similar rewards in the labour force. In fact, returns are actually estimated to be slightly greater for people of colour (Alboim, Finnie, and Ming 2005).

These results suggest that a foreign degree held by an immigrant who belongs to a visible minority group is heavily discounted in the Canadian labour market. However, they go further to suggest that there is little difference in the returns on degree obtained in Canada for both immigrants of colour and White immigrants. Additionally, native-born members of visible minority groups holding degrees achieve income levels that are again a little higher than their White counterparts. From this, researchers conclude that direct racial discrimination seems unlikely to be the reason—or at least the sole reason—for this gap. Finally, researchers cannot discern why non-White immigrants with foreign degrees consistently earn low returns for their schooling, and cannot rule out some discrimination towards foreign education obtained in certain countries. However, differences in the type and quality of schooling, or the inability of Canadians to accurately judge the worth of foreign degrees seem to be more likely explanations (Alboim, Finnie, and Ming 2005).

Interestingly, research has found that while foreign-born visible minority members are at a disadvantage in the wage labour force, those who are native-born and self-employed do substantially better than self-employed Canadian-born persons (Maxim 1992). It has been suggested that the decline of manufacturing jobs and the erosion of opportunities for advancement within the labour force for immigrants are tied to entrepreneurship within an ethnic economy (Satzewich and Wong 2003). This situation is reminiscent of earlier times when entrepreneurship was chosen by members of Chinese and Jewish communities because of blocked mobility in the mainstream labour market.

There is some evidence to suggest that contemporary ethnoracial entrepreneurship is also consistent with the new global formation of the "transnational" actor, and the related formation of the international approach to social life and citizenship (Portes 1999). Previously, international migrants made radical breaks from their ancestral homes to start life afresh in their new homeland. Currently, the new paradigm of transnationalism emphasizes the link that immigrant and ethnic communities retain and cultivate with families, institutions, and political economies abroad (Satzewich and Wong 2003). Ethnic entrepreneurship and related transnational economic enterprises may offer opportunities to immigrants of modest backgrounds for escaping dead-end, menial jobs and making their way into the middle class (Portes 1999:471). This would seem to support the individual factor approach to the examination of immigrant earnings inequality.

Some research has referenced demographic and motivational factors in regard to the selectivity of immigration procedures. For instance, it has been found that Asian immigrants have experienced the greatest social economic advancement in Canada in recent years. This appears to imply that there is a place in Canada's vertical mosaic for the upward mobility of some visible minority groups (Shamai 1992). However, there are studies that attribute this apparent success to the selectivity of the immigration points system and an increase in the number of Asian immigrants over the last three decades (Basavarajappa, Ravi, and Verma 1985:32–35). It has also been suggested that new immigration regulations may have been more stringently applied in the selection of non-European immigrants, thereby increasing entry levels of human capital (Kalbach and Richard 1988). In view of these potential variables, it is possible that some minority groups may have high educational attainments due to the selectivity of immigration, or to high aspirations and individual efforts.

Hou and Balakrishanan (1996) found that the selectivity of immigration only contributes partly to the achievement of visible minorities in education. They argue that income inequality on the basis of qualifications is probably related to discrimination rather than demographic factors. This finding is substantiated in two ways. First, while there is some evidence of variability within both non-visible minority groups and visible minority groups in terms of the effects of various individual factors on their income levels, patterns of integration into Canadian society for non-visible minorities and visible minorities are different and clearly distinct. Second, while income equality has materialized in spite of educational differences for some European groups, it has not for visible minority groups. Specifically, in Canada, differences in income exist between and within non-visible and visible minority groups. After adjusting for variations in educational and occupational distributions, most visible minorities receive less income for equal levels of employment and skills. In this sense, we can say that visible minorities follow a different path of integration into contemporary Canadian society (Hou and Balakrishanan 1996:282).

The Second Research Theme Stresses Structural Factors: Accentuating the importance of higher education in postindustrial societies is thought to be consistent with an "open society" concept based on the principle of meritocracy. This mandates that an individual's accomplishments are basically determined by personal attributes and efforts. Income, for instance, is the reward for an individual's investment in human capital. Therefore, income differences between individuals should reflect differences in education, profession, age, and other achieved social and economic characteristics. The ascribed statuses of individuals, including visible ethnicity and race, should not be factors. Consequently, racialized differences in income may be an important indicator of discrimination.

In this approach, structural factors that contribute to racialized patterns of difference are noted as indicators of discrimination in the recognition of foreign credentials. This suggests, in conjunction with "the discrimination thesis," that control of entry into professions has caused systematic exclusion and occupational disadvantages for professional immigrants (Boyd 1985; McDade 1988; Trovato and Grindstaff 1986; Rajagopal 1990; Ralston 1988; Beach and Worswick 1989). Specifically, Boyd provides an analysis of differences between Canadian-born and foreign-born workers in the acquisition of occupational status. Boyd (1985) argues that Canadian-born people receive a greater return for their education compared to foreign-born individuals because of "difficulties of transferring educational skill across national boundaries" (p. 405).

Several studies use census data to demonstrate the difficulties in translating educational achievements into occupational advantage that are faced by selected cohorts of immigrants

(Trovato and Grindstaff 1986). Pendakur and Pendakur's research suggests that even when controlling for occupation, industry, education, experience, official language knowledge, and household type, visible minorities earn significantly less than native-born white workers (1998:26). Reitz argues that the cause of low earnings among immigrants is overwhelmingly pay inequity, with some underutilization of skills (2003).

DYNAMIC INTERPLAY OF SOCIAL FORCES AND THE COLLECTIVE EXPERIENCES OF INDIVIDUALS

Although the individual approach has elucidated some personal difficulties, it cannot explain how structural factors pertaining to policies, criteria, and evaluation procedures also contribute to occupational disadvantages for foreign-trained professionals. In a Durkheimian sense, failure to locate individual barriers in social conditions and structural arrangements tends to blame immigrant professionals for their problems in Canada. However, individual behaviour does not evolve in a vacuum. For example, lacking Canadian experience is an individual attribute, but it is related to employers refusing to recognize foreign credentials and failing to hire immigrants for jobs suited to their training. Samuels (2004) notes that the use of "Canadian experience" is used as a euphemism for racism. From the vantage point of visible minority foreign-trained professionals, it would not be accurate to consider their occupational disadvantages as resulting from these two types of barriers in isolation. Instead, their visible status can have the effect of precluding a smooth transition into Canadian society, while public reaction to their visible status and cultural differences can complicate the settlement process.

Faviola Fernandez, of the Policy Roundtable Mobilizing Professions and Trades (PROMPT), affirmed that earnings disadvantages can be particularly egregious for visible minority immigrants whose physical appreareance and cultural backgrounds are most distant from the White mainstream population. Immigrants from non-European, racialized communities face the steepest downward shift in career mobility and the highest levels of poverty (Second Annual Law and Diversity Conference 2004).

Fernandez recounted her personal baptism in social and economic inequities and the racialization of poverty she encountered in Canada that eventually shocked her into a greater level of community involvement. After immigrating to Canada three years ago in possession of an honours degree in Literature and Linguistics from the University of Singapore and a masters degree in Applied Linguistics from the University of Essex, UK, Fernandez discovered her foreign-acquired degrees were not recognized toward the procurement of an Ontario Teaching Certificate. Instead, since her arrival she has struggled to work in part-time and/or contract positions as a second language (ESL) teacher, an after-school program coordinator, and a recreation project coordinator for newcomer children. As is common among visible minority job seekers, Fernandez first experienced employment discrimination in a unique form of Canadian "low-grade racism," embodied by "people who could be polite even when they were being impolite" (Second Annual Law and Diversity Conference 2004).

Visible minority natives and newcomers are regularly exposed to subtle and informal exploitation in the Canadian workplace that can lead to a demoralizing sense of despair and loss of dignity. However, visible minority newcomers are further exposed to the immobilizing "catch-22" of the "Canadian experience" rule, which holds that you need Canadian experience to get a job, but you cannot get a job because you do not have Canadian experience. All of this means that immigrants from racialized communities are typically relegated to the most "vulnerable place in society … where there is a loss of control over your life … with a limited right to participate in the processes to gain a right to participate" (Second Annual Law and Diversity Conference 2004).

Reitz (2003:5–6) argues that even when occupational or educational standards in the immigrant's place of origin are not questioned, traditional prejudice may be operant, and the institutional development of society may present barriers.

Education may be valued for reasons other than its functional relevance, including prestige or authority-enhancing capacity. Some employers may tend to distrust the relevance of foreign qualifications because they lack familiarity with them, and because of the fear involved in taking a chance on the unknown. Bureaucratic procedures in hiring may be tailored to local or conventionally esteemed educational institutions. Since these traditional prejudices and conventional standards of authority tend to break down along geographic and colour lines, they represent a form of racialization of skill recognition that compounds other obstacles faced by immigrants. It has been suggested that the contemporary workplace phenomenon of managerial cloning might be a related tendency which further functions to entrench Whiteness at the level of corporate power and decision-making (Arrow, Bowles, and Durlauf 2000).

"The Voices of Visible Minorities: Speaking out on Breaking down Barriers" (2004) summarize seven focus group discussions with successful immigrant and Canadian-born managers and professionals. Participants in these focus groups reported that organizations in Canada have regularized use of duplicitous terms like "lack of fit" to exclude talented visible minorities from senior positions. Immigrants of colour face particularly daunting, albeit unspoken, barriers to achieving career success that goes beyond psychometric career counseling strategies. These range from lost opportunities because they speak with an accent to non-recognition of their work experience or credentials. Many immigrants felt that in Canada, speaking with an accent or owning foreign credentials is often used by employers as an excuse to screen them out of job competitions. Consequently, many talented immigrants are prevented from working in their fields, even in professions where labour shortages exist.

The low valuation of foreign credentials, together with the demand for Canadian experience, is ethnocentric and cannot be separated from the ethnoracial dimension of disparity. European and American credentials are easily translatable because they are part of the dominant "whitestream" culture. Furthermore, public perception of visible minority immigrants who are forced to compete for menial jobs is shaped negatively, which in turn serves to negate government responsibility for the problem (Keung 2005). While skilled jobs go unfilled, this vicious circle also creates heightened competition for menial jobs. Immigrants living in poverty could create pressures—or at least the perception of pressures—on the social safety net (Keung 2005). This might result in public demands for a reduction in social programs and other support for immigrants (Keung 2005).

Even those visible minority immigrants who succeed continue to feel undervalued and underappreciated, looked down upon by the dominant class, and torn between the cross-cutting pressures of affirming their distinctiveness while accepting the norms and practices of White middle-class society (Fleras and Elliott 1999:276).

While it is sometimes difficult to separate individual factors from structural factors, ethnoracial stratification must be examined dynamically. We live in a world where the dynamics of human enterprise and social outcomes are primarily filtered through a techno-coloured lens which is not always responsible to individual skills, aptitudes, values, personality traits, and/or interests. Objective research consistently reveals that a commitment to social justice must recognize the need for collective as opposed to individual initiatives where appropriate.

It also endorses the principle of social intervention for true equality, since equal outcomes in the workplace are unlikely to arise from competitive market forces.

TWO KEY APPROACHES USED TO STUDY STRUCTURAL BARRIERS

The first approach to the study of structural barriers focuses on the policies, regulations, and procedures that control entry and advancement in the workplace. Even when education-based skills are important and meritocracy is espoused in a labour market, immigrants may experience structural difficulties. The first key approach to the study of these difficulties focuses specifically on governmental practices and policies (Task Force on Access to Professions and Trades in Ontario 1989; Reitz 1997). Access to information on accreditation procedures, agencies involved in assessment, and the nature of these evaluations are some of the factors considered through this approach.

Culminating with Ontario's 1989 "ACCESS! Report" and the 1997 federal government "Not Just Numbers Report," most reputable structurally oriented research now seems to agree on the barriers foreign-trained immigrants face in having their skills and credentials recognized. Particularly, much research notes the problematic nature of the various, confounding rules/regulations/requirements of provincial regulatory bodies, the obtuse requirements of education institutions and the subjective hiring and promotion rules of employers. The current problem is not to be found in identifying barriers, but establishing effective strategies for eliminating these barriers.

The "ACCESS! Report" (1989) also includes an examination of whether the Charter of Rights and Freedoms applies to regulatory bodies. It contains a review of admissions criteria, appeal requirements, and additional examinations for internationally trained candidates and concludes that the Charter may apply if the licensing practices are found to be discriminatory. The report acknowledges that the primary obligation of professional bodies is to protect the public interest with respect to health, safety, and welfare. However, in fulfilling this obligation the bodies must also consider the duty to respect an individual's right to equality of opportunity and to equal treatment without unreasonable discrimination. The report goes to review barriers to entry, including:

- the lack of clear information on professional standards and registration requirements;

- the lack of recognition of related academic qualifications and experience;

- inappropriate and/or unfair registration exams that might not provide a fair reflection of knowledge and skills;

- language tests that do not measure the skills actually required for appropriate, safe, and effective professional practice;

- the lack of upgrading and bridging training opportunities; and

- the lack of internal appeal mechanisms.

According to the "ACCESS! Report," the assessment of equivalency is the stage that is the least standardized and most difficult for applicants. This report recommends a Prior Learning Assessment Network (PLAN) to address problems in assessing equivalency. The PLAN proposal was recommended as a move away from a certificate-based system toward a competency-based system.

Subsequent analyses into the problem of assessing equivalency have built on this recommendation. For example, in the medical profession, Joan Atlin, Executive Director, Association of International Physicians and Surgeons of Ontario (AIPSO), has emphasized the importance of focusing on the doctor shortage in Ontario through a lens of competence and rights—human rights and the Charter of Rights. The question is, why is medical licensure a right for Canadians and a privilege for internationally trained physicians (Second Annual Law and Diversity Conference 2004)?

At present, internationally trained physicians compete for the limited assessment and training positions available, with only 10 to 15 percent of these professionals finding placement. At the end of this process, those who do succeed in obtaining a license to practice are also required to fulfill a five-year return of service contract with the government. In other words, the present licensure system has created two classes of Canadians. One class has full access, and the other class must compromise and compete before they can gain access to the steps to prove competency. According to Atlin, Canada's doctor shortage is not only a regulatory and assessment problem, but an equity problem that requires a "paradigm shift" to eliminate the double standards that are embedded in the medical profession and society. Internationally trained physicians are "treated like labour market commodities and not like citizens with equality rights" (Foster 2004). The potential for the development of a self-sufficient health-care system that provides adequate service to all Canadians lies in organizing social policy principles around fair practices that actualize existing human resources (Foster 2004).

The Council of the College of Physicians and Surgeons of Ontario has recently taken steps toward addressing Canada's health-care problem, and has forwarded recommendations to the health ministry proposing a new assessment program for foreign-trained physicians. This assessment tool was created by Ontario's five medical schools, and includes a fast-tracking process that is to be coupled with other initiatives, including location incentives for underserviced areas and tuition subsidies.

However, Atlin argues for a new "equality rights" action plan as well. This recommends the provision of adequate training opportunities and emphasizes competencies that reflect clear and concise criteria that are equally applied to all physicians. Atlin notes that for many internationally trained physicians, this was the "working assumption" about this country before they emigrated. Only after their arrival did they realized they had been seduced and abandoned by the immigration system (Second Annual Law and Diversity Conference 2004). Some sociologists maintain that the removal of overt and covert systemic barriers in a way that preserves human rights and professional standards would involve the implementation of government administered programs and policies, for example, a "licensing equity plan" for regulatory and licensing bodies and/or the implementation of an "employment equity plan" (Foster 1998).

The second approach to the study of structural barriers focuses on experience and perceptions. An attitudinal survey conducted in 1990 by Decima Research Ltd. showed that 90 percent of Canadians agreed with the statement, "All races are created equal" (cited in Reitz and Breton 1994:68). Nevertheless, a 2005 Ipsos-Reid poll conducted on a randomly selected sample of 1,001 Canadians found that one in six adults, or 17 percent of those surveyed, had personally experienced racism. The survey also found that 7 percent (1.7 million) of Canadians would not welcome someone of another race as a next door neighbour. Further, 13 percent (3.1 milllion) said they would never marry or have a relationship with a person of another race, and 15 percent (3.4 million) said skin colour makes a difference in their workplace.

Today most Canadians tend to believe that all races are created equal, and the dominant White majority is generally open to residency, citizenship, and commingling with and among ethnic and racial minorities in public. Nevertheless, studies also indicate that many people are hesitant about minorities marrying into their families, and they strongly resist the admittance of minorities to prestigious professional structures. A report released by the Canadian Race Relations Foundation (2000), entitled "Unequal Access: A Canadian Profile of Racial Differences in Education, Employment and Income," confirmed that ethnoracial diversity is generally seen at the bottom and middle level of the labour force pyramid, but, "the higher the pyramid, the less diverse and the Whiter it becomes."

Further, research also suggests that most professions would prefer to restrict supply so that members can continue to enjoy higher income levels. This seems to be particularly true among physicians, surgeons, dentists, and veterinarians (Samuels 2004).

Basran and Zong's (1998) research emphasized the importance of personal experience and perceptions in understanding both individual and structural barriers. In their study of 404 Indo and Chinese immigrant professionals residing in the Vancouver area, they found only 18 percent of this population to be working in their profession in Canada. Only 6 percent agreed that the provincial government fairly assessed and recognized their foreign credentials. When asked about possible sources of discrimination in the accreditation process, 65 percent noted colour, 69 percent listed nationality or ethnic origin, and 79 percent cited the inability to speak English as issues of concern.

Samuels (2004) interviewed nine foreign-trained graduates of various disciplines from developing countries who now reside in Ontario. Eight of the nine respondents feel that undertones of racism have hindered their ability to become credentialed. Veterinarians and dentists are particularly affected. They stated that there is a "strong element of exclusion" felt by graduates from developing countries since internship positions are very limited and there are not many visible minorities who own animal hospitals. A lack of Canadian experience, combined with accents of varying notability and differences in culture block visible minority immigrants from internship positions, even when their help is offered free of charge. Most of the respondents stated "somewhere race is coming into play" (Samuels 2004).

The Ethnic Diversity Survey (2003) offers a portrait of the experience and perception of discriminatory barriers in Canada. Respondents were asked how often they felt out of place in Canada because of their ethnicity, culture, race, skin colour, language, accent, or religion. The finding show several distinctive ethno-cultural patterns. First, visible minorities were more likely than others to say that they felt uncomfortable or out of place at least some of the time. Second, it found that one in five visible minorities experienced discrimination or unfair treatment "sometimes" or "often," while only one in twenty non-visible minorities reported experiencing discrimination or unfair treatment "sometimes" or "often." Further, among indicators of discrimination or unfair treatment, race, or colour was the most commonly cited reason for perceived discrimination or unfair treatment. Finally, the research found that discrimination or unfair treatment was most likely to occur in the workplace.

Twenty-four percent of visible minorities in Canada said they felt uncomfortable or out of place because of their ethno-cultural characteristics "all," "most," or "some" of the time. This is almost three times higher than any other reporting group. Generational differences also indicate that visible minorities may feel uncomfortable for a longer period than their non-visible minority counterparts after they or their families arrive in Canada. Twenty-nine percent of first-generation visible minorities who arrived between 1991 and 2001 said they felt uncomfortable or out of place in Canada "some," "most," or "all" of the time. This proportion was only slightly lower, at 23 percent, for visible minorities who came before 1991. In contrast, among the population who were not visible minorities, a higher proportion of recent arrivals than of those who had resided in Canada for over 10 years (18 percent versus 9 percent) felt uncomfortable or out of place because of their ethno-cultural characteristics.

TABLE 9.1

Population Reporting Discrimination or Unfair Treatment in Canada in the Past Five Years Because of Ethno-cultural Characteristic, by Generation in Canada and Visible Minority Status, 2002

		FREQUENCY OF DISCRIMINATION		
	TOTAL POPULATION	SOMETIMES OR OFTEN	RARELY	DID NOT EXPERIENCE DISCRIMINATION
Total population	**22,445,000**	**7%**	**6%**	**86%**
Not a visible minority	19,252,000	5%	5%	90%
Visible minority	3,000,000	20%	15%	64%
First generation	5,272,000	13%	10%	77%
Not a visible minority	2,674,000	5%	6%	89%
Visible minority	2,516,000	21%	14%	65%
Second generation or more	16,929,000	6%	5%	89%
Not a visible minority	16,349,000	5%	5%	90%
Visible minority	480,000	18%	23%	59%

Note: Refers to Canada's non-Aboriginal population aged 15 and older.
Source: Statistics Canada, Ethnic Diversity Survey, 2002.

Finally, respondents who had reported discrimination or unfair treatment because of their ethno-cultural characteristics in the previous five years were questioned about where the incident took place. Regardless of the location, a significantly higher proportion of visible minorities reported discrimination or unfair treatment in the precious five years in comparison to all other groups. The survey found that approximately 35 percent of people 15 years and older had "sometimes" or "often" been discriminated against. The workplace was noted as the most common location where perceived discrimination or unfair treatment occurred. Fifty-six percent of those who had "sometimes" or "often" experienced discrimination or unfair treatment because of their ethno-cultural characteristics in the past five years said they had experienced such treatment at work or when applying for work.

* * * * *

RE-THINKING ACCREDITATION

Anti-racism activists and sociological researchers are now in the process of trying to re-think Canadian society and immigration/emigration in terms of ethnoracial reality. This requires that research provides analyses that come from the standpoint of racialized persons. Additionally, this research must consider other stakeholders, including governments, regulating bodies, employers, unions, educational institutions, and credential assessment services.

Alboim (2003) explored the social implications of the under-utilization of immigrant skills at the individual, ethnoracial, and societal level for the design and implementation of public policy. In conjunction with prior research, she found that when large numbers of visible immigrants are prevented from practicing their professions, society experiences higher levels of inter-group tensions, individual and collective alienation, and generalized perceptions of institutional discrimination. Ultimately, Alboim argues for the implementation of a public discourse that moves beyond competency assessment to qualifications recognition.

Accordingly, The Maytree Foundation developed a ten-point action plan for implementation at federal, provincial, and local levels that would better provide for the integration of immigrants and their skills into the Canadian economy:

1. Create an Internet resource that contains employment, certification, and educational information to assist skilled immigrants with employment;

2. Improve collaboration on the assessment of academic credentials to increase employer confidence;

3. Provide incentives for educational institutions and licensing bodies to develop competency-based assessment tools;

4. Review post-secondary funding formulas and the statutory framework so that educational institutions are encouraged to provide bridging programs as part of their mainstream services;

5. Expand student loan programs;

6. Fund labour market language training to be delivered by employers and educational institutions;

7. Provide incentives to employers, employer associations, and labour to become more active in the integration of immigrant skills;

8. Sustain the collaborative efforts of self-regulated professions to improve access for international candidates;

9. Initiate multi-lateral discussions between levels of government, regulating bodies, employer's associations, unions, educational institutions, and academic credential assessment servers in order to develop agreements on the labour market integration of immigrants; and

10. Support local initiatives to integrate immigrant skills (Alboim 2003).

This plan, provided through The Maytree Foundation, is an example of a holistic and dynamic approach to the contemporary social problem of foreign accreditation barriers. It emphasizes skills utilization and fair practice and assumes an equity paradigm. The equity paradigm states that all qualified persons should be able to work within their fields. Further, it assumes all regions that adopt this paradigm and a congruent plan of action will reap the many benefits that immigrants have to offer society.

CONCLUSIONS

Despite the international marketing tool of multicultural diversity, many Canadians have not confronted the reality and challenges of a racially and culturally diverse society. The need to be more inclusive in our thinking about the importance of immigration for society-building and economic development in the global age is often compromised by public pressure to preserve the entrenched interests of the status quo. Immigrants no longer typically endure legislated racial abuse and overt discrimination. Nevertheless, in the new world order, the furtive de-racialization of political economy discourse disregards visible minority experiences through the discounting of qualifications and restricting access to gainful employment in the professions. This results in social marginalization, alienation, and disillusionment.

REFERENCES

Alboim, Naomi. 2003. *Integrating Immigrant Skills into the Ontario Economy: A Ten Point Plan.* Toronto: The Maytree Foundation.

Alboim, Naomi, Ross Finnie, and Ronald Meng. 2005. "The Discounting of Immigrants' Skills in Canada: Evidence and Policy Recommendations." Institute for Research on Public Policy. 11, 2.

Arrow, K., S. Bowles, and S. Durlauf, eds. 2000. *Meritocracy and Economic Inequality*. Princeton: Princeton University Press.

Baker, M., and D. Benjamin. 1994. "The Performance of Immigrants in the Canadian Labor Market." *Journal of Labor Economics* 12:369–405.

Basavarajappa, K.G., B. Ravi, and P. Verma. 1985. "Asian Immigrants in Canada: Some Findings from 1981 Census." *International Migration* 23(1):97–121.

Basran, Gurcharn, and Li Zong. 1998. "Devaluation of Foreign Credentials as Perceived by Non-White Professional Immigrants." *Canadian Ethnic Studies* 30(3):6–23.

Beach, Charles, and Christopher Worswick. 1989. "Is There a Double Negative Effect on the Earnings of Immigrant Women?" *Canadian Public Policy* 16(2):36–54.

Boyd, Monica. 1985. "Immigration and Occupational Attainment in Canada." Pp. 393–445 in *Ascription and Achievement: Studies in Mobility and Status Attainment in Canada*, edited by Monica Boyd et al. Ottawa: Carleton University Press.

———. 1992. "Gender, Visible Minority, and Immigrant Earnings Inequality: Reassessing an employment Equity Premise." Pp. 279–321 in *Deconstructing a Nation: Immigration, Multiculturalism & Racism in the '90s Canada*, edited by Vic Satzewich. Halifax: Fernwood.

Canadian Race Relations Foundation. 2000. "Unequal Access: A Canadian Profile of Racial Differences in Education, Employment and Income." Canadian Race Relations Foundation.

Conference Board. 2004. "The Voices of Visible Minorities: Speaking Out on Breaking Down Barriers." Conference Board's e-Library (http://www.conferenceboard.ca/boardwise).

Durkheim, Emile. 1964/1895. *The Rules of Sociological Method*. Translated by Sarah A. Solovay and John H. Mueller. New York: The Free Press.

Fleras, Augie, and Jean Leonard Elliott. 1999. *Unequal Relations: An Introduction to Race and Ethnic, and Aboriginal Dynamics in Canada*. 3rd ed. Toronto: Prentice Hall.

Foster, Lorne. 1998. *Turnstile Immigration: Multiculturalism, Social Order & Social Justice in Canada*. Toronto: Thompson Educational Publishing.

———. 2002. "The Race Paradox of Our Time." *Share*. 25, 24: September 19.

———. 2004. "Breakthrough for Foreign-trained Docs?" *Share*, February 4.

Government of Ontario, Task Force on Access to Professions and Trades in Ontario. 1989. *Access!* Toronto: Ministry of Citizenship.

Herberg, Edward N. 1990. "The Ethno-racial Socioeconomic Hierarchy in Canada. Theory and Analysis of the New Vertical Mosaic." *International Journal of Comparative Sociology* 31:206–221.

Hou, Feng, and T.R. Balakrishnan. 1996. "The Integration of Visible Minorities in Contemporary Society." *Canadian Journal of Sociology* 21(3):307–326.

Kalbach, Warren E., and Madeline A. Richard. 1988. *Ethnic-Religious Identity, Acculturation, and Social and Economic Achievement of Canada's Post-war Minority Populations*. Report for the Review of Demography and Its Implications for Economic and Social Policy. Toronto: University of Toronto Population Research Laboratory.

Keung, Nicholas. 2005. "Immigrants Better Trained, Worse Off." *The Toronto Star*, February 1.

Maxim, Paul. 1992. "Immigrants, Visible Minorities, and Self-Employment." *Demography* 29:181–198.

McDade, Kathryn. 1988. *Barriers to Recognition of the Credentials of Immigrants in Canada*. Ottawa: Institute for Research on Public Policy.

Pendakur, K., and R. Pendakur. 1998. "The Colour of Money: Earnings Differentials among Ethnic Groups in Canada." *Canadian Journal of Economics* 31(3):518–548.

Portes, Alejandro. 1999. "Towards a New World—The Origins and Effects of Transnational Activities." *Ethnic and Racial Studies* 22(2):463–477.

Rajagopal, Indha. 1990. "The Glass Ceiling in the Vertical Mosaic: Indian Immigrants to Canada." *Canadian Ethnic Studies/Etudes Ethniques au Canada* 22(1):96–105.

Ralston, Helen. 1988. "Ethnicity, Class, and Gender among South Asian Women in Metro Halifax: An Exploratory Study." *Canadian Ethnic Studies/Etudes Ethniques au Canada* 20(3):63–83.

Reitz, Jeffrey. 1997. "Priorities for Immigration in a Changing Canadian Economy: From Skill Selectivity to Skill Utilization." Pp. 189–206 in *New Selection Criteria for Economic Stream Immigrants*, edited by the Ministry of Citizenship and Immigration Canada, workshop held October 30–31. Ottawa: Citizenship and Immigration Canada.

———. 2003. "Occupational Dimensions of Immigrant Credential Assessment: Trends in Professional, Managerial, and other Occupations, 1970–1996." The Monk Centre for International Studies (http://www.utoronto.ca/ethnicstudies/reitz.html).

———. 2005. "Tapping Immigrant Skills: New Directions for Canadian Immigration Policy in the Knowledge Economy." *Institute for Research on Public Policy* 11(1):1–18.

Reitz, J.G., and R. Breton. 1994. *The Illusion of Difference: Realities of Ethnicity in Canada and the United States*. Toronto: C.D. Howe Institute.

Reitz, J.G., and Sherrilyn M. Sklar. 1977. "Culture, Race, and the Economic Assimilation of Immigrants." *Sociological Forum* 12(2):233–277.

Richmond, Anthony H. 1984. "Immigration and Unemployment in Canada and Australia." *International Journal of Comparative Sociology* 25(3–4):243–255.

Samuels, John. 2004. *Are There Racial Barriers to Access to Professions and Trades for the Foreign-Trained in Ontario?* Toronto: Queen's Printer for Ontario.

Satzewich, Vic, and Lloyd Wong. 2003. "Immigration, Ethnicity, and Race: The Transformation of Transnationalism, Localism, and Identities," Pp. 263–290 in *Changing Canada: Political Economy as Transformation*, edited by Wallace Clement and Leah F. Vosko. Montreal: McGill-Queen's University Press.

Second Annual Law and Diversity Conference. 2004. "Making the Mosaic Work." January 2004. Second Annual Law and Diversity Conference held at the University of Toronto.

Shamai, Shmuel. 1992. "Ethnicity and Educational Achievement in Canada 1941–1981." *Canadian Ethnic Studies* 24:43–51.

Simmons, Alan, and Dwaine Plaza. 1995. "Breaking through the Glass Ceiling: The Pursuit of University Training among Afro-Caribbean Migrants and Their Children in Toronto." Presented at the Annual Meeting of Canadian Population Society, Montreal, Quebec.

Statistics Canada. 2003. *Ethnic Diversity Survey: Portrait of a Multicultural Society*. Ottawa: Statistics Canada.

Trovato, Frank, and Carl F. Grindstaff. 1986. "Economic Status: A Census Analysis of Immigrant Women at Age Thirty in Canada." *Review of Sociology and Anthropology* 23(4):569–687.

CHAPTER TEN

Racism/Anti-racism, Precarious Employment, and Unions

Tania Das Gupta

Precarious employment is a highly gendered and racialized phenomenon. Large numbers of women, immigrants, refugees, and people of colour labour under precarious conditions in Canada (Vosko 2000; Zwarenstein 2002). All workers who belong to unions have better working conditions, including wages, than those who are not unionized (Galabuzi 2001; Jackson 2002). Unfortunately, only 22 per cent of workers of colour[1] were covered by a collective agreement in 1999, while the rate for all other workers was 32 per cent (Jackson 2002, 16). This finding is consistent with trends in the 1980s and early 1990s (Leah 1999).

* * * * *

This chapter contests this assessment regarding racism, arguing that systemic racism in the labour movement is indeed one contributing factor, among many, to the lower unionization rate of workers of colour compared to white workers. It suggests, as Jackson does, that the racism may not be conscious—but racism is not always conscious. Systemic racism refers to standard and apparently neutral policies, procedures, and practices that disadvantage people of colour. Reproduced over time through written policies and laws, these practices become institutionalized. Other factors contributing to the low unionization rate of workers of colour include systemic racism practised by employers, which is demonstrated in racist hiring and promotional practices; fear and intimidation tactics of employers; and legal prohibitions or barriers against the unionization of certain groups of workers, along with anti-union sentiment in the community. The chapter argues further that the efforts of equity-seeking groups within the labour movement, including those of anti-racism activists, contribute to changes that could be more conducive to organizing workers in precarious employment.

* * * * *

PRECARIOUS EMPLOYMENT, PRECARIOUSNESS AMONG WORKERS OF COLOUR

For most workers of colour, immigrant and refugee workers, precarious employment is not a new or an unusual phenomenon. In fact, before World War II, most people of colour in Canada held precarious jobs, since only a minority were entrepreneurs and professionals (Das Gupta

2000). This concentration reflected contemporary labour market requirements, which focused on land clearing, railway building, and farming.

Because of systemic discrimination and exclusion from professional sectors, people of colour were, historically, allocated to jobs that were the least desirable—jobs with low pay, insecurity, and gross exploitation. People of African heritage were brought over as slaves or entered Canada as refugees from slavery and war in the United States; they also held precarious jobs in the service and agricultural sectors. Workers of First Nations backgrounds were marginalized, disenfranchised, and relegated to precarious employment as well (Muszynski 1996).

For Aboriginal peoples, people of colour, and immigrant workers, the precarious labour market conditions in which they worked were an extension of their precarious condition in society at large, where they were socially constructed as dependants, as non-citizens, and as non-workers, those deemed to be "others" in relation to employed white male citizens. Their otherness was marked by the colour of their skin, their "strange" customs and languages, their immigration status, and their lack of citizenship rights. While white women were also considered inferior under white patriarchy, they were valued as "mothers of the nation," as vehicles of reproduction of white Canada (Dua and Robertson 1999). Women of colour, in contrast, with their capacity to reproduce non-white citizens, were viewed as threats to the whiteness of the nation. They were, therefore, until the post-war period, either excluded or restricted from entering Canada (Das Gupta 2000), other than in small numbers in domestic work (Calliste 1991)—a highly precarious occupation characterized by a lack of citizenship status. Apart from domestic work, the few women of colour who entered the country worked under precarious conditions either as unpaid family workers in fishing, laundries, and restaurants or as waged workers in the fishing or garment industries. Before 1985, status Aboriginal women lost their status when they married anyone who did not have status—including non-status Aboriginal men. This policy was not only sexist but designed to assimilate Aboriginal members into white patriarchal values. Many Aboriginal women and men were forced to find jobs in non-Aboriginal enterprises because of the destruction of indigenous economies and ways of living, and they worked in deplorable conditions. The precariousness of immigrants, people of colour, and Aboriginal workers, including women, in the labour marker was produced by their precarious citizenship status in Canada—and that lack of citizenship was due, in turn, to their racialization, their gender, their immigration status, to all the legal and social locations they occupied.

This precarious status was maintained by well-thought-out racist and sexist ideologies that characterized these groups as subhuman and unfit to be members of the nation. And these ideologies were institutionalized in both laws and policies. People of colour were said to be so inferior that they were biologically and culturally capable of working under subhuman working conditions, at super-exploitative wages (Creese 1992; Muszynski 1984; Ward 1978), thereby threatening the wages and working conditions of white male workers of nation. They were viewed as threats to the nation by their otherness and as threats to the organized working class by their racialized capacity and supposed "willingness" to work at wages below those paid to white workers. Creese (1992) documents that white unionists considered Asians to be "unorganizable," leading unions to adopt a strategy of exclusionism (Das Gupta 1998; Leah 1999; White 1990). In so doing, they contributed actively to precarious employment among workers of colour as well as to their social precariousness. They spearheaded such groups as the Anti-Chinese Union, the Asiatic Exclusion League, and the White Canada Association. In addition to lobbying white politicians to restrict the entry of non-white workers to Canada, they also instigated popular hostility and violence against them (Das Gupta 1998).

By excluding workers of colour and, in some cases, reaching collective agreements that instituted labour standards differentiated by race, white unions took part in reproducing a racially segregated labour market. Creese (1992) writes that unions representing white tailors, garment workers, laundry workers, and restaurant workers were the most vociferous against Chinese and other Asian workers, who were paid much less because of employer racism and the lack of union protection. Instead of including Asian workers in existing unions in order to eliminate the wage competition, these unions took an exclusionary stance. The Hotel and Restaurant Employees Union, for instance, remained exclusionary until 1938, when a Chinese organizer was hired for one month.

Only a few radical, leftist unions were inclusive of workers of colour, including the One Big Union (OBU) and the Workers' Unity League, which actively recruited Chinese workers and opened leadership positions for them (Creese 1991). Unfortunately, these unions were short lived. Some research indicates that not all communist-inspired unions were egalitarian. For instance, Frager (1992) points to sexism in the Toronto cloak makers union in the inter-war years, while Muszynski's (1996) research into fishing unions in British Columbia shows racist and sexist preferences in organizing practices and differential wage rates. She writes that, in 1968, an experienced female general fish worker received 9.3 per cent less than an inexperienced male fish worker, and 24.5 per cent less than an experienced male fish worker (8). Women fish workers were initially Aboriginal and later included Japanese and other non-English-speaking immigrant women.

Workers of colour did not acquiesce to this reality despite popular stereotypes of their passivity and lack of interest in organizing. They formed organizations of their own, including unions, relying on their ethnic, racial, and kin networks (Creese 1991; Ward 1978). Chinese workers struck for higher wages, shorter working hours, and licensing rights and against discrimination and the contracting system. The Amalgamated Association of Japanese Fishermen contested the government's proposal to reduce Japanese fishing licenses, over time eliminating them altogether (Das Gupta 1998; Ward 1978). The Native Brotherhood of British Columbia negotiated the first agreement with canners on behalf of Aboriginal fish workers (Muszynski 1996). Many of these organizations exerted pressure on the labour movement, on government, and on other institutions to remove the racial bar against workers of colour. These groups were simultaneously fighting for labour rights as well as for social justice, specifically against racism and exclusion.

According to Ward (1978), racism in the labour movement began to be less overt around the 1920s. The movement began to dissociate itself from the rabid white supremacist organizations of previous decades. In its 1931 convention, the Trades and Labour Congress dropped its racially exclusionary position and called for extending voting rights to all Canadian-born people, including people of colour. The Cooperative Commonwealth Federation (CCF), also formed around this time, pushed for greater inclusion of Asian Canadians. The Jewish Labour Committee (JLC), founded in 1935, as well as the National Unity Association formed in 1943 by Black residents in Dresden, Ontario, and civil liberties associations, some unions, and women's and ethnic associations, were predominantly responsible for bringing pressure to bear on the labour movement as well as on the Ontario government of the time (Lukas and Persad 2004; Hill 1977).

In the 1930s, groups such as the Jewish Labour Committee pushed the Canadian Labour Congress to bring in human rights legislation. The National Committee on Human Rights was formed within the Canadian Labour Congress. Trade union committees for human rights were set up in Winnipeg, Toronto, Montreal, and Vancouver, and these committees worked against discrimination outside the scope of collective bargaining. They investigated and documented cases of discrimination in employment, housing, and services (Das Gupta 1998; Hill 1977) and conducted public educational programs. In addition, they organized for the enactment of human rights legislation provincially and federally. They supported those who suffered from discrimination in their jobs and in the community at large and negotiated anti-discrimination clauses in collective agreements.

INCLUDED, BUT NOT EQUAL

Feminist labour studies scholars and labour activists have illustrated the continuing gender segregation and discrimination faced by women workers, even those who are unionized. In fact, they have demonstrated how union policies and practices perpetuated such divisions in some cases (Briskin and McDermott 1993; Forrest 1993; Frager 1992; Sugiman 1993). Parallels can be seen for workers of colour.

Although formal equality reigned in trade unions in the 1930s and 1940s, racism continued. Even in the years of supposed equality and access to unions, Muszynski (1984, 91) reports that one of the organizers of the Hotel and Restaurant Employees Union practised selective recruitment where white waiters and busboys were organized, to the neglect of waitress and Chinese men working as kitchen help. The union signed agreements without any protection for Chinese and Japanese workers.

In 1940 the United Fishermen's Federal Union approached the BC government to force companies to hire white herring packers rather than Japanese packers. When the government refused, white women packers at one cannery walked off their jobs in protest. After fishers and cannery workers were unionized by the United Fishermen and Allied Workers' Union, Chinese workers were covered for first time in 1947, when the union signed a supplement to the master agreement. In 1949 Chinese workers were included under the Male Cannery Workers' Supplement. Of the four groups in the supplement, Chinese workers were included in group IV (sundry workers) and were paid a maximum of $183 a month, while group I (machine workers) and II (boiler house) workers were paid to a maximum of $245 a month (Muszynski 1984, 99). Even so, by 1949, very few Chinese workers remained in fishing because many companies had stopped hiring them.

In the railway, Black males were segregated in portering (Calliste 1987). They were also paid lower wages compared to white porters. Black porters could not join porters' unions. Countering racist exclusion by the Canadian Brotherhood of Railway Employees (CBRE) until 1919, Black porters employed on the Canadian National Railways formed the Order of Sleeping Car Porters (Calliste 1987). As a result of pressure by the order on the CBRE for racial integration, the brotherhood incorporated the order as an auxiliary. Moreover, the CBRE created two separate units, where unit I was made up of higher-paid white conductors, inspectors, and stewards, while unit II was made up of lower-paid Black porters and cooks. Promotions could happen only within the same unit. This racial segregation lasted till 1964. Thus, the union reproduced practices of racial segregation adopted by employers.

Supported by the Toronto Labour Committee for Human Rights and the *Fair Employment Practices Act* of 1953, Black porters within various unions, such as the Brotherhood of Sleeping Car Porters and the Canadian Brotherhood of Railway Transport and General Workers, won promotional rights. Initially, however, they lost their seniority if they were promoted, though this practice was overturned after it was challenged by a local as racism. According to Calliste

(1987), the Order of Railway Conductors resisted opening its organization to Black members, and the other related unions mentioned above never took responsibility for their own racism. Promotional and seniority rights of Black porters were won through legal challengers and supported by human rights committees and community organizations.

Industries with significant numbers of immigrant women and women of colour witnessed structural inequalities based on gender and/or race. Frager (1992), writing on the garment industry between 1900 and 1939, observes that Toronto's Jewish unions failed to include predominantly Jewish female workers and that the Canadian feminist movement failed to support them too. There were very few women in leadership positions, since the union did not provide any support for women who had childcare responsibilities. In 1933 the average woman cloak maker earned 44 per cent of what a man earned in the same trade (121). This practice was perpetuated largely because of women's confinement to jobs that were predominantly performed by women workers.

Winnie Ng (1995, 35), the first organizer of Chinese heritage hired by the International Ladies Garment Workers' Union (ILGWU) in 1977, commented on the continuing sexism and racism in the industry as well as in the union at the same time:

> In a union that represented a membership made up of over 85% immigrant women, the ILGWU, at the time, operated very much like an old boys' network. All the executive members were white men of European backgrounds within the Cutters and Pressers' Locals. In the union office, aside from the clerical staff, all the staff representatives and business agents were men. Servicing the membership was done in a patriarchal and patronizing manner such as "I'm going to take care of the girls" or "these poor girls, they don't speak the language...." The union as a workplace was no different from a garment factory in upholding the pattern of occupational segregation on the basis of gender and race.

In 1979 Ng resigned from the union. She said it operated as a business union, making deals with the manufacturers and thwarting any challenges to their style of operation.

PRECARIOUS EMPLOYMENT AMONG WORKERS OF COLOUR AFTER 1967

Although not all people of colour immigrating to Canada under the Points System introduced in the *Immigration Act* in 1967 engaged in precarious employment, a significant proportion of immigrants and non-whites, including women, were compelled to take up precarious jobs, even though many arrived with university degrees and professional qualifications. Their middle-class characteristics in terms of education level, languages spoken, and professional experiences should have resulted in secure employment. However, systemic discrimination in the forms of devaluation of previous education and professional experiences, demand for "Canadian experience," and lack of access to language and professional training streamed them into precarious employment. This trend continues. [...]

A number of studies document racism in the Canadian labour marker. Using 1999 data from the Survey of Labour and Income Dynamics, Jackson (2002) reports that people of colour[2] earned $19,895 in 1999, while all other workers earned $23,764, a difference of 16.3 per cent. On the basis of Census data from 1996, Galabuzi (2001) notes that individuals of colour had poverty rates of 35.6 per cent, compared to a general poverty rate of 17.6 per cent, and argues that economic apartheid exists in Canada.

Another study of the City of Toronto by Ornstein (2000), based on the 1996 Canadian Census, concludes that non-European groups suffered a family poverty rate of 34.3 per cent, one more than double that for Europeans and self-identified Canadians. Income disparities and high poverty levels reflect other factors such as higher unemployment rates and the segregation of workers of colour in low-end jobs in processing and manufacturing, sales and service, and industries such as clothing and textiles. Many of these sectors often have high concentrations of women of colour. High unemployment rates, overrepresentation in low-end jobs and industries, and underrepresentation in high-end jobs and industries occur through systemically racist hiring and promotional processes as well as through the devaluation of foreign education and professional experience. Henry and Ginzberg (1984) and Das Gupta (1996) demonstrate that racism in the form of exclusion or segregation in workplaces can result from such systemic practices as word-of-mouth hiring, differential treatment at the screening or pre-screening stages, biased interview processes, and the use of vague and subjective criteria in hiring, performance appraisals, and promotions. These policies, procedures, and practices amount to systemic racism as they disproportionately disadvantage people of colour. This issue is not restricted to immigrants (Pendakur and Pendakur 1995) but applies also to non-white, Canadian-born citizens.

Although racism is much more systemic and subtle in 2004 than it was in the past, it is very much present in the labour market. Precarious employment is still highly prevalent among non-whites, including non-white women. Many of these women are new immigrants or refugees, desperately trying to attain the "Canadian experience" that is demanded of them. Often their only recourse is to take up a job with a temporary agency, sell products and services door to door on commission, work as security guards, or drive a taxi—jobs that are synonymous with non-white workers and that often entail false self-employment or independent work. Many, lacking an adequate level of spoken English and denied the opportunity to learn the language, are left with no option but to work in factories, warehouses, farms, or in their own homes as homeworkers. Others, even more marginalized, enter Canada in semi-indentured conditions to work as live-in caregivers or as farm workers (Zwarenstein 2002). These sectors are usually non-unionized. Only the fortunate few are lucky enough to get a unionized job, with acceptable working conditions and benefits.

MOVING BEYOND INCLUSION

The days of overt exclusion of workers of colour, Aboriginal workers, and immigrant workers by labour unions no longer exist, given the anti-racist efforts of these communities, a process documented by a number of authors, including Calliste (1987), Das Gupta (1998), and Leah (1999). However, a focal question of anti-racist activism in the post-1980s relates to the nature of involvement of those workers of colour fortunate enough to be union members. Despite the move towards greater inclusion, the continued marginalization of many workers of colour within unions remains a pressing issue.

One key indicator of the marginalization of workers of colour is the predominantly white leadership in the movement, despite the number of dynamic non-white activists in local areas. This imbalance is reproduced systemically through old-boys' networks that are predominantly white. White women began organizing in the post-war period, particularly in the 1960s and

1970s (Briskin and McDermott 1993; Ng 1995; White 1990), against blatant sexism in the movement. However, Ng (1995, 38) writes that feminist activism within the labour movement did not incorporate the issue of immigrant women and of women of colour: "'women' meant white women only." Although white women were getting organized into committees within the labour movement and were able to push for staff positions dealing with women's issues, workers of colour remained marginalized. As Ng (1995, 38) states, racism remained a "taboo topic." This bifurcation in labour politics is reflected in labour studies scholarship. Leah (1999) writes that there are few integrated studies of the organizing experiences of women workers of colour. Studies of workers of colour generally exclude the experiences of women, while feminist studies on labour organizing neglect questions of race and racialization.

The role of women of colour within the labour movement has been, historically, to create the connections between anti-racism and anti-sexism as they embody this unity in their everyday lives. They experience both sexism and racism, in addition to exploitation as workers (Leah 1999). In making this connection, women of colour within the movement have had to confront racism from many white women. Some talk about not being supported in their anti-racist activities because it is not seen as a priority, or of not being supported in their leadership aspirations (Das Gupta 1998; Leah 1999). Nevertheless, a number of statements, policies, and conferences organized by both national and provincial trade union bodies attest to progress in developing links between feminist and anti-racist efforts within the labour movement (Leah 1993; Leah 1999). One of the most concrete indications was the collaborative work done by women and human rights committees within the labour movement for employment equity in the 1990s in Ontario, a collaboration discussed below in relation to coalition building with communities outside unions. Another convergence occurred in the Women's Work Project (Canadian Labour Congress 1998), which generated a report, written by Winnie Ng, on the effects of restructuring on women's work. The report outlined an approach and generated recommendations for organizing more women, women of colour, and immigrants who were precarious workers.

Affirmative action and equitable representation within union structures are major points of organizing among anti-racism activists. Anti-racism activists within the movement argue that equity policies can be better interpreted and applied if union staff and elected representatives at various levels reflect the membership.

Representation for What

Equitable representation in union leadership is not an end in itself. Still, it indicates a recognition of racism and provides a means to challenge the historical marginalization of workers of colour and to change the basic structure and practices of unions. As Briskin and McDermott (1993, 95) note in discussing "separate" organizing by feminist unionists, the aim is "unions changing" rather than "individual women changing." They further argue that separate organizing by women has changed organizing practices and educational programs, brought in more social unionism, and enabled coalition building with groups outside the labour movement. At the level of strategy, separate organizing by workers of colour has similar objectives. Kike Roach (Rebick and Roach 1996, 113) says it most succinctly in characterizing anti-racist organizing within the National Action Committee on the Status of Women (NAC): "We shouldn't think that becoming an anti-racist organization just means having more women of colour members and executive. It has to be about the anti-racist perspective, the analysis, the alliances created and the ongoing campaigns NAC develops and carries forth.... Many are happy to 'include' but ignore, so our inclusion alone can be superficial unless our presence makes a difference."

Anti-racism includes a reformulation of the hiring and servicing priorities of unions. According to June Veecock, human rights and anti-racism coordinator of the Ontario Federation of Labour (OFL): "Those in leadership need to understand that their unions need to reflect the membership.... Unions will do a better job if stewards were doing a better job. They [white stewards] don't understand how systemic racism works. They say there is no racism. They don't recognize racial segregation."[3] Veecock is contacted by workers of colour because they feel more comfortable with her than with their own shop stewards or staff members. More diverse representation would enable more effective service and support for members of colour and immigrant workers. More diverse staffing in unions would also influence organizing priorities. Bev Johnson of the Ontario Public Service Employees Union (OPSEU) observes that anti-racism and affirmative action have implications for union organizing: "Either pay attention or die.... How are you going to organize workers who are predominantly people of colour when you don't have any organizers who are people of colour? How are you going to service members effectively when they don't see themselves reflected in the union staff?"[4]

Hiring organizers of colour is crucial for organizing workers of colour in precarious employment, according to union organizers who have successfully reached them. Michael Cifuentes of the Hotel Employees and Restaurant Employees (HERE), whose members are largely immigrant women workers of colour, says: "The community workers are leaders. They are insiders. We explain to them the meaning of a union. What does a union stand for? The first meeting will be with them. These leaders are very important. These leaders have respect in the community."[5] Bryan Neath from the United Food and Commercial Workers Union (UFCWU), which has organized farm workers, had this to say about the representation of organizers: "For example, in the mushroom plant the main groups were Cambodian, Sudanese, and Canadians.... If you want to be successful in organizing you need to find a leader in each community so they can communicate with the larger working community. If you don't find these leaders, you can forget it."[6] Some unions are starting to hire men and women of diverse racial and ethnic backgrounds to recruit members from those same communities. For instance, Neath notes: "We introduced something called SPUR (special project union representatives). This reflected the need to make the right contacts with [the] community. If we were organizing part-time workers, then we could get part-timeworkers who are unionized to go out and meet with them.... If the workers were workers of colour, we need workers of colour organizing.... If they are women, then we need women organizing."[7] The program trains selected workers as organizers. They are then involved in organizing drives in workplaces similar to theirs. They are paid their regular wages and they return back to their own workplaces once the organizing is over (CLC 1998).

Although SPUR is a highly successful program that has resulted in dramatic increases in membership in UFCWU, including the precarious sectors, not all such programs function so effectively. Some concerns remain generally with contracting temporary organizers of colour. Some of them are contracted or "borrowed" for limited periods of time to sign up new members. Once that is done, their contracts are over. Although they may have been members of organizing committees, they were not treated like full-time organizers. When the organizers left, the new members, many of whom speak minimal or no English, have no one to connect with in the union. Community groups with workers who speak different languages get called by workers of colour unable to get through to their unions. Opportunistic methods of organizing often end up in failures, as workers have been known to decertify under such conditions or to end up with bad agreements. For example, after an intensive organizing drive of predominantly non-English-speaking contract workers of colour, a union signed a "bad deal," according to an organizer of colour, one in which she did not have any input. Similarly, a local of another union, composed predominantly of workers of colour, wanted to decertify because the union had no staff members who could represent them and it provided no translation services.[8] This point is captured by Hasan Yussuff of the CLC, who says that we need to consider "how we do organizing that is not just about bringing in a new membership dues base but integrates workers of colour fundamentally at every level" (CLC 1998, 28).

Anti-racism activists in the labour movement feel that more workers of colour in staff and elected positions will initiate changes in organized labour's priorities, practices, and policies. More emphasis will be given to the needs and issues of workers located in the most precarious forms of employment in society—immigrants, refugees, and workers of colour in unorganized sectors or in workplaces poorly serviced by unions. Greater effort will be put into working in coalitions with community groups, many of which are in touch with unorganized workers of colour in precarious employment, whether self-help organizations, ethnic networks, support groups in neighbourhoods, or worker centres. Trade unionists of colour self-organized within the labour movement, such as the Ontario Coalition of Black Trade Unionists in 1986, the Coalition of Black Trade Unionists (Ontario Chapter) in 1996, and the Asian Canadian Labour Alliance in 2000, have links with communities outside the labour movement. The Asian Canadian Labour Alliance, for instance, has a two-pronged strategy of bringing labour leaders and rank-and-file members of Asian heritage together, as well as bringing Asian activists together to create a union-friendly culture overall. The Coalition of Black Trade Unionists has been active on the campaign against racial profiling in the Black community. Bev Johnson, ex-president of the union, wants to reach out particularly to Black youth to bring them into the labour movement as future leaders. She articulates a concern shared by a number of people interviewed about the younger generation of labour leaders being largely white. Marie Clarke Walker, executive vice-president of the Canadian Labour Congress, says that she spent a year trying to connect her union with community issues when she was elected onto the Canadian Union of Public Employees (CUPE) executive committee in Ontario in 1999: "Members belong to communities before they belong to unions.... People don't just see you as a dues-grabbing institution. They see you as genuinely concerned."[9]

A brief but important period of coalition-based organizing among various segments of the labour movement and community organizations occurred around the issue of employment equity in the early part of the 1990s in Ontario. The Ontario Federation of Labour and affiliated unions became integrally involved in drafting Bill 79, the precursor to the *Employment Equity Act,* which the New Democratic Party (NDP) would steer forward into law in 1994. The provincial labour movement and its equity activists were at the forefront of this development along with community organizations of women, people of colour, people with disabilities, and Aboriginal people. Union activists spent hundreds of hours on equity issues, and grassroots community activists facilitated workshops, prepared brochures, and informed people about the concept, fostering the environment for the successful adoption of legislation (Das Gupta 1998). The movement was pushed into taking this position by activists from outside and from within. Sadly, with the defeat of the Ontario NDP government in 1995, the *Employment Equity Act,* even the watered-down version that was passed, and all its infrastructure were scrapped overnight.

Another example of a community-labour coalition was the Coalition for Fair Wages and Working Conditions for Homeworkers, initiated by the International Ladies Garment Workers' Union (now Union of Needletrades Industrial and Textile Employees, or UNITE) in 1991, which engaged in various public activities to voice the concerns of this very precarious group of workers (Borowy, Gordon, and Lebans 1993). Made up of labour, women's, immigrant, and church communities, the coalition focused on public education through press conferences and a large conference on homework. It put pressure on retail firms to improve the wages and working conditions of homeworkers, and it pressured the government for stronger legislative protection of homeworkers and for sectoral bargaining. In addition, the coalition spearheaded a campaign to raise the awareness of consumers about the exploitation of homeworkers for the production of garments and to develop a consumer campaign, called the "Clean Clothes Campaign," for fair wages and working conditions for homeworkers.

Changing Structures

The labour movement has made significant progress in addressing racism. In the words of the CLC's Yussuff: "The labour movement is dealing with equity. It is in the mainstream. There is recognition that it [racism] is a problem and that resources must be allocated to deal with it. Twenty years ago it may have been dismissed.... People of colour have tremendous opportunity to be confident in shaping the direction of the labour movement."[10]

While it is true that workers of colour are much better represented today (CLC 1997, 98; CLC 2003) than they were 20 years back, there are still lingering problems and resistance to equity in some quarters. Some of the interviewees, particularly women of colour activists, spoke about problems of co-optation, tokenism, harassment of women of colour, and their silencing.[11] Groups like the Coalition of Black Trade Unionists and the Asian Canadian Labour Alliance are still viewed by some as community groups because they are outside the labour structure and do not always agree with the labour movement. One member said that there is still a strong sense of control over caucuses through "report back" processes. There is still a fear among some people that community groups threaten the labour movement. These reactions all indicate resistance against anti-racism and change, as well as a lack of openness and democracy.

Anti-racism activists would like to see structural changes (CLC 1997, 6) in the way in which the labour movement works, including how decisions are made and how meetings are conducted. The supposedly democratic structures are, in reality, often exclusionary. Marie Clarke Walker[12] told how a resolution to bring in two designated seats on the executive of CUPE, one for workers of colour and the other for Aboriginal workers, was defeated because it was brought in at the end of the day, when the audience had dwindled and no one was there to debate it. June Veecock, of the Ontario Federation of Labour, noted that leadership "education is good, but it does nothing to change the structure.... There are systemic barriers that need to be removed. They [people of colour] feel uncomfortable with those structures ... the onus is on people of colour to go back and make changes in structures."[13] Carol Wall, a former human rights director with the Communications, Energy and Paperworkers Union of Canada (CEP), observed that "structures don't help around equity and human rights issues. The democratic structures are used to silence."[14] A turning point in anti-racism within the Canadian Labour Congress occurred in Montreal during the 1990 convention. Dory Smith, a black male member, ran against the white slate and received over a thousand votes. As one activist said, it "made the white boys sit up and take note." A resolution was passed to review the constitution and recommend changes to it. In the 1992 convention, a recommendation was brought forth to create a position on the executive committee for a member of colour. Many felt that this recommendation was tokenism. The Ontario Coalition of Black Trade Unionists and other anti-racist activists organized and achieved, instead, the designation of two seats. But structural change threatens many old-timers who want to maintain the status quo.

Exclusion—New Style

Just as union structures have sometimes resulted in the marginalization and silencing of unionists of colour, traditional methods of organizing exclude workers in precarious employment today. Most unions still function on the model of a traditional workplace and a standard worker who works 9 to 5 and is white, male, and English-speaking. Although these received practices and frameworks have been modified, to a certain extent, by the intervention of women and by non-whites, they need to be challenged even more. In order to organize workers in precarious employment, the assumptions that are taken for granted in the organizing process need to be examined and changed if necessary, and more creative strategies need to be incorporated. Ideas around organizing precarious workers have been greatly influenced by the writings of Kate Bronfenbrenner, director of Labour Education Research at Cornell University (CLC 1998). In 1995 she spoke at a conference on community unionism organized by the Ontario Federation of Labour. The following discussion is a reflection of some of her insights.

In order to include workers in precarious employment within the labour movement, organizing has to be seen as a longer-term project, not something that can be accomplished by speedy weekend campaigns or "blitzes" followed by worker sign-ups. The outreach process has to be more innovative, often requiring labour-intensive methods of contacting workers and then of building trust, a sense of community, and indigenous leadership through training and education programs. The current approaches do not allow that process in most unions. Longer, labour-intensive organizing campaigns require more resources—resources that are not always forthcoming. One success story is the organizing drive at Purdy's Chocolates (Ghosh 2003) in Vancouver, a campaign that included a minority of white, mainly full-time workers and part-time workers who were originally from China, the Philippines, Vietnam, and Latin America. That campaign took six years to conclude under the Communications, Energy and Paperworks Union of Canada (CEP). [...]

All organizers interviewed about organizing workers in precarious employment spoke about the intensive and sometimes lengthy nature of the organizing process, particularly given the high level of employer intimidation tactics with immigrant workers and workers of colour and the stringent requirements for union certification under the former Progressive Conservative government in Ontario. These insights are substantiated by experiences in other successful organizing drives with precarious workers that have been documented by the CLC (1998). Those insights are unable, for whatever reason, to allocate significant resources to organizing "stake out familiar territory," according to Galabuzi (Ghosh 2003), where it is easier to organize, mobilize, and develop leadership. Workers in this territory are also often better-paid standard workers and, consequently, their dues paying is more regular and reliable.

One informant[15] provided an even more critical perspective of this approach. Her union would take on organizing drives based on what, in effect, were ethnic and racial stereotypes. They assumed that workers of colour were more prone to unionizing if they came from a situation of collective struggle. In this mindset, Latin Americans, Filipinos, and Sri Lankans would unionize much faster than Chinese, for instance, The union would then prioritize its organizing strategy based on such assumptions. This approach is not only tantamount to racialized thinking but also opportunistic. It promotes competition among organizers working within different communities, emanating from the "How many members have you signed up today?" mentality. It promotes organizing as piecework rather than a long-tem process of building on a union base in a workplace or a community. This organizer, who challenged the mode of operation within her union by laying down different principles, was isolated and marginalized. By this logic, some workers of colour are still being excluded, although more systemically. It appears that certain groups are still being labelled by some unions as "unorganizable."

CONCLUSION

Systemic racism persists in the labour movement, although the movement has come a long way from the blatant exclusionism practised in the early 20th century. Racism today is characterized by authors as a "new" or "democratic" variety of racism (Henry et al. 2000) that employs non-racial discourses to "otherize" immigrants and people of colour. These discourses allow the co-existence of progressive policies and laws with racist practices and effects. Such discourses include "denial of racism," blaming the victim," or "pathologizing the victim." While unions have been in the forefront of advocating for equity and combating racism, sexism, and various other discriminatory practices in the larger society, they have been slower in acknowledging racism within their own organizations. This trend is exemplified by the persistence of old structures, procedures, and practices that prevent unionists of colour from becoming central actors in the movement, despite the emergence of strong equity policies. At the same time, old union practices around organizing keep many workers in precarious employment out. Anti-racist union activists want a labour movement that moves issues confronting workers of colour to the centre of the agenda, including challenging racism and sexism in the workplace and in society at large, mitigating precarious working conditions, and facilitating greater access to the labour movement so more scope exists for their participation and leadership. The structural changes and union democracy desired by equity-seeking groups within the labour movement are the same changes that workers in precarious employment require to participate fully in the movement.

ENDNOTES

1. Jackson notes that this category does not include Aboriginal workers and those workers who reported "didn't know" when asked about visible minority status.

2. This category does not include Aboriginal workers or those who answered "didn't know" when asked about visible minority status.

3. Interview with June Veecock, Ontario Federation of Labour, June 17, 2003, Toronto.

4. Interview with Bev Johnson, Ontario Public Service Employees Union, June 17, 2003, Toronto.

5. Interview with Michael Cifuentes, HERE, September 25, 2003, Toronto.

6. Interview with Bryan Neath, UFCWU, September 4, 2003, Toronto.

7. Ibid.

8. Interview with anonymous organizer, September 8, 2003, Toronto.

9. Interview with Marie Clarke Walker, CLC, September 19, 2003, Toronto.

10. Interview with Hassan Yussuff, CLC, June 19, 2003, Ottawa.

11. Another article by this author describes in more detail these problems that exist in the labour movement. It is a chapter in *Union Responses to Equity in Canada*, edited by Gerald Hunt and David Rayside (Toronto: University of Toronto Press, forthcoming).

12. Interview with Marie Clarke Walker.

13. Interview with June Veecock, OFL, June 17, 2003, Toronto.

14. Interviews with Carol Wall, Public Sector Alliance of Canada (PSAC), September 22, 2003, Ottawa.

15. Interview with anonymous organizer, September 24, 2003, Toronto.

BIBLIOGRAPHY OF SECONDARY SOURCES

Borowy, Jan, and Teresa Johnson. 1993. "Are These Clothes Clean? The Campaign for Fair Wages and Working Conditions for Homeworkers." In L. Carty, ed., *And Still We Rise: Feminist Political Mobilizing in Contemporary Canada*, 299–332. Toronto: Women's Press.

Briskin, Linda, and Patricia McDermott. 1993. *Women Challenging Unions: Feminism, Democracy, and Militancy*. Toronto: University of Toronto Press.

Calliste, Agnes. 1987. "Sleeping Car Porters in Canada: An Ethnically Submerged Split Labour Market." *Canadian Ethnic Studies* 19 (1): 1–20.

———. 1991. "Canada's Immigration Policy and Domestics from the Caribbean: The Second Domestic Scheme." In Jesse Vorst et al., eds., *Race, Class, Gender: Bonds and Barriers*. Toronto: Society for Socialist Studies and Garamond Press.

Canadian Labour Congress. 1997. *Challenging Racism: Going beyond Recommendations*. Report of the CLC National Anti-racism Task Force.

———. 1998. *No Easy Recipe: Building the Diversity and Strength of the Labour Movement: Feminist Organizing Models*. CLC Women's Symposium, November 1–3.

———. 2003. Falling Unemployment Insurance Protection for Canada's Unemployed. March. Ottawa: CLC or www.unemployed.ca.

Creese, Gillian Laura. 1991. "Organizing against Racism in the Workplace: Chinese Workers in Vancouver before the Second World War." In Ormond McKague, ed., *Racism in Canada*, 33–44. Saskatoon: Fifth House Publishers.

———. 1992. "Exclusion or Solidarity? Vancouver Workers Confront the 'Oriental Problem.'" In Laurel Sefton MacDowell and Ian Radforth, eds., *Canadian Working Class History: Selected Readings,* 311–32. Toronto: Canadian Scholars' Press.

Das Gupta, Tania. 1996. *Racism and Unpaid Work*. Toronto: Garamond Press.

———. 1998. "Anti-Racism and the Organized Labour Movement." In Vic Satzewich, ed., *Racism and Social Inequality in Canada*, 315–34. Toronto: Thompson Educational.

———. 2000. "Families of Native Peoples, Immigrants, and People of Colour." In Nancy Mandell and Ann Duffy, eds., *Canadian Families: Diversity, Conflict, and Change*, 141–74. Toronto: Harcourt Brace.

Das Gupta, Tania, and Franca Iocavetta. 2000. "Whose Canada Is It? Immigrant Women, Women of Colour, and Feminist Critiques of 'Multiculturalism.'" *Atlantis* 24 (2): 1–4.

Dua, Enakshi, and Angela Robertson, eds. 1999. *Scratching the Surface: Canadian Anti-racist Feminist Thought*. Toronto: Women's Press.

Forrest, Anne. 1993. "A View from outside the Whale: The Treatment of Women and Unions in Industrial Relations." In Linda Briskin and Patricia McDermott, eds., *Women Challenging Unions: Feminism, Democracy, and Militancy*, 325–42. Toronto: University of Toronto Press.

Frager, Ruth A. 1992. *Sweatshop Strife: Class, Ethnicity, and Gender in the Jewish Labour Movement of Toronto, 1900–1939*. Toronto: University of Toronto Press.

Galabuzi, Grace-Edward. 2001. *Canada's Creeping Economic Apartheid*. Toronto: Center for Social Justice. Available from www.socialjustice.org.

Ghosh, Sabitri. 2003. "Immigrant Workers and Unions." *This Magazine* (January/February).

Henry, Frances, and Effie Ginzberg. 1984. *Who Gets the Work? A Test of Racial Discrimination in Employment*. Toronto: Urban Alliance on Race Relations and Social Planning Council of Toronto.

Henry, Frances, and Carol Tator. 2000. *The Colour of Democracy: Racism in Canadian Society*. Toronto: Harcourt Brace.

Hill, Dan. 1977. *Human Rights in Canada: A Focus on Racism*. Canadian Labour Congress.

Jackson, Andrew. 2002. "Is Work Working for Workers of Colour?" Canadian Labour Congress, Research Paper 18.

Ladd, Deena. 1998. *No Easy Recipe: Building the Diversity and Strength of the Labour Movement*. Feminist Organizing Models: Canadian Labour Congress Women's Symposium.

Leah, Ronnie. 1993. "Black Women Speak out: Racism and Unions." In Linda Briskin and Patricia McDermott, eds., *Women Challenging Unions: Feminism, Democracy, and Militancy*, 157–72. Toronto: University of Toronto Press.

———. 1999. "Do You Call Me 'Sister'? Women of Colour and the Canadian Labour Movement." In Enakshi Dua and A. Robertson, eds., *Scratching the Surface: Canadian Anti-racist Feminist Thought*, 97–126. Toronto: Women's Press.

Lukas, Salome, and Judy Persad. 2004. *Through the Eyes of Workers of Colour: Linking Struggles for Social Justice*. Toronto: Women Working with Immigrant Women and the Toronto and York Region Labour Council.

Muszynski, Alicja. 1984. "The Organization of Women and Ethnic Minorities in a Resource Industry: A Case Study of the Unionization of Shoreworkers in the B.C. Fishing Industry, 1937–1949." *Journal of Canadian Studies* 19 (1): 89–107.

———. 1996. *Cheap Wage Labour: Race and Gender in the Fisheries of British Columbia*. Montreal: McGill-Queen's University Press.

Ng, Winnie Wun Wun. 1995. "In the Margins: Challenging Racism in the Labour Movement." MA thesis, University of Toronto.

Ornstein, Michael. 2000. *Ethno-racial Inequality in Toronto: Analysis of the 1996 Census*. Toronto: York University.

Pendakur, K., and R. Pendankur. 1995. *The Colour of Money: Earning Differentials among Ethnic Groups in Canada*. Ottawa: Department of Canadian Heritage.

Rebick, Judy, and Kike Roach. 1996. *Politically Speaking*. Vancouver: Douglas & McIntyre.

Sugiman, Pamela H. 1993. "Unionism and Feminism in the Canadian Auto Workers Union, 1961–1992." In Linda Briskin and Patricia McDermott, eds., *Women Challenging Unions: Feminism, Democracy, and Militancy*, 172–88. Toronto: University of Toronto Press.

Vosko, Leah F. 1995. "Recreating Dependency: Women and UI Reform." In D. Drache and A. Ranikin, eds., *Warm Heart, Cold Country*, 213–31. Toronto: Caledon Press.

———. 2000. *Temporary Work: The Gendered Rise of a Precarious Employment Relationship*. Toronto: University of Toronto Press.

Vosko, Leah, Nancy Zukewich, and Cynthia Cranford. 2003. "Precarious Jobs: A New Typology of Employment." *Perspective on Labour and Income*. Ottawa: Statistics Canada. October 16–26.

Ward, Peter. 1978. *White Canada Forever: Popular Attitudes and Public Policy towards Orientals in British Columbia*. Montreal and Kingston: McGill-Queen's University Press.

White, Julie. 1990. *Mail and Female: Women and the Canadian Union of Postal Workers*. Toronto: Thompson Educational Publishing.

Yates, Charlotte. 2001. *Making It: Your Economic Union and Economic Justice*. Toronto: The CSJ Foundation for Research and Education and the Ontario Federation of Labour.

———. 2002. "Expanding Labour's Horizons: Union Organizing and Strategic Change in Canada." *Just Labour* 1 (2): 31–40.

Zeytinoglu, Isik Urla, and Jacinta Khasiala Muteshi. 1999. "Gender, Race, and Class Dimensions of Nonstandard Work." *Relations Industrielles/Industrial Relations* 55 (1): 133–67.

Zwarenstein, Carolyn. 2002. "Smalltown Big Issues." *Our Times* 21 (3): 14–21.

CHAPTER FIVE, *Grace-Edward Galabuzi*

Further Reading

Lee, K. (2000). *Urban Poverty in Canada: A Statistical Profile.* Ottawa: Canadian Council on Social Development.

> This study uses recent statistics available to compare poverty rates among Canadian cities and provide a profile of Canada's urban poor. Special attention is given to poverty rates among visible minorities, immigrants, and Aboriginal peoples living in urban areas.

National Council of Welfare. (2000). *Justice and the Poor.* Ottawa: National Council of Welfare.

> The report notes the huge gap between the realities and public perceptions of crime, and it calls on governments and politicians to stop using crime as a political weapon. Canada is one of the safest countries in the world, but it has a very poor record when it comes to the huge number of people it sends to jail, often for very minor offences or non-payment of fines. The report contains 21 recommendations for improving the criminal justice system.

Saloojee, A. (2003). *Social Inclusion, Anti-racism, and Democratic Citizenship.* Toronto: Laidlaw Foundation.

> This paper identifies racism as a form of social exclusion. Exclusion in the form of racial discrimination results in unequal access for racialized groups to rights, goods and services, employment, and all areas of public life.

Related Web Sites

Canadian Feminist Alliance for International Action (FAFIA)
www.fafia-afai.org

> The Canadian Feminist Alliance for International Action (FAFIA) is a dynamic coalition of over 50 Canadian women's equality-seeking and related organizations. FAFIA's mandate is to further women's equality in Canada through domestic implementation of its international human rights commitments.

DisAbled Women's Network Ontario (DAWN)
www.dawn.thot.net

> DAWN Ontario is a progressive, volunteer-driven, feminist organization promoting social justice, human rights, and the advancement of equality rights through education, research, advocacy, coalition building, resource development, and information technology. DAWN's mission is to generate knowledge, information, and skills to advance the inclusion, citizenship, and equality rights of women and girls with disabilities.

National Anti-poverty Organization (NAPO)
www.napo-onap.ca

> The National Anti-poverty Organization (NAPO) is a non-profit, non-partisan organization that represents the interests of low-income people in Canada.

CHAPTER SIX, *Roxana Ng*

Further Reading

Johnson, L., and R. Johnson. (1982). *The Seam Allowance: Industrial Home Sewing in Canada.* Toronto: Women's Educational Press.

This book tells the story of homeworkers in Canada, most of whom are immigrant women who toil the garment industry and make dresses on a piecework basis for about $1 apiece. They are the last vestiges of 19th-century sweatshops.

Ng, R., R. Wong, and A. Choi. (1999). *Homeworking: Home Office or Home Sweatshop? Centre for the Study of Education and Work*, OISW/UT, http://hdl.handle.net/1807/2720.

By examining the working conditions of women who sew garments at home (heretofore home-workers) in the Greater Toronto Area, this study challenges the view painted by the media and encouraged by governments and employers that homeworking is a positive and viable alternative for everyone who does homework. Using in-depth and telephone interviews with 30 homework-ers who are immigrant women from Asia (Hong Kong, China, and Vietnam), this study adds to present knowledge on the conditions of homeworkers in Toronto and raises questions about the popular image of homeworking as the desired alternative to full-time, stable, and office- or factory-based employment.

Yanz, L., et al. (1999). *Policy Options to Improve Standards for Garment Workers in Canada.* Ottawa: Status of Women Canada.

This research report looks at a variety of possible responses to the deterioration of standards and labour practices in the garment industry caused by globalization, trade liberalization, restructur-ing, and deregulation.

Related Web Sites

Canadian Labour Congress
www.canadianlabour.ca

The Canadian Labour Congress is the largest democratic and popular organization in Canada with over 3 million members. The Canadian Labour Congress brings together Canada's national and international unions, the provincial and territorial federations of labour and 136 district labour councils.

International Labour Organization
www.ilo.org

The International Labour Organization is the UN specialized agency that promotes social justice and internationally recognized human and labour rights.

UNITE HERE!
www.unitehere.org

UNITE (formerly the Union of Needletrades, Industrial, and Textile Employees) and HERE (Hotel Employees and Restaurant Employees International Union) merged on July 8, 2004, forming UNITE HERE. UNITE HERE boasts a diverse membership comprised largely of immigrants and including high percentages of racialized Canadian workers. The majority of UNITE HERE members are women. Organizing the unorganized is a top priority for UNITE HERE.

CHAPTER SEVEN, *Jo-Anne Lee*

Further Reading

Bakker, I. (ed.). (1996). *Rethinking Restructuring: Gender and Change in Canada*. Toronto: University of Toronto Press.

This collection essays presents a critical exploration of the question of political and economic restructuring from the vantage point of gender. The authors argue that the present shift in the global order is revealing the contradictory effects of what is a dual process of both gender erosion and intensification. With the convergence of male and female job experience in polarized labour markets, gender appears to be less important in understanding the global political economy; at the same time, gender becomes more of a determining factor in the transformation of politics and markets, owing to the changing role of women as workers, caregivers, and consumers.

Tator, C. (1996). "Anti-racism and the Human Service Delivery System." In Carl E. James (ed.), *Perspectives on Racism and the Human Services Sector: A Case for Change*. Toronto: University of Toronto Press.

Today's social services agencies are faced with the challenge of responding to the diverse needs and expectations of a growing multicultural population. This book contains a collection of articles that examine race and racism in Canada from historical and contemporary perspectives and explore the extent to which these factors operate within social services systems related to immigration, settlement, the justice system, health, and education. The contributors, including practitioners, educators, and policy makers, argue for specific changes in current approaches to service delivery and provide practical suggestions for services that make it possible for various communities to be served more effectively. The collection also proposes an anti-racism approach to service provision to produce a system that is beneficial to all Canadians, particularly Aboriginals and racial and ethnic minorities.

Richmond, T. (1996). *Effects of Cutbacks on Immigrant Service Agencies*. Toronto: Public Health Department.

This is a report that features the planning and delivery of health and social services in Metro Toronto, and the current and long-term effects of the cutbacks on immigrant service agencies and their clients. The report addresses the following questions, including the scope of the cutbacks: Is there any particular pattern in terms of types of services, or agencies, or clients groups that are most severely threatened? How are immigrant service agencies responding to the cutbacks? And what potential exists for productive collaboration in defending essential settlement, social, and health services for immigrants and refugees in Metro Toronto?

Related Web Sites

Chinese Canadian National Council (CCNC)
www.ccnc.ca

> The Chinese Canadian National Council was formed to promote the rights of all individuals, in particular those of Chinese Canadians, and to encourage their full and equal participation in Canadian society.

Council of Agencies Serving South Asians (CASSA)
www.cassa.on.ca

> CASSA is an umbrella organization that supports and advocates on behalf of existing as well as emerging South Asian agencies, groups, and communities in order to address their diverse and dynamic needs. CASSA's goal is to empower the South Asian Community. CASSA is committed to the elimination of all forms of discrimination from Canadian society.

Ontario Council of Agencies Serving Immigrants (OCASI)
www.ocasi.org

> OCASI was formed in 1978 to act as a collective voice for immigrant-serving agencies and to coordinate response to shared needs and concerns. Its membership is comprised of more than 170 community-based organizations in the province of Ontario.

CHAPTER EIGHT, *Nandita Sharma*

Further Reading

Basok, T. (2003). *Tortillas and Tomatoes: Transmigrant Mexican Harvesters in Canada*. Montreal: McGill-Queen's University Press.

> This book explores the vital role played by Mexican seasonal workers in Canadian agriculture and how they have become a structural necessity in some sectors. This book also argues that mechanisms exist that make Mexican seasonal workers unfree and shows that the workers' virtual inability to refuse the employer's demand for their labour is related not only to economic need but to the rigid control exercised by the Mexican Ministry of Labour and Social Planning and Canadian growers over workers' participation in the Canadian guest worker program, as well as the paternalistic relationship between the Mexican harvesters and their Canadian employers.

Morely, D. (2000). *Home Territories: Media, Mobility, and Identity*. New York: Routledge.

> This book looks at the complex constructions of both "home" territories (or zones of safety) and the "uncanny" spaces of the unfamiliar, at the macro (nation) and micro (family) level. It examines how these are impacted by the new spaces and routes of communication and forms of community engendered by globalization and new technologies, as well as how people distinguish themselves from "others."

Torpey, J. (2000). *The Invention of the Passport: Surveillance, Citizenship, and State*. Cambridge and New York: Cambridge University Press.

This book introduces the notion and process of how state authorities have circumscribed, registered, regimented, and observed people within their jurisdictions. The passport deserves special attention not only because of the bureaucratic control it entails, but also because it implies establishment of citizenship, relatively unambiguous identification of individuals at a national scale, but it also profoundly altered relations between citizens and their governments.

Related Web Sites

Commission for Labour Cooperation
www.naalc.org/migrant/english/pdf/mgintro_en.pdf

This site offers documents on employment guides and employment laws for migrant workers in North America (Canada, United States, and Mexico).

New Socialist
www.newsocialist.org/

This is a web site of an organization of socialist activists. It publishes *New Socialist*, a magazine offering radical analysis of politics, social movements, and culture. It covers a variety of information in relation to racism, poverty, women, work, and migration.

Women and the Economy: A Project of Platform for Action Committee Manitoba (UNPAC)
www.unpac.ca/economy/g_migration.html

This site contains information on globalization and migration in Canada. It covers topics and resources on domestic migrant workers, domestic labour, and farm labour in Canada. It also provides links to United Nations' international conventions of protection of migrant workers.

CHAPTER NINE, *Lorne Foster*

Further Reading

Bauder, H. (2003). "'Brain Abuse,' or the Devaluation of Immigrant Labour in Canada." *Antipode* 35 (4), 669–717.

Based on data from interviews with institutional administrators and employers in Greater Vancouver who service or employ immigrants from South Asia, the author of this article found that many professional and skilled Canadian immigrants suffer from deskilling, non-recognition of their foreign credentials, and dismissal of their foreign work experience. Consequently, they are underrepresented in and systematically excluded from the upper segments of the Canadian labour market.

Kalbach, M.A., and W.E. Kalbach (eds.). (2000). *Perspectives on Ethnicity in Canada*. Toronto: Harcourt Canada.

This book is a collection of articles that covered various areas of systemic racism in Canadian society. Such racism could be found at workplace, media coverage, and politics.

Reitz, J. (2002). "Addressing Systemic Racial Discrimination in Employment: The Health Canada Case and Implications of Legislative Change." *Canadian Public Policy* 28 (3), 373–394.

This article introduced a case study of the 1997 Human Rights Tribunal decision on "systemic" racial discrimination at Health Canada, specifically addressing "glass-ceiling" barriers to the promotion of visible minorities to senior management, provides an effective illustration of the subtle and elusive nature of this form of discrimination. Under the 1996 amendments to the Employment Equity Act and the Canadian Human Rights Act, responsibility for systemic discrimination has changed, replacing the demonstrated potential of the human-rights complaints process with the broader coverage of a new audit-based employment equity process. The Health Canada experience shows a trade-off has taken place. Enhanced opportunities for public input would increase accountability.

Related Web Sites

Manitoba Labour and Immigration
www.gov.mb.ca/labour/immigrate/newcomerservices/8.html

This site offers information and materials on job preparation programs and volunteer work experiences in Manitoba that may be useful to newcomers as they settle in Canada.

Maytree Foundation
www.maytree.com/index.asp?section=3

This site features reports and publications in the areas of poverty and inequality of employment to immigrants in Canada.

Toronto Region Immigrant Employment Council
www.triec.ca

This site provides information to employers, immigrants, regulators, post-secondary institutions, immigrants, agencies, and all levels of government that enable skilled immigrants to find appropriate employment so they are better able to use the skills, education, and experience they bring with them to Canada.

CHAPTER TEN, *Tania Das Gupta*

Further Reading

Pocock, B. (ed.). (1997). *Strife: Sex and Politics in Labour Unions*. Sydney: Allen Unwin.

This book examines the problem of women who are chronically underrepresented at every level of the Australian trade union movement. Women are less likely than men to join unions and when women do join, women remain disproportionately underrepresented in each level in the movement. The higher up the organizational hierarchy and the more political and organizational power a position wields, the less likely it is that a woman will hold it.

Reitz, J., and A. Verma. (2004). "Immigration, Race, and Labour: Unionization and Wages in the Canadian Labour Market." *Industrial Relationship* 43 (4), 835–854.

In Canada, most racial minorities have lower rates of unionization than do members of the majority workforce. This article, using the data from the Survey of Labour and Income Dynamics, shows that racial minority immigrants assimilate into unionization over time. However, unionization reduces net minority wage disadvantages only slightly. Union race relations policies should place more emphasis on collective bargaining as well as on unionization.

Vosko, Leah. (2000). *Temporary Work: The Gendered Rise of a Precarious Employment Relationship.* Toronto: University of Toronto Press.

This book analyzes the history and recent growth of temporary work in Canada. It examines the relationship between varied forms of temporary work and the erosion of terms of employment for the standard employment relationship. Furthermore, the author uses archetypes of feminized employment (more casual, lower pay) to characterize this trend.

Related Web Sites

Canadian Labour Congress, Women's and Human Rights Department
canadianlabour.ca/index.php/Women

This site offers information and reports on various issues related to the labour movement and women in Canada.

Coalition of Labour Union Women (CLUW)
www.cluw.org/

This site is the homepage of the United States' only national organization for unionized women. The objectives of CLUW is to unify all unionized women in determining common problems and concerns and to develop action programs to promote affirmative action in the workplace; to strengthen the role of women in unions; to organize the unorganized women; and to increase the involvement of women in the political and legislative process.

Status of Women Canada
www.swc-cfc.gc.ca/pubs/pubspr/0662281608/index_e.html

This site provides a research report in 2000 that reviews employment equity policy at the federal and provincial levels; examines variations in employment equity policy and practice; and recommends ways to rectify a perceived impasse in the effective implementation of employment equity policy.

PART THREE

Crime, Policing, Surveillance, and Social Exclusion

OBJECTIVES

To comprehend how poverty in Canada is criminalized

To understand how racial profiling gets accomplished

To critically analyze the "moral panic" regarding Asian youth gangs in Canada

To make the connections between wars and the murder of people, domestic violence against women, and the right to participate in public life

INTRODUCTION

In addition to the economic consequences of "race" and gender, there are other social ways that racialized people, specifically women, are socially constructed to experience their lives as second-class Canadian citizens. In this third part, we will examine how poverty, race, and gender are criminalized.

In Chapter 11, Kiran Mirchandani and Wendy Chan document the experiences of people of colour on welfare. In the 1990s, Canadian welfare policy was characterized as a "war against poverty" due to attempts to criminalize the poor. Welfare budgets were slashed, resulting in increased poverty and homelessness. Workforce programs create degrading rituals to target poverty as deviant. The authors note that this dismantling and transformation of the welfare state is occurring in an era of mass joblessness and precarious employment. Increasingly, as a result of the racialization and feminization of poverty, welfare policies tend to be gendered and racialized. Through interviews with racialized welfare recipients, Mirchandani and Chan's analysis provide a critical understanding of the ways in which racism structures welfare enforcement and control in Canada.

In Chapter 12, Scott Wortley and Julian Tanner examine the racial profiling debate in Toronto. Racial profiling, in the criminological literature, is said to exist when the members of certain racial or ethnic groups become subject to greater levels of criminal justice surveillance than others. The authors examine the work of a sociologist hired by the Toronto Police who claimed that racial profiling did not exist in Toronto. Wortley and Tanner critique his "data-cleaning procedures," lack of transparency, and lack of references to academic studies in the field. They demonstrate how the police expert's data in fact show the existence of racial profiling in Toronto. The authors conclude by calling on the criminological community to take a much more active role in the racial profiling debate in Canada.

In Chapter 13, Siu-ming Kwok and Dora Tam write that, since the late 1980s, law enforcement personnel have increasing concerns about the rise of youth violence, especially among Asian youth. This moral panic is fuelled by various reports. For example, the Canadian Criminal Intelligence Service reported that Asian-based organized crime groups were very active in British Columbia, Ontario, and Quebec; were major controllers of illegal drug supplies; and were among the fastest-growing gangs in Canada. However, despite these concerns and the volume of research into the ethnic youth gang phenomenon undertaken in North America over the past decade, there are many gaps in our understanding of Asian youth gangs. In this article, Kwok and Tam review the existing literature on delinquency of Asian youth in Canada to provide a framework to understand this underresearched population.

Finally, in Chapter 14, Sunera Thobani documents the vicious Canadian media response to her speech at a women's conference on violence against women after the September 11, 2001, attacks on the World Trade Center in New York. In that speech, Thobani described President Bush's new war as a racialized construction, rooted in colonialism and imperialism, that would result in an increase in violence against all women both in the North and South. After this speech, Thobani was vilified in the Canadian press. She was even the subject of a hate crime complaint made to the RCMP, alleging that her speech amounted to a hate crime against Americans. The intensity of the personal attacks reveals the power that racialized women confront when their interpretation of their own reality is articulated in public. Thobani had the courage to analyze how the United States' violence against some people, including women, is ultimately violence to many others—both women and men. Sunera Thobani, a Canadian, was questioned about her citizenship, her authority to speak, and was charged with a hate crime when she exercised her right to express facts about the track record of U.S. foreign policy.

Experiences of poverty are criminalized by welfare policies, police stop-and-searches, and the surveillance of gangs. In addition, people speaking out against other forms of poverty—as a result of war, for example—can in turn become the subjects of complaints to police. These experiences, at the present time, are increasingly gendered and racialized. Further, poverty stigmatizes and results in other consequences. We will examine these other consequences in the final section of this book.

CHAPTER ELEVEN

The Racialized Impact of Welfare Fraud Control in British Columbia and Ontario

Kiran Mirchandani and Wendy Chan

INTRODUCTION

Canadian welfare policy and anti-fraud measures in the 1990s have been characterized by many activists and researchers as representing a devastating "war against poverty." In October 2002, the National Anti-poverty Association (NAPO) issued a press release in which they noted:

> While the United Nations marks October 17th, the International Day for the Eradication of Poverty, the relevance of such an occasion goes virtually unacknowledged by parliamentarians, governments and media in Canada.... The concept of poverty elimination has been lost in Canada. Instead of attacking the root causes of poverty and establishing viable mechanisms which would lead to an end to poverty in Canada, federal and provincial/territorial governments advance treacherously towards the wholesale criminalization of poverty.... "They are not the least bit interested in solving problems," said Linda Lalonde, NAPO President, "They're more concerned with making people afraid of poverty and blaming the individuals for it."

This project serves to illustrate the ways in which the "criminalization of poverty" mentioned in the NAPO press release is in fact not only a war against poverty but also fundamentally a war against people of colour. This research study examines the racialized effects of government policies on the policing of "welfare fraud" in two provinces in Canada—Ontario and British Columbia. Through interviews with welfare recipients of colour, the researchers demonstrate how current welfare enforcement measures rely on racial stereotypes and myths about recipients in order to refuse or suspend access to welfare benefits.

* * * * *

METHODOLOGY

Introduction

This research study has been informed by both feminist and anti-racist writings about the welfare state. The importance of gender, race, and class issues in the context of welfare "fraud" cannot be understated since within Canada, racialized women are more likely to be poor and seek assistance from the state. This section begins by outlining the theoretical framework underpinning the project. A discussion of the research methods follows.

Feminist Anti-racist Approach to Welfare Enforcement Practices

Racialization refers to the historical emergence of the idea of "race" and to its subsequent reproduction and application (Miles, 1989, p. 76). Racialization is part of a broader process whereby "categories of the population are constructed, differentiated, inferiorized, and excluded" (Anthias, 1998, p. 7). Conceptualizing racialization in this manner allows for an analysis of how "privilege and oppression are often not absolute categories but, rather, shifts in relation to different axes of power and powerlessness" (Friedman, 1995, p. 114). The criminalization of certain racialized groups within the Canadian context can be understood in two ways: 1) in light of the construction of white, majority groups as "race-less" and 2) within the context of historical relations between First Nations People, early settlers, and recent immigrants and migrants.

* * * * *

At the same time, it should be noted that while "the poor" in Canada are not a uniform group, higher rates of poverty amongst certain groups do not correspond with proportionally higher welfare rates. Given the heterogeneity amongst those living in poverty, further sections of this report highlight the ways in which welfare control policies do not have uniform effects on "the poor." These policies are fundamentally racialized and gendered.

Interviewing Welfare Recipients of Colour

This research on welfare fraud adopts a qualitative research approach, using interviews as the primary tool for data collection.

* * * * *

The sample consisted of individuals occupying a diverse range of social locations. Respondents ranged from 24 to 55 years of age; three-quarters of the sample had child-care and/or eldercare responsibilities. Individuals self-identified as Black, African, Chinese, Aboriginal, Somali, Sri Lankan, Caribbean, and Mixed Race. One quarter of the sample was Aboriginal. The majority of respondents were female, although a few men were also interviewed. Some respondents were hesitant in their use of English while others were extremely fluent. Considerable overlap was found between the experiences of respondents from British Columbia and Ontario; therefore findings from both provinces are discussed together.

The process of data analysis reflects the principles of qualitative analysis. Data gathered from interviews were subject to on-going analysis throughout the fieldwork phase and into the process of writing the report. In approaching the interview data, it is recognized that the data does not reflect an external reality of the interviewee, but is an internal reality constructed by both the interviewer and interviewee in order to produce an event that is recognizable to both parties. Meanings that emerge from the interviews are the negotiated tensions between the research participants' and researcher's assumptions about reality (Fielding, 1993, p. 163). The mechanics of analyzing the data involved using a qualitative computer software package, NVivo, to code the interviews. The focus of the report now turns to the presentation of research findings.

THE EFFECTS OF THE WELFARE CONTROL SYSTEM ON PEOPLE OF COLOUR

Introduction

In order to provide a context within which people of colour are criminalized in their intersection with welfare fraud policies, a discussion of the ways in which the welfare system itself operates to maintain the oppression and subordination of people of colour is pertinent. An awareness of the ways in which policing, sentencing, and imprisonment practices affect people of colour has been well documented by scholarly research. However, the racialized impact of welfare control, as a site of investigation, has remained largely unexcavated. Much of the Canadian literature on welfare fraud has focused on the ways in which recent social assistance program changes and fraud policies negatively affect poor women. As Carruthers (1995, p. 241) has noted, the "'welfare cheater' does not present a genderless face to the public." Martin (1992) argues that women are significantly over-represented in the prosecution of welfare fraud, and many receive sentences involving imprisonment. Women who are offered plea bargains often plead guilty to fraud, whether or not there is a convincing case against them. As Martin notes, "to a woman already traumatized by poverty, the added stigma of a criminal record is not worth disputing if failure means going to prison and leaving one's children without care, or in the hands of child welfare authorities" (1992, p. 68).

* * * * *

Inadequate Financial Support

Almost all the respondents interviewed mentioned the utter inadequacy of the welfare payments that they received, leading to difficulties making ends meet. Many regularly visited food banks and relied on community support agencies. Respondents noted:

* * * * *

> The money they give me is not all that enough. Like, I have five children. My rent is nine hundred and sixty. And they give me six hundred and sixty. Where am I going to get the rest of the money for myself and five children? (BC4F)

Given that funds received cannot pay for all of their expenses, respondents noted that they could understand why some may choose to commit fraud in order to make ends meet:

> Sometimes I'm actually for saying, all the credit to the people who can actually cheat the system out of a couple more dollars. Because people have to live, they have bills to pay and, really, Ontario Works just doesn't cut it. (ON3M)

As one woman respondent explains, not disclosing extra income makes it possible to make up the difference between what welfare provides and what is needed to survive:

> I mean I know people who if they do get a few shifts, or if they do get a job, they don't report it right away. Or they don't report all of what they make. Just to get by. And really that is what you are trying to do is to get by. It's not even to live above your means. It's just to get by. (ON9F)

Language Barriers

Advocating for higher payments or attempting to ensure the continuity of welfare payments was challenging for a large portion of recipients who do not have strong English language skills:

> When I tried to apply for welfare, I had difficulties because it's only the educated people who know English. Like how to apply for welfare, you have to make an appointment through the phone first and you have to go through the process of applying for welfare over the whole ... we didn't know any people who would actually help us to apply. (ON13M)

* * * * *

Negative Interactions with Case Workers

Much of the stress of being and staying on welfare was attributed to the interactions which individuals had with their "case workers." Respondents reported that workers were insensitive, not compassionate, and often racist:

> The more needs you acquire, the more they can stigmatize you. They get too much up here with all these drug addicts and alcoholics.... That's why those people are trained to be very aggressive, very hard, and very uncompassionate people. They are trained like that. Because they have so much up to here and they don't care about anyone. (ON10F)

In a few cases, respondents reported positive experiences with case workers:

> I found this worker I got here—he took the time to talk to me and explain things to me. He gave me goals, told me by next time I saw him he needed that done and I basically did what was required of me. (ON11F)

Insufficient funds combined with an unsupportive case worker are not the only problems respondents encountered. Many women and men on social assistance also face numerous structural barriers to employment.

Structural Barriers to Employment

* * * * *

In addition, immigrants noted the significant barrier they faced in gaining Canadian experience:

> It was hard for me to get a job ... because whenever I applied they said that they need Canadian experience.... Where am I going to get the Canadian experience? (BC4F)

Respondents of colour noted that regardless of their qualifications or education levels, they were confronted by the expectation that they would be most suited to deskilled and/or precarious employment:

> There's this cashier training course and business skills not only means cashier. But that's I guess what I'm supposed to do because I'm an immigrant. That's what they assume.

Well, you're an immigrant and that's what you're supposed to do. That's the only thing you can do and that's the only thing that all immigrants can do. So I'll just give you this information. You're an immigrant and there's a cashier that is not a computerized cashier training course but it's at Goodwill. And this is what you'll be doing for six weeks. You'll be folding clothes and putting bags of clothes away and work in labour. And yeah, you can do that for the rest of your life. (ON10F)

As Shields notes, "in the new labour market, immigrants … are coming to be used increasingly as a part of a new 'flexible' and disposable labour force suited to the demands of the globalized just-in-time economy" (2003, p. iii). In order to avoid the trap of precarious minimum-wage jobs, many respondents reported turning to education in an attempt to gain more meaningful work:

I would love to get a job and support myself, but at the same time we need to go to school. You can't go, you can't get a good job that you want, or you can't pursue a career or anything unless you go to school. (ON1F)

* * * * *

One of the most significant barriers to employment mentioned was the racism within the Canadian labour market itself. As will be discussed in greater detail, […] employer racism was an important factor in excluding women and men from obtaining fulfilling jobs:

Well, people always assume that I'm Hispanic and I'm dumb. They always assume that, well, she looks Latino or Latina, Hispanic, so she is a dumb immigrant.... [About her supervisor] Why is he giving other people cashier positions and for me it's a food prep position and I'm much older than these students, these kids? They're actually kids, a lot younger than me. Already have been to one year college and I didn't understand why the misled information was towards me but I just assumed, well, it could be because I look Hispanic so maybe he thinks I should just work in food and to clean up and that's what I was doing in this job. I was food prep and cleaning up, and never was allowed to go near the cash register, touch it, or help out or anything (ON10F)

These experiences both within the welfare system and in society at large have a direct impact on the mental health of women and men on welfare.

Depression and Shame

Many respondents noted feeling depressed or ashamed about being on welfare. Rather than providing support, however, the systems and structures in place served to exacerbate these feelings.

The process is, it is difficult to, it is very impersonal first of all. It is a very impersonal process. You go in and you feel like utter crap first of all. It is very demoralizing. I don't care who says, it is very demoralizing to be on social assistance. (ON3M)

I need to buy a pillow, a bed, or whatever. People told me that you could make a list and take it to the welfare worker and they will give you some money about for that. So I did that and then a white worker actually interviewed me and said, well, you have spent so much money to come from Sri Lanka, from Sri Lanka to Canada, so don't you have money to get these things? (ON14M)

* * * * *

While many of the experiences reported above are a direct result of poverty, women and men of colour are particularly stigmatized. As discussed in the following section, the existing criminalization of people of colour (Chan and Mirchandani, 2002) facilitates the enhanced surveillance of women of colour who are on social assistance.

CRIMINALIZING WELFARE RECIPIENTS OF COLOUR

Introduction

While there is no shortage of discussion and debate on the state of welfare systems, there have been remarkably few discussions both within and outside of Canada regarding the enforcement practices of welfare provisions and virtually none that address, in a sustained fashion, the racialized nature of welfare enforcement (with the exceptions of Neubeck and Cazenave, 2001 and Quadagno, 1994). Within the literature, attention centres on recipients' views and perspectives regarding having their behaviour monitored and policed. Some writers have noted that the increased policing of welfare fraud continues to reinforce a negative view of people in need, thereby legitimizing their stigma and discrimination in the public eye. Moreover, while it is widely acknowledged that gender plays a significant role in determining persons who are more likely to be in need, and as a result, surveilled, there is less attention paid to the racialized nature of welfare provisions and enforcement.

* * * * *

The Impact of Fraud "Policing"

Government methods to combat the increasing "fraud problem" have led several commentators to critically examine the social and political impact of surveillance and policing methods on welfare recipients. The implementation of finger-printing programs and mandatory addiction screening and treatment programs have raised concerns about the ways in which poverty and the need for welfare are being constructed. Murray (2000) claims that finger-printing welfare recipients sends a strong message regarding the connections between poverty and welfare dependency to deviance and criminality. […] Paul Bobier (1998) explores whether the problem of welfare fraud justifies the high costs of purchasing a biometric identification system to finger-print welfare recipients. He notes that in New York City, out of a million recipients, there were only 36 detected cases of "double-dippers" in 1996. Canada's experience with biometric identification also reveals that such programs have little cost-saving potential. Toronto, for example, introduced a Client Identification Benefits Program (CIBS); this program was operational between 1996–1999 and then cancelled due to the withdrawal of private sector consortium members (Barry, 2002, p. 98). Aside from the financial costs, there are also privacy considerations raised by the use of such programs as well as reservations about protecting the rights of people living in poverty. Philip Berger (2001) expresses a similar concern about the use of mandatory addiction screening and treatment for welfare recipients. Despite overwhelming objections from civil rights advocates and no solid evidence that welfare recipients are more likely to have drug- or alcohol-related problems, the Ontario Government has nonetheless singled out welfare recipients as particularly affected by substance abuse problems. [...]

While Canada continues to grapple with these concerns, in the United States, such measures and practices are commonplace. Charlotte Twight's (2002) study of federal control and surveillance of ordinary Americans paints an Orwellian picture of a nation that no longer enjoys any privacy rights. Expanding the use of people's Social Security Numbers (SSN) to a broad range of non-employment-related transactions highlights a way in which the problem of welfare fraud can be used to shore up legitimacy for intrusive data collection and data-sharing programs (Twight, 2002, p. 247). John Gilliom (2001) concurs with Twight's analysis in his own study of welfare surveillance. He states that the emphasis of the American welfare state on deterring those who can fend for themselves, on adhering to strict eligibility requirements combined with a disdain for welfare recipients, has resulted in a situation where "the welfare poor are subject to forms and degrees of scrutiny matched only by the likes of patients, prisoners, and soldiers" (Gilliom, 2001, p. 28). [...]

The Role of the State

Several writers have undertaken to understand the nature and functioning of the administrative state in the control of welfare fraud. In most developed countries, a large bureaucratic machine has been established in order to manage the distribution of welfare benefits and control problematic human behaviours. [...] Pemberton (1990) questions the need for the apparatus of surveillance in the welfare system when the annual rate and cost of welfare fraud in Australia has not increased significantly in the past six years. He questions whether there is much "disciplining" or "pacification" of the welfare recipient taking place given the low incidence of welfare fraud and, consequently, whether the concept of "disciplinary technologies" is useful to an understanding of the modern "Administrative State" (Pemberton, 1990, p. 138).

Recipients' Views

Attempts to provide an understanding of the fraud issue from the perspectives of those using the welfare system have begun to emerge. Interestingly, and perhaps not surprisingly, welfare recipients are more than aware that theirs is a no-win situation. Whether they rely on the state for assistance or attempt to make ends meet by taking on extra work to top up their inadequate benefits, they are confronted with a system that is confusing, degrading, full of hassles, and one in which they are demonized as undeserving, lazy, and stigmatized because they need help. Evanson and Woods's (1995) study of claimants' experiences in the social security system in Northern Ireland demonstrates that making ends meet requires dependency on family members and/or charity organizations or "doing the double" (working while receiving benefits). They document the resentment that claimants have towards a system that leaves them with no choice but to "do the double," since real jobs are lacking and the benefits provided are wholly inadequate to meet basic needs. John Gilliom's (2001) interviews with fifty welfare mothers in Ohio and Seccombe, James, and Walters's (1998) stories of forty-seven women on welfare in Florida reveal a similar situation. These studies (as well as Zucchino, 1997) highlight the constant struggles these women experience while being under constant surveillance as they attempt to meet their family's needs. Finally, Cherlin et al.'s (2002) study of welfare recipients' experiences with sanctions and case closings points to the confusion many recipients experience while trying to understand the complex administrative rules they are required to adhere to and how easily people can lose access to their benefits for bureaucratic reasons, such as missing a meeting or failing to produce a document.

Our research study echoes many of the themes described above. In particular, the recent emphasis in welfare reforms on enforcement has resulted in more punitive and criminalizing tendencies. The impact of these policy changes are acutely felt by racialized people, particularly women. That a gap exists between welfare policies concerning enforcement and the realities of many welfare recipients should perhaps come as no surprise, since there are many indications that the provision of welfare for those "most in need" is a politically loaded statement. The main themes associated with the enforcement of welfare provisions—welfare surveillance and dehumanizing treatment—will now be detailed.

WELFARE SURVEILLANCE

According to the twenty-four recipients of colour interviewed, welfare surveillance occurred at two main sites in the system—during application for benefits, and in order to continue receiving benefits over a period of time.

Accessing Welfare Benefits

At the time of application, the respondents noted that welfare workers often demanded extensive documentation, which related not only to their financial situation, but to every aspect of their lives. Respondent reported that it was not uncommon for them to provide pay slips, birth certificates, letters from landlords, bank transcripts, and landed immigrant papers in an effort to demonstrate need. Yet, for both first-time applicants and those who had previously received benefits, while they recognized the need to provide some of this information, they found the process demeaning:

> They just, I allowed them to ask me stupid questions and I answered. And they said, "We'll only allow you to do it this one time, but you have to have your landed immigrant papers." And I said, "Oh, okay." I acted dumb and that was it. But it was an awful experience because it makes you feel like you're a criminal 'cause that's the way I was being treated. (ON10F)

* * * * *

Ensuring Compliance

The surveillance of welfare recipients also occurred while respondents were receiving assistance. The three main areas of surveillance were: 1) compliance with training and workshop obligations, 2) ensuring that there wasn't another adult living in the house with the recipient ("spouse in the house"), and 3) reporting any income earned while receiving assistance.

Most provincial welfare programs require that recipients undergo training programs, attend workshops, and actively seek employment. Respondents in this study noted that these demands were made on them by welfare workers, despite various difficulties in meeting these obligations:

> Welfare wants me to go to work, but I really can't work. I am afraid that they will cut me off. My doctor can't find any "proof" that there is a real health problem. I am always anxious and sweating and that this has been for a year. (BC10F, translated)

In addition, welfare recipients are required to attend appointments with their case workers. Many respondents felt that these appointments were unnecessary, prevented them from meeting other obligations, and were time consuming as there were long waits to see their case workers:

> Sometimes I have a test, but I still have to go see him. And he will make me wait for two hours sometimes. There was a time when my appointment was at, I think, 8:30, no no no, 9:30. It was very early in the morning. He made me wait for two hours and when I went and sat there, I asked him, "Why did you make me wait for all this time?" He goes, "Oh, I had more important things to do." (ON1F)

* * * * *

Many of the respondents have had their welfare cheques suspended at one time or another because they failed to provide adequate documentation. Respondents noted that the documents they were asked to provide were often difficult to obtain, and that they were often given confusing and contradictory information about exactly which documents they needed to present. Since their main interaction with the welfare system was through their case workers, respondents attributed much of the dehumanizing treatment they received to the actions and attitudes of case workers.

Dehumanizing Treatment

The effects of being forced to comply with every regulation, often without any flexibility or consideration, left many respondents with a negative experience of the welfare system.

* * * * *

Respondents reported that welfare workers tended to assume that they were lying about their circumstances and the information they provided in order to receive assistance:

> I think sometimes it appears to me that the welfare system seems to think that everybody is a liar, everybody is trying to fraud them, everybody is lazy and not wanting to do anything about their situation instead of taking each case as, you know, looking at each case individually. (ON9F)

In some cases respondents noted difficulties in attempting to contact their welfare workers. Phone calls would go unanswered and respondents' attempts to set up meetings would be refused:

> He never answered the message. That's his habit. He's not going to answer. He's going to leave with the answering machine and then if he wants it that time, he's going to call you back. (ON2F)

Many respondents stated that they thought their welfare workers could have been a lot more helpful with letting them know about various programs they could have access to, the regulations regarding receiving assistance, and other benefits associated with receiving assistance:

They do not mention those things that are helpful. I mean, I had to hear from talking to different people that you can get a free computer if you have children. You can get a start-up package if you are moving. All these things were not knowledge to me until I spoken with different people. (ON9F)

* * * * *

Some of the experiences discussed above may be shared by all people on welfare, regardless of "race" or ethnicity. The people of colour interviewed for the present study, however, noted that the dehumanizing treatment they received from their welfare workers was the result of being both poor and racialized. One woman believed that the lack of access to programs was the result of being non-white:

Because my friend, she's white, and we have the same worker and she's the same age as I am and she gets a lot more things going for her than I do. (BC5F)

* * * * *

The punitive treatment directed towards respondents by the welfare system is consistent with the literature. As various governments tighten access to the welfare system, those who fail to abide by the rules and regulations are either penalized or criminalized for their behaviour. The intense surveillance and control of welfare recipients also ensures that only a small proportion of those in need will actually receive assistance. For racialized people, the problem is exacerbated by racist comments and treatment within the welfare system. The next section discusses the effects of racism on respondents' interactions with the welfare system.

RACISM AND THE CANADIAN WELFARE SYSTEM

Introduction

An examination of welfare systems across North America and Europe reveals a similar pattern of stereotyping, scapegoating, and marginalization of welfare recipients. The current political discourse of welfare entitlement highlights the prevalence of a neo-liberal agenda shaping public policy. The promotion of free markets and reduced state social responsibility has allowed governments to articulate the kinds of people that are entitled to assistance and protection. As many writers note, the dichotomy of the "deserving" and the "undeserving" person has played a significant role in shaping debates and policies for the last several decades (Mandell, 2001; Mosher, 2000; Sidel, 2000; Sales, 2002). Janet Mosher (2000) reveals that the Canadian government's retreat from social programs has been made possible through the adoption of several strategies—one of which is the active construction of deeply negative stereotypes of welfare recipients, particularly welfare mothers. Fuelling and maintaining this stereotype is the state's "anti-fraud" campaign.

* * * * *

In our interviews with racialized welfare recipients, racism was regarded as a problem both indirectly and directly. Indirectly, language barriers made it difficult for respondents to fill out application forms and communicate with welfare workers; finding interpreters was often difficult. This resulted in numerous delays and confusion. Direct forms of racism could be found in the belief many respondents held that they were treated differently because of their racial or ethnic background. Indirect and direct racism, experienced as language barriers and/or differential treatment, will now be explored in further detail.

LANGUAGE BARRIERS

Many of the respondents in this study required interpreters in order to communicate in English. In some cases, though, deadlines needed to be met; the welfare system did not provide interpreters to help respondents complete tasks:

> He say that they suggested that he has to apply for ODSP within 90 days, right? And they don't give him any kind of resources in a sense that they don't have an interpreter, they don't have a person who is actually able to help him because he doesn't know how to do that process itself. (ON8F, translated)

The need for translation services exacerbated the effects of the bureaucratic rules and mechanisms that people on welfare are expected to follow. Having to rely on a network of friends, community support workers, and translators, the bureaucratic rules and regulations required in order to receive social assistance form yet another literacy barrier for people with limited English skills:

> I also don't know English so I asked one of my friends.... He took a day off and [I] took him to the welfare office. And they said, no, this is not the office, you have to go to another office, which is at Finch. So then we went to that office. That office said no, this is not the office, you have to go to another office. And so we went to four offices and the fourth office actually told [us] that you can't make an appointment here. You have to call these people first and make an appointment. (ON14M)
>
> The worst part was I don't know the language and I have to look for someone to interpret for me. The worst part is that. (ON8F, translated)

An inability to explain problems to their workers meant that respondents were unable to access their benefits quickly:

> One thing is that I would say language because it is very hard to get the welfare worker on the phone or to meet them. When you meet them you can't tell everything all at once. So if you don't tell everything at once you don't get the services properly. So I would prefer that opportunity to be utilized well. In order to utilize well, you need a person who can speak English also. (ON14M)

* * * * *

Differential Treatment

In addition to the subtle, indirect forms of racism experienced by respondents, more direct forms of racism and sexism were noted by respondents, who were aware that not everyone received the same type of treatment within the welfare system:

> They come and they investigate and then they leave and that was it ... but I mean, you're native, you're either an alcoholic, or you're a drug addict or you're? which not everybody is. (BC3F)

* * * * *

Another respondent explains that racism fuels the belief that people of colour are not entitled to welfare benefits. Stereotypes and prejudices make it difficult for people of colour to assert their rights:

> See, a lot of people, a lot of white society, the way they look at it is that welfare is basically for those who are refugee status who basically, people who are new to the country and don't have education when it comes down to being Toronto-educated or Ontario-, Canadian-educated, North American-educated. They feel basically that people of colour, because Orientals are people of colour too. They think basically it's, we're taking advantage of that, we're wasting tax-paying money, you know? Like Black folks and Orientals don't pay taxes either? (ON12M)

According to the respondents, overt racist treatment by welfare workers was not uncommon:

> I know some of the ladies that they told me, we had the same worker. They told me they don't know that much the language. They told me whenever we came to interview while he was sitting in the chair, he start dropping our bag and throw it and say, what's this, what's this, what's this [dumping the contents of their bag, going through their bag].... Because of the way I dress, because of my religion, because of my colour, because I'm a minority and everything. Otherwise, if there was a white people, he wouldn't do that. (ON2F)

The differential treatment of people of colour is further compounded by the stigma surrounding welfare, thereby ensuring that equitable treatment remains elusive. The next section describes the ways in which neo-liberal Canadian society promotes and sustains a situation in which people of colour are more likely to live in poverty.

RACISM AND NEO-LIBERALISM IN CANADIAN SOCIETY

Introduction

A close examination of who is most likely to be disadvantaged in the labour market and thus live in poverty highlights the centrality of race to the issues surrounding welfare. Since racial politics are deeply embedded in the disenfranchisement of the poor, welfare reform is not just an attack on the poor, but importantly, an attack against people of colour. [...]

A "Racism-Centred" Perspective of Welfare Policy

The need to challenge welfare debates that routinely exploit the use of racist stereotypes has led Neubeck and Cazenave (2002) to argue that only a "racism-centred" perspective of welfare policy and its consequences will shed light on the nature of welfare reforms and the effects they have on communities of colour. They use the term "welfare racism" to refer to the various reforms and manifestations of racism associated with means-tested programs of public assistance for poor families (Neubeck and Cazenave, 2002). The authors argue that public assistance attitudes, policymaking, and administrative practices are racialized, and it is only by uncovering and naming the racism that occurs that perceptions surrounding welfare entitlement and welfare fraud may change (Neubeck and Cazenave, 2002).

Canada's "New" Racism

The analyses found in the previous sections provide vivid illustrations of the racism that pervades the welfare system in Canada. In the name of fraud protection, people of colour are treated in dehumanizing ways and face surveillance and scrutiny that construct them as criminals. Welfare policies ignore the structural racism faced by many immigrants and people of colour, which filters them into precarious and poorly paid employment, regardless of their qualifications. Giroux argues that in the past few decades, racism has undergone a significant shift and now takes new forms: "In its current manifestation, racism survives through the guise of neo-liberalism, a kind of repartee that imagines human agency as simply a matter of individual choices, the only obstacle to effective citizenship and agency being the lack of principled self-help and moral responsibility" (2003, p. 191). In this context, neo-liberal racism manifests itself through the shift from welfare to workfare, in the construction of welfare recipients who face language or labour market barriers as "cheats," and in the distinction made between the so-called "deserving poor" and "undeserving poor."

The criminalization of poor, racialized people is but one dimension of the way in which neo-liberal ideology has reshaped our lives. The dismantling of the social state and the erasure of the economic state work in concert with the strengthening of the penal state to manage poverty in an era of mass joblessness and precarious employment (Wacquant, 2001, p. 404). The intense pursuit and surveillance of welfare recipients is, Wacquant (2001) argues, part of a broader trend by the state to warehouse, through criminalization and penalization, those who refuse to accept the precarious nature of wage labour. The public campaign against welfare fraud in Ontario is an example of how governments, in an era of neo-liberalism, no longer feel any discomfort in placing blame on targeted groups like immigrants and single mothers for their misfortune. Their poverty is blamed not on structural inequalities of the new marketplace, but on their own personal shortcomings in being unable to overcome the racism and sexism of the marketplace.

Case Workers: The Agents of Neo-liberal Policies

As frontline agents of the welfare system, case workers are often identified as the perpetrators of the racism which exists within the welfare system. The discussion of the changes in welfare policy in Section Two of this report, however, suggests that case workers' treatment of people on welfare must be situated within the broader context of policy changes that have occurred in the Canadian welfare system over the past ten years. Guided by neo-liberalism, state policy has focused on reducing social spending and challenging welfare "dependency." As Shields (2003, p. xxxi) notes, "welfare policy has been reshaped to encourage market dependence, while de-emphasizing any nurturing roles for the state." Studies have indicated that welfare workers themselves struggle with unreasonably high caseloads, poor resources, and unstable work environments. Morgen's interviews with welfare workers show, for example, that "workers commonly shared stories about themselves or coworkers who were on antidepressants or medications for anxiety, had taken unpaid 'stress leaves' or early retirement, or were seeking other jobs to escape the burdens of welfare work" (2001, p. 756).

Neo-liberal racism privatizes the discourse about race and focuses on individuals rather than groups. As a result, individual case workers are put in positions where they can exercise discretion and their racism appears to be merely an expression of their individual prejudice rather than of institutional discrimination.

CONCLUSION

Giroux argues that "racial discourse is not simply about private speech acts or individualized modes of communication … racist discourses and expressions should alert us to the workings of power and the conditions that make particular forms of language possible" (2003, pp. 204–5). Through interviews with racialized welfare recipients, this report serves to provide a systematic understanding of the ways in which racism structures welfare enforcement and control in Canada. As one respondent noted:

> The reason why I wanted to be part of this project is that I hope it gets written up in such a way that it is going to be used to confront the provincial government with some of their problems, or the problems with these systems. To actually show perhaps how visible minority groups, more than any other, feel the pain and carry the burden of being on [welfare], of being in a sense harassed. (ON3M)

REFERENCES

Anthias, F. (1998). The Limits of "Ethnic Diversity." *Patterns of Prejudice, 32(4)*, 6–19.

Barry, D.G. (2002). Neo-liberalizing Welfare: Politics and Information Technology in a New Era of Governance. In M. Pendakur and R. Harris (Eds.), *Citizenship and Participation in the Information Age*. Aurora, ON: Garamond Press.

Berger, P. (2001). Science Misapplied: Mandatory Addiction Screening and Treatment for Welfare Recipients in Ontario. *Canadian Medical Association Journal*, 164(4), 443–444.

Bobier, P. (1998). Privacy at Risk: Finger-scanning for ideology and profit. *Media Awareness Network*, Government Computer. Retrieved February 20, 2005, from http://www.mediaawareness.ca/eng/issues/priv/resource/govcomp.htm.

Carruthers, E. (1995). Prosecuting Women for Welfare Fraud in Ontario: Implications for Equality. *Journal of Law and Social Policy*, 11, 241–262.

Chan, W., and Mirchandani, K. (Eds.). (2002). *Crimes of Colour: Racialization and the Criminal Justice System in Canada*. Peterborough, ON: Broadview Press.

Cherlin, A., Bogen, K., Quane, J., and Burton, L. (2002, September). Operating within the Rules: Welfare Recipients' Experiences with Sanctions and Case Closings. *Social Service Review*, 76(3), 387–405.

Evanson, E., and Woods, R. (1995). *Poverty, Charity, and "Doing the Double."* Aldershot, U.K.: Avebury Press.

Fielding, N. (1993). Qualitative Interviewing. In N. Gilbert (Ed.), *Researching Social Life*. London: Sage.

Friedman, S.S. (1995). Beyond White and Other: Relationality and Narratives of Race in Feminist Discourse. *Signs* 21(1), 109–157.

Gilliom, J. (2001). *Overseers of the Poor: Surveillance, Resistance, and the Limits of Privacy*. Chicago: University of Chicago Press.

Giroux, H.A. (2003). Spectacles of Race and Pedagogies of Denial: Anti-Black Racist Pedagogy under Reign of Neo-liberalism. *Communication Education*, 52(3/4), 191–211.

Mandell, B. (2001). Welfare Reform: The War against the Poor. *New Politics*, 8(2), 1–23.

Martin, D.L. (1992). Passing the Buck: Prosecution of Welfare Fraud: Preservation of Stereotypes. *Windsor Yearbook of Access to Justice*, 12, 52–97.

Miles, R. (1989). *Racism*. London: Routledge.

Morgen, S. (2001). The Agency of Welfare Workers: Negotiating devolution, privatization, and the meaning of self-sufficiency. *American Anthropologist*, 103(3), 747–761.

Mosher, J. (2000). Managing the Disentitlement of Women: Glorifies Markets, the Idealized Family, and the Undeserving Other. In S. Neysmith (Ed.), *Restructuring Caring Labour: Discourse, State Practice, and Everyday Life*. Don Mills, ON: Oxford University Press.

Murray, H. (2000). Deniable Degradation: The Finger-Imaging of Welfare Recipients. *Sociological Forum*, 15(1), 39–63.

National Anti-poverty Association. (2002, October 17). Press release. Ottawa: National Anti-poverty Association.

Neubeck, K., and Cazenave, N. (2001). *Welfare Racism: Playing the Race Card against America's Poor*. New York and London: Routledge.

Neubeck, K., and Cazenave, N. (2002). Welfare Racism and Its Consequences. In F. Fox-Piven, M. Hallock, and S. Morgen (Eds.), *Work, Welfare, and Politics: Confronting Poverty in the Wake of Welfare Reform*. Portland: University of Oregon Press.

Pemberton, A. (1990). Discipline and Pacification in the Modern Administrative State: The Case of Social Welfare Fraud. *Journal of Sociology and Social Welfare*, 17(2), 125–142.

Quadagno, J. (1994). *The Color of Welfare: How Racism Undermined the War on Poverty*. New York: Oxford University Press.

Sales, R. (2002). The Deserving and the Undeserving? Refugees, Asylum Seekers, and Welfare in Britain. *Critical Social Policy*, 22(3), 456–478.

Seccombe, K., James, D., and Walters, K. (1998). They Think You Ain't Much of Nothing: The Social Construction of the Welfare Mother. *Journal of Marriage and the Family*, 60, 849–865.

Shields, J. (2003). *No Safe Haven: Markets, Welfare, and Migrants*. Toronto: Joint Centre of Excellence for Research on Immigration and Settlement (CERIS).

Sidel, R. (2000). The Enemy within: The Demonization of Poor Women. *Journal of Sociology and Social Welfare*, 27(1), 73–84.

Twight, C. (2002). *Dependent on D.C.: The Rise of Federal Control over the Lives of Ordinary Americans*. New York: Palgrave Press.

Wacquant, L. (2001). The Penalization of Poverty and the Rise of Neo-liberalism. *European Journal on Criminal Policy and Research*, 9, 401–412.

Zucchino, D. (1997). *Myth of the Welfare Queen*. New York: Scribner.

CHAPTER TWELVE

Data, Denials, and Confusion: The Racial Profiling Debate in Toronto

Scot Wortley and Julian Tanner

On 19 October 2002 the *Toronto Star* began publication of a series of articles on the controversial topic of race and crime. In addition to reviewing previous Canadian research on this issue, the *Star* provided its own, original analysis of data derived from the Toronto Police Service's Criminal Information Processing System (CIPS). The CIPS data set, received from the police through a freedom of information request, contains information on over 480,000 incidents in which an individual was either charged with a crime or ticketed for certain types of traffic offences.[1] The final data set is supposed to represent the *total population* of criminal charges (approximately 800,000) laid by the Toronto Police Service from "late" 1996 until "early 2002" (see Rankin, Quinn, Shephard, Simmie, and Duncanson 2002a).

The *Star*'s analysis revealed that black Torontonians are highly over-represented in certain charge categories—including drug possession. The *Star* maintains that this pattern of over-representation is consistent with the idea that the Toronto police engage in racial profiling (Rankin et al. 2002b). The *Star*'s analysis also reveals that blacks may be treated more harshly *after arrest* than their white counterparts. In particular, white offenders are more likely to be released at the scene, while black offenders are more likely to be detained and taken to the station for processing. Furthermore, once at the station, black offenders are much more likely than whites to be held in custody for a bail hearing. The *Star* maintains that these racial differences remain after other relevant legal factors have been taken into statistical account (Rankin et al. 2002a)

In response to the *Star* series, the Toronto police vehemently denied all allegations of racial bias. Chief Fantino declared that "[w]e do not do racial profiling ... There is no racism ... We don't look at, nor do we consider race or ethnicity, or any of that, as factors of how we dispose of cases, or individuals, or how we treat individuals" (quoted in "There Is No Racism" 2002: A14). Craig Brommel, president of the Police Association, stated in a news release that "[n]o racial profiling has ever been conducted by the Toronto Police Service and we question the *Toronto Star*'s interpretation of its statistical information" (quoted in Porter 2002: A6). These sentiments were echoed by several local politicians. Mayor Lastman, for example, declared that: "I don't believe that the Toronto police engage in racial profiling in any way, shape, or form. Quite the opposite, they're very sensitive to our different communities" (quoted in "Analysis" 2002: A9). Even Norm Gardiner, chair of Toronto's civilian—and supposedly non-partisan—police oversight board, claimed that he was confident that the Toronto police did not engage in racial profiling. In fact, he went so far as to suggest that the researchers involved in the *Star* series just wanted to stir up controversy during a period of excellent police-minority relations: "Some of the people involved, who keep on bringing this stuff up … they make a living out of social unrest" (quoted in "Analysis" 2002: A9).

Nonetheless, despite all of their denials, police officials provided no systematic critique of the *Star*'s analysis in the four months following the release of the race-crime series. Nor did they provide any new information that might challenge the racial-profiling hypothesis. All that changed, however, at a Police Services Board meeting held on 20 February 2003. On this occasion Chief Fantino produced his own "experts" on racial profiling, who subsequently slammed the *Star* report as being based on faulty research. Edward Harvey, the University of Toronto sociology professor hired by the police to conduct the re-analysis of the *Star* data, concluded that his "independent review results do not provide evidence of systemic racial profiling being practiced by the Toronto Police Service" (Harvey 2003; see also Granatstein 2003: 22). Lawyer Alan Gold added that "the *Star* articles are what we would call junk science" (Moloney 2003: A1). Although newspaper headlines the next day screamed that "allegations of racial profiling are junk science" and "Study finds races treated equally" (Blatchford 2003: A1), Harvey did not actually release his full report to the public until more than a month after his well-publicized presentation. This strategy served to prevent interested academics from commenting on his work in the immediate aftermath of his controversial statements. However, on the day of the presentation, the Police Service Web site did provide an "executive summary" of the Harvey report. This summary provided very few details about Harvey's actual re-analysis of the data, but it did include the following text:

> The *Star*'s allegations of systemic police bigotry, based upon claims of statistical disparity in the particular examples it has publicized, are scientifically unsound and an unfair selection of the available data. In a word they are bogus, bogus and bogus…. The truth is that the *Star*'s conclusions are simply false based upon the data that they had and the *Star*'s mistakes in considering the matter are fundamental, basic and simply embarrassing. Their whole project is fundamentally flawed. Their articles will enter the junk science hall of fame. ("Text" 2002: A19)

It is the purpose of this article to review—in detail—Edward Harvey's re-examination of the *Star* data and his conclusion that racial profiling does not exist in the Toronto area. It is our opinion that, in his report, Professor Harvey (1) does not properly define racial profiling and totally ignores the published criminological literature on this topic; (2) makes several incorrect and/or misleading statements designed to discredit the *Star*'s analysis; (3) engages in questionable "data-cleaning" procedures that may dramatically reduce racial disparities in the arrest statistics; (4) provides neither a transparent nor a complete re-analysis of the *Star*'s major findings; and (5) provides no concrete evidence that can disprove the *Star*'s allegations of racial bias. Indeed, many of the findings produced by Harvey are completely consistent with the racial-profiling argument. We conclude with a brief discussion of what this racial-profiling debate—a debate fought largely in the media rather than academic journals—could mean for the reputation of criminology in Canada.

RESEARCH ON RACIAL PROFILING

In his report, Professor Harvey claims to provide evidence that systematic racial profiling does not exist in the Toronto area (Harvey 2003: 39). In fact, Harvey does not actually examine racial-profiling data at all. Indeed, his entire report is based on an examination of the Toronto police *arrest* data set (CIPS). It is our contention that such arrest data are only produced *after racial profiling has already taken place*. In the criminological literature, racial profiling is said to exist when the members of certain racial or ethnic groups become subject to greater levels of criminal justice surveillance than others. Racial profiling, therefore, is typically defined as a racial disparity in police stop-and-search practices, racial differences in customs searches at airports and border crossings, increased police patrols in racial minority neighbourhoods and undercover activities, or sting operations that selectively target particular ethnic groups (see Weitzer and Tuch 2002; Meehan and Ponder 2002; Engel, Calnon, and Bernard 2002; Harris 1999). Racial profiling, therefore, is associated with racial bias in police investigation—not racial bias in arrest decisions or racial bias in police treatment after arrest. [...]

Do black people come under greater criminal justice surveillance than people from other racial backgrounds? Are black people more likely to be stopped, questioned, and searched by the police? Police data from both England (Bunyan 1999) and the United States (see Engel et al. 2002; Harris 1997) suggest that they are. In England, for example, the passage of the *Police and Criminal Evidence Act (PACE)* gave the police the authority to stop and search persons or vehicles on the reasonable suspicion that they would find drugs, stolen goods, or other prohibited items. However, the *PACE* legislation also mandated that the police make a written record of the racial background of all people who were subjected to police stops and searches. Police statistics from 1997–1998 reveal that black people were stopped and searched at a rate of 142 per 1,000 compared to 45 per 1,000 for Asians and 19 per 1,000 for whites. Overall, the English data suggest that blacks are approximately eight times more likely to be stopped and searched by police than whites (Bunyan 1999; Brown 1997).

Unfortunately, unlike England and the United States, the police in Canada are not required to record the race of the people they stop and/or search. Thus, official police statistics cannot be used to investigate the presence or absence of racial profiling in this country. However, a number of field studies have uncovered evidence that racial profiling may exist. For example, James (1998) conducted intensive interviews with over 50 black youth from southern Ontario. Many of these youths reported that being stopped by the police was a common occurrence for them. James concludes that the adversarial nature of these police stops contributes strongly to black youths' hostility towards the police. Neugebauer's (2000) interviews with 63 black and white teenagers from Toronto produced very similar results. Although the author found that teenagers from all racial backgrounds often complain about being hassled by the police, both white and black youth agreed that black males are much more likely to be stopped, questioned, and searched by the police than youths from other racial backgrounds.

Although these ethnographic studies provide great detail about police encounters and document the "lived experiences" of black youth, they are based on rather small, non-random samples. They thus risk being dismissed as anecdotal and not truly representative of police behaviour. However, similar evidence of racial profiling has been recently uncovered by two surveys that utilized much larger, random samples. To begin with, a 1994 survey of over 1,200 Toronto residents found that black people are much more likely to report involuntary police contact than either whites or Asians. For example, almost half (44%) of black male respondents reported that they had been stopped and questioned by the police at least once in the past two years, and one third (30%) reported that they had been stopped on two or more occasions. By contrast, only 12% of white males and 7% of Asian males reported multiple police stops. Multivariate analyses reveal that these racial differences in police contact cannot be explained by racial differences in social class, education, or other demographic variables (Wortley forthcoming; see also Commission on Systemic Racism 1995). In fact, two factors that seem to protect white males from police contact—age and social class—do not protect blacks. In general, whites with high incomes and education are much less likely to be stopped by the police than whites who score low on social class measures. By contrast, blacks with high incomes and education are actually more likely to be stopped than lower-class blacks. Black professionals, in fact, often attribute the attention they receive from the police to their relative affluence. As one black respondent stated, "If you are black and you drive something good, the police will pull you over and ask about drugs" (Wortley forthcoming).

* * * * *

These findings strongly suggest that racial profiling does, in fact, exist in Toronto. Our research further suggests that, due to racial profiling, black people are much more likely to be caught when they break the law than white people who engage in similar forms of criminal activity. For example, 65% of the black drug dealers in our high school study reported that they had been arrested at some time in their lives, compared to only 35% of the white drug dealers (Wortley and Tanner 2002). This finding is completely *consistent* with the fact, reported by the *Star*, that blacks are highly over-represented in drug-related arrests (Rankin et al. 2002a). It must be stressed that Harvey totally ignored these stop-and-search findings when writing his report—despite the fact that these studies were extensively covered by the *Toronto Star* as part of their investigative series on race and crime (see Rankin et al. 2002b; Quinn 2002; Moloney and Shephard 2002; Contenta 2002; Wortley 2002). The fact that Professor Harvey totally ignored previous Canadian, American, and British research on racial profiling is very difficult to explain. How could he come to a "no profiling" conclusion without examining all of the empirical evidence? At best, this situation *might* be viewed as unprofessional and reflecting a general ignorance of the academic literature on racial profiling. At worst, it might represent a deliberate attempt to mislead the public about the true nature of the racial-profiling debate. Nonetheless, we now turn to a critique of the analysis that Professor Harvey did conduct.

HARVEY'S "CLEANING" OF THE TORONTO ARREST DATA

Harvey begins his "independent analysis" of the police data set by noting that, in their original investigative report, "The *Toronto Star* generally did not provide specific information on its management of CIPS data and the analytic procedures used" (Harvey 2003: 5). We agree totally with this statement. The *Star*'s description of its data is rather vague and the newspaper provides very few details about the statistical analysis that was conducted in order to uncover evidence of racial bias in police treatment. The *Star* may have made an editorial decision not to present its multivariate analyses because they felt such advanced quantitative methods would go beyond the understanding of its readership. However, to our knowledge, the *Star* has never released any form of technical report to the public that might have better explained its methodology to interested social scientists. As Harvey notes, this makes it very difficult to evaluate the soundness of the *Star*'s analysis or replicate its findings.

Although we agree with Harvey's initial statement about the lack of transparency in the *Star*'s analysis, we fundamentally disagree with a number of other observations he makes about the police data. To begin with, Harvey complains that "as a database, CIPS was designed as an administrative tool to assist TPS officers in the conduct of their duties. It is not and was never intended to be a research database" (Harvey 2003: 10).[2] Harvey seems to be implying that this arrest data should never have been examined by the *Star* and that any conclusions drawn from such data are questionable. We believe that this statement is completely incorrect. Indeed, any cursory glance at the published literature in the social sciences—including history, political science, sociology, and criminology—would reveal that a great deal of research examines administrative or archival data that was not originally intended for research purposes. For example, many important court-processing studies—including research that examines racial and gender bias in bail decisions and sentencing—effectively use court records that were not originally designed for empirical analysis (see reviews in Bowling and Phillips 2002; Kellough and Wortley 2002; Cole 1999; Williams 1999; Roberts and Doob 1997; Mann 1993; Hood 1992). As long as arrest data are adequately described and subjected to appropriate analysis, there is absolutely no intrinsic problem with using them for research purposes.

* * * * *

After questioning whether the data should be used for research at all, Harvey states that he will, nonetheless, attempt to replicate the *Star*'s analysis. He begins by outlining the various "data-cleaning" procedures he utilized to prepare the data for analysis (see Harvey 2003: 10–13). Firstly, Harvey eliminated all cases with missing information. This is a perfectly acceptable social science practice. However, in our opinion, Harvey then engages in some very questionable "data-cleaning" procedures. For example, he eliminates all "multiple offenders" from the CIPS data. This strategy eliminates over half the completed cases from the offender data set (reducing it from 418,148 completed cases to 204,373). Harvey's only justification for dropping 213,775 "multiple offenders" from his analysis is that their inclusion "has the potential of skewing the data and biasing analytical outcomes" (Harvey 2003: 11). Although we do not understand this reasoning (advanced statistical analyses could easily control for multiple offenders), we do agree that excluding these offenders from the analysis could have a major impact on the results. Specifically it could greatly reduce the size of the racial disparities that emerge in the subsequent analysis.

Harvey first eliminates all offenders who were charged with a crime on more than one occasion during the six-year study period. In other words, if a person was charged with one crime in 1996 and another crime in 2002, s/he was automatically eliminated from the analysis (Harvey 2003: 11–13). However, if racial profiling exists—and black people do come under greater police surveillance than whites—we would expect that black people would have a much higher probability of being arrested on multiple occasions. Furthermore, by focusing exclusively on those who had been charged with a "single count" of a criminal offence, it appears that Harvey also eliminated those offenders who were charged with more than one crime during a specific arrest incident (Harvey 2003: 12). For example, if an offender was charged with both assault and drug possession at the time of their arrest, they were apparently left out of Harvey's investigation. Interestingly, previous research suggests that black people are much more likely to be charged with multiple crimes than whites—a phenomena referred to as over-charging (Commission on Systemic Racism 1995; Kellough and Wortley 2002). In sum, we feel that by eliminating multiple offenders, Professor Harvey likely excluded from his analysis the very population that experienced the greatest degree of police discrimination and thus reduced the extent of the racial disparities in his findings. If racial profiling exists, blacks should be greatly over-represented among multiple offenders.

While the *Star* focused on racial differences in arrest statistics at the aggregate level, Harvey decided to focus on racial differences at the division level. His only rationalization for this decision is that there are "extensive sociodemographic differences among the various TPS divisions" (Harvey 2003: 13). We can see no reason for not looking at the data at the divisional level. In fact, it might produce some interesting comparisons. However, we totally disagree with Harvey's decision to focus only on those divisions that have a black population of greater than 6% (see Harvey 2003: 20). Harvey justifies this decision by stating that the exclusion of divisions with less than 6% black population "is based on concerns about the validity of statistical analysis based on such small proportions" (Harvey 2003: 20). Importantly, we could not locate a single statistics manual or academic publication that would support this position—and Harvey does not provide a single reference to justify his argument. Furthermore, we must remember that the CIPS data set is not a random sample—it represents the total population of arrests made by the police from 1996 to 2002. It is, therefore, not subject to the normal statistical concerns related to probability theory. Secondly, Harvey's decision suffers from a basic methodological problem known as the *ecological fallacy*. He seems to assume that all offenders are arrested for crimes and charged with traffic offences in the very same areas that they live in. There is absolutely no evidence to support such a claim. Indeed, research suggests that people often travel outside of their neighbourhoods to engage in certain types of criminal behaviour—including prostitution and drug use (see Wortley, Fischer, and Webster 2002). In addition, it is logical to assume that many traffic charges are administered to citizens while they are travelling in their automobiles, some distance away from their home residences. Finally Harvey's exclusion of those police divisions with less than 6% black population totally ignores the previous research which supports the "out-of-place" hypothesis—the idea that minorities are actually treated more harshly by the police when they live in or venture into predominantly white neighbourhoods (see Meehan and Ponder 2002). In other words, Harvey's elimination of police divisions with small black populations—and his refusal to discuss the data at the aggregate level—may further reduce the size of the racial disparities revealed in his analysis. Nonetheless, despite Harvey's extremely questionable "data-cleaning" procedures, we ultimately feel that his results remain quite consistent with the *Star*'s conclusion that racial profiling exists.

INTERPRETING ARREST STATISTICS

The original *Star* analysis focused on racial differences with respect to four different types of offence: simple drug possession, cocaine possession, out-of-sight traffic offences, and violence (see Rankin et al. 2002a; 2002b; 2002c; 2002d). The over-representation of minorities in drug arrests has long been linked—both theoretically and empirically—to the racial-profiling debate (see Mauer 1999; Harris 1999; Harris 1997; Tonry 1995). Out-of-sight traffic offences (including driving without a licence, driving with a suspended licence, and driving without proper insurance) have also been linked to racial profiling. After all, such behaviours can only be discovered *after* the police have stopped and questioned a driver. Thus, racial differences in out-of-sight charges may reflect racial differences in police stop-and-search activities. This is particularly true when the police have not charged the driver with a moving violation like speeding or running a red light (violations that would justify the initial traffic stop). Although the *Star* articles also discuss black over-representation in violent crimes, Harvey decides not to focus on such arrests because they include too many multiple offenders (see Harvey 2003: 17). However, Harvey, does include both prostitution and impaired driving in his independent analysis—two offences that were not discussed by the *Star*. Harvey provides no justification for including these two new offences.[3]

Harvey's findings suggest that while blacks are over-represented in charges for simple drug possession, cocaine possession, and out-of-sight traffic offences, whites are over-represented in charges for both prostitution and impaired driving (Harvey 2003: 39). Harvey seems to suggest that white over-representation in certain crime categories constitutes proof that racial profiling does not exist. We disagree totally with this assessment. First of all, the fact that Harvey only focuses on police divisions with a greater than 6% black population completely distorts his analysis. Fortunately, Harvey actually does provide complete arrest data for all divisions—and a summary table for the entire city—in Appendix B of his report. This allows us to scrutinize his findings more closely.

TABLE 12.1

Selected Arrest Statistics for 42 Division, by Race of Offenders

OFFENCE CATEGORIES	% BLACK OFFENDERS	% BLACKS IN POPULATION	RATIO OF BLACK OFFENDERS/ BLACK POP-ULATION	% WHITE OFFENDERS	% WHITES IN POPULATION	RATIO OF WHITE OFFENDERS/ WHITE POP-ULATION
Out-of-sight traffic charges	42.9	10.9	3.936	36.1	39.8	0.907
Drug possession	23.3	10.9	2.138	50.6	39.8	1.271
Cocaine possession	41.0	10.9	3.761	48.7	39.8	1.224
Prostitution	6.7	10.9	0.615	60.4	39.8	1.518
Impaired driving	10.2	10.9	0.936	54.3	39.8	1.364

TABLE 12.2

Selected Arrest Statistics for 52 Division, by Race of Offenders

OFFENCE CATEGORIES	% BLACK OFFENDERS	% BLACKS IN POPULATION	RATIO OF BLACK OFFENDERS/ BLACK POP-ULATION	% WHITE OFFENDERS	% WHITES IN POPULATION	RATIO OF WHITE OFFENDERS/ WHITE POP-ULATION
Out-of-sight traffic charges	29.7	4.2	7.071	50.7	69.4	0.731
Drug possession	15.8	4.2	3.762	73.4	69.4	1.058
Cocaine possession	17.0	4.2	4.048	73.0	69.4	1.052
Prostitution	12.2	4.2	2.905	66.9	69.4	0.964
Impaired driving	5.9	4.2	1.405	74.8	69.4	1.078

TABLE 12.3

Selected Arrest Statistics for All Police Divisions, by Race of Offenders

OFFENCE CATEGORIES	% BLACK OFFENDERS	% BLACKS IN POPULATION	RATIO OF BLACK OFFENDERS/ BLACK POP- ULATION	% WHITE OFFENDERS	% WHITES IN POPULATION	RATIO OF WHITE OFFENDERS/ WHITE POP- ULATION
Out-of-sight traffic charges	34.3	8.1	4.235	51.8	62.7	0.826
Drug possession	24.3	8.1	3.000	63.3	62.7	1.010
Cocaine possession	29.6	8.1	3.654	61.2	62.7	0.976
Prostitution	11.9	8.1	1.496	68.1	62.7	1.086
Impaired driving	7.0	8.1	0.864	73.6	62.7	1.174

Tables 12.1 through 12.3 present arrest statistics from the City of Toronto. These data were drawn directly from Appendix B of Harvey's report. In order to illustrate the extent of racial over-representation, we calculated a ratio statistic by dividing the percentage of blacks and whites in the various charge categories by their percentage in the total population. Table 12.1 provides the arrest figures for 42 Division—one of the divisions Harvey focuses on because it has a relatively large black population. Consistent with Harvey's conclusions, the statistics from this division reveal that blacks are indeed over-represented in the drug possession and out-of-sight traffic offences, while whites are over-represented in both prostitution and impaired driving charges. However, what Harvey fails to discuss in his report is the fact that the level of black over-representation in drug and out-of-sight traffic offences is much greater than the level of white over-representation for either prostitution or impaired driving. For example, our calculations reveal that blacks are almost 4 times over-represented in out-of-sight driving offences, 3.8 times over-represented in cocaine possession, and 2.1 times over-represented in simple drug possession. By contrast, whites are only 1.5 times over-represented in prostitution offences and 1.4 times over-represented in impaired driving charges. It is, therefore, difficult to understand how Harvey could imply that these figures cancel each other out and prove that racial profiling does not exist.

The situation gets more problematic when we examine those divisions that Harvey deliberately dropped from his analysis. Table 12.2, for example, presents data from 52 Division—an area of the city with a relatively small black population. In our opinion, this is a very important division to include in the analysis because it incorporates much of the downtown core. It is the heart of Toronto's business, shopping, and entertainment district. Thus, while only 4% of the permanent residents of this area are black, it is logical to assume that many more blacks regularly travel to this area of the city to work, shop, and seek entertainment (including sports events, nightclubs, restaurants, and the theatre). Interestingly, data from this division indicate that blacks are over-represented in all five offence categories—including prostitution and impaired driving. This finding totally contradicts Harvey's conclusions. Furthermore, the ratios suggest that blacks are even more over-represented in police divisions with low black populations than in divisions in which they make up a larger proportion of the total population. For example, while blacks are approximately four times over-represented in out-of-sight traffic offences for 42 Division (Table 12.1), they are more than seven times over-represented in this offence category for 52 Division (Table 12.2). This finding is consistent with the idea that blacks are treated more harshly by the police when they venture into predominantly white areas.

Table 12.3 presents arrest data for Toronto at the aggregate level. It includes statistics for all police divisions. These data clearly indicate that Harvey's final conclusions are both misleading and inaccurate. First of all, contrary to Harvey's statements, blacks are actually overrepresented with respect to prostitution charges. Importantly, blacks are more over-represented (1.5 times) in this offence category than whites (1.1 times). Additional analysis reveals that impaired driving is, in fact, the only offence category in which blacks are under-represented and whites over-represented. However, it must be stressed again that the degree of black over-representation in drug and out-of-sight offences is much greater than the degree of white over-representation in impaired driving charges. Indeed, blacks are 4.2 times over-represented in out-of-sight traffic offences, 3.7 times over represented in cocaine charges, and 3.0 times over-represented with respect to simple drug possession. By contrast, whites are only slightly over-represented (1.2 times) in impaired driving arrests.

Clearly these findings do not in any way disprove the existence of racial profiling. Indeed, researchers have long argued that black over-representation in both drug offences and out-of-sight traffic violations is completely consistent with the racial-profiling hypothesis. Experts maintain, for example, that drug offenses are often discovered by the police when they engage in racially biased stop-and-search tactics. This argument is supported by survey research that consistently reveals that although blacks are over-represented in drug arrests, whites actually have higher rates of illegal drug use (see Tonry 1995; Mauer 1999). By contrast, neither prostitution nor impaired driving arrests have been theoretically linked to racial profiling. For example, prostitution arrests are often made during sting operations in which prostitutes or their clients must approach and communicate their intentions to undercover police officers (see Wortley et al. 2002). In other words, prostitution is rarely uncovered by police stop-and-search practices. Similarly, impaired driving charges often result from RIDE programs in which all drivers—regardless of their race—are stopped and questioned. This is not to say that Harvey's findings actually prove that racial profiling exists. We feel that more data—including official police statistics on stop-and-search practices—are needed before such a conclusion can be reached. However, we do feel that Harvey's findings are completely consistent with the idea that racial profiling may be a problem in the Toronto area. Harvey's manipulation and interpretation of the CIPS data only serves to mask this reality and deflect charges of racial bias.

POLICE TREATMENT AFTER ARREST

The *Toronto Star* also used the CIPS data set to examine the treatment of offenders by the police after they had been charged with a crime. The *Star* found that for simple drug possession (over 10,000 cases), blacks were less likely to be released at the scene (61.8%) than their white counterparts (76.5%). Of those taken to the station for processing, blacks (15.5%) were held for a bail hearing at twice the rate of whites (7.7%). The *Star* maintains that if the drug in question was cocaine (over 2000 cases), the police treatment of blacks became even harsher. For example, only 41.5% of blacks charged with cocaine possession were released at the scene, compared to 63% of whites charged with the same offence. Similarly, over 40% of blacks charged with one count of cocaine possession were held for a bail hearing, compared to only 20% of their white counterparts. The *Star* maintains that these racial differences in police treatment persist after statistically controlling for other relevant factors—including the offender's criminal history, age, employment status, immigration status, and whether or not the suspect had a permanent home address (see Rankin et al. 2002a).

In his report, Harvey argues that the *Star's* analysis is not transparent and that his re-analysis of the CIPS data reveals no evidence of racial bias in police treatment. It is interesting to note that in his 156-page report (including appendices) Harvey devotes only a half page to this important issue. In fact, we feel that Harvey's re-analysis of the *Star's* treatment data is so poorly done and incomplete that we have reproduced the entire section of the report below. Harvey writes,

> In its reporting on possession of cocaine, the *Toronto Star* states, "If the drug was cocaine, the treatment was tougher: 63 percent of Whites were released at the scene but only 41.5% of Blacks." Using the cleaned-up CIPS database, I re-analysed the numbers controlling for a number of factors available in the CIPS database. These factors are: CIPS, MANIX, BAIL, PROBATION, PREVIOUS CONVICTION, TAP PAROLE, WARRANT. The purpose of these controls was to come up with a population of Blacks and a population of Whites who were "clean" with respect to police records and the criminal justice system. Put in plain language, I wanted to ensure I was comparing "apples" with "apples." This analysis revealed no difference in the "release-at scene" (Form 9) rates for Blacks and Whites. The rate for Blacks was 74.0% and the rate for Whites was 74.3%. (Harvey 2003: 36–37)

That is all that Harvey has to say about the matter. In our opinion, this is a totally misleading attempt to discredit the *Star's* analysis. First of all, by stating that he has controlled for "a number of factors available in the CIPS database," Harvey suggests that he has actually conducted a multivariate analysis. However, he does not directly discuss the multivariate procedures that he has employed, nor does he present his results in tabular form. Harvey goes on to identify the names of the variables that he has apparently taken into statistical account. However, he does not provide any definitions for these variables—a tactic that can only serve to confuse the reader. Finally, Harvey suggests that he has eliminated all offenders with any kind of criminal history from his analysis. It is among this group that he apparently finds no evidence of racial bias in the release decision. However, Harvey does not exactly define what he means by offenders who are "clean" with respect to police records and the criminal justice system. Has he only eliminated those offenders with previous criminal convictions—or has he eliminated all offenders with a previous record of arrest or other form of contact with the justice system? It is unclear. Importantly, Harvey does not disclose how many of the original 2000-plus cocaine offenders remain after he has eliminated those with a criminal history. What is his final sample? We suspect that his selective "cleaning" procedures may have greatly reduced the total number of offenders in his analysis and consequently rendered his findings meaningless. Finally, we find it particularly disturbing that Harvey blasts the *Star* for lack of transparency, then produces his own analysis which is equally—if not more—vague and difficult to follow.

* * * * *

It is clear that the debate concerning racial bias in police treatment after arrest cannot be resolved with the current data provided by either the *Toronto Star* or Professor Harvey. What is required is a properly reported multivariate analysis—perhaps a series of logistic regression models—that would investigate whether race is a significant predictor of both the release and the bail decision, after other relevant legal factors have been taken into statistical account. Such a procedure would simultaneously control for variables like criminal record and current charges, without eliminating multiple offenders and artificially reducing the size of the data set. Such an approach would also permit us to examine whether blacks with a criminal record are treated differently than whites with a similar criminal history. To our knowledge, such standard analyses have not yet been conducted.

DISCUSSION

As our above review suggests, Harvey's re-analysis of the CIPS database is plagued with both methodological issues and problems of interpretation. Unfortunately, critics of Harvey's report have not yet had a full opportunity to discuss these issues in the public arena. They were supposed to be given that opportunity at a special meeting of Toronto's Police Services Board on 28 April 2003—more than two months after Harvey originally presented his findings. However, a coalition of minority organizations actually walked out of this meeting after learning that the Board would only give them five minutes to respond to Harvey's report and his conclusion that the police do not engage in racial profiling (see Lakey and Duncanson 2003: A1). Harvey and his colleagues, incidentally, were given over two hours to present their results to the very same Police Services Board (Blatchford 2003: A1).

In the meantime, social science in general—and the discipline of criminology in particular—has taken a beating over its part in the racial-profiling debate. Most damaging are accusations that social scientists can be hired to provide support for any side of an argument. This sentiment was perhaps best expressed by Councillor Gloria Luby—the vice-chair of the Toronto Police Services Board. In response to the *Star's* analysis, Luby claimed that statistics can be used to prove anything (see "Analysis" 2002: A9). We obviously disagree with this argument. However, we strongly believe that, under ideal circumstances, statistical analyses of sensitive issues (like racial profiling) should be subject to intensive review by academic experts *before the figures are released to the public*. This is why academic journals usually adopt a strict peer-review process that ensures the basic integrity of published research. Clearly, such a system of quality control has not been applied to media discussions of racial profiling.

Almost as damaging to the reputation of criminology are accusations that research can actually cause social problems. Chief Fantino expressed this opinion when he was initially asked to comment on the *Star's* investigation: "It seems that … no matter what honest efforts people make, there are always those who are intent on causing trouble. Obviously this (story) is going to do exactly that" (quoted in "There Is No Racism" 2002: A14). Consistent with this view, Fantino recently dismissed community attempts to further discuss the racial-profiling issue as "mischief-making" (Lakey and Duncanson 2003: A20). Councillor Luby expanded on this theme when she stated that "we've been getting along quite well. Police discrimination has not been an issue. So why should it suddenly become one? Because the *Star* did this research?" (quoted in "Analysis" 2002: A9). The argument seems to be that studies that document racism within the justice system do more harm than good. That public discussion of evidence of racism creates distrust, damages relationships with specific minority communities, and lowers morale among criminal justice personnel ("There Is No Racism" 2002: A14). We could not disagree more. Good, objective social research does not create social problems—it merely documents them. Research has not caused the apparent problems that exist between certain racial minority groups and the police. It has only documented a situation that already exists. The discomfort of having to talk about racism—and deal with it in the policy arena—should not be used as an excuse to prevent further research in this area.

In conclusion, it is clear that the controversy over the issue of racial profiling is far from over. It is also clear that the criminology community must take a much more active role in this debate. We must provide more detailed commentary on the research than has already been conducted—and demand that research funds be set aside to conduct more thorough investigations of this phenomenon. Most importantly, we must vigorously defend our right to examine sensitive topics and conduct research that may not coincide with the interests of major players within the criminal justice system.

ENDNOTES

1. It is very unclear which "traffic offences" are included in the CIPS data set. Although the data do not seem to have information on speeding tickets or other moving violations, they do contain information on such out-of-sight offences as driving without a licence and driving without insurance.

2. Harvey used "TPS" to refer to the "Toronto Police Service."

3. Why did Harvey focus on prostitution and impaired driving? Why did Harvey not focus on other types of crime—like theft, vandalism, and car theft? We suspect that he purposely tried to identify crimes that would show an over-representation of white offenders.

REFERENCES

Analysis raises board hackles. 2002 *Toronto Star*. October 20: A9.

Blatchford, Christie 2003 Fantino report says allegations of racial profiling are "junk science"—Study finds races treated equally. *National Post*, February 21: A1.

Bowling, Ben and Coretta Phillips 2002 *Racism, Crime, and Justice*. London: Pearson Education.

Brown, David 1997 *PACE Ten Years on: A Review of the Research*. London: Home Office.

Bunyan, Tony 1999 The cycle of UK racism: Stop and search, arrest and imprisonment. *Statewatch* 9: 1–4.

Cole, David 1999 *No Equal Justice: Race and Class in the American Criminal Justice System*. New York: New Press.

Commission on Systemic Racism 1995 *Report of the Commission on Systemic Racism in the Ontario Criminal Justice System*. Toronto: Queen's Printer for Ontario.

Contenta, Sando 2002 U.K. to target police racism: Study finds blacks more likely to be searched. *Toronto Star*, November 8: A1.

Engel, Robin Shepard, Jennifer M. Calnon, and Thomas J. Bernard 2002 Theory and racial profiling: Shortcomings and future directions in research. *Justice Quarterly* 19(2): 249–273.

Granatstein, Rob 2003 Police study slams report. *Toronto Sun*, February 21: 22.

Harris, David 1997 Driving while black and all other traffic offences: The Supreme Court and pretextual traffic stops. *Journal of Criminal Law and Criminology* 87: 544–582.

Harris, David 1999 The stories, the statistics, and the law: Why "driving while black" matters. *Minnesota Law Review* 84: 265–326.

Harvey, Edward 2003 An Independent Review of the Toronto Star Analysis of Criminal Information Processing System (CIPS) Data Provided by the Toronto Police Service (TPS). Report available on the Toronto Police Service Web site. http://www.torontopolice.on.ca.

Hood, Roger 1992 *Race and Sentencing: A Study in the Crown Court.* Oxford: Clarendon Press.

James, Carl 1998 "Up to no good": Black on the streets and encountering police. In Victor Satzewich (ed.), *Racism and Social Inequality in Canada: Concepts, Controversies, and Strategies of Resistance.* Toronto: Thompson.

James, Royson 2001 Why I fear for my sons. *Toronto Star,* October 21: A1.

Kellough, Gail and Scot Wortley 2002 Remand for plea: The impact of race, pre-trial detention and over-charging on plea bargaining decisions. *British Journal of Criminology* 42(1): 186–210.

Lakey, Jack and John Duncanson 2003 Groups walk out at race-crime summit. *Toronto Star,* April 29: A1.

Mann, C.R. 1993 *Unequal Justice: A Question of Color.* Bloomington: Indiana University Press.

Mauer, Marc 1999 *Race to Incarcerate.* New York: New Press.

Meehan, Albert and Michael Ponder 2002 Race and place: The ecology of racial profiling African-American motorists. *Justice Quarterly* 19: 399–429.

Moloney, Paul 2003 Police attack *Star's* race articles. *Toronto Star,* February 21: A1.

Moloney, Paul and Michelle Shephard 2002 Summit urged on police arrests. *Toronto Star,* October 21: A1.

Neugebauer, Robynne 2000 Kids, cops, and colour: The social organization of police-minority youth relations. In Robynne Neugebauer (ed.), *Criminal Injustice: Racism in the Criminal Justice System.* Toronto: Canadian Scholars' Press.

Porter, Catherine 2002 Police union blasts *Star. Toronto Star,* October 22: A6.

Quinn, Jennifer 2002 New Jersey shooting spurred real reform. *Toronto Star,* October 21: A6.

Rankin, Jim, Jennifer Quinn, Michelle Shephard, Scott Simmie, and John Duncanson 2002a Singled out: An investigation into race and crime. *Toronto Star,* October 19: A1.

Rankin, Jim, Jennifer Quinn, Michelle Shephard, Scott Simmie, and John Duncanson 2002b Police target black drivers. *Toronto Star,* October 20: A1.

Rankin, Jim, Jennifer Quinn, Michelle Shephard, Scott Simmie, and John Duncanson 2002c Black crime rates highest. *Toronto Star,* October 26: A1.

Rankin, Jim, Jennifer Quinn, Michelle Shephard, Scott Simmie, and John Duncanson 2002d Life and death on mean streets. *Toronto Star,* October 27: A1.

Roberts, Julian, and Anthony Doob 1997 Race, ethnicity, and criminal justice in Canada. In Michael Tonry (ed.), *Ethnicity, Crime, and Immigration: Comparative and Cross-National Perspectives,* Vol. 21. Chicago: University of Chicago Press.

Tanner, Julian and Scot Wortley 2003 *The Toronto Youth Crime and Victimization Survey: Overview Report.* Toronto: Centre of Criminology.

Text from Toronto Police Service Web site 2002 *Toronto Star,* February 21: A19

There is no racism. We do not do racial profiling 2002 *Toronto Star,* October 19: A14

Tonry, Michael 1995 *Malign Neglect: Race, Crime, and Punishment in America.* New York: Oxford University Press.

Weitzer, Ronald and Steven Tuch 2002 Perceptions of racial profiling: Race, class, and personal experience. *Criminology* 40: 435–456.

Williams, Toni 1999 Sentencing black offenders in the Ontario criminal justice system. In J.V. Roberts and D.P. Cole (eds.), *Making Sense of Sentencing.* Toronto: University of Toronto Press.

Wortley, Scot 2002 Profiling one source of alienation: Both sides of debate get support in recent survey. *Toronto Star*, November 25: B1.

Wortley, Scot Forthcoming. The usual suspects: Race, police contact, and perceptions of criminal injustice. *Criminology.*

Wortley, Scot, B. Fischer, and C. Webster 2002 Vice lessons: A survey of prostitution offenders enrolled in the Toronto John school diversion program. *Canadian Journal of Criminology* 44(4): 369–402.

Wortley, Scot and Julian Tanner 2002 November 28 The good, the bad, and the profiled: Race, deviant activity, and police stop and search practices. Paper presented at the University of Toronto Faculty of Law Conference on Systemic Racism in the Criminal Justice System, Toronto.

CHAPTER THIRTEEN

Delinquency of Asian Youth in Canada

Siu-ming Kwok and Dora Mei-Ying Tam

The purpose of this article is twofold: (1) to review the literature on delinquency of Asian youth in North America, and (2) to identify the areas for future research with respect to Asian delinquency in Canada.

Research on the delinquency of Asian youth and their experience with the criminal justice system is surprisingly limited (Zhang, 1993) within the North American and especially the Canadian literature. This paucity of literature is curious given that the cultural contexts of Asians are markedly different from other ethnic groups (Wong, 1997, 1998, 1999, 2000; Zhang, 1993); Asians are one of the fastest-growing populations in the United States, and Asians are the largest ethnic minority in Canada (Statistics Canada, 2000).

DEFINITION OF ASIAN AND DELINQUENT BEHAVIOURS

Definition of "Asian"

Asian refers to those who come from East Asia (i.e., People's Republic of China, Taiwan, Hong Kong, Japan, and Korea) and Southeast Asia (i.e., Vietnam, Cambodia, and Laos). Not included in this review are populations from South Asia (e.g., India and Pakistan), other parts of Southeast Asia (e.g., the Philippines, Indonesia, and Thailand) and West Asia (e.g., Iran). The criteria used to select the countries to be assumed under the term "Asians" included previous research studies, as well as the cultural context and practice of social service providers.

The use of this definition was evident in most studies. Many studies distinguished between Asian/East Asian populations that included the People's Republic of China, Hong Kong, Taiwan, Japan, and Korea (Song, 1988; Wang, 1994), and those that identified the populations from India and Pakistan as South Asians (Bagley, 1972). However, some research defines "Asian" as both East Asians and Southeast Asians (Adlaf, Smart, & Tan, 1989; Barnes & Welte, 1986).

Several common characteristics between East Asian and Southeast Asian ethnic groups emerged despite their diversity in linguistic and cultural backgrounds. For example, trends of lower crime, delinquency, and other deviances were identified compared to other ethnic groups (Wong, 2000). Moreover, East and Southeast Asia, in particular China, Japan, Korea, and Vietnam, have long been under the influence of Confucianism, which is keen on conformity, family solidarity, maintaining harmonious relationship, and respect for authority, particularly the unconditional respect for parents or filial piety (Fong, 1973). Perhaps, it is an overgeneralization to assume that all East and Southeast Asians would accept and follow all these cultural traditions. There is, however, evidence that this cultural explanation is still viewed as important in interpreting research findings; that is, it is used to account for the differences found between the Asian groups and those from other ethnic backgrounds (Chin, 1996; Wong, 1997, 1998, 1999, 2000; Zhang, 1993).

In cities with high percentage of Asian populations (e.g., San Francisco), social service providers use the term "Asian" to cover East Asians and Southeast Asians as well, and people from India and Pakistan should be considered South Asians (Ja & Aoke, 1993). Statistics Canada also uses the term "South Asian" (e.g., Indians, Pakistanis) to distinguish these populations from Southeast Asian (e.g., Vietnamese, Cambodians, and Laos), Chinese, Japanese, and Koreans (Statistics Canada, 2001).

Defining Delinquent Behaviours

The term "delinquent behaviours" is less controversial in the research literature and covers behaviours ranging from stealing to physical assault as outlined from major research studies such as the Rochester Youth Development Study (Thornberry, Lizotte, Krohn, Farnworth, & Jang, 1991), the National Youth Survey (Elliott, Huizinga, & Ageton, 1985), and the Denver Youth Survey (Huizinga, Esbensen, & Weiher, 1991). Here delinquent behaviours refer to those law-breeding behaviours/crimes which are outlined under the Canadian Criminal Code and adopted under the Young Offenders Act of Canada (YOA), or the proposed Youth Criminal Justice Act of Canada.

SIGNIFICANCE OF STUDIES ON DELINQUENCY OF ASIAN YOUTH

Distinctiveness of Studies on Asian Delinquency

Numerous researchers have proposed the necessity of using a "minority model" in the study of visible minority children. The reason propelling the use of such a model is that the stresses in the developmental process for ethnically minority children is not exactly the same as those for children within the ethnic majority (Coll et al., 1996; Gonzales & Cauce, 1995). Examples of stress faced by youth from visible minorities include a disadvantaged minority status, such as discrimination in school and biases from the criminal justice system, and acculturation stress and strains within the larger society. Moreover, Asian youth have some unique stressors to face in addition to those commonly shared with other ethnic minority youth. Each of these categories of stressors will be reviewed separately.

1. DISADVANTAGED MINORITY STATUS

Findings of some researchers suggest that a disadvantaged minority status is a significant stressor (Vega & Rumbaut, 1991), particularly for youths as they are more likely to encounter discrimination and racial prejudices (Gonzales & Cauce, 1995). Problems within Asian communities to which these youths belong can aggravate the stress that marginality causes. These problems include lack of status, political power, economic opportunity, and discrimination from law enforcement officers (Hunt, Joe, & Waldorf, 1997; Song, 1988). There has been a long history of discrimination, unfair treatment, exploitation, and oppression of the Asians in North America (Li, 1988; Wong, 1999). Such treatment is a likely source of stress that can impact delinquent behaviours (Go, 1998; Wong, 1999).

On the other hand, other researchers have found that social and economic disadvantages do not necessarily translate into increased behavioural deviance. There are studies which found that Asian youth, especially the Chinese, were less involved in delinquency and other behavioural deviances than the general youth population (Chi, Kitano, & Lubben, 1988; Li & Rosenblood, 1994; Pogrebin & Poole, 1989).

Some researchers such as Toy (1992) have attempted to explain this contradictory evidence through concepts such as the resiliency of children and of their ethnocultural backgrounds. Toy argues that a disadvantaged status due to ethnic minority membership creates stress and strains for such youth, but that their psychological strength, strong commitment to family, and other cultural factors may serve as buffers and mitigate some of the stress experienced.

2. ACCULTURATION STRAIN

Pressures of adapting to a new culture are more pronounced for the ethnic minority youth than for younger or older persons. These youth may experience daily conflict and stress as they discover that their cultural values and behaviours at home are not recognised or valued among peers or at school. They often encounter among their peers a wide range of values and cultural orientations that may conflict with and challenge the values and expectations of their parents (Go, 1998; Gonzales & Cauce, 1995; Kelley & Tseng, 1992). Such cultural conflicts with the parents were strongly related to the delinquent behaviours among Asian youth (Wong, 2000).

3. DIFFERENCES BETWEEN ASIAN AND OTHER ETHNIC YOUTH

Despite the stress shared among all ethnic minorities when faced with the ethnic majority in a society, some aspects of Asian delinquency were found to be unique, such as their pathway to delinquency and their coping strategies with the criminal justice system. In a study among high school students in the United States, Harberth (1999) found that the delinquent behaviours of Asian youth often went undetected, whereas youths from African or Hispanic ethnic backgrounds readily received attention from schoolteachers. In another study, Zhang (1993) found that parents of Asian delinquents differed from African parents in their strategies for coping with the criminal justice system.

The Growing Asian Population in North America

The proportion of Asian immigrants in the United States and Canada has increased over the past few decades. In the U.S., the Asian population increased by 128 per cent, from 1.5 million to 3.5 million, between 1970 and 1980 (Trimble, Padilla, & Bell, 1987). In 1990 the population of Asian/Pacific Islanders exceeded 7.2 million (Rosenblatt, 1996). It has been estimated that the population of Asian/Pacific Islanders in the United States is increasing at a rate of 380,000 per annum, including 235,000 immigrants (Rosenblatt, 1996). In spite of the population statistics documenting that Asians are a growing segment of the American society, very little is known about delinquent behaviours within this sector.

In Canada, the number of immigrants arriving from Asian destinations has also increased substantially over the past two decades. Immigrants from Asian countries such as Hong Kong, Taiwan, the People's Republic of China, and Korea represented 25 per cent of all immigrants who came to Canada between 1997 and 1999 (Statistics Canada, 2000). Moreover, these Asian immigrants tended to be young with approximately one-quarter under 15 years old (Statistics Canada, 1997). Given this surge in the numbers of the Asian sector in both Canada and the United States, it is difficult to understand the lack of attention to this population within the research literature in general and the study of delinquency among Asian youths in particular.

Despite research findings that indicate lower crime rates among Asian youths, there remains a strong concern or perception among the general public that crime among Asian youths is rampant.

Prevalence of Asian Delinquency and the Concerns of Public of Asian Gangs

With the exception of a few studies (Barnes & Welte, 1986; Murray, Perry, O'Connel, & Schmid, 1987; Wong, 1997), there has been a paucity of research concerning the delinquency rates for Asians.

The Asian gang problem has been characterised as small in comparison with the overall gang problem (McCurrie, 1999). However, public perception of crimes committed by "Asian" youth gangs in both the United States and Canada continues despite this finding. Although youth gangs are not unique to contemporary society, the prevalence and diversity of Asian gangs that emerged in the late 1980s and early 1990s has spurred public interest and concerns in the United States (U.S. Senate, 1992). Recently, the same concerns have surfaced in Canada (Wittmeier, 1999).

The media has been named a primary source of rising concerns about this problem as they have been keenly interested in youth gang activities, especially among Asian youths (Fasiolo & Leckie, 1993; Smith & Tarallo, 1995). In a study on the coverage of gang stories in Canadian print media, Fasiolo and Leckie (1993) found that the most frequently cited type of gang affiliation was the Asian gang. Most of these stories did not mention potential causes of these delinquent behaviours.

Regardless of the reasons underlying the concerns of Asian delinquency, law enforcement officers tend to act upon these public anxieties (Wittmeier, 1999). The level of tolerance for youth crimes has decreased over the past two decades, which has impacted the youth justice system in North America and the number of youths involved with this system.

ASIAN DELINQUENCY IN EXISTING LITERATURE

Most studies on the causes of delinquency were mainly focused on the social- psychological and cultural context, whereas the involvement of delinquent youth with criminal justice system was mainly studied in the political context of racial discrimination.

Social-Psychological Context

The social control theory of Travis Hirschi and Edwin Sutherland's theory of differential association were the two dominant social psychological perspectives on deviant behaviours found in the contemporary delinquency literature (Marcos, Bahr, & Johnson, 1986; Massey & Krohn, 1996; Warr & Stafford, 1991).

Social bonding theory focuses on the role of social institutions and institutional relationships in constraining deviant behaviours. These constraining institutions usually revolve around family relationships and school involvement. The theory suggests that when any element of the social bond is weakened, the probability of involvement in delinquent behaviours is increased (Massey & Krohn, 1996).

In general, research findings support the social bonding theory in regards to the relationship between family relationship and Asian delinquency. In a comparison study (N = 62) of Japanese-American delinquents and non-delinquents in California, Kitano (1973) found that Japanese-American delinquent boys had weak attachment to their families. They were less subject to discipline by their parents, were less obedient, spent less time, and had less communication with their parents. In a qualitative study conducted in Boston, Kendis and Kendis (1976) noted that Chinese delinquents were detached from their parents and tended to be peer-oriented. They had difficulty mastering the Chinese language and found communication with their parents and other family members difficult and bothersome. In a study on New York Chinatown, Sheu (1986) found Chinese delinquents had tense relationships with their family members.

More recent studies have also provided evidence to support the relationship between a weak attachment to family and delinquency. In an unpublished doctoral dissertation, Wang (1994) found that delinquent behaviours among Asian high school students (N = 358) in the United States were negatively correlated with parental supervision. In another unpublished doctoral dissertation, Go (1998) found that delinquent behaviours among Southeast Asian high school students (N = 106) in California were correlated with the time spent with their parents and the conflicts within the family. In a Canadian qualitative study of 13 Chinese juvenile gang members in Vancouver, Joe and Robinson (1980) reported that the lack of parental supervision, the absence of traditional Chinese extended kinship group[s], and conflict relationship with family members were among the most probable explanations of ganging and delinquent behaviours. In a community survey of 315 Chinese adolescents in Winnipeg, Wong (2000) found that there was evidence to support that the less the parental supervision and communication the parents had with the children, the more likely the children would demonstrate delinquent behaviours.

Further research findings lend support to the social bonding theory when the association between weak school attachment and delinquent behaviours are considered (Chin, 1996; Go, 1998; Harberth, 1999; Sayasane, 2000; Sheu, 1986; Wang, 1994, 1995; Vigil & Yun, 1996). However, these findings must be qualified by the observation that schoolteachers usually paid less attention to the school and behavioural problems of Asian youth than youth from other ethnic backgrounds (Harberth, 1999). Potential explanations for this phenomenon were the stereotyping of Asian students as hardworking and having fewer troubles at school (Toupin, 1991; Wong, 1999).

The strongest predictor of delinquent behaviour identified in the research was negative peer influence as defined in the differential association theory (Marcos, Bahr, & Johnson, 1986). Association with delinquent peers was positively related to delinquency of Asian youth. Similar results were found in studies on delinquent behaviours of Asian high school students (Wang, 1994, 1995), gang members (Sayasane, 2000; Song, Dombrink, & Geis, 1992), and young offenders in prison (Kitano, 1973). In other words, youths who had more delinquent friends were more likely to be involved in delinquent behaviours.

Some researchers attempted to combine the two theories to explain the delinquency of Asian youth (Toy, 1992; Wang, 1994; Wong, 1999): the failure of constraining social institutions on the youths made them more vulnerable to the influence of delinquent peers. Several research studies on Asian gangs found that youths who had family and school problems were more likely to be targeted and recruited by gangs (Hunt, Joe, & Waldorf, 1997; Toy, 1992). Cultural explanations have also been used in the literature to account for the delinquent behaviours of youths with the level of acculturation and cultural conflicts with the family as important variables.

Cultural Context

Studies have shown that delinquency is related to acculturation: those who detach themselves from their ethnic culture and identify themselves more to the mainstream culture are more likely to engage in delinquency. In a study of Japanese-American delinquency in California prisons, Kitano (1973) found that delinquent boys had fewer Japanese friends; fewer preferred ethnic activities and fewer Japanese customs. Hisame (1980) found that Asian-American children, who had rejected their ethnic cultures and identified themselves with the mainstream culture, were more likely to show anti-social behaviours. Similar results were found in a qualitative study in Boston's Chinatown where many native-born Chinese-Americans with delinquent behaviours had rejected part of their ethnic cultural heritage and identified with the American mainstream culture (Kendis & Kendis, 1976). In a community survey of Chinese delinquency in Winnipeg, Canada, Wong (2000) found that there was a correlationship between acculturation and delinquency: the more the youths identified themselves with the mainstream culture, the more likely they demonstrated delinquent behaviours. This relationship was explained by researchers on the premise that no matter how hard the Asian youths tried to identify themselves with the mainstream cultures, they were not totally accepted by the host society (Kendis & Kendis, 1976; Song, Dombrink, & Geis, 1992; Toy, 1992).

If acculturation is positively related to delinquency, parents should be advised to monitor the acculturation process of their children. However, studies found that the correlationship between acculturation and parental supervision is weak (Wong, 2000). Acculturation was associated with the child's individual orientation rather than the effect of parental control. That is, children would acculturate to the larger society regardless of the supervision from parents.

Apart from acculturation, cultural conflict within the family was another predictor of delinquency among Asian youths. The relationship was such that parents who were less acculturated to the host culture (Charron & Ness, 1981; Go, 1998; Toy, 1992) and were less proficient in English (Go, 1998; Wong, 1997) increased the probability of their children displaying delinquent behaviours. It is assumed that the different rates of acculturation between the two generations would create cultural conflicts within the family (Go, 1998; Wong, 1997). In particular, for those parents who were less proficient in English, language acculturation had a strong relation with delinquency (Wong, 1997). That is, those youths who used English more often were more likely to have committed delinquency, possibly due to a widened language gap between themselves and their parents. Moreover, role reversal might happen. The role reversal experienced by many of the youths afforded them both satisfaction and a considerable amount of unease (Go, 1998; Song, Dombrink, & Geis, 1992). In essence, the parents did not approve of the Westernisation of their offspring, yet they were forced to rely on their children for help in accommodating to the host society.

Political Context

Compared to studies on the pathway to delinquency, the studies on the Asian youth after they have been involved in the criminal justice system were noticeably scant (Zhang, 1993). Some researchers explained this phenomenon in terms of the methodological challenges involved (Biernacki & Waldorf, 1981; Zhang, 1993). Using survey methods with high school students was considerably easier to obtain access to Asian youths once they had been arrested and involved with the criminal justice system (Zhang, 1993). Additionally, these studies suggested that the relationship between ethnic delinquency and criminal justice system should be understood in the political context of racial discrimination.

Nevertheless, the small sample of existing research provides a value to the area of Asian delinquency through increasing our understanding of the attitudes of Asian youths towards the criminal justice system and how they cope with the system once they have become involved with it.

1. PERCEPTION OF THE CRIMINAL JUSTICE SYSTEM BY VISIBLE MINORITIES

Generally, visible minorities have the perception that they were being discriminated against by the criminal justice systems in North America (Currie & Kiefi, 1994; Doob, Marinos, & Varma, 1999; Ioannou, 1995; Parsons, Simmons, Shinhoster, & Kilburn, 1999). Some research evidence supported the notion that the visible minority, especially the African youths, were being discriminated against throughout the whole process of the criminal justice system (Frazier, Bishop, & Henretta, 1992; Huizinga & Elliott, 1987).

Predictions of racial discrimination in the administration of justice were often based on traditional conflict theory, primarily the works of Chanbliss and Seidman (1971) and Quinney (1970) (as cited in Frazier, Bishop, & Henretta, 1992). According to these theorists, members of minority races are more vulnerable to discrimination because they are relatively powerless; that is, they lack political, economic, and social resources (Frazier, Bishop, & Henretta, 1992). Research on ethnic minorities, in particular the ethnic groups with African backgrounds, have provided adequate evidence to support the premise that African youths were more easily targeted and arrested by police (Bolton, 1999), received harsher punishment (Frazier, Bishop, & Henretta, 1992), and were overrepresented in prisons (Austin, 1995; Ioannou, 1995).

The perception of unfair treatment in the criminal justice system was also found among Asian populations. In an Ontario study, almost one-third of the Chinese respondents (31 per cent) believed judges do not treat visible minorities the same as white people (Ioannou, 1995). More specifically, close to three in 10 of the Chinese respondents (29 per cent) believed that judges do not treat Chinese people the same as white people (Ioannou, 1995). Some studies with young Asian gang members also reported that the behaviours of criminal justice functionaries, especially the police, have been characterised as biased and insensitive in regard to Asian youth (Song, 1988; Song, Dombrink, & Geis, 1992). Even more, they were also treated with contempt despite some of the police officers being from the same ethnic background (Hunt, Joe, & Walforf, 1997).

Interviews with 52 community leaders and surveys of Asian immigrant communities (mostly Chinese and Vietnamese) in two southern California counties indicated that language barriers and cultural differences exacerbate tensions between the law enforcers and the Asian residents (Song, 1988). Moreover, some law enforcement officials in California developed "gang profiles" which are steeped in racial stereotypes and based on questionable data (Song, Dombrink, & Geis, 1992).

Racism against visible minorities was even recognised by the government. A Canadian government report admitted that members of ethnocultural minorities appear to believe that racism is pervasive within the justice system. While there was no conclusive evidence of racism in the justice system from the empirical research, racism was widely believed to be covert rather than overt (Currie & Kiefi, 1994). Moreover, there was widespread fear among ethnic minorities of approaching the justice system, of seeking the protection of the justice system, or of cooperating with the justice system among minorities. This is very important with respect to relations between the minority groups and the justice system (Currie & Kiefi, 1994).

2. COPING WITH THE CRIMINAL JUSTICE SYSTEM

Hitherto, very few published research reports have focused directly on Asian delinquents and their coping with the criminal justice system. Findings from other related research regarding coping strategy of Asians have been used as references.

Studies examining responses to stressful situations were usually based on the coping theory of Billings and Moos (1981), Folkman and Lazarus (1980), and Pearlin and Schooler (1978) (as cited in Banyard, 1995). According to these theories, coping consists of several stages, including cognitive appraisal of the situation, assessment of available coping options, and implementation of a response. Within this framework, one would choose a problem-oriented solution such as help-seeking or an emotion-oriented solution such as denial or self-blaming (Banyard, 1995). Asians were found to be more often using emotion-focused coping strategies when faced with stressful situations such as migration (Noh, Beiser, Kaspar, Hou, & Rummens, 1999), having mental health problems (Herrick & Brown, 1998), and having substance abuse problems (Ja and Aoke, 1993).

Similar results were found for Asian parents of delinquent youths when coping with the criminal justice system. For example, in a comparison study in California, Zhang (1993) examined how 50 Black and 50 Asian parents perceive and respond to their delinquent children who were on probation in Los Angeles county. Asian parents were found to perceive the incident of arrest and subsequent probation as a far more serious and emotionally upsetting event than the Black parents. Asian parents were more inclined than the Black parents to blame themselves for having failed in their parenting efforts and felt responsible for and ashamed of the incident. Black parents were found to be less willing to accept the fact that their children did something wrong and more likely to attribute the reasons to the larger society. To explain the different responses between the two ethnic groups, the researcher used a cultural explanation.

Moreover, poor family attachment, which was one of the contributing factors to delinquency, has been found to correlate with the coping strategies of both parental groups: the weaker the attachment of the children to the family, the less likely the parents would use both formal and informal resources to deal with their delinquent children. Therefore, it was suggested that it was necessary to examine the contributing factors to the delinquency in order to fully comprehend how the parents cope with the incidents.

Apart from this study on the coping mechanism of Asian parents, no other research studies, however, were found from the perspective of Asian youth and the criminal justice system that they perceived discriminated against them.

CONCLUSION

There is an increasing concern on the surge of Asian delinquency; however, the general paucity of research on delinquency and Asian youth and their involvement with the criminal justice system does not permit a full understanding of the subject. Given the increasing public concern about the way in which the criminal justice system handles Asian delinquency, studying the perception of Asian youths and their coping strategies with the criminal justice system is an area deserving further research.

REFERENCES

Adlaf, E.M., Smart, R.G., & Tan, S.H. (1989). Ethnicity and Drug Use: A Critical Look. *The International Journal of the Addictions, 24(1),* 1–18.

Austin, J. (1995). The Overrepresentation of Minority Youths in the California Juvenile Justice System: Perceptions and Realities. In K.K. Leonard, C.E. Pope, & W.H. Feyerherm (eds.), *Minorities in Juvenile Justice* (pp. 153–78). Thousand Oaks, CA: Sage Publications.

Bagley, C. (1972). Deviant Behavior in English and West Indian School Children. *Research in Education, 8,* 47–55.

Banyard, V.L. (1995). "Taking Another Route": Daily Survival Narratives from Mothers Who Are Homeless. *American Journal of Community Psychology, 23(6),* 871–91.

Barnes, G., & Welte, J. (1986). Patterns and Predictors of Alcohol Use among 7–12 Grade Students in New York State. *Journal of Studies on Alcohol, 47(1),* 53–61.

Biernacki, P., & Waldorf, D. (1981). Snowball Sampling: Problems and Techniques of Chain Referral Sampling. *Sociological Methods and Research, 10,* 141–63.

Bolton, K.H., Jr. (1999). "Everyday Racism" in Policing: Interview with African American Law Enforcement Officers. Unpublished doctoral dissertation, University of Florida.

Charron, D.W., & Ness, R.C. (1981). Emotional Distress among Vietnamese Adolescents. *Journal of Refugee Resettlement, 1,* 7–15.

Chi, I., Kitano, H.L., & Lubben, J.E. (1988). Male Chinese Drinking Behavior in Los Angeles. *Journal of Studies on Alcohol 49,* 21–25.

Chin, K. (1996). *Chinatown Gangs Extortion, Enterprise, and Ethnicity.* New York: Oxford University Press.

Coll, C.G., Lamberty, G., Jenkins, R., Mcadoo, H.P., Crnic, K., Wasik, B.H., & Garcia, H.V. (1996). An Integrative Model for the Study of Developmental Competencies in Minority Children. *Child Development, 67,* 1891–914.

Currie, A., & Kiefi, G. (1994). *Ethnocultural Groups and the Justice System in Canada: A Review of the Issues.* Ottawa: Department of Justice Canada.

Doob, A.N., Marinos, V., & Varma, K. (1999). *Youth Crime and the Youth Justice System in Canada: A Research Perspective.* Toronto: Centre of Criminology, University of Toronto.

Elliott, D., Huizinga, D., & Ageton, S. (1985). *Explaining Delinquency and Drug Use.* Beverly Hills, CA: Sage.

Fasiolo, R., & Leckie, S. (1993). *Canadian Media Converage of Gangs: A Content Analysis.* Ottawa: Solicitor General of Canada.

Fong, S.L.M. (1973). Assimilation and Changing Social Roles of Chinese Americans. *Journal of Health and Social Behavior, 33,* 66–76.

Frazier, C.E., Bishop, D.M., & Henretta, J.C. (1992). The Social Context of Race Differentials in Juvenile Justice Dispositions. *The Sociological Quarterly, 33(3),* 447–58.

Go, C.G. (1998). The Relationship of Acculturation, Parent and Peer Relations to Delinquency and Depression: An Exploratory Study of Adaptation among Southeast Asian Youth. Unpublished doctoral dissertation, the California State University, Davis, California.

Gonzales, N.A., & Cauce, A.M. (1995). Ethnic Identity and Multicultural Competence: Dilemmas and Challenges for Minority Youth. In W.D. Hawley & S.W. Jackson (eds.), *Toward a Common Destiny: Improving Race and Ethnic Relation in America* (pp. 131–62). San Francisco, CA: Jossey-Bass Inc.

Harberth, T. (1999). School Problems with Delinquent Youth: A Cross-cultural Comparison Findings. Unpublished doctoral dissertation, University of California, Long Beach.

Herrick, C., & Brown, H. (1998). Underutilization of Mental Health Services by Asian Americans Residing in the United States. *Issues in Mental Health Nursing, 19*, 225–40.

Hisame, T. (1980). Minority Group Children and Behavior Disorders: The Case of Asian- American Children. *Behavior Disorder, 5*, 186–96.

Huizinga, D., & Elliott D.S. (1987). Juvenile Offenders: Prevalence, Offender Incidence, and Arrest Rates by Race. *Crime and Delinquency, 33(2)*, 206–23.

Huizinga, D., Esbensen, F.A., & Weiher, A.W. (1991). Are There Multiple Paths to Delinquency? *Journal of Criminal Law and Criminology, 82*, 83–118.

Hunt, G., Joe, K., & Waldorf, D. (1997). Culture and Ethnic Identity among Southeast Asian Gang Members. *Free Inquiry in Creative Sociology, 25(1)*, 9–21.

Ioannou, G. (1995). *Report of the Commission on Systemic Racism in the Ontario Criminal Justice System*. Toronto: Queen's Printer for Ontario.

Ja, D., & Aoke, B. (1993). Substance Abuse Treatment: Culture and Barriers in the Asian American Community. *Journal of Psychoactive Drugs, 25(1)*, 67–71.

Joe, D., & Robinson, N. (1980). Chinatown's Immigrant Gangs. *Criminology, 4*, 337–45.

Kelly, M.L., & Tseng, H.M. (1992). Cultural Differences in Child Rearing: A Comparison of Immigrant Chinese and Caucasian American Mothers. *Journal of Cross-cultural Psychology, 23*, 445–55.

Kendis, O.K., & Kendis, R.J. (1976). The Street Boy Identity: An Alternate Strategy of Boston's Chinese-Americans. *Urban Anthropology, 29(10)*, 1–17.

Kitano, H.H.L. (1973). Japanese-American Crime and Delinquency. In S. Sue & N.N. Wagner (eds.), *Asian-Americans: Psychological Perspectives*. Palo Alto, CA: Science and Behavior Books.

Kwong, P. (1990). The Challenge of Understanding the Asian-American Experience. *Ethnic and Racial Studies, 13*, 594–590.

Li, P. (1988). *The Chinese in Canada*. Toronto: Oxford University Press.

Li, H.Z., & Rosenblood, L. (1994). Exploring Factors Influencing Alcohol Consumption: Patterns among Chinese and Caucasians. *Journal of Studies on Alcohol, 55*, 427–33.

Maddahian, E., Newcomb, M.D., & Bentler, P.M. (1986). Adolescents' Substance Use: Impact of Ethnicity, Income, and Availability. *Advances in Alcohol and Substance Abuse, 5*, 63–78.

Marcos, A.C., Bahr, S.J., & Johnson, R.E. (1986). Test of a Bonding and Association Theory of Adolescent Drug Use. *Social Forces, 65(1)*, 135–61.

Massey, J.L., & Krohn, M.D. (1996). A Longitudinal Examination of an Integrated Social Process Model of Deviant Behavior. *Social Forces, 65(1)*, 106–34.

McCurrie, T.F. (1999). Asian Gangs: A Research Note. *Journal of Gang Research, 6(2)*, 47–51.

Murray, D.M., Perry, C.L., O'Connel, C., & Schmid, L. (1987). Seventh-Grade Cigarette, Alcohol, and Marijuana Use: Distribution in a North Central U.S. Metropolitan Population. *The International Journal of the Addictions, 22, 357–76.*

Noh, S., Beiser, M., Kaspar, V., Hou, F., & Rummens, J. (1999). Perceived Racial Discrimination, Depression, and Coping: A Study of Southeast Asian Refugees in Canada. *Journal of Health and Social Behavior, 40(3),* 193–207.

Parsons, S., Simmons, W., Shinhoster, F., & Kilburn, J. (1999). "A Test of the Grapevine: An Empirical Examination of Conspiracy Theories among African Americans." *Sociological Spectrum, 19(2),* 201–222.

Pearson, G. (1983). *Hooligan.* London: Macmillan.

Pogrebin, M.P., & Poole, E.D. (1989). South Korean Immigrants and Crime: A Case Study. *The Journal of Ethnic Studies, 17,* 47–80.

Portes, A., & Zhou, M. (1993). The New Second Generation: Segmented Assimilation and Its Variants. *Annals, American Academy of Political and Social Sciences, 530,* 74–96.

Rosenblatt, R.A. (1996, March 13). *Latinos, Asians to Lead Rise in U.S. Population* (pp. Al, A4). *Los Angeles Times.*

Sayasane, P. (2000). Correlates of Gang Membership: Southeast Asian Gang and Nongang Youth. Unpublished doctoral dissertation, University of Denver.

Sheu, C.J. (1986). *Delinquency and Identity: Juvenile Delinquency in an American Chinatown.* New York: Harrow and Heston.

Smith, M.P. & Tarallo, B. (1995). Who Are the "Good Guys"? The Social Construction of the Vietnamese "Other." In P.M. Smith & J.R. Feagin (eds.), *The Bubbling Cauldron: Race, Ethnicity, and the Urban Crisis* (pp. 50–76). Minneapolis, MN: University of Minnesota Press.

Song, J.H.L. (1988). No White Feathered Crows: Chinese Immigrants' and Vietnamese Refugees' Adaptation to American Legal Institution. Unpublished doctoral dissertation, University of California, Irvine.

Song, J.H.L., Dombrink, J., & Geis, G. (1992). Lost in the Melting Pot: Asian Youth Gangs in the United States. *Gang Journal, 1(1),* 1–12.

Statistics Canada. (1997). *1996 Census of Canada: The Nation Series.* Ottawa, ON: Minister of Government Works and Government Service.

Statistics Canada. (2000). *1999 Facts and Figures: Immigration Overview.* Ottawa, ON: Minister of Government Works and Government Service.

Statistics Canada, Canadian Centre for Justice Statistics. (2001). *Youth Court Data Tables* (Catalogue no. 85F0030X1E). Ottawa, ON: Minister of Industry.

Thornberry, T.P., Lizotte, A.J., Krohn, M.D., Farnworth, M., & Jang, S.J. (1991). Testing Interactional Theory: An Examination of Reciprocal Causal Relationship among Family, School, and Delinquency. *Journal of Criminal Law and Criminology, 82,* 3–35.

Toupin, E.W. (1991). Preliminary Findings on Asian American: "The Model Minority" in a Small Private East Coast College. *Journal of Cross-cultural Psychology, 22(3),* 403–17.

Toy, C. (1992). Coming out to Play: Reason to Join and Participate in Asian Gang. *Gang Journal 1(1),* 13–29.

Trimble, J.E., Padilla, A.M., & Bell, C.S. (1987). *Drug Abuse among Ethnic Minorities*. Rockville, MD: National Institute on Drug Abuse.

U.S. Senate. Committee on Governmental Affairs. (1992). *The New International Criminal and Asian Organized Crime*. Washington, DC: U.S. Government Printing Office.

Vega, W.A. & Rumbaut, R.G.M. (1991). Ethnic Minorities and Mental Health. *Annual Review of Sociology, 17*, 351–83.

Vigil, J.D., & Yun, S.C. (1996). Southern California Gangs: Comparative Ethnicity and Social Control. In C.R. Huff (ed.), *Gangs in America*. Thousand Oaks, CA: Sage Publication.

Wallace, J.M., & Bachman, J.D. (1991). Explaining Racial/Ethnic Differences in Adolescent Drug Use: The Impact of Background and Lifestyle. *Social Problems, 38*, 333–57.

Wang, Z. (1994). Factors Affecting Gang Affiliation among Asian-American High School Students: An Examination of Fagan's Social Development Model. Unpublished doctoral dissertation, Indiana University of Pennsylvania.

Wang, Z. (1995). Gang Affiliation among Asian-American High School Students: A Path Analysis of Social Development Model. *Journal of Gang, 2(3)*, 1–13.

Warr, M., & Stafford, M. (1991). The Influence of Delinquent Peers: What They Think or What They Do? *Criminology, 29*, 851–66.

Wittmeier, C. (October 1999). Criminal Credentials: Are the City's Police as Well Prepared as Its Asian Gangs? *Alberta Report*, 27–28.

Wong, S.K. (1997). Delinquency of Chinese-Canadian Youth: A Test of Opportunity. Control and Intergeneration Conflict Theories. *Youth & Society, 29(1)*, 112–34.

Wong, S.K. (1998). Peer Relations and Chinese-Canadian Delinquency. *Journal of Youth and Adolescence, 27(5)*, 641–64.

Wong, S.K. (1999). Acculturation, Peer Relations, and Delinquent Behavior of Chinese-Canadian Youth. *Adolescence, 34(133)*, 107–19.

Wong, S.K. (2000). Acculturation and Chinese Delinquency. In L. Driedger & S.S. Halli (eds.), *Race and Racism: Canada's Challenge* (pp. 235–52). Montreal, QC: McGill-Queen's University Press.

Zhang, X.D. (1993). Coping with Delinquency in a Cultural Context: The Perceptions and Coping Behaviors of Black and Asian Parents of Juvenile Delinquents. Unpublished doctoral dissertation, University of Southern California.

CHAPTER FOURTEEN

War Frenzy

Sunera Thobani

My recent speech at a women's conference on violence against women has generated much controversy.[1] In the aftermath of the terrible attacks of September 11, I argued that the US response of launching "America's new war" would increase violence against women. I situated the current crisis within the continuity of North/South relations, rooted in colonialism and imperialism. I criticized the American foreign policy, as well as President Bush's racialized construction of the American Nation. Finally I spoke of the need for solidarity with Afghan women's organizations as well as the urgent necessity for the women's movement in Canada to oppose the war.

Decontextualized and distorted media reports of my address have led to accusations of me being an academic imposter, morally bankrupt and engaging in hate-mongering. It has been fascinating to observe how my comments regarding American foreign policy, a record well documented by numerous sources whose accuracy or credentials cannot be faulted, have been dubbed "hate speech." To speak about the indisputable record of US-backed coups, death squads, bombings, and killings ironically makes me a "hate-monger." I was even made the subject of a "hate crime" complaint made to the RCMP, alleging that my speech amounted to a "hate crime" against Americans.

Despite the virulence of these responses, I welcome the public discussion my speech has generated as an opportunity to further the public debate about Canada's support of America's new war. When I made the speech, I believed it was imperative to have this debate *before* any attacks were launched on any country. Events have overtaken us with the bombing of Afghanistan now underway and military rule having been declared in Pakistan.[2] The need for this discussion has now assumed greater urgency as reports of casualties are making their way into the news. My speech at the women's conference was aimed at mobilizing the women's movement in Canada against this war. I am now glad for this opportunity to address wider constituencies and in different fora.

First, however, a few words about my location: I place my work within the tradition of radical, politically engaged scholarship. I have always rejected the politics of academic elitism, which insist that academics remain above the fray of political activism and use only disembodied objectified language and a "properly" dispassionate professorial demeanor to establish our intellectual credentials. This insistence on disembodied, objectified language is itself a discourse of power, claiming objectivity even as it strives for increased power. My work is grounded in the politics, practices, and languages of the various communities I come from, and the social justice movements to which I am committed.

ON AMERICAN FOREIGN POLICY

In the aftermath of the terrible September 11th attacks on the World Trade Center and the Pentagon, the Bush administration launched "America's War on Terrorism." Eschewing any role for the United Nations and the need to abide by international law, the US administration initiated an international alliance to justify its unilateral military action against Afghanistan. One of its early coalition partners was the Canadian government, which committed its unequivocal support for whatever forms of assistance the United States might request.[3] In this circumstance, it is entirely reasonable that people in Canada examine carefully the record of American foreign policy.

As I observed in my speech, this record is alarming and does not inspire confidence. In Chile, the CIA-backed coup against the democratically elected Allende government led to the deaths of over 30,000 people. In El Salvador, the US-backed regime used death squads to kill about 75,000 people. In Nicaragua, the US-sponsored terrorist contra war led to the deaths of over 30,000 people. The initial bombing of Iraq left over 200,000 dead, and the bombings have continued over the last ten years. UNICEF estimates that over one million Iraqis have died, and that 5,000 more die every month as a result of the UN-imposed sanctions, enforced in their harshest form by US power. The list does not stop there. 150,000 were killed and 50,000 disappeared in Guatemala after the 1954 CIA-sponsored coup; over 2 million were killed in Vietnam; and 200,000 before that in the Hiroshima and Nagasaki nuclear attacks. Numerous authoritarian regimes have been backed by the United States including Saudi Arabia, Egypt, the apartheid regime in South Africa, Suharto's dictatorship in Indonesia, Marcos in the Philippines, and Israel's various occupations of Lebanon, the Golan Heights, and Palestinian territories. The US pattern of foreign intervention has been to overthrow leftist governments and to impose right-wing regimes, which in turn support US interests, even if this means training and using death squads and assassinating leftist politicians and activists.[4] To this end, it has a record of treating civilians as entirely expendable.

It is in this context that I made my comment that the United States is the largest and most dangerous global force, unleashing horrific levels of violence around the world, and that the path of US foreign policy is soaked in blood. The controversy generated by this comment has surprisingly not addressed the veracity of this assessment of the US record. Instead, it has focused on my tone and choice of words (inflammatory, excessive, inelegant, un-academic, angry, etc.).

Now I have to admit that my use of the words "horrific violence" and "soaked in blood" is very deliberate and carefully considered. I do not use these words lightly. To successive United States administrations, the deaths resulting from its policies have been just so many statistics, just so much "collateral damage." Rendering invisible the humanity of the peoples targeted for attack is a strategy well used to hide the impact of colonialist and imperialist interventions. Perhaps there is no more potent a strategy of dehumanization than to proudly proclaim the accuracy and efficiency of "smart" weapons systems, and of surgical and technological precision, while rendering invisible the suffering bodies of these peoples as disembodied statistics and mere "collateral damage." The use of embodied language, grounded in the recognition of the actual blood running through these bodies, is an attempt to humanize these peoples in profoundly graphic terms. It compels us to recognize the sheer corporeality of the terrain upon which bombs rain and mass terror is waged. This language calls on "us" to recognize that "they" bleed just like "we" do, that "they" hurt and suffer just like "us." We are complicit in this bloodletting when we support American wars. Witness the power of this embodiment in the shocked and horrified responses to my voice and my words, rather than to the actual horror of these events. I will be the first to admit that it is extremely unnerving to "see" blood in the place of abstract, general categories and statistics. Yet this is what we need to be able to see if we are to understand the terrible human costs of empire-building.

We have all felt the shock and pain of repeatedly witnessing the searing images of violence unleashed upon those who died in New York and Washington. The stories we have heard from their loved ones have made us feel their terrible human loss. Yet where do we witness the pain of the victims of US aggression? How do we begin to grasp the extent of their loss? Whose humanity do we choose to recognize and empathize with, and who becomes just so much "collateral damage" to us? Anti-colonial and anti-imperialist movements and theorists have long insisted on placing the bodies and experiences of marginalized others at the centre of our analysis of the social world. To fail to do so at this moment in history would be unconscionable.

In the aftermath of the responses to my speech, I am more convinced than ever of the need to engage in the language and politics of the embodied thinking and speaking. After all, it is the lives, and deaths, of millions of human beings we are discussing. This is neither a controversial nor a recent demand. Feminists (such as Mahasweta Devi, Toni Morrison, and Gayatri Spivak and Patricia Williams) have forcefully drawn our attention to what is actually done to women's bodies in the course of mapping out racist colonial relations. Franz Fanon, one of the foremost theorists of decolonization, studied and wrote about the role of violence in colonial social organization, and about the psychology of oppression; but he described just as readily the bloodied, violated black bodies and "searing bullets" and "blood-stained knives" which were the order of the day in the colonial world. Eduarda Galeano entitled one of his books *The Open Veins of Latin America* and the post-colonial theorist Achille Mbembe talks of the "mortification of flesh," of the "mutilation" and "decapitation" of oppressed bodies. Aime Cesaire's poetry pulses with the physicality of blood, pain, fury, and rage in his outcry against the domination of African bodies. Even Karl Marx, recognized as one of the founding fathers of the modern social sciences, wrote trenchant critiques of capital, exploitation, and classical political economy, and did not flinch from naming the economic system he was studying "vampire capitalism." In attempting to draw attention to the violent effects of abstract and impersonal policies, I claim a proud intellectual heritage.

INVOKING THE AMERICAN NATION

In my speech I argued that in order to legitimize the imperialist aggression which the Bush administration is undertaking, the President is invoking an American nation and people as being vengeful and bloodthirsty. It is *de rigeur* in the social sciences to acknowledge that the notion of a "nation" or a "people" be socially constructed. The American nation is no exception.

If we consider the language used by Bush and his administration to mobilize this nation for the war, we encounter the following: launching a "crusade"; operation "infinite justice"; fighting the forces of "evil and darkness"; fighting the "barbarians"; "hunting down the evildoers"; "draining the swamps of the Middle East," etc., etc. This language is very familiar to peoples who have been colonized by Europe. Its use at this moment in time reveals that it is a fundamentalist and racialized western ideology which is being mobilized to rally the troops and to build a national and international consensus in defence of "civilization." It suggests that anyone who hesitates to join is also "evil" and "uncivilized." In this vein, I have repeatedly been accused of supporting extremist Islamist regimes merely for criticizing US foreign policy and western colonialism.

Another tactic to mobilize support for the war has been the manipulation of public opinion. Polls conducted in the immediate aftermath of the September 11 attacks were used to repeatedly inform us that the overwhelming majority of Americans allegedly supported strong military retaliation. They did not know against whom, but they purportedly supported the strategy anyway. In both the use of language and these polls, we are witnessing what Noam Chomsky has called the "manufacture of consent." Richard Lowry, editor of the *National Review* opined, "If we flatten part of Damascus or Tehran or whatever it takes, this is part of the solution." President Bush states, "We will bear no distinction between those who commit the terrorist acts, and those who harbour them." Even as the bombing began, he declared that the war is "broader" than against just Afghanistan, that other nations have to decide if they side with his administration or if they are "murderers and outlaws themselves."

We have been asked by most public commentators to accept the calls for military aggression against "evil-doers" as natural, understandable, and even reasonable, given the attacks on the United States. I reject this position. It would be just as understandable a response to re-examine American foreign policy, to address the root causes of the violent attacks on the United States, and to make a commitment to abide by international law. In my speech, I urged women to break through this discourse of "naturalizing" the military aggression, and recognize it for what it is, vengeful retribution and an opportunity for a crude display of American military might. We are entitled to ask: Who will make the decision regarding which "nations" are to be labeled as "murderers" and "outlaws"? Which notions of "justice" are to be upheld? Will the Bush administration set the standard, even as it is overly institutionalizing racial profiling across the United States?

I make very clear distinctions between people in America and their government's call for war. Many people in America are seeking to contest the "national" consensus being manufactured by speaking out and by organizing rallies and peace marches in major cities, about which there has been very little coverage in Canada. Irresponsible media reporting of my comments which referred to Bush's invocation of the American nation as a vengeful one deliberately took my words out of this context, repeating them in one television broadcast after another in a grossly distorted fashion.

My choice of language was, again, deliberate. I wanted to bring attention to Bush's right-wing, fundamentalist leanings and to the neo-colonial/imperialist practices of his administration. The words "bloodthirsty" and "vengeful" are designations most people are quite comfortable attributing to "savages" and to the "uncivilized," while the United States is represented as the beacon of democracy and civilization. The words "bloodthirsty" and "vengeful" make us confront the nature of the ideological justification for this war, as well as its historical roots, unsettling and discomforting as that might be.

THE POLITICS OF LIBERATING WOMEN

I have been taken to task for stating that there will be no emancipation for women anywhere in the world until western domination of the planet ended. In my speech I pointed to the importance of Afghanistan for its strategic location near central Asia's vast resources of oil and natural gas. I think there is very little argument that the West continues to dominate and consume a vast share of the world's resources. This is not a controversial statement. Many prominent intellectuals, journalists, and activists have pointed out that this domination is rooted in the history of colonialism and rests on the ongoing maintenance of the North/South divide, and that it will continue to provoke violence and resistance across the planet. I argued that in the current climate of escalating militarism, there will be precious little emancipation for women, either in the countries of the North or the South.

In the specific case of Afghanistan, it was the American administrator's economic and political interests which led to its initial support for, and arming of Hekmatyar's Hezb i Islami and its support for Pakistan's collaboration in, and organization of, the Taliban regime in the mid-1990s. According to the Pakistani journalist Ahmed Rashid, the United States and Unocal conducted negotiations with the Taliban for an oil pipeline through Afghanistan for years in the mid-1990s. We have seen the horrendous consequences this has had for women in Afghanistan. When Afghan women's groups were calling attention to this US support as a major factor in the Taliban regime's coming to power, we did not heed them. We did not recognize that Afghan women's groups were the front line resisting the Taliban and its Islamist predecessors, including the present militias of the Northern Alliance. Instead, we chose to see them only as "victims" of "Islamic culture," to be pitied and saved by the West. Time and time again, third world feminists have pointed out to us the pitfalls of rendering invisible the agency and resistance of women of the South, and of reducing women's oppression to various third world "cultures." Many continue to ignore these insights. Now, the US administration has thrown its support behind the Northern Alliance, even as Afghan women's groups oppose the US military attacks on Afghanistan, and raise serious concerns about the record of the Northern Alliance in perpetuating human rights abuses and violence against women in the country. If we listen to the voices of these women, we will very quickly be disabused of the notion that US military intervention is going to lead to the emancipation of women in Afghanistan. Even before the bombings began, hundreds of thousands of Afghan women were compelled to flee their homes and communities, and to become refugees. The bombings of Kabul, Kandahar, Jalalabad, and other cities in the country will result in further loss of life, including the lives of women and children.[5] Over three million Afghan refugees are now on the move in the wake of the US attacks. How on earth can we justify these bombings in the name of furthering women's emancipation?

My second point was that imperialism and militarism do not further women's liberation in western countries either. Women have to be brought into line to support racist imperialist goals and practices, and they have to live with the men who have been brutalized in the waging of war when these men come back. Men who kill women and children abroad are hardly likely to come back cured of the effects of this brutalization. Again, this is not a very controversial point of view. Women are taught to support military aggression, which is then presented as being in their "national" interest. These are hardly the conditions in which women's freedoms can be furthered. As a very small illustration, just witness the very public vilification I have been subjected to for speaking out in opposition to this war.

CLOSING WORDS

I have been asked by my detractors that if I, as a woman, am so critical of western domination, why do I live here in Canada? It could just as readily be asked of them that if they are so contemptuous of the non-western world, why do they so fervently desire the oil, trade, cheap labour, and other resources of that world? Challenges to the presence of women of colour in the West have long been answered by people of colour who say, "We are here because you were (are?) there!" Migrants find ourselves in multiple locations for a myriad of reasons, personal, historical, and political. Wherever we reside, however, we claim the right to speak and participate in this public life.

My speech was made to rally the women's movement in Canada to oppose the war. Journalists and editors across the country have called me idiotic, foolish, stupid, and just plain nutty. While a few journalists and columnists have attempted balanced coverage of my speech, too many sectors of the media have resorted to vicious personal attacks. Like others, I must express a concern that this passes for intelligent commentary in the mainstream media.

The manner in which I have been vilified is difficult to understand, unless one sees it as a visceral response to an "ungrateful immigrant" or an uppity woman of colour who dares to speak out. Vituperation and ridicule are two of the most common forms of silencing dissent. The subsequent harassment and intimidation which I have experienced, as have some of my colleagues, confirms that the suppression of debate is more important to many supporters of the current frenzied war rhetoric than is the open discussion of policy and its effects. Fortunately, I have also received strong messages of support. More importantly, the opposition to this unconscionable war is growing day by day in Canada and all over the world.[6]

ENDNOTES

1. The conference was organized by the Elizabeth Fry Society, a national organization working with women prisoners and on issues of prison reform, and the Canadian Association of Sexual Assault Centres (CASAC). The conference took place in Ottawa, on 1–4 October, 2001. The full text of the speech has been published in *Meridiens: Feminism, Race, & Transnationalism*, Vol. 2.2 (2002) and at the CASAC website—www.casac.ca/conference01/conf01_thobani.

2. Following the Pakistani incursion and withdrawl from Kargil at the Line of Control, General Musharraf came to power as a result of a coup on 12 October 1999. He subsequently promised to hold elections in Pakistan. The declaration of military rule in September 2001, which preceded the bombing of Afghanistan, could be considered an extension of the previously existing state of emergency and worked in favour of the General consolidating his power. In response to Pakistan's support for the War on Terrorism, the United States provided military and financial aid to Pakistan.

3. This support reflects both the historical continuity of shared economic and security interests of the two closely related societies, as well as the accelerated integration of the Canadian economy into the US in the current phase of globalization.

4. See, for example, Chomsky (2000); Herman and Chomsky (1988); Johnson (2000); Nelson-Pallmeyer (2001); and Landau (1993).

5. The bombings in Afghanistan have resulted in a significant loss of civilian lives. Estimates range from a few hundred to tens of thousands. As there are no official releases on the number of civilian casualties, we can anticipate that it will be some time before the actual number of civilian deaths can be accurately calculated.

6. The anti-war movement in North America grew for a brief period of time after the United States initiated the bombing of Afghanistan. The movement has declined significantly since then for various reasons. However, we can anticipate a reinvigoration of the anti-war movement should the United States engage in an attack on Iraq.

REFERENCES

Ahmed, Leila. *Women and Gender in Islam: Historical Roots of a Modern Debate*. New Haven: Yale University Press, 1992.

Amos, Valerie & Pratibha Parmer. "Challenging Imperial Feminism," *Feminist Review* 17 (1984): 3–20.

Anderson, Benedict. *Imagined Communities*. London: Verso, 1996.

Bannerji, Himani. *The Dark Side of the Nation: Essays on Multiculturalism, Nationalism, and Gender*. Toronto: Canadian Scholars' Press, 2000.

Bello, Walden. *Dark Victory: The United States, Structural Adjustment on Global Poverty*. London: Pluto Press, 1994.

Chomsky, Noam. *The Fateful Triangle*. Sydney: Pluto Press, 2000.

Collins, Patricia Hill. *Fighting Words: Black Women & the Search for Justice*. Minneapolis: University of Minnesota Press, 1998.

Fanon, Frantz. *The Wretched of the Earth*. New York: Grove Press, Inc., 1963.

———. *Black Skin, White Masks*. London: Pluto Press, 1986.

Hardt, Michael & Antonio Negri. *Empire*. Cambridge: Harvard University Press, 2000.

Herman, Edward & Noam Chomsky. *Manufacturing Consent: The Political Economy of the Mass Media*. New York: Monthly Review Press, 1988.

hooks, bell. *Ain't I A Woman: Black Women and Feminism*. Boston: South End Press, 1981.

Johnson, Chalmers. *Blowback: The Costs and Consequences of American Empire*. New York: Henry Holt & Co., 2000.

Klare, Michael. *Resource Wars: The New Landscape of Global Conflict*. New York: Metropolitan Books, 2001.

Landau, Saul. *The Guerilla Wars of Central America*. London: Weidenfield and Nicholson, 1993.

Mohanty, Chandra Talpade. "Cartographies of Struggle: Third World Women and the Politics of Feminism," Mohanty, C.T. et al., eds., *Third World Women and the Politics of Feminism*. Bloomington: Indiana University Press, 1991, pp. 51–80.

Nelson-Pallmeyer, Jack. *School of Assassins: Guns, Greed, and Globalization*. New York: Orbis Books, 2001.

Rashid, Ahmed. *Taliban: Militant Islam, Oil, & Fundamentalism in Central Asia*. New Haven: Yale University Press, 2000.

Razack, Sherene. *Looking White People in the Eye: Gender, Race, and Culture in Courtrooms and Classrooms*. Toronto: University of Toronto Press, 1998.

Smith, Dorothy. *The Conceptual Practices of Power*. Toronto: University of Toronto Press, 1990.

Spivak, Gayatri Chakravorty. *The Post-colonial Critic: Interviews, Strategies, Dialogues*, Sarah Harasym, ed. New York: Routledge, 1999.

Thobani, S. "Nationalizing Canadians, Bordering Immigrant Women in Late Twentieth-Century Canada," *Canadian Journal of Women and the Law*, Vol. 12.2 (2000): 279–312.

CHAPTER ELEVEN, *Kiran Mirchandani and Wendy Chan*

Further Reading

Batsleer, J., and B. Humphries (eds.). (2002). *Welfare, Exclusion, and Political Agency.* London: Routledge.

This book nicely sets out a number of interrelated theories to critique professional practice in a modern inequalitarian society. It helps professionals with a critical perspective to promote the voice and agency of those increasingly excluded from the full benefits of citizenship and to develop alliances with clients/users, which challenge and resist dominant regulatory welfare discourses and practices.

Marchevsky, A., and J. Theoharis. (2000). "Welfare Reform, Globalization, and the Racialization of Entitlement." *American Studies* 41 (23), 235–265.

This book notes that welfare reform of the United States hinges on pitting the interests of the White citizenry against the delegitimized claims of an "undeserving" and "alien" underclass. One of the key myths that governments rely on in demonizing women is the belief that most of these impoverished, single, child-bearing women are Black. The stigmatization of mainly low-income women of colour has allowed successive American governments to dismantle the welfare state and increase surveillance and policing of welfare recipients.

Wacquant, L. (2001). "The Penalization of Poverty and the Rise of Neo-liberalism." *European Journal on Criminal Policy and Research* 9, 401–412.

This article argues that the generalized increase of incarcerated populations in advanced societies is due to the growing use of the penal system as an instrument for managing social insecurity and containing the social disorders created at the bottom of the class structure by neo-liberal policies of economic deregulation and social-welfare retrenchment. It retraces the steps whereby this "neo-liberal penality" was elaborated in the United States and then diffused throughout the world.

Related Web Sites

Dawn Ontario Disabled Women's Network Ontario
dawn.thot.net/Kimberly_Rogers/

This site contains information and comments on the death of Kimberly Rogers in 2001. Ms. Rogers had been serving six months under house arrest for welfare fraud. She was eight months pregnant at the time of her death.

Legal Services Society (LawLINK)
www.lawlink.bc.ca/links/welfare.asp

This site provides information related to application to welfare assistance as well as the procedures of how to appeal in case welfare fraud is involved.

PovNet
www.povnet.org/welfare.htm

This web site features information on how to apply for welfare assistance in different provinces in Canada. It also provides other updates news in relation to recent welfare reforms across Canada.

CHAPTER TWELVE, *Scot Wortley and Julian Tanner*

Further Reading

Bowling, B., and C. Phillips. (2002). *Racism, Crime, and Justice.* London: Pearson Education.

This book offers a comprehensive critical analysis of racism and the criminal justice process from crime and victimization to policing, punishment, and probation in Britain. Criminological research and official statistics produced by the Home Office, police, courts, and prisons are closely examined and are balanced by documentary accounts published by minority community organizations and the experiences of practitioners in the criminal justice system. The conclusion critically examines New Labour's crime control polices and argues that "zero tolerance," the "culture of control," and "institutional racism" will intensify injustice and the criminalization of ethnic minority communities in Britain.

Neugebauer, R. (2000). "Kids, Cops, and Colour: The Social Organization of Police-Minority Youth Relations." In Robynne Neugebauer (ed.), *Criminal Injustice: Racism in the Criminal Justice System.* Toronto: Canadian Scholars' Press Inc.

This volume examines racism within the process of criminal justice. In every society criminal justice plays a key role in establishing social control and maintaining the hegemony of the dominant economic classes. The contributors to this anthology argue that the differential treatment of people of colour and First Nations peoples is due to systemic racism within all levels of the criminal justice system, which serves these dominant classes. Ideological and cultural changes are preconditions for the success of anti-racist policies and practices within the criminal justice system and within other state institutions.

Weitzer, R., and S. Tuch. (2002). "Perceptions of Racial Profiling: Race, Class, and Personal Experience." *Criminology* 40, 435–456.

Racial profiling by the police has become an increasingly controversial issue in recent years in the United States, but we know little about the extent of the problem and even less about public perceptions of profiling. This article analyzes recent national survey data on citizens' views of racial profiling. We find that both race and personal experience with profiling are strong predictors of attitudes toward profiling and that, among Blacks, social class affects views of the prevalence and acceptability of the practice. The findings on social class point to the need for further investigation and explanation of class influences on evaluations of the police.

Related Web Sites

African Canadian Legal Clinic
www.aclc.net

The African Canadian Legal Clinic (ACLC) is a community legal clinic based in Toronto, Ontario. Its primary mandate is to engage in test case litigation in the areas of racial discrimination and anti-Black racism. It also acts as an advocacy agency and resource centre for individuals and other organizations dealing with racial discrimination.

Canadian Arab Federation
www.caf.ca

> The Canadian Arab Federation (CAF) is a national, non-partisan, non-profit, and membership-based organization that represents Canadian Arabs on issues relating to public policy. Through education, public awareness, media relations, and non-partisan government relations, CAF raises awareness of domestic issues that affect the Arab community.

Canadian Council of Muslim Women
www.ccmw.com

> The Canadian Council of Muslim Women is a national non-profit organization established to assist Muslim women in participating effectively in Canadian society and to promote mutual understanding between Canadian Muslim women and women of other faiths.

CHAPTER THIRTEEN, *Siu-ming Kwok and Dora Mei-Ying Tam*

Further Reading

Chin, K.L. (2000). *Chinatown Gangs: Extortion, Enterprise, and Ethnicity*. New York: Oxford University Press.

> This book presents a closed society and a rare portrait of the underworld of New York City's Chinatown. Based on first-hand accounts from gang members, gang victims, community leaders, and law enforcement authorities, this book reveals the pervasiveness, the muscle, the longevity, and the institutionalization of Chinatown gangs. Moreover, this book argues that Chinatown's informal economy provides yet another opportunity for street gangs to become "providers" or "protectors" of illegal services. These gangs, therefore, are the pathological manifestation of a closed community, one whose problems are not easily seen—and less easily understood—by outsiders.

Howell, J.C. (2003). *Preventing & Reducing Juvenile Delinquency: Comprehensive Framework*. Thousand Oaks: Sage.

> This book presents research studies and the most effective programs for understanding, preventing, and controlling juvenile delinquency. It also examines key myths about juvenile violence and the ability of the juvenile justice system to handle modern-day juvenile delinquents.

Winterdyk, J. (ed.). (2004). *Issues & Perspectives on Young Offenders in Canada*. Toronto: Harcourt Brace Canada.

> This book is a collection of reading that covers legislature, research studies, and the criminal justice system relating to the issues of young offenders in Canada.

Related Web Sites

Department of Justice, Programs and Initiatives, Youth Justice Renewal
www.justice.gc.ca/en/ps/yj/index.html

> This site contains information on the youth justice system in Canada and about the roles and responsibilities of the federal, provincial, and territorial governments and other youth justice partners.

National Gang Crime Research Center
www.ngcrc.com/resource/resource.html

> This site provides comprehensive information and research reports with respect to the prevention of gang crime in the United States.

Public Safety Canada, Research
www.psepc.gc.ca/policing/publications_e.asp

> This web site features various report studies in the areas of youth gang crimes and crime prevention in Canada.

CHAPTER FOURTEEN, *Sunera Thobani*

Further Reading

Ahmed, L. (1992). *Women and Gender in Islam: Historical Roots in a Modern Debate*. New Haven: Yale University Press.

> This book adds a new perspective to the current debate about women and Islam by tracing what Islamic texts throughout history have had to say about women and gender. Using the analytical tools of contemporary gender studies, the author surveys Islamic discourse on women and places it in its social and historical context, focusing on Arabia during the period in which Islam was founded, Iraq during the classical age, and Egypt during the modern era.

Anderson, B. (1996). *Imagined Communities*. London: Verso.

> The author explains why nationalism has become so prevalent in the world. What factors have led us to take pride in someone dying for our nation while we don't take the same pride in someone dying for our political beliefs? This book also discusses "official" nationalism in some depth, focusing on Europe and making some quite surprising comments regarding the penetration of the various vernacular languages into their respective empires. This analysis seems a little more forced at times, but the general point remains that a "nation" is essentially a modern and "imagined" community.

Klare, M. (2001). *Resource Wars: The New Landscape of Global Conflict*. New York: Metropolitan Books.

> The author analyzes the most likely cause of war in the century just begun: demand by rapidly growing populations for scarce resources. The strength of the author's presentation is its concreteness. His analyses of likely conflicts, for example, among Syria, Jordan, and Israel for the limited water delivered by the Jordan River, are informed by detailed research into projected usage rates, population growth, and other relevant trends. As the author shows, the same pattern is repeated in dozens of other locations throughout the world. Finite resources, escalating demand, and the location of resources in regions torn by ethnic and political unrest all combine as preconditions of war.

Related Web Sites

Herizons
www.herizons.ca (search for Winter 2002 issue)

> Sunera Thobani's original speech is published in its entirety in *Herizons*, a Canadian feminist magazine.

Justice for Girls
www.justiceforgirls.org/press/ltrs_10052001_september11.html

> A response to Sunera Thobani's speech.

Vancouver Rape Relief and Women's Shelter
"Unmasking the Bigotry behind the Hysteria"
By Michele Landsberg
www.rapereliefshelter.bc.ca/issues/us_violence/us_violence27.html

> Michele Landsberg's analysis of the Canadian response to Sunera Thobani's speech.

PART FOUR

Other Exclusion and Inequality

OBJECTIVES

To understand how poverty excludes low-income women of colour from public space in Canada, and thereby constrains them from exercising their rights and enjoying their privileges as citizens

To comprehend the "spatiality and naturalization" of violence and the resulting reproduction of a colonial social order

To gain insight into the structural reasons for students' disengagement from school

To understand individual freedom as a social commitment; to comprehend society's responsibilities for substantive freedoms, that is, the social conditions for the development of individual capacities

INTRODUCTION

In this final part, we will examine in the first three articles some other consequences of the racialized and gendered nature of poverty. These consequences fundamentally affect people's quality of life. Then with the last article in this part, we begin our reflections, continued in the conclusion, on how we can address these structural forms of poverty in Canada.

In Chapter 15, Punam Khosla highlights what she calls "the largely underground realities of low-income and racialized women" (2003:10). Homelessness is a devastating effect of women's poverty. In addition, access to public transit and public space such as community programs, due to increasing user fees, isolate women who are poor. These consequences, in turn, help contribute to the poor physical and mental health of low-income women. In this article, Khosla documents how social, economic, and political segregation based on class, race, and gender is becoming an undeniable feature of Canadian life.

In Chapter 16, Sherene Razack analyzes how poor racialized women, and, in this case, the murder of Pamela George, a woman of the Saulteaux (Ojibway) nation, experience violence that is "naturalized" and obscures relations of domination. Laws that sustain and reproduce a colonial social order were used in the murder trial to dehumanize Pamela George and to abstract her out of the historical context of a "White settler" society. In contrast, the two men accused and found guilty of her murder were constructed as "respectable" and entitled to lenient sentences. White privilege and complicity in reproducing current Aboriginal realities are made invisible in narratives that treat people as autonomous individuals standing outside history. In this article, Razack details how race, social position, and gender were made to disappear during the trial and in sentencing. In this way, both accountability and social justice also disappear.

In Chapter 17, George Dei examines the myth of the school "dropout." He rejects the exclusive focus on the individualized and meritocratic world view that emphasizes the free choice to drop out. Dei examines how structural factors such as teachers' low expectations, an alienating curriculum, adverse economic conditions, and other emotional and psychological conditions of Black students result in low self-esteem, boredom, and disengagement from school. Such students can be said to be "pushed out," which ultimately restricts their employment and other life chances. George Dei's empirical research supports other studies that emphasize that once students get on the track of fading out (e.g., skipping classes, sitting in the back of class, hanging out in hallways, "acting out," being truant), schools often help them out the door. Schools, however, individualize these systemic and structural failures as "lack of motivation" and a "poor work ethic." In this way schools "rationalize the policies and practices of exclusion" (Fine quoted in Dei, 1997:62).

Chapter 18, by Amartya Sen, winner of the Nobel Prize in economics, helps us conceptualize how we can begin addressing the increasing structural poverty in Canada. Amartya Sen addresses the claim that people are responsible for themselves and society need not be involved. Sen argues that while there is no substitute for individual freedom, freedom is required for individual responsibility. Society—both the state and various organizations in civil society—has a social responsibility for ensuring that individuals have substantive freedoms, that is, the freedom to develop their capacities to lead the kind of lives they have reason to value (1999:285). Amartya Sen makes a strong argument for public policy, dealing with poverty, inequality, and assessments of social performance, to be seen in the perspective of freedom. Sen writes, "[T]he capabilities that a person does actually have (and not merely theoretically enjoys) which can be crucial for individual freedoms. And there the state and the society cannot escape responsibility" (1999:288).

In this part we highlight other consequences of racialized and gendered poverty. Homelessness, spatial segregation, colonial reproduction, and school "dropouts" are the result of poverty and the subsequent stigma and devaluation. With the help of Amartya Sen's article, we reflect on the question: What are the substantive freedoms all citizens of Canada ought to enjoy?

REFERENCES

Dei, George J. Sefa, Josephine Mazzuca, Elizabeth McIsaac, Jasmin Zine. (eds.). (1997). *Reconstructing "Drop-Out": A Critical Ethnography of the Dynamics of Black Students' Disengagement from School*. Toronto: University of Toronto Press.

Khosla, P. (2003). *If Low-Income Women of Colour Counted in Toronto*. Toronto: Community School Planning Council of Toronto.

Sen, Amartya. (1999). *Development as Freedom*. New York: Alfred A. Knopf.

CHAPTER FIFTEEN

If Low-Income Women of Colour Counted in Toronto

Punam Khosla

THIS REPORT

This document is designed to be an impetus to action among policy-makers and women's, social justice, and municipal advocates alike. It provides an initial sketch of the realities, perspectives, and ideas of low-income women, mainly women of colour, rarely seen in the public eye. As such it is a rich resource for those working for progressive change in neighbourhoods and at City Hall.

* * * * *

SECTION ONE

Women in Toronto—The Big Picture

POVERTY, INCOME, AND EMPLOYMENT

There are 1.3 million women[1] living in Toronto and a good half of them are women of colour.[2] Across the City, women's poverty is at a critical and urgent stage. Women make up 60% of Toronto's caseload for Ontario Works,[3] and are over-represented among low-wage earners living below the poverty line, including the unemployed and under-employed. Many women of colour who are recent immigrants don't qualify for social assistance and have no income at all.

As we struggle with the socio-economic devastation of the past decade, differences within equity-seeking groups are becoming more pronounced. Among women, for example, some face far tougher hurdles than others. All women are still significantly more likely to be poor than men,[4] and women's poverty rates have seen little improvement over the years. But women of colour, immigrant women, single mothers, women with disabilities, older women, young mothers, and women on their own are strikingly poor.

The median income of single parent families in Toronto fell by 17.7% during the nineties.[5] Sole-support mothers face deep poverty with incomes $10,000 below the poverty line. Here too, racism creates significant separations. Racialized women raising children on their own are far worse off than women of European heritage.[6] Recorded poverty rates for Ethiopian, Ghanaian, Somali, Tamil, Vietnamese, and Central American single mothers are well above 80%.[7] Table 15.1 shows the broad breakdown of poverty among groups of lone-parenting mums:

TABLE 15.1

Incidence of Poverty Lone Mothers by Ethno-Racial Group, Toronto 1996[8]

| | % BELOW LOW INCOME CUT-OFFS | | | | | |
	LATIN AMERICAN ORIGINS	ARAB AND WEST ASIAN	AFRICAN, BLACK, AND CARIBBEAN	EAST AND SOUTHEAST ASIAN, PACIFIC ISLANDER	SOUTH ASIAN	EUROPEAN
FEMALE LONE PARENTS WITH ONE OR MORE CHILDREN UNDER 19	75.4	74.1	70.8	60.2	58.7	47.7

Source: Statistics Canada, 1996 Census. Tabulation by Michael Ornstein, Institute for Social Research, York University.

* * * * *

Short-term, contract, and part-time employment that is both insecure and low-paying has become the mainstay for large numbers of working women. In 1999 two thirds of the part-time workforce in Toronto were women.[9] The distribution of "good" versus undesirable jobs falls conspicuously along class, race, and gender lines.

The people most likely to end up in low-skill jobs are women and men of colour, and Portuguese people. Lack of English language skills is also an important factor contributing to poverty. The vast majority of non-English speaking immigrants who came to Toronto between 1991 and 1996 were women.[10] Without English language capacity, immigrant women's employment choices are severely restricted. The majority of women of colour in Toronto work in either manual or non-manual low-skill occupations.

* * * * *

HOUSING AND NEIGHBOURHOOD SEGREGATION

It is well known that rental housing is desperately lacking in the City of Toronto. Waiting lists for subsidized housing are climbing daily. As of early 2003, there were 68,409 people on the City's social housing waiting list. Although the City does not keep track of how many of these are women or people from racialized communities, women of colour who are raising children on their own are among those most dependent on affordable rental housing. [...]

Given that women are disproportionately poor and dependent on a dwindling stock of rental housing, the threat of homelessness looms large. However, the trajectory of homelessness that plays out in public discourse is largely based on images of white men who are down on their luck. This belies the realities of homelessness for women, Aboriginal people, and racialized communities.

* * * * *

As the housing crisis worsens, women are turning to shelters. The report goes on to note that Aboriginal and Black women are predominant among those who have reached this point of last resort.

Discrimination plays a substantial role in determining who gets and is able to keep affordable and quality housing. Few groups in the housing sector address this key dimension of the problem. CERA has taken a lead in this area providing support to those affected, as well as documenting housing discrimination based on race, gender, and income status. They have found that people of colour, single mothers, immigrants, refugees, and people with disabilities all face particular discrimination at the hands of landlords. Even those willing to pay higher rents run into a wall of excuses and lies.[11] As CERA's Executive Director Leilani Farah told us in a key informant interview, focusing on supply of rental housing will not solve the housing crisis if those that most need housing are still turned away by the unchecked discrimination of landlords.

* * * * *

Other recent studies have shown rising income-based segregation in Canadian cities.[12] In Toronto, where gender and race are major factors in determining who is poor, women of colour are most likely to find themselves living outside of the mainstream of the city life, isolated into communities of poor and racialized people.

CHILDCARE

Access to affordable, quality childcare is a key factor affecting women's ability to overcome poverty and isolation. In a recent Toronto study, childcare management was cited as one of the top five barriers low-income immigrant women face in accessing a paid job, and a key reason for problems retaining a job.[13]

Public subsidies are a crucial bridge making childcare affordable for working low-income women. These are harder and harder to get. In all there are only 22,600 subsidized childcare spaces in the City, and the gap between need and available services is growing. At any given time there are 15,000 children on the waiting list and Provincial rules on who can apply have become more and more narrow.

* * * * *

Increasing numbers of women are forced to use expensive, private, and informal babysitting arrangements to fill this gap. Although studies tell us that the vast majority of parents using care would prefer to have their children in licensed care, the Provincial government is strengthening the casual approach by diverting funds to Early Years Centres where parents can go with their children, but which don't provide the relief women need to allow them to get jobs and increase their economic and social independence.

PUBLIC TRANSIT

Public Transit is the only distance transportation option for low-income women in Toronto. Working women make up a steady 60% of those who rely on transit to travel to work and back,[14] but rising fares are putting a major dent into their already stretched paycheques.

The Toronto Transit Commission (TTC) depends more heavily on fare revenues than any other transit system in the western world. Well over 80% of its operating budget now comes from the fare box and a good portion of this revenue comes out of the pockets of working and other women who are significantly less likely to own cars. The government subsidy per rider dropped from 61 cents in 1991 to 35 cents in 2001. [...]

In everyday terms this means the system is just too expensive for low-income people. Most fares have doubled in the past ten to fourteen years. Adult cash fares have risen from $1.10 to $2.25 and seniors now pay $80 for a metropass compared to $32.00 in 1989.[15] Incomes have not kept pace and, because of service cuts due to the budget squeeze, every year riders pay more for poorer quality service.

* * * * *

Low-income people with no alternative options are at the mercy of the system. Women's safety is compromised particularly in the former suburbs where transit service has traditionally been weak. High fares further trap them in their homes, and poor service means women must walk longer distances, and stand for long periods at isolated bus stops. One survey pointed out that walking is the only way low-income people can make it to appointments, food banks, and services.

* * * * *

Women with disabilities are even more dependent on Transit. The Wheel-Trans system operated by the TTC is critical, as many would be utterly housebound and unable to function with any degree of independence without the service. Although access to the Wheel-Trans service was severely restricted in the mid-nineties, the demand virtually doubled in the years since. Service access is still problematic. Rides have to be booked at least a day in advance and the unaccommodated rate for 2001 was officially 4.1%,[16] translating into nearly 45,000 unmet trip requests.

PUBLIC RECREATION

Public Parks and Recreation programs and facilities have the potential to become a much-needed meeting ground for people across barriers of race, language, gender, and income. Rather than cultivating this potential, the City has opted to commercialize the recreation system.

Since amalgamation the mandate of the recreation system has been hotly contested at City Hall. Large numbers of residents from across the City have repeatedly told Council that the recreation programs, swimming pools, community centres, parks, and public spaces are crucial to the health of their neighbourhoods. An early City Council Task Force on recreation user fees recommended that programs be offered without fees to encourage participation by all residents regardless of income, age, race, gender, language, and ability. This was rejected by senior staff and Councilors who see public recreation as a limited program for the privileged, offered only on the condition that it pays for itself through added charges.

As a result, fees have been increased for most programs and facilities. The few programs that are still offered without fees are shorter in length, poorer quality, and quickly filled up. Drop-in programs that provide informal and flexible opportunities for residents are being cut back. More time in public centres is shifting to private clubs as the City tries to make money through permits, and save money by reducing the number of recreation staff. Each year more fees are added and programs are whittled away. In 2003 alone, seventeen permanent staff positions are being cut, and user fees for fitness programs and adult recreation programs are being increased to follow rates charged in the private sector.

* * * * *

Initiatives in low-income neighbourhoods are too often focused on crime-prevention. Programs such as a midnight basketball at recreation centers and police-youth basketball, which aim to keep youth off the streets, are almost exclusively aimed at young men. These are singled out for funding even as hours for regular youth programs are cut back. Not only does this approach pre-judge the young people in low-income communities as potential criminals, it leaves young women out of the equation entirely. In the rush to keep boys busy and distracted from breaking the law, options for young women are actually shrinking. Since amalgamation, community programming for girls and women has been dropped from the City's priorities. Instead of encouraging empowerment, pride, skill development, and solidarity among girls, it renders them passive spectators and hangers-on for the activities of boys.

Encouraging participation among women of any age is a challenge in low-income neighbourhoods. They are overworked, pressed for time, money, childcare, and everyday support. Only accessible public programs designed around their schedules and needs have any hope of drawing them out of their isolation. Young women of colour in low-income neighbourhoods face many barriers to participation in recreation and community life.

* * * * *

COMMUNITY SUPPORTS AND SERVICES

There are few public places available for women to gather and meet within their communities. The women's programs that do exist are facing critical shortages of resources, few staff, and little space.

Women's Centres, which operate in some areas in the City, are seldom located within low-income areas, making access difficult for women without funds for transportation. As well, they lack the flexibility to creatively address the material pressures defining women's lives. Operating on tight budgets made up of a patchwork of unstable project-oriented grants, they are faced with heavy reporting requirements and demands from funders for concrete and extraordinary "outcomes" for each small grant they receive. This becomes increasingly impossible as the economic and social situation of women worsens due to Government decisions to shred the social safety net. Positive outcomes are difficult to achieve among women whose difficulties are rooted in systemic issues of worsening poverty and growing racism.

In recent years the Provincial Government has cut back core funding of women's centres in favour of specific job training projects and programs. As a result, most centres cannot offer drop-in support to neighbourhood women looking for informal and flexible opportunities to meet each other. Ethno-specific women's groups are particularly strapped. The only steady funding available for them comes through contracts with the Federal Government to run English as a Second Language (ESL) programs. Except in rare cases, this work takes up almost all their time and energy and leaves them no room to work with women in their communities on the other pressing issues in their lives.

* * * * *

There is a severe shortage of local, community-based services addressing issues of violence against women in low-income neighbourhoods. The only independent rape crisis centre in the entire City of Toronto is located downtown and is facing a problem of shrinking resources. Almost all the services that exist within the neighbourhoods are gender neutral and issues of sexual violence are rarely addressed in any open or systematic manner. Women's shelters are an option for some women, but most are operating at capacity as demand grows and waiting times for affordable housing gets longer.

Cuts to legal aid mean access to the justice system is shrinking for women. Community Legal Aid Clinics, which provide free support, are flooded with poverty, welfare, housing, evictions, and related complaints. They have no mandate to support women looking for help with divorce or family issues. Women experiencing violence can get family law legal aid certificates, but they cover only a very limited number of hours with a lawyer. No allowance is made for translation, which eats up a lot of time and may or may not even be available. Women who want to take action to remove themselves from an unhealthy relationship *before* it turns violent are not eligible for support.

Women who are not proficient in English have difficulty accessing community programs of any description. Although the City offers third-party translation of its Access Toronto hotline, the City's corporate budget for translation has been targeted for cuts on an annual basis. On some pamphlets the only sentence translated tells people to call the City for more information, but residents are not provided any clue as to what they are to call about. Publications and services that are translated are rarely publicized effectively in areas where non-English speakers live.

LAW AND ORDER, SAFETY, AND PUBLIC SPACE

Across the western world law and order is replacing social and economic equality measures as the centrepiece of Government social policy. In Toronto, law and order policies cut a wide swath through the city, creating a growing divide between those residents considered worthy of protection, and those cast as the source of disorder. Race, gender, and poverty are the determining fault lines.

* * * * *

As crime rates fall, Councillors and Police use public perceptions and fears of crime and the notion of "crime prevention" to justify increased spending. During the summers of 1999 and 2000 City Council approved funds for a targeted police initiative dubbed "Community Action Policing" aimed at neighbourhoods identified as crime "hot spots."[17] Police officers, working at overtime rates, were deployed into racialized low-income neighbourhoods such as Regent Park, Parkdale, Jane-Finch, Rexdale, and Glendower on foot, in cars, on bicycles and motorbikes. Most of the targeted communities are home to large numbers of people of colour, new immigrants, single mothers, and young people. A survey conducted by the community-based Committee to Stop Targeted Policing found that residents experienced harassment, intimidation, threats, and violence in the period of the initiative.

Young, racialized, and homeless people, sex trade workers, and poor white residents reported being unduly stopped and harassed by police officers in public areas such as parks and the streets. This criminalizing of large numbers of people, and ongoing public portrayal of them as potential criminals, leaves them more vulnerable to public discrimination, harassment, and violence.

Low-income women who are victims of sexual assault or domestic violence are caught in a lethal catch 22. They are caught between legitimate concerns for their safety as women and their well-founded distrust of the police. Young women who see their neighbours and friends roughly treated by police are less likely to call for help or report assaults. Dual charging in cases of domestic violence is becoming commonplace, particularly among racialized and low-income women. Anti-violence advocates are raising the alarm at the numbers of cases where women call the police for assistance and end up facing charges themselves.

SECTION TWO

What Women Told Us

This part of the report presents the views of the one hundred and fifty women who partici-pated in the *Breaking Isolation, Getting Involved* Project as well as the advocates, researchers, and front-line workers employed in projects and services who interact with them on a regular basis. [...]

2.1 Making Ends Meet

POVERTY

Lack of money was, not surprisingly, the number one concern raised by the women.

Most of the participants said they are unemployed and, with the exception of the seniors, all of them said they want to find paid work.

* * * * *

Even without paid work, women reported heavy workloads and stress in caring for children and extended families, with little resources or support. Without exception, women said they do not have enough money to meet basic expenses. They noted that their incomes from all sources have remained constantly low or gone down, while costs and expenses rise each year. A number said healthcare costs are very high, especially prescription drugs.

* * * * *

A number of the women have no income at all and are completely dependent on relatives. Sponsored immigrants are automatically disqualified for social assistance, housing, and other supports. They expressed much distress about having no options, having to endure exploitation and abuse, and being hemmed into situations that allow them no sovereignty over their lives.

This puts women experiencing violence at the hands of partners or family members in real danger. Community workers report that there has been a significant shift from emotional counseling to practical support for women survivors of sexual and intimate violence. Battered women are reportedly returning to abusive husbands because they know they cannot care for their children on social assistance.

* * * * *

Health problems caused by long-term poverty, abuse, and isolation leave some women practically unable to work. They end up with few options outside of social assistance, where they are often listed as "employable" in spite of their ailments.

EMPLOYMENT BARRIERS

Women in poor neighbourhoods who are on Social Assistance want to work, but they face multiple barriers to finding jobs. No childcare, husbands who do not allow women to work, lack of mobility, language barriers, lack of recognition for their qualifications, Canadian experi-ence requirements, were all cited as factors. Some of these amount to clear discrimination. The requirement of Canadian experience, even in cleaning jobs, has become a less than subtle way of eliminating women from even applying for positions.

* * * * *

Parenting responsibilities are a predicament for mothers with small children wanting to improve their financial position. Many said they need childcare but didn't have any information about childcare centres, subsidies, or waiting lists.

* * * * *

Women who have tried volunteering as a way of getting paid work said they are stuck in unpaid roles. They noted that it is not in employers' interests to hire them into paid positions as this would mean losing an unpaid worker. This appears to be a chronic problem in the social service sector where racialized women say they are relegated to menial tasks and never have the opportunity to develop the skills needed to be hired on as paid staff.

JOB DISCRIMINATION
Some participants were professionals in their country of origin but are unable to work in their field.

* * * * *

In some cases women who have extensive education are pressured to stay in low-skilled factory jobs by partners and families who care little about the woman's working conditions and don't want any interruption in their overall family income.

Women between the ages of 40 and 65, who are on their own, said they are in an untenable position. They are caught between employers who say they are too old to hire and the fact that they do not qualify for seniors benefits and so cannot retire.

* * * * *

Racism and discrimination was raised as a factor in finding work. A Somali woman was refused a job when she went to the interview wearing a hijab. Suspecting discrimination and desperate for work, she went back the next day without the headscarf and was hired. Others said it is racism that closes down their options and forces them into low-skill jobs.

* * * * *

LACK OF ACCESS TO EDUCATION AND SKILLS TRAINING
Many women want to go to school to increase their employability and access to better jobs, but have neither the money nor the time. A number of women wanted job training but said they do not meet the criteria. Job readiness and pre-employment programs are few and far between, and often far out of the women's neighbourhoods. Low-income women have very restricted mobility. They neither have the time or the transit money to travel out of their immediate communities.

Some existing employment training programs were criticized as taking a cookie-cutter approach that is too stiffly formal and does not account for the particular needs of the women. In one instance, the trainer of a local workshop was very rude to women participants, declaring aloud that they didn't speak English well enough to be in her workshop. In the words of one interviewee, women need to have places to go "more like an aunt's place" where they feel respected and are comfortable grappling with what they need to learn.

ONTARIO WORKS AND THE ONTARIO DISABILITY SUPPORT PROGRAM

* * * * *

Women on social assistance programs said they simply do not have enough money to survive. Whether they are on Ontario Works (OW), the Ontario Disability Support Program (ODSP), or the Canada Pension Plan (CPP), they all said the rates are far below what they need to meet their basic living requirements. They cannot cover basics such as rent, food, and transportation.

A number of women are facing evictions because they cannot pay the rent and are in desperate need of more money and benefits. The shelter allowance under Ontario Works is far below what landlords are charging for rent. The Ontario Disability Support Program has very onerous application requirements, and women facing mental health barriers find that depression and mental health issues are not taken seriously.

* * * * *

They noted that as single women, they are heading family units and carrying all the responsibility for children and households on their own. Many said it has become too easy for officials to arbitrarily cut the amount of their assistance. Some had had funds deducted from their cheques without any prior explanation.

* * * * *

CRIMINALIZATION OF WOMEN ON SOCIAL ASSISTANCE

There was much chagrin amongst women about the degree of monitoring and invasion of privacy in Ontario Works. They overwhelmingly agreed that the welfare system is too punitive and intrusive. They complained of regular lack of respect and mistreatment by social assistance workers and pointed out that they are now invariably treated as potential criminals although they have committed no crime.

* * * * *

Community workers, too, take offense at the now well-entrenched presumption that people are cheating the social assistance system. When women are cut off or threatened with it, they say it's usually because they didn't send in a piece of paper or didn't realize it was required. More women are facing fraud charges for the most minor and unwitting infractions. In one case a woman was charged because she and her children were still under her ex-husband's benefits plan for dental coverage.

* * * * *

2.2 A Roof of One's Own

THE HOUSING CRISIS FOR WOMEN

The most devastating effect of women's poverty is their inability to secure decent affordable housing. It generated the most debate across the nine neighbourhoods, and women were keen to articulate their housing issues and recommend action on their concerns.

The key informants' assessments of women's housing are even more dire. Their front-line role gives them a particularly graphic perspective. Reinforcing the issues raised by residents, they elaborated at length on exorbitant rents, overcrowding, poor maintenance, lack of options for women, discrimination, and evictions. Many said they feel powerless under the circumstance.

* * * * *

The cost of housing is too high for most women. Rents eat up almost all of their incomes and the current legislation is ineffective in keeping rents from skyrocketing. They talked about large recent rent hikes in spite of so-called rent controls. In St. Jamestown, women told us they were being slapped with illegal rent increases—a story confirmed shortly afterwards when it broke in the media. Worries about eviction are ever-present. Many didn't know their rights or how to protect themselves, and said rent subsidies are urgently needed to keep roofs over their heads. According to women, landlords use intimidation and fear and are too quick to punish people for late payment of rent.

Advocates said that government policies have created a huge, but largely invisible, housing crisis for women. They point out that the Province's decisions to cut social assistance rates, eliminate rent controls for new units, and make evictions easier through the introduction of the so-called "Tenant Protection Act" are all largely responsible for women's position.

* * * * *

THE PRIVATE RENTAL MARKET

As a Somali community advocate told us, when owners and managers realize that the ethno-racial community they rent to has few options, rents go up and maintenance of the units goes down. In the Dixon and Kipling area, where there is a large Somali community, people are paying high prices for units that are rarely repaired. They have trouble renting in higher quality buildings nearby because of landlord discrimination. They are also stuck because many seniors in the community need to live close to each other for a basic level of social connection. Kids and adults all go out during the day, but the seniors are not able to get around—especially in winter. In any case, the community does not believe in putting seniors in homes.

* * * * *

Front-line workers say there is ample evidence to show a systematic pattern of discrimination against racialized people, low-income people, women with children, and recent immigrants. The Centre for Equality Rights in Accommodation (CERA) has done some tests on racial discrimination with the North York Housing Help Centre. The Help centre refers people of colour to vacant apartments. If they are told the place is rented when they arrive, a white person is sent out and suddenly the apartment is available again. This is not just in a handful of cases but in many situations. CERA's experience is that this happens everywhere.

* * * * *

WOMEN'S HOMELESSNESS

The net effect of the housing crisis is that many women of colour with kids have no address. They move from place to place in the community and stay with whomever they can, but have great difficulty finding secure housing. Those who don't have good enough credit ratings have to rely on someone to sign as a guarantor for them. Some stay with people in exchange for childcare, but find they lose control over their lives, as they are required to do more and more domestic labour to earn their stay. This type of homelessness is rarely acknowledged as such but, along with overcrowding, is as much of a problem for women as street homelessness.

* * * * *

ISSUES IN SOCIAL HOUSING

The situation in social housing is not much better. Lack of subsidized units and the long waiting list for social housing mean women who cannot afford the rental market have very few options. Some said they do not bother to apply even though their need is desperate. They called social housing a bad bureaucracy that does not help women. Lack of information in appropriate languages conspires to make the situation worse. It was noted that the priority system in social housing does not recognize the pressing needs of immigrant women or single mothers.

* * * * *

Women who are survivors of violence are a designated priority on the social housing waiting list, but many run into trouble when they try to access it. One settlement worker told us there are too many hoops for women to jump through to even be considered.

* * * * *

Another woman was running from a violent ex-husband in Ottawa who was threatening to kill her. She was very high risk and had police reports, but did not qualify because she did not share a place with her husband in Toronto.

Women who are living in social housing and being abused are very reluctant to leave their homes and go to shelter. Women fear they will become homeless by losing their internal status and being bumped to the bottom of the waiting list, so they feel they have to stay in unsafe situations. Advocates say the Toronto Community Housing Corporation provisions for internal transfers for women in abusive situations need to be expanded and improved.

* * * * *

HARASSMENT AND ABUSE

Racial and sexual harassment by landlords, supervisors, and neighbours was a recurring theme, with women saying they are infuriated at these violations, but have no idea what can be done because they often take place behind closed doors, are subtle, or are supported and tolerated by neighbours. Women say they are treated with racism in everyday life interactions around their homes. Women of colour talked about building managers and security guards that repeatedly ask them and their children if they are dealing drugs. This adds a layer of non-stop anxiety for the women.

* * * * *

The stories of older immigrant women sponsored by siblings or children can be tragic. Some are abandoned as families move on without them, leaving them behind with nowhere to live. In Rexdale and other communities outside downtown Toronto, there are no homeless shelters. It is very difficult for women in this situation to find temporary accommodation. Older women are too often staying in relationships that are not good for them—where they are verbally abused and mistreated.

2.3 Body and Soul

EXCESSIVE RESPONSIBILITY AND OVERWORK

The personal, domestic, and family sphere for low-income and racialized women is often a place of little solace, much work, and staggering loneliness. Lack of personal supports, sexist role expectations, abuse, and mistreatment within their families are compounded by the hard reality that there is really nowhere for them to go.

Even though the vast majority of women we met did not have paid jobs, almost all said they are overloaded with unreasonable responsibilities that they must cope with alone. Mothers say caring for their children with so few resources is exhausting and leaves them trapped in their homes. Those in extended families are primary caregivers for elderly and sick relatives, who often need detailed and intensive medical attention at home. It's more than a full-time job.

* * * * *

ISOLATION AND LONELINESS

Too often women are facing these responsibilities completely on their own. Isolation and loneliness were issues raised by women in every neighbourhood. A number of the women have no family supports and are on their own. Widows, some fleeing war, are often completely alone, as are others who have been abandoned by their husbands and families, and are now living on their own in cramped and marginal housing. Some told of being abandoned by their families and left on the street after years of surviving abuse in their marriages. Suffering from deep depression and distress, some develop deep fear of society and become shut-ins, not trusting any form of human contact.

Women living with partners and husbands are not immune to the depression and stress of loneliness. Many are here without their extended family and spend extraordinary amounts of their limited time and resources trying to sponsor family members for immigration into Canada, running into roadblocks because they either don't have jobs or are poorly paid. This is tragic for women, a number of whom are used to relying on their own parents, friends, and relatives as a source of protection and support in dealing with the families they marry into.

* * * * *

Women rarely have a chance to meet as neighbours in a supportive and friendly environment. In one project session, two residents who had lived down the hall from each other for ten years met for the first time. Over the years they had developed an antagonism towards one another based on stereotypes and lack of contact. The meeting and discussion allowed them to finally move beyond the hostilities and develop a new respect for each other, signaling the positive effect that supported social interaction can have in women's everyday lives.

* * * * *

FAMILY CARE, PARENTING, AND CHILDREN

Parenting responsibilities, language difficulties, and the inability to pay for babysitting keep women trapped in their homes. Young single mums outside of the downtown area are particularly stuck, as are many older women who told us they are saddled with unpaid care of their grandchildren while their adult children work. Staff at local agencies say they see too many elderly women with limited mobility and independence, exploited by family members.

* * * * *

Women of colour say relationships with their own children become conflicted as their kids absorb sexist values from seeing fathers engage in degrading behaviour towards them. They also internalize their experiences of racism at school.

Advocates confirm this saying that immigrant children adapt much faster than adults to Canadian language and cultural norms. Women find the changes in their children scary and try to rein them in without knowing the problems the kids are having at school. Women and their children sometimes barely understand one another as mothers speak only their original language and children speak only English. There are few supports for either of them in dealing with what can quickly become hostile relationships, and there are few alternatives for women in getting outside translation for important meetings or documents.

MENTAL AND PHYSICAL HEALTH

Overworked, abandoned, abused, heartbroken, destitute, and lonely, women become understandably depressed and anxious. The downward spin that leads to persistent mental health problems is only accelerated by the absolute lack of accessible, supportive, and therapeutic counseling available to them. Unable to afford even the sliding scale fees charged by public counseling agencies, women end up in the medical system and become unnecessarily psychiatrized and dependent on prescription medications. Lack of mental health support also affects women as caregivers who are left to care for mentally ill relatives on their own.

* * * * *

PROBLEMS WITH DOCTORS AND HEALTH CARE

When they turn to their doctors for help, however, women say they are too often mistreated, misunderstood, and dismissed. A vast majority of women in the neighbourhood meetings shared serious concerns about their experiences with health professionals.

Some said there is no language interpretation available for their doctors' visits and this means doctors frequently misunderstand the nature of their ailments. Coupled with their own lack of ability to communicate in English, this turns appointments into a dangerous game of charades. Other women told us they travel across the City to see a physician that speaks their language. This is far from satisfactory because it takes a whole day to get to and from the appointment, and if they are unhappy with the doctor, they're left with no alternative.

Women's relationships with their bodies, and their unwillingness to expose themselves in front of strangers, particularly men, are rarely met with consideration and sensitivity. According to the women, medical staff are too quick to fall back on racist stereotypes, becoming harsh and dismissive when they don't understand women's cultural values and customs. Not enough time with doctors during regular appointments was also a widespread concern.

* * * * *

VIOLENCE AND ABUSE

Women did talk extensively about how poverty leaves them vulnerable to abuse, and makes it difficult for them to make proactive decisions to protect themselves and their children. And community workers were quite forthcoming.

* * * * *

Despite the many gains of the women's movement in opening up the public discourse on violence, the issue remains personally difficult and largely taboo for women of all backgrounds. Women of colour are very afraid of losing face and relationships within their communities. And their own experiences of racism have taught them that they are unlikely to be well received outside in the mainstream. A more sustained initiative, which could take place over a longer period of time to allow for the required level of trust to be built, is needed to encourage women to open up on these issues. There is a clear vacuum of resources and work at this level in the neighbourhoods.

* * * * *

On the other hand, women of colour also reported that they have been referred to women's anti-violence services where they had bad experiences with staff who act out of racist attitudes and assumptions about them. This is just one of the many barriers stopping them from using women's shelters. A shelter worker pointed out that women of colour who end up at battered women's shelters have often endured years of repeated and escalating abuse before they make the move—a reality not always understood by shelter staff.

* * * * *

The situation is made more difficult by the trend among funders to support gender-neutral multi-service agencies to deliver anti-violence programs. This threatens to compromise well-proven understandings of violence against women as systemic abuses of power by men. The resulting misconceptions can lead to strategies aimed at family mediation and reconciliation, which, when used as formulaic prescriptions, only serve to further compromise women's safety.

There are many powerful reasons why women of colour are unable to leave abusive situations. Mothers fear losing custody of their children, because they cannot show enough independent income to demonstrate their ability to provide for them. Some have neither the financial means nor the social capacity to live alone and survive outside of family and community supports. Others have no idea what their rights, what supports are available for them are, and where they can go.

* * * * *

SEXUAL VIOLENCE

Sexual assault, rape, and sexual abuse within families are even more rarely discussed in low-income communities where public policy and resources are increasingly being concentrated into preventing young people, largely men, from committing crimes. Crime prevention approaches not only increase the stigma of criminalization attached to young men, they can have quite retrograde effects on women and girls.

* * * * *

Many said that they see a number of young women who are, once again, becoming dependent on their sexual relationships with boys for their sense of self-worth. Low self-esteem and lack of community and social supports for their independent pursuits also encourages them to internalize sexual violence and abuse in their relationships and families as being their own fault.

* * * * *

In some communities, parents fear sexual assault of, or sexual activity by their daughters to such an extent that they forbid them from having any social contact. One worker pointed out that South Asian girls are particularly affected by this, saying it results in a virtual imprisonment of girls where they must spend most of their time indoors and at home. This not only isolates them from their peers, but robs many of them of the opportunity to build the self-esteem and confidence they need to become independent beings. The girls who rebel can end up very alone, alienated from family and community, and unsupported as they encounter the barriers created by racism in mainstream society.

2.4 Getting Out and About

CHILDCARE

There were many complaints that waiting lists for subsidized childcare are too long. But a large proportion of the women said they were not even aware that subsidized childcare spaces exist, and have no idea of the qualification criteria or how to apply. Translated information is hard to come by, and there are few advocates to help them get through the bureaucratic maze.

Women on social assistance pointed out that Ontario Works requires them to go to job placements, but doesn't provide daycare to allow women to get there. As noted in the unemployment section of this report, lack of childcare was cited as the single biggest and most pervasive obstacle to women getting paid work in all neighbourhoods.

The few women that had children in regulated care said the system is too expensive and inflexible. Even those with subsidy said they have a hard time keeping up with payments. The few that tried unsubsidized care so they could work were forced to quit both because the cost was too high. One woman said she lost her subsidized spot because of her child's absences and illness. Others agreed that it is too easy to be dropped from the rolls for minor reasons.

A number of women said their only option is support from neighbours, relatives, or friends, which is hard to arrange and not dependable. Most others pay for informal babysitting done by elderly or unemployed women in their neighbourhoods, but are worried that the poor quality of care is harming their children. These caregivers are likely taking on too many children in order to make ends meet. The result is that children are, too often, put in front of the television rather than offered stimulating and engaging activities.

* * * * *

PUBLIC SPACE

Participation in community activities eludes many of the women who took part in our sessions. In most neighbourhoods women said there is simply nowhere for them to go where they can connect with others without having to spend money. Outdoor spaces are out of the question for much of the year because of the weather, and malls—which are already difficult for most women because they cannot afford to buy anything—are increasingly discouraging of residents using them as community meeting places.

PUBLIC RECREATION

In spite of the potential benefits of public recreation in counteracting stress, providing community involvement and social contact, few of the women we met use City recreation facilities and programmes. Those that do said their local ethno-specific women's groups had pre-arranged access for them and they largely come to the centres for activities planned by the group, as well as a few children's programs. Hardly any of the women participate individually in the adult offerings. A variety of reasons were given, some specific to the neighbourhoods and centres in question, others were echoed city-wide. Overall we found that the barriers inhibiting low-income women of colour from using City-run public recreation are tangible and avoidable.

* * * * *

Many were not aware of the City's so-called "welcome policy," which waives some fees for those who show proof of their low-income status, and, when told about it, recoiled at the thought of having to publicly declare their poverty. Advocates said they have seen situations in which part-time student staff of Parks and Recreation have humiliated people asking about the welcome policy by yelling across a crowded room for special forms—a clear deterrent for the others still waiting in line who would not want their low-income status announced publicly.

Advocates said the automated telephone system of registration is a real obstacle for low-income women—a number of whom cannot afford telephones. Women said that additional fees are often charged in children's programs over and above the registration costs. One woman reported having to pay a daily surcharge for her child's food in the local after-school program, but said she was not refunded the money for the days he did not attend.

* * * * *

PUBLIC TRANSIT—THE TORONTO TRANSIT COMMISSION (TTC)

Public transit was among the topics that generated the most animated discussion among women in all neighbourhoods. The high cost of taking transit, as well as racism and discrimination by drivers and passengers on the transit system in all parts of the City, were the top concerns. In addition, route planning in some areas is very inconvenient, and women reported feeling unsafe because of increasingly long waits for buses. The unreliability of WheelTrans and poor treatment of vulnerable passengers was raised as a critical problem for older women and women with disabilities.

Across the board, women stressed that the TTC is too expensive and their mobility is severely restricted by constantly rising TTC fare prices. Many said they are forced to resort to walking as much as they can because they simply cannot afford to take public transit.

* * * * *

In the accounts we were able to record, women said that drivers regularly humiliate them with mockery and verbally abusive comments. This, in turn, gives passengers permission to do the same. Some women said drivers have refused to stop for them, passing by their stops without even slowing down.

A couple of young Black Muslim women told of an altercation earlier that day with a TTC driver who was refusing to allow them to board the bus because they were wearing hijab.

Disparagement of women who wear the veil was a complaint echoed in all the other neighbourhoods where Muslim women participated in sessions.

* * * * *

ADVOCACY, COMMUNITY SUPPORTS, AND FUNDING LIMITATIONS

A major theme arising in the conversations with residents and community workers was the need for advocacy initiatives. Participants said they are too often pathologized or medicalized for the problems they face. And while they need immediate help and support in a number of areas, they want to be able to interact with their communities as more than clients.

Women said they want to be recognized as full, contributing members of society. They emphasized that they rarely have opportunities to meet as adults and discuss social issues in their lives, or consider joint actions to press for needed changes.

* * * * *

Very few community or women's groups now have the money to hire community development staff to work with residents on broader issues. Front- line direct service staff said they are burning out trying to solve problems created by systemic policy directions one person at a time. As deepening poverty, reduced social programs, and lack of available supports mount around them, they can't keep up with the numbers of people affected and have few solutions to offer those they do serve. The result is they too often end up falling sick themselves.

* * * * *

Many women told us that that the supports they need are simply not there in the large agencies. Advocates said the trend needs to be stemmed as it is creating a growing gap between a few, established, highly bureaucratic agencies that are increasingly removed from their constituency, and the many smaller, more dynamic groups run by, for, and about the people they serve.

* * * * *

Many of the community workers we collaborated with are low-paid, part-time, insecure, and casual workers. Hired as funds become available, they sometimes find themselves treated as nothing more than glorified volunteers. Many disclosed that they experience a great deal of racism and sexism in their workplaces and their homes. A number are mothers having trouble juggling childcare responsibilities, accessing services, and finding decent housing.

Some can't access the education or training they need to become eligible for more stable permanent positions. Others have more than average educational qualifications, but find themselves stuck in a "revolving door" of project positions, piecing together multiple part-time jobs. This precarious status means they can't participate in networks that allow them to build connections and skills or access necessary training. Many said they simply cannot do the much-needed consistent, long-term, community development work with women that goes beyond rudimentary project funding requirements.

LANGUAGE, SETTLEMENT, AND CULTURALLY APPROPRIATE INFORMATION
Women said the intermittent programming and shallow support available to them also means they are unable to get their hands on crucial information that would allow them to help themselves.

* * * * *

A community worker told us that, even when information is circulated by public agencies, it misses those that need it the most.

* * * * *

Translation and culturally appropriate materials, messages, and approaches are essential in reaching multiply marginalized women. Over and over again women told us that language barriers and discrimination stop them from being able to negotiate everyday interactions, get jobs, and participate in society. They expressed frustration at being left dependent on friends and family, simply because they cannot operate in English.

* * * * *

Community workers agreed strongly that conversational English opportunities are desperately needed, saying that there needs to be community, cross-cultural follow-up. But they also pointed out that too many women miss out on taking even the initial classes funded by the Federal Government. Under the Language Instruction for Newcomers to Canada (LINC) guidelines, immigrant women have a three-year window within which they are eligible to enroll in these classes. But culture shock, responsibilities for children, lack of mobility, and a host of other responsibilities mean large numbers of them can't even think about going out to a program. By the time they have adjusted enough to make time, it's too late.

* * * * *

One worker pointed out that most of the supports that do exist for immigrant women and women of colour in their own language are one-on-one appointments. These don't connect them with women in similar circumstances from other communities, and therefore cannot go beyond short-term problem-solving to address the deep and destructive isolation women are living with. What is needed, she said, are spaces and opportunities for women to gather in a less structured environment, to learn English, while also discovering more about the broader society of which they are now a part.

* * * * *

ACCESS TO JUSTICE AND POLICING

Many women were not aware of their legal rights and didn't know how to access the legal system. A number of women, both in the neighbourhood meetings and over the phone at the project office, called to find out where to go for support on how to pursue a separation or a divorce. Some said that their marriage relationship had broken down and they wanted to prevent an escalation of their partner's anger and hostility by removing themselves, but were afraid of losing their children.

They were frustrated to learn that Legal Aid does not cover divorce or property matters unless there is demonstrated abuse or a custody dispute. Even where certificates are provided, the number of hours allocated are severely limited, and no provision is made for women who require extra time and support for translation.

There is an almost complete lack of options for poor women to get legal support on family law issues. In searching for places to refer women in need, we found only one legal aid clinic in the City of Toronto that provides a family law clinic, and that only for a very limited number of hours per week.

* * * * *

There was strong concern that the Police have adopted a gender-neutral attitude in dealing with male violence, and that this means women are met with the attitude that they are potential criminals, rather than getting the protection and support they need in critical moments of danger. As well, advocates and residents alike noted that low-income areas, where large numbers of women live, are treated as zones of criminal activity in which people of colour are in constant fear of police harassment.

* * * * *

SECTION THREE

Ideas for Change

An explicit goal of the *Breaking Isolation, Getting Involved* project was to recommend policy and program changes that would begin to address the issues and concerns emerging from the discussions, interviews, and research. To this end women were encouraged to go beyond articulating the problems they encounter and to think creatively about ways in which the City and other community institutions can make a difference in the lives of multiply marginalized women in Toronto.

* * * * *

3.1 EIGHT INITIATIVES TO KICK-START CHANGE
1. A Community-Based Network of Women's Houses
City Hall spearheaded the establishment of a network of full-time, core-funded, cross-cultural, women's drop-in houses in low-income neighbourhoods across the City.

Backed by support from both foundations and government, they would operate as full-time, drop-in, community-based facilities designed to serve multiply marginalized and low-income women, specifically women of colour, immigrant, and refugee women. Shaped as public spaces that provide resource, relief, civic education, engagement, and advocacy support, the houses would not provide individual direct social services. They would, instead, make referrals and links to appropriate community services as needed by participants. They would initially operate during daytime hours with some evening events programming, with scope for expansion of hours in the long term.

* * * * *

Key program offerings of the houses would include:

- A community kitchen with daily communal lunch preparation to contribute to food security, cooperation, and sharing between women.

- Community gardens with access to plots of land for women to grow food for themselves and for use in the community kitchen.

- A source of information, resource, and support for women to access community programs, supports, and services, including current and ongoing information on community activities, civic campaigns, employment and training opportunities, and advocacy support for written and verbal English communications with officials, agencies, and bureaucracies.

- Conversational English sessions based on topics of interest to participants.

- Discussions, films, speakers, and activities developed in conjunction with participants with an active focus on adult civic education and participation.

- Joint activities and programming with local libraries, recreation centres, public health staff, schools, and other community facilities.

- Open drop-in time for women to connect informally.

- Allowance for use of space during evenings and weekend days for women to hold private events such as birthday parties, etc.

- Allocation of time, programming, and space by, for, and about young women.

- To be an effective first point of contact for women who may be at risk of, or experiencing, violence within the home to develop relationships of trust and seek support.

- Referrals to emergency, urgent care, or other one-to-one services, programs, and facilities as needed.

2. Livesafe—A Rental Housing Standards Campaign

The City undertakes a priority campaign, titled LiveSafe, to ensure proper maintenance in Toronto's rental housing.

Similar to DineSafe, the clean restaurants campaign run by the public health department, City by-law Inspectors would prioritize low-income areas of the City to check and enforce minimum housing standards. Public, non-profit, and private housing would be evaluated on a pass/fail basis, with fines imposed on those landlords who refuse to ensure that their buildings are maintained to a high public standard, which guarantees a healthy and humane living environment for tenants.

* * * * *

3. TTC Access Initiative

The Toronto Transit Commission and the City's Social Services Division implement a two-pronged transit access initiative, including:

- Provision of discounted Metropasses to social assistance recipients at 30% of retail cost or $33 monthly passes.

- Establishment of a Human Rights Inquiry into residents' experiences of discrimination on the Toronto public transit system, with a special emphasis on soliciting the views of multiply marginalized women.

* * * * *

4. Women of Colour Anti-Violence Training Initiative

The City initiate a citywide training program for women who are front- line workers in ethno-specific and settlement agencies, as well as low- income women's advocates and community activists who are in contact with survivors of violence against women.

The program would provide staff training to volunteer, casual, part-time, and full-time workers in three areas:

- a gender-based analysis of the root causes of violence against women

- baseline skills in referral procedures, risk assessment, support protocols, criminal justice procedures, and the limitations of a criminal justice approach

- the differential impacts of gender-based violence on low-income women, women of colour, immigrant, and refugee women

* * * * *

5. Getting Women Active and Involved through Public Recreation

The Parks and Recreation Department place a high priority on women's access to City programs and facilities with a publicity campaign to increase use of public recreation centres by low-income women, women of colour, and refugee women and their children. This would involve:

- Eliminating recreation fees for single parents and their children across the City for all adult and children's programs

- Establish women-only programs in sports, fitness, and other activities at recreation centres across the City

- Commit to the building of full-service recreation centres in low-income neighbourhoods where they currently do not exist

- Conduct mandatory, independent, anti-racism, and anti-oppression training for supervisors and managers at all levels, and in all aspects of the Parks and Recreation Department

- Linguistically/culturally appropriate mass outreach to women to let them know about the availability of programs designed for them (e.g., radio and TV spots, newspaper ads, billboards, etc.)

* * * * *

6. Multi-lingual Information on Women's Rights and Services

The City conduct a multi-lingual, citywide information campaign specifically aimed at women whose first language is not English.

The campaign would inform women of their rights, as well as available services and supports in key areas such as: housing help, social housing access, social assistance, public health, sexual health, Community Health Centres and dental care, childcare, violence against women, legal aid, education, and recreation.

* * * * *

7. A Public Health Review of Low-Income Women's Experiences with Health Services

The Public Health Department conduct a review to document and detail the difficulties, experiences, and obstacles encountered by low-income women, women of colour, and immigrant and refugee women in their interactions with all manner of health services and health professionals.

The aim would be to propose comprehensive actions needed at all levels of public decision-making to remedy the most persistent and overarching problems.

* * * * *

8. A Cross-cultural Women's Social Planning Group

The City's Community and Neighbourhood Services Division encourage and support the development of an independent cross-cultural Women's Social Planning Group.

The group would be dedicated to addressing the combined effects of racialization, poverty, and gender disparities on women in Toronto through qualitative and quantitative research, policy analysis, and community development projects. It would seek to engage low-income women, women of colour, and immigrant and refugee women in efforts to transform their situations in the home, their communities, neighbourhoods, workplaces, and within the City as a whole.

ENDNOTES

1. Statistics Canada, Census, *2001 Community Profiles*.

2. Women in Canada 2000, *A Gender-Based Statistical Report*, Statistics Canada, 2000 p. 235.

3. Heather McVicar, General Manager, Toronto Social Services, Letter to the Editor, NRU Publishing, June 4, 2002.

4. Kevin Lee, *Urban Poverty in Canada*, Canadian Council on Social Development, 2000.

5. United Way of Greater Toronto & Canadian Council on Social Development, *A Decade of Decline, Poverty, and Income Inequality in the City of Toronto in the 1990s*.

6. Michael Ornstein, *Ethno-Racial Poverty in the City of Toronto, An Analysis of the 1996 Census*, City of Toronto, May 2000.

7. Ibid. pp. 88, 89.

8. Ibid.

9. Alice de Wolff, *Breaking the Myth of Flexible Work: Contingent Work in Toronto*, Contingent Workers Project, September 2000 p. 6.

10. CIC Recent Immigrants in the Toronto Metropolitan Area—May 2000.

11. The Hugh Burnett Report, *Discrimination and Systemic Barriers in Accessing Rental Housing*, Centre for Equality Rights in Accommodation, January 2001.

12. J. Myles, G. Picot, W. Pyper, *Neighbourhood Inequality in Canadian Cities*, Statistics Canada, 11f0019MPE, No. 160, December 2000.

13. *Challenges and Connections: Meeting the Information Needs of Professionals Working with Immigrant Women*, by Advocates for Community-Based Training and Education for Women (ACTEW), July 2001.

14. Statistics Canada, Mode of Transportation, Highlight Tables, Census Metropolitan Area/Census Agglomeratiosn accessed online March 29, 2003.

15. Steve Munro and The Rocket Riders Transit User Group, *Transit's Lost Decade: How Paying More for Less Is Killing Public Transit*, 2002.

16. Steve Munro and The Rocket Riders Transit User Group, *Transit's Lost Decade: How Paying More for Less Is Killing Public Transit*, 2002.

17. Who's the Target? An Evaluation of Community Action Policing, Committee to Stop Targeted Policing, August 2000.

BIBLIOGRAPHY

Advocates for Community-Based Training and Education for Women (ACTEW). July 2001. *Challenges and Connections: Meeting the Information Needs of Professionals Working with Immigrant Women*, Maytree Foundation. Toronto.

Callaghan, M., Farha, L., Porter, B. 2002. *Women and Housing in Canada: Barriers to Equality*. Centre for Equality Rights in Accommodation. Toronto.

Citizenship and Immigration Canada. May 2000. *Recent Immigrants in the Toronto Metropolitan Area*. Citizenship and Immigration Canada.

City of Toronto. 2001. *The Toronto Report Card on Homelessness 2001*. Toronto: City of Toronto.

City of Toronto. January 2003. *Preserving Child Care in Toronto: The Case for New Ontario Government Funding*. Toronto: City of Toronto.

Committee to Stop Targeted Policing. 2000. *Who's the Target? An Evaluation of Community Action Policing*. Toronto: Committee to Stop Targeted Policing.

De Wolff, Alice, and The Contingent Workers Project. 2000. *Breaking the Myth of Flexible Work: Contingent Work in Toronto*. Toronto: The Contingent Workers Project.

Drolet, Marie. 1999. *The Persistent Gap: New Evidence on the Canadian Gender Gap*. Canada: Statistics Canada, Income Statistics Division.

Fong, Eric, and Kumiko Shibuya. 2000. The Spatial Separation of the Poor in Canadian Cities. *Demography* 37(4) 449–459.

Hill, Diane. 1998. *Freedom from Violence: Helping Abused Women and Their Children. A Review of Services for Abused Women and Their Children in Toronto*. Toronto: The United Way of Greater Toronto.

Kitchen, Harry. November 2000. *Municipal Finance in a New Fiscal Environment*. C.D. Howe Institute Commentary No. 147, ISSN 0824-8001.

Kunz, Jean Lock, Anne Milan, and Sylvain Schetagne. 2000. *Unequal Access: A Canadian Profile of Racial Differences in Education, Employment, and Income*. Canada: Canadian Race Relations Foundation & Canadian Council on Social Development.

Lee, Kevin. 2000. *Urban Poverty in Canada. A Statistical Profile*. Canada: Canadian Council on Social Development.

Lochhead, Clarence, and Katherine Scott (Canadian Council on Social Development). 2000. *The Dynamics of Women's Poverty in Canada*. Canada: Status of Women Canada.

Mathien, Julie, and Leela Viswanathan. 2000. *Taking Stock, The Status of ChildCare Services in Toronto*. Toronto: City of Toronto & the Community Social Planning Council of Toronto.

Munro, Steve and the Rocket Riders Transit User Group. 2002. *Transit's Lost Decade: How Paying More for Less Is Killing Public Transit*. Toronto Environmental Alliance. Toronto.

Murdie, R.A., A.S. Chambon, J.D. Hulchanski, and C. Teixeira. 1999. *Differential Incorporation and Housing Trajectories of Recent Immigrant Households: Towards a Conceptual Framework*. Toronto: Housing New Canadians Research Working Group, Discussion Paper.

Myles, J., G. Picot, and W. Pyper. 2000. *Neighbourhood Inequality in Canadian Cities*. Canada: Statistics Canada, Analytical Studies Branch—Research Paper Series.

National Council of Welfare. 2000. *Justice and the Poor*. Canada: National Council of Welfare.

Novac, Sylvia. *Immigrant Enclaves & Residential Segregation, Voices of Racialized Refugee and Immigrant Women*.

Novac, Sylvia, Joyce Brown, and Gloria Gallant. 1999. *Women on the Rough Edge: A Decade of Change for Long-Term Homeless Women*. Ottawa: Canada Mortgage and Housing Corporation.

O.A.I.T.H. 1996. *Locked in Left out. Impacts of the Progressive Conservative Budget Cuts and Policy Initiatives on Abused Women and Their Children in Ontario*. Toronto: Ontario Association of Interval and Transition Houses.

Ornstein, Michael. 2000. *Ethno-Racial Inequality in the City of Toronto: An Analysis of the 1996 Census*. Toronto. City of Toronto, Access and Equity Unit.

Statistics Canada. *The Daily*. March 11, 2003.

Statistics Canada. 2000. Women in Canada 2000: A Gender based Statistical Report.

Statistics Canada. 2001 *Census Community Profiles*.

Statistics Canada. 2003. *Mode of Transportation, Highlight Tables, Census Metropolitan Area/Census Agglomerations*. Accessed online March 29, 2003: http://wwwl2.statcan.ca/English/census0l/products/highlight/Pow/RetrieveTable.cfm?Lang=E&T=601&GH=8&D1=1&D2=1&SC=1.

The Hugh Burnett Report. January 2001. *Discrimination and Systemic Barriers in Accessing Rental Housing*. Centre for Equality Rights in Accommodation.

Toronto Transit Commission. March 2003. *Ridership Growth Strategy*. Toronto.

Townson, Monica. 2000. *A Report Card on Women and Poverty*. Canadian Centre for Policy Alternatives.

Tsang, Beryl & Sfeir, M. July 2000. *Custody and Access and Immigrant and Refugee Women: Preliminary Recommendations for Change*. Education Wife Assault. Toronto.

United Way of Greater Toronto, Canadian Council on Social Development. 2002. *A Decade of Decline: Poverty and Income Inequality in the City of Toronto in the 1990's*.

Workfare Watch. 1999. *Broken Promises: Welfare Reform in Ontario*. Toronto: Workfare Watch.

Yalnizyan, Armine. 2000. *Canada's Great Divide: The Politics of the Growing Gap between Rich and Poor in the 1990's*. Ontario: Centre for Social Justice.

AUTHOR'S NOTE

"If Low-Income Women of Colour Counted in Toronto" was the outcome of "Breaking Isolation, Getting Involved," an action-research project conducted between 2000 and 2003. The full report is based on meetings with more than 150 women in nine low-income neighbourhoods, interviews with community workers and advocates, and a critical analysis of municipal policies and practices in the newly amalgamated megacity of Toronto. In July 2004, the city's Policy and Finance Committee voted "in principle" to support the report and its recommendations.

CHAPTER SIXTEEN

Gendered Racial Violence and Spatialized Justice: The Murder of Pamela George

Sherene H. Razack

On Easter Weekend, April 17, 1995, Pamela George, a woman of the Saulteaux (Ojibway) nation and a mother of two young children, was brutally murdered in Regina, Saskatchewan. Beyond the fact that Pamela George came from the Sakimay reserve on the outskirts of the city, and that she occasionally worked as a prostitute, something she was doing that weekend, few details of her life or the life of her community are revealed in the court records of the trial of the two white men accused of her murder or in the media coverage of the event. More is known about her two murderers—young middle-class white men. Easter marked the first weekend since the end of their university exams. There was a week or so of freedom before summer jobs began, and nineteen-year-old university athletes Steven Kummerfield and Alex Ternowetsky set out to celebrate the end of term. They went out drinking in isolated areas under bridges and behind hockey arenas, and then cruised "the Stroll," the city's streets of prostitution. Eventually, after failing to persuade one Aboriginal woman working as a prostitute to join the two of them in a car, one man hid in the trunk. Approaching her twice and being refused twice, they finally succeeded in persuading another Aboriginal woman, Pamela George, to enter the car.

The two men drove George to an isolated area outside the city, a place littered with bullet casings and condoms. Following oral sex, they took turns brutally beating her and left her lying with her face in the mud. They then drove to a fast-food restaurant and later to a cabin on the Saskatchewan Beach, which belonged to one of their grandfathers. The next morning, upon returning to town, they heard a radio report describing a body found outside the city. After both first confided their involvement to the murder to a number of friends and to one of their parents, one man left town to take up his summer job planting trees in the northern forests of British Columbia. The other man flew to the mountain resort of Banff, Alberta, where he joined other white male university athletes celebrating the end of the term. In early May, nearly one month later, after following a tip and having exhausted the lists of suspects who were mostly Aboriginal or of the "streets" of the Stroll, the Royal Canadian Mounted Police (RCMP) arrested both men for the murder of Pamela George. The arrest of two young middle-class white men for the murder of an Aboriginal woman working as a prostitute sent shock waves through the white population of this small prairie city. Pamela George's own family endured the pain of losing a loved one violently.

At the trial two years later, the defence at first tried to argue that Pamela George managed to walk away from the isolated field and was killed by someone else, an Aboriginal man. They also argued that since both men were highly intoxicated, they bore diminished responsibility for the beating. The boys did "pretty darn stupid things," but they did not commit murder.

Both the Crown and the defence maintained that the fact that Pamela George was a prostitute was something to be considered in the case.[1] The judge sparked a public furor when he instructed the jury to bear this in mind in their deliberations. The men were convicted of manslaughter and sentenced to six-and-a-half years in prison, having already spent twenty months in prison. The objections of the Native community and some members of the white community stemmed from their belief that the crime was, at the very least, one of second-degree murder and that the judge acted improperly in directing the jury to a finding of manslaughter.[2] Alex Ternowetsky was paroled in 2000 after having served only two-thirds of his sentence. In August 2001, he faced new charges of assault, robbery, mischief, impaired driving, and refusing to take a Breathalyzer test.[3]

Why write about this trial as spatialized justice and this murder as gendered racial or colonial violence? Some readers of early versions of this essay have commented that the prison sentences for manslaughter meted out to the two accused were not highly unusual and therefore not indicative of the court's leniency. Others noted that a finding of murder would have required more evidence than was available. In agreement with this latter view, in 1998, the Saskatchewan Court of Appeal rejected an appeal by the Crown that the trial judge had failed to fairly present the Crown's position that the two men had murdered Pamela George. The Appeal Court concluded that Mr. Justice Malone had made it clear to the jury that a finding of murder, whether first or second degree, would require evidence that the accused intended to commit murder or knew that their actions would result in Pamela George's death. There is some indication, according to the Appeal Court, that the jury did indeed carefully consider whether there was enough evidence to convict on a charge of murder rather than manslaughter. Further, the Appeal Court continued, the trial judge's direction to the jury to consider that Pamela George was working as a prostitute the night of the murder did not degrade her in any way and thus cannot be considered to have led the jury to its conclusion that the men committed manslaughter and not murder.[4]

I propose to show that a number of factors contributed to masking the violence of the two accused and thus diminishing their culpability and legal responsibility for the death of Pamela George. Primarily, I claim that because Pamela George was considered to belong to a space of prostitution and Aboriginality, in which violence routinely occurs, while her killers were presumed to be far removed from this zone, the enormity of what was done to her and her family remained largely unacknowledged. My argument is, in the first instance, an argument about race, space, and the law. I deliberately write against those who would agree that this case is about an injustice but who would de-race the violence and the law's response to it, labeling it as generic patriarchal violence against women, violence that the law routinely minimizes. While it is certainly patriarchy that produces men whose sense of identity is achieved through brutalizing a woman, the men's and the court's capacity to dehumanize Pamela George came from their understanding of her as the (gendered) racial Other whose degradation confirmed their own identities as white—that is, as men entitled to the land and the full benefits of citizenship.

In the same vein, I trace the argument made by some feminist scholars that women working as prostitutes are considered in law to have consented to whatever violence is visited upon them.[5] While I wholeheartedly agree, I underline how prostitution itself (through enabling men to mark the boundary between themselves and the degenerate[6] Others) and the law's treatment of it as a contract sustain a colonial social order. Finally, I reject the view that the specialized justice I describe, the values that deem certain bodies and subjects in specific spaces as undeserving of full personhood, has more to do with class than it does with race. In this view, it is her poverty and her location in the inner city that most influenced how Pamela George was treated in life and in law.[7] A white woman in a similar circumstance and place would be treated the same way, or perhaps only slightly better. Again, while I would not disagree (indeed, I would argue that a white woman working as a prostitute on the Stroll would be racialized), I emphasize here that race overdetermined what brought Pamela George *and her murderers* to this brutal encounter. Equally, race overdetermined the court's verdict that the men bore diminished culpability for their actions.

The racial or colonial aspects of this encounter are more prominently brought into view by tracing two inextricably linked collective histories: the histories of the murderers, two middle-class white men, and of Pamela George, a Saulteaux woman. Significantly, history is precisely what was absent in the trial. Pamela George stood abstracted from her history and remained for the court only an Aboriginal woman working as a prostitute in a rough part of town. The two men, Alex Ternowetsky and Steven Kummerfield, were also abstracted from their histories. They were simply university athletes out on a spree one Easter weekend. As abstractions, neither side could be seen in the colonial project in which each was embedded. The history of dispossession, and its accompanying violence, that brought both Pamela George and her murderers to the Stroll; white people's historic participation in and benefit from that dispossession and violence; and the law's complicity in settler violence, particularly through an insistence on racelessness and on contract, all remained invisible. At the end of the day, the record showed only that two white "boys" lost control and an Aboriginal woman got a little more than she bargained for. That an Aboriginal woman was brutally murdered sometimes seemed lost during the trial.

The collective histories I trace are also geographies. In examining the transcripts of the case, one can hardly miss the spatiality of the violence and its relationship to identity as well as to justice. The men leave the university and their families' and girlfriends' middle-class homes in the suburbs to spend time with each other, in places that are "outside" civilized society. From drinking under bridges, beside airports, and behind hockey arenas, they proceed to the Stroll, the streets of prostitution occupied by racial Others, and ultimately to the murder scene. In the elite spaces of middle-class life (the university, suburban homes, chalets, and cottages), they learn who they are, and, more important, who they are not. Moving from respectable space to degenerate space and back again is an adventure that confirms that they are indeed white men in control who can survive a dangerous encounter with the racial Other and who have an unquestioned right to go anywhere and do anything.

These journeys of transgression are deeply historical ones. White settlers displaced Pamela George's ancestors, confining her Saulteaux nation and others to reserves. Pamela George's own geographies begin here. Colonization has continued apace. Forced to migrate in search of work and housing, urban Aboriginal peoples in cities like Regina quickly find themselves limited to places like the Stroll. Over-policed and incarcerated at one of the highest rates in the world, their encounters with white settlers have principally remained encounters in prostitution, policing, and the criminal justice system. Given the intensity of this ongoing colonization, white men such as Kummerfield and Ternowetsky had only a very small chance of seeing Pamela George as a human being. When the court itself undertook the same journey from respectable to degenerate space during the trial, as it reviewed the events surrounding the murder, her personhood again remained invisible. White complicity in producing the harsh realities of her life never surfaced, and the men's own activities were subjected to very little critical scrutiny. The "naturalness" of white innocence and of Aboriginal degeneracy remained firmly in place as the conceptual framework through which this incident of gendered racial violence could be understood.

I propose to unmap these journeys. That is to say, I want to denaturalize the spaces and bodies described in the trial in an effort to uncover the hierarchies that are protected and the violence that is hidden when we believe such spatial relations and subjects to be naturally occurring. To unmap means to historicize, a process that begins by asking about the relationship between identity and space.[8] What is being imagined or projected on to specific spaces, and I would add, on to bodies? Further, what is being enacted in those spaces and on those bodies? In the first section of this chapter, I discuss the factors that brought Pamela George to the Stroll and those that brought two white men to it. I suggest that the encounter between the white men and Pamela George was fully colonial—a making of the white, masculine self as dominant through practices of violence directed at a colonized woman. In the second section, I explore how various legal and social constructs naturalized these spatial relations of domination, highlighting in the process white respectability and entitlement and Aboriginal criminality. In the conclusion, I explore how we might contest these practices of domination through a resurrection of historical memory of colonization and its continuing effects. In essence, I suggest that we insist that in law, as in life, we inhabit histories of domination and subordination for which we are accountable.

SPACE, GENDERED RACIAL VIOLENCE, AND THE MAKING OF WHITE SETTLER SOCIETIES

* * * * *

Two white men who buy the services of an Aboriginal woman in prostitution, and who then beat her to death, are enacting a quite specific violence perpetrated on Aboriginal bodies throughout Canada's history, a colonial violence that has not only enabled white settlers to secure the land *but to come to know themselves as entitled to it.* In the men's encounter with Pamela George, these material (theft of the left hand) and symbolic (who is entitled to it) processes shaped both what brought Pamela George to the Stroll and what white men from middle-class homes thought they were doing in a downtown area of prostitution on the night of murder. These processes also shaped what sense the court made of their activities.

* * * * *

Regina, a city of almost two hundred thousand people in which Aboriginal peoples make up approximately 8 percent of the population,[9] is estimated to have a higher urban Aboriginal population per capita than all major Canadian cities. The Aboriginal population is also the youngest one in Canada—43 percent of Aboriginals are fifteen years old or younger.[10] However, the presence of a significant Aboriginal population in an urban centre is a relatively recent historical development. Canada's colonizing endeavours confined the majority of Aboriginal peoples to reserves by the second half of the nineteenth century, establishing in the process the geographical configuration of the Regina today as a primarily white city in the midst of the reserves of the Qu'appelle Valley. This nineteenth-century spatial containment of a subject population was never secure and often required brutal policing and settler violence. In 1885, for example, white settlers of Regina who were fearful of Native rebellions organized a Home Guard and pressed vigorously for the North West Mountain Police (NWMP) to police Natives and to hang Native leaders arrested after the Riel Rebellion.[11]

Sexual violence towards Aboriginal women was an integral part of nineteenth-century settler strategies of domination. In her research on the appearance during this time of captivity narratives (stories about the abduction of white women and children by Aboriginal peoples), Sarah Carter documents the important role that stereotypical representations of Aboriginal women played in maintaining the spatial and symbolic boundaries between settlers and Natives. Prior to1885 there had been relative co-existence between fur traders and Aboriginal peoples, but the Metis rebellion and general Aboriginal resistance to their spatial confinement, as well as the increasing presence of white women on the Prairies, led to powerful negative images of Aboriginal women that portrayed them as licentious and bloodthirsty. These images helped to justify the increasing legal regulation of Aboriginal women's movements and their confinement to reserves. As Carter demonstrates, "the squalid and immoral 'squaw'" helped to deflect criticism away from the brutal behaviour of government officials and the NWMP, and it enabled government officials to claim that the dissolute character of the Aboriginal women and the laziness of the men explained why reserve land was not used to capacity and were pockets of poverty.

* * * * *

The nineteenth-century spatial containment of Aboriginal peoples to reserves remained in place until the 1950s. As professor Jim Harding of the University of Regina noted in his presentation to the Royal Commission on Aboriginal Peoples (RCAP), a white boy growing up in Regina in the 1950s would know Regina as almost exclusively white and as bordered by the reserves of the Qu'Appelle Valley: "two different worlds."[12] By the 1960s, however, a steady stream of Aboriginal peoples flowed from the reserves to the city. With a high birth rate, Aboriginal peoples left reserves in increasing numbers, impoverished among other things, by a series of federal government cutbacks for housing. In 1971, the census indicated only 2,860 Aboriginal peoples living in Regina, but unofficial estimates placed the number closer to thirty thousand by mid-decade.[13]

* * * * *

Pamela George's homeland, the Sakimay reserve, is typical of the spatial configurations that emerged in Canadian colonialism and produced the migration from reserves to the city. The link between the material privilege of white settlers in the cities and Aboriginal marginalization is a direct one, as the Indian Claims Commission (an independent body set up by the federal government to aid in the settlement of land claims) established with respect to the Sakimay and other reserves in the area. The Commission found that, in the 1940s, the federal government failed to consult the six First Nations involved before passing the *Prairie Farm Rehabilitation Act*, which authorized the construction of dams and the flooding of the reserve lands along the Qu'Appelle River. The government also failed to expropriate or obtain surrenders of affected reserve lands. These practices left the Sakimay reserve tremendously impoverished, while white farmers profited from their enhanced irrigation.[14]

* * * * *

There are perhaps no better indicators of continuing colonization and its accompanying spatial strategies of containment than the policing and incarceration of urban Aboriginal peoples, a direct continuation of the policing relationship of the nineteenth century. Between the late 1960s and the early 1970s, the number of Aboriginal peoples in Regina's jails increased by 10 percent. In 1971 the city stepped up downtown patrols, and in 1975 created a special task force for the purpose of policing Aboriginal peoples. By 1994, the province of Saskatchewan (of which Regina is the capital) had the highest level of incarceration of Aboriginal peoples in Canada: 72 per cent of the population in the province's jails were Aboriginal.[15] According to a "One-Day-Snapshot" survey taken in October of 1996, 76 per cent of Saskatchewan's inmates on register in adult correctional facilities were Aboriginal.[16] In 1999, Patricia Monture-Angus tells us that Aboriginal men made up approximately 80 per cent of the population at Saskatchewan Penitentiary.

The rates of incarceration are even more dramatic for Aboriginal women. Ten years ago it was estimated that in Saskatchewan a treaty Indian women was 131 times more likely to be incarcerated than a non-Aboriginal woman, while Metis women were twenty-eight times more likely to be incarcerated. According to Jim Harding's 1993 testimony to the Royal Commission, Aboriginal women then made up 80 to 90 per cent of the prison population at Pinegrove, a correctional facility in Regina. Thus, while the number of admissions to correctional centers increased in Saskatchewan by 46 per cent between 1976 and 1992, the rate of increase for Aboriginal women was 111 percent for the same period.[17] Looking to a national scale, and to more recent statistics, First Nations women (registered or "Status" Indians) made up only 1 to 2 per cent of the Canadian population in 1997, but represented 19 per cent of federally sentenced women.[18] Harding connected Saskatchewan's provincial carceral scene, in particular, to the history of colonization, reminding RCAP commissioners that it was in Saskatchewan that Louis Riel was hanged and eight Indian leaders were executed in 1885. Perhaps, he speculated, the lessons of 1885 remain "deeper in our psyche [and] in our social structure than we would like to realize."[19]

* * * * *

Although there is no systematic study of the sexual violence Aboriginal women endure today on the streets at the hands of white men,[20] the cases that do surface suggest that the nineteenth-century perception of the Aboriginal woman as a licentious and dehumanized squaw (a perception described by Missy near the end of the twentieth century) continues to prevail. The Aboriginal Justice Inquiry's discussion of the 1971 murder of Helen Betty Osborne in The Pas, Manitoba, elaborates on its prevalence. Brutally murdered by two white men, Osborne, an Aboriginal student who was walking along a downtown street, was picked up in town and driven to a more secluded spot where she was assaulted and killed. As the Commissioners of the Aboriginal Justice Inquiry concluded, Osborne's attackers "seemed to be operating on the assumption that Aboriginal women were promiscuous and open to enticement through alcohol or violence. It is evident that the men who abducted Osborne believed that young Aboriginal women were objects with no human value beyond [their own] sexual gratification."[21]

* * * * *

THE MAKING OF WHITE MEN: THE TWO ACCUSED

Alex Ternowetsky and Steven Kummerfield's histories begin in the colonial practices described above. In their everyday life, they would have had almost no chance of encountering an Aboriginal person. Absent from university, the ordered suburbs of their families, the chalets and cottages, Aboriginal bodies had to be sought out in the marginal spaces of the city. Why would white men seek out these bodies? Why would they leave their own spaces of privilege? How do young white men such as Alex Ternowetsky and Steven Kummerfield come to know themselves as beings for whom the definition of a good time is to travel to the parts of the city inhabited by poor and mostly Aboriginal peoples and there to purchase sexual services from an Aboriginal woman? I argue that the subject who must cross the line between respectability and degeneracy and, significantly, return unscathed, is first and foremost a colonial subject seeking to establish that he is indeed in control and lives in a world where a solid line marks the boundary between himself and racial/gendered Others. For this subject, violence establishes the boundary between who he is and who he is not. It is the surest indicator that he is a subject in control.

I have argued elsewhere[22] that the spatial boundaries and transgression that enable the middle-class white male to gain mastery to self-possession are generally evident in his use of a woman in prostitution. When they purchase the right of access to the body of a prostitute, men, whether white and middle-class or not, have an opportunity to assert mastery and control, achieving in the process a subjectivity that is intrinsically colonial as well as a patriarchal. Naturalized as necessary for men with excess sexual energy, prostitution is seldom considered to be a practice of domination that enables men to experience themselves as colonizers and patriarchs, that is, as men with the unquestioned right to go anywhere and do anything to bodies of women and subject populations that they have conquered (or purchased). Instead, the liberal idea that we are autonomous individuals who contract with each other is used to annul the idea that prostitution is non-reciprocal sex and thus a violation of the personhood of the prostitute. The contract cancels the violence, although we readily recognize the violence of other financial transactions (such as Third World youth who sell their corneas to First World buyers). The space of prostitution, which Malek Alloula describes as "*the very space of orgy*: the one that the soldier and the coloniser obsessively dream of establishing on the territory of the colony,"[23] is the space of license to do as one pleases, regardless of how it affects the personhood of others.

How did the two men enact their colonial histories? Race is not, at first glance, as evident as gender, although neither exists independently. The men's behaviour bears some resemblance to the young hockey athletes researched by Laura Robinson in her book *Crossing the Line: Violence and Sexual Assault in Canada's National Sport*. Robinson describes the masculinity that is actively fostered in the world of young athletes as one where violence and sexual aggression, and a hatred of the softness that is female, are positive signs of masculinity. The normalizing of abusive relationships and male-bonding rituals designed to foster team relationships help to produce men for whom relationships with other men become the primary source of intimacy. Drawing on the work of scholars researching sports and masculinity, notably Peggy Reeves Sanday, Robinson suggests that sexual violence collectively enacted enables the men to get as close to each other as they can without endangering their sense of themselves as heterosexuals. To debase and degrade a woman in the presence of other men secures the masculinity that must be aggressive and that must disavow sexual feeling for other men.[24]

* * * * *

Steven Kummerfield confided to his best friend Tyler Stuart, with whom he had once gone to the area of prostitution, that "we beat the shit" out of "an Indian hooker." In Tyler Stuart's account, Kummerfield also elaborated that he said to Pamela George, "If you don't give us head, we're going to kill you." Stuart, apparently mostly concerned about the transmission of disease to Kummerfield's white girlfriend, advised his friend to break up with her if he hadn't worn a condom the night of the murder.[25] In none of these conversations was there any indication that the men acknowledged that a woman had been brutally murdered; her death seemed almost incidental and simply inconvenient. The men seemed to possess a collective understanding of Pamela George as a thing, an objectification that their exclusively white worlds would have given them little opportunity to disrupt.

* * * * *

Although there are several instances which neither of the accused can recall, they generally agreed that once at the country field, Pamela George was frightened and tried to defend herself. They talked to her and gave her false names. She ultimately agreed to perform oral sex and all three remained in the front seat of the car while this was in progress. While George was performing oral sex on Ternowetsky (having finished with Kummerfield), Kummerfield announce that they should leave. Ternowetsky asked that George be allowed to finish but a short time later, Kummerfield dragged her from the car and hit her. Ternowetsky, at first surprised, joined in. Neither recalled the extent of the violence, but each remembered her face in the mud and the fact that she tried to defend herself. They later claimed that when they drove off (after having bent the license plate to conceal the numbers), Pamela George was still standing.[26]

During the trial, the murder scene and the Stroll were described as spaces somehow innately given to illicit and sexual activity. The bodies of Charlene Rosebluff, Pamela George, and a number of Aboriginal men were represented variously as bodies that naturally belonged to these spaces of prostitution, crime, sex, and violence. This degenerate space, into which Kummerfield and Ternowetsky ventured temporarily, was juxtaposed to the spaces of respectability. Each space required a different legal response. In racialized space, violence may occur with impunity. Bodies from respectable spaces may also violate with impunity, particularly if the violence takes place in the racialized space of prostitution.

UNMAPPING LAW: GENDERED RACIAL VIOLENCE IN ANOMALOUS ZONES

When I identify Ternowetsky and Kummerfield's transgression into racial space as an identity-making process (the men entered the zone, came into close contact with its degenerate occupants, and survived to tell the tale), it is worth reiterating the important connection between prostitution, race, space, and justice. Prostitution emerged in its modern form as distinct and confined to sharply demarcated areas of the city at the historical moment when liberal nation-states emerged. Bourgeois subjects, the new citizens of the nation-state, knew themselves as respectable and civilized largely through a spatial separation from those deemed to be degenerate and uncivilized. Degenerate spaces (slums, colonies) and the bodies of prostitutes were known as zones of disorder, filth, and immorality. The inhabitants of such zones were invariably racialized,[27] evacuated from the category human, and denied the equality so fundamental to liberal states.

During the trial, Pamela George came to be seen as a rightful target of the gendered violence inflicted by Kummerfield and Ternowetsky. Put another way, her murder was characterized as a natural by-product of the space and thus of the social context in which it occurred, an event that is routine when the bodies in question are Aboriginal. This naturalizing of violence is sustained by the legal idea of contract, an agreement between consenting and autonomous individuals. Because she consented to provide sexual services, the violence became more permissible. The moment of violence is contained within the moment of the contract and there can be no history or context, for example, the constraints on her choice and the historical conditions under which the bargain was made. Trapped in the moment in time of the contract, Pamela George remained simply "the prostitute" or the "Indian."

* * * * *

It is no small irony that racism, so rarely named during the trial, only emerged explicitly during sentencing. The defense reported that Alex Ternowetsky had taken a course on Native literature while in prison and had written a paper on Aboriginal–white relations that proved that he had "no clear motive of hatred towards someone of a particular racial origin."[28] Racelessness was pursued to the bitter end, however. When there were complaints made against him after the trial, Mr. Justice Malone confirmed (in a letter to Chief Justice Allan McEachern) that race overdetermined the trial, but noted that only a strategy of racelessness (ignoring everyone's race) countered it:

> I suspect the real basis for most of the complaints, including the two that I have dealt
> with, is the underlying feeling that because the two accused were white and the victim
> was a First Nations person they received special treatment and the jury's verdict [of man-
> slaughter and not murder] was based on racism. This was certainly the reaction of several
> First Nations spokesmen and extensive media coverage was given to their remarks in this
> regard. Furthermore, both accused came from financially secure homes and enjoyed the
> material benefits associated therewith. Their position in life was in striking contrast to the
> position of the victim. Every effort was made during the trial by counsel and myself to
> deal with the case strictly on the basis of relevant evidence and not on the financial and
> social positions of the accused and their victim or their race.[29]

Here, colour-blindness as a legal approach, the belief that justice can only be achieved by treating all individuals as though they were the same, held full sway.

Race, social position, and, I would add, gender were indeed made to disappear during the trial and in the sentencing. The social meaning of spaces and bodies were deliberately excluded as evidence that would contaminate the otherwise pure process of law, evidence that was not relevant. It was not then possible to interrogate what white men thought they were doing in journeying to the Stroll to buy the services of an Aboriginal prostitute. It was also not possible to interrogate the meaning of consent and violence in the space of prostitution and between white and Aboriginal bodies. Since bodies had no race, class, or gender, the constructs that ruled the day, heavily inflected with these social relations, coded rather than reveal them explicitly. Thus "prostitute" and people of "the street" came to signify the racial Other and the spaces of violence. In contrast, the university, the chalet, the cottage, the suburban home, the isolated spaces in which the men socialized were unmarked. When Pamela George's mother Ina and her sister Denise respectively commented in their victim impact statement, "so what if she was a prostitute?" and "it felt she was on trial because she was a prostitute," they were identifying two domains of law—the domain of justice and the domain beyond it.[30] This spatial configuration was explicitly geographical and quite deliberately mapped. It was also explicitly raced, classed, and gendered. Bodies that engage in prostitution and the spaces of prostitution are racialized, as I have argued elsewhere, regardless of the actual race of the prostitute. In this sense, it is possible, as Ternowetsky's lawyer suggested at sentencing, that Pamela George's race made no difference, but only in the sense that any woman engaging in prostitution loses her status as white. What a spatial analysis reveals is that bodies in degenerate spaces lose their entitlement to personhood through a complex process in which the violence that is enacted is naturalized. Even when the trial judge at sentencing acknowledged that Pamela George was the victim of mindless violence and that her murderers "cast her aside as if she were something less than human," these observations did not alter his ultimate positions that the accused deserved a punishment of six and a half years, given the time of twenty months already served.[31]

Uncovering this spatialized view of justice helps us to see how race shapes the law by informing notions of what is just and who is entitled to justice. It enables us to see how whiteness is protected and reproduced through such ideas as a contract between autonomous individuals standing outside of history. What would it mean to deliberately introduce history and social context into this trial? In the first instance, we would have to ask questions about the activities of the accused. How did they routinely conduct themselves? What is the role of violence against woman in their activities? Who were the women who were seen as targets of the violence? These questions would have to be raised within the historical and social context of Aboriginal–white relations in Regina. Secondly, to appreciate that a person has been brutally murdered, details about Pamela George's life, once again historically contextualized, would have to be on the record to counter the historically produced response to her as a woman whose life was worth very little. Efforts to introduce these two lines of evidence would be thwarted by the notion that prostitution is a contract and not violence, and the notion that individuals must be judged as though they were not embedded in historical and contemporary relations of domination. These approaches would also be resisted by the deeply entrenched notion that colonization simply happened a long time ago, if at all, and that it has ended, without colonizers enacting it and benefiting from it and, most of all, without their continuing to do so. If this exploration of Pamela George's murder trial does anything at all, my hope is that it raises consciousness about how little she mattered to her murderers, their friends and families, and how small a chance she had of entering the court's and Canadian society's consciousness as a person.

ENDNOTES

1. *R. v. Kummerfield and Ternowetsky,* "Transcript of 12–15, 18–22, 25–28 November, and 2–5, 9–12, and 17–20 December 1996" [1997] (Regina, Sask. Prov. Ct. [Crim. Div.]), 3469, 4755 (hereafter "Transcript").

2. B. Pacholik, "Relief, and Anger, Aboriginal Spokesperson Demands Appeal," *Leader Post* (Regina), December 21, 1996, p. A1.

3. Barb Pacholik, "Ternowetsky in Ontario Jail, Facing New Charges," *Leader Post,* October 3, 2001, p. A1.

4. *R. v. Kummerfield,* [1998] 9 W.W.R. 619; *R. v. Kummerfield. (S. T.) & Ternowetsky (A.D.),* [1998] 163 Sask. R. 257.

5. See, for example, B. Balos and M. L. Fellows, "A Matter of Prostitution: Becoming Respectable," *New York University Law Review* 74 (1999). The authors write: "The unstated assumption is that if a woman enjoyed a benefit, she 'assumed the risk' and therefore bears responsibility for the violence, leaving the alleged perpetrator less accountable for his behavior" (p. 1231).

6. I use the term "degeneracy" in this article to denote those groups Foucault describes as the "internal enemies" of the bourgeois state—women, racial Others, the working class, people with disabilities—in short, all those who would weaken the vigorous bourgeois body and state. For a discussion of the concepts of respectability and degeneracy, see Sherene Razack, "Race, Space, and Prostitution: The Making of the Bourgeois Subject," *Canadian Journal of Women and the Law* 10, 2 (1998), pp. 335–52.

7. For a general argument of this kind, made with respect to Aboriginal people in the inner city, see C. La Prairie, *Seen But Not Heard: Native People in the Inner City* (Ottawa: Minister of Justice and Attorney General of Canada, 1994). La Prairie writes, "Overall, the research suggests that social stratification and the experience of people have in their families dictate the role they play in cities. It is the ill-equipped who are mostly seen on the streets of the inner city" (p. 19). Similar to the deficit model in educational theory, this view places the problems Aboriginal peoples have in cities squarely on their own shoulders, leaving little room for the ongoing effects of colonial practices emphasized in this article.

8. Phillips, *Mapping Men and Empire: A Geography of Adventure* (New York: Routledge, 1997), p. 338.

9. *Canada, Profile of Census Tracts in Regina and Saskatoon* (Ottawa: Statistics Canada, 1999). Regina's total population for 1996 was 193,652. Of that total 14,565 persons identified as Aboriginal. On the problems associated with Aboriginal census data, see J. Saku, "Aboriginal Census Data in Canada: A Research Note," *Canadian Journal of Native Studies* 19, 2 (1999). In coming years Saskatchewan is expected to have a greater proportion of population with Aboriginal identity: 13 per cent by 2016. See M. J. Norris, D. Kerr, and F. Nault, *Projections of the Population with Aboriginal Identity, Canada, 1991–2016* (Ottawa: Statistics Canada and Population Projections Section, Demography Division, 1996).

10. D. Anaquod and V. Khaladkar, "Case Study: The First Nations Economy in the City of Regina," in *For Seven Generations: An Information Legacy of the Royal Commission on Aboriginal Peoples,* CD-ROM (Ottawa: Libraxus, 1997), p. 6.

11. J.W. Brennan, *Regina: An Illustrated History* (Toronto: James Lorimer and Company and the Canadian Museum of Civilization with the Secretary of State, 1989), p. 37; Sarah Carter, *Capturing Women: The Manipulation of Cultural Imagery in Canada's Prairie West* (Montreal: McGill-Queen's University Press, 1997), pp. 20–1. The brutality of the NWMP and the RCMP towards Aboriginal peoples and their sexual brutality towards Aboriginal women are described in L. Brown and C. Brown, *An Unauthorized History of the RCMP* (Toronto: James Lewis and Samuel, 1973), pp. 143–81.

12. Jim Harding, "Presentation to the Royal Commission on Aboriginal Peoples," May 11, 1993, Regina, Saskatchewan, in *For Seven Generations,* p. 321.

13. Brennan, *Regina*, p. 165.

14. "Qu'Appelle Valley Indian Development Authority Inquiry Report on: Flooding Claim Cowessess First Nation, Muscowpetung First Nation, Ochapowace First Nation, Pasqua First Nation, Sakimay First Nation, Standing Buffalo First Nation." *Indian Claims Commission.* http://www.indianclaims.ca/english/claimsmap/prov_sask.htm. May 2000.

15. Harding, "Presentation to the Royal Commission on Aboriginal Peoples"; Brennan, *Regina*, p. 165; J. Hylton cited in *Royal Commission on Aboriginal Peoples, Bridging the Cultural Divide: A Report on Aboriginal People and Criminal Justice in Canada* (Ottawa: Supply and Services Canada, 1996), pp. 31 n 41.

16. A. Finn et al., "Female Inmates, Aboriginal Inmates, and Inmates Serving Life Sentences: A One-Day Snapshot," *Juristat* 19, 5 (Ottawa: Canadian Centre for Justice Statistics/Statistics Canada, 1999), p. 9. In addition, "at the provincial/territorial level, a larger proportion of Aboriginal than non-Aboriginal inmates were segregated from the rest of the inmate population (11 percent versus 4 percent)."

17. Patricia Monture-Angus, "Women and Risk: Aboriginal Women, Colonialism, and Correctional Practice," *Canadian Woman Studies* 19, 1 and 2 (1999), p. 28 n 3; Manitoba, *Report of the Aboriginal Justice Inquiry of Manitoba: The Justice System and Aboriginal People,* vol. 1 (Winnipeg: Queen's Printer, 1991), p. 498. In describing the Saskatchewan situation, Manitoba's commissioners were highlighting the fact that the disproportionate rate of Aboriginal women represented in Manitoba's Portage Correctional Institution (at the time 70 percent) was by no means unique, particularly when considered within the prairie regional context; Harding, "Presentation to the Royal Commission on Aboriginal Peoples," p. 323; Hylton cited in *Royal Commission on Aboriginal Peoples, Bridging the Cultural Divide,* pp. 31–2 (notes omitted).

18. "Fact Sheets: Alternatives to Incarceration." *Elizabeth Fry Society.* http://www.elizabethfry.ca/facts1_e.htm. July 21, 2000. According to the Society, in 1998 "41 percent of federally sentenced women who are classified as maximum security women are Aboriginal, whereas Aboriginal women represent only 18.7 percent of the total population of federally sentenced women, and less than 2 percent of the population of Canada." See "Position of the Canadian Association of Elizabeth Fry Societies (CAEFS) Regarding the Classification and Carceral Placement of Women Classified as Maximum Security Prisoners." *Elizabeth Fry Society.* http://www.elizabethfry.ca/maxe.htm. July 21, 2000.

19. Harding, "Presentation to the Royal Commission on Aboriginal Peoples," pp. 324–6.

20. Of course Aboriginal women also endure considerable violence from the men of their communities. I would urge that such violence is of a different order than the violence discussed here, although the obvious link is that both emerge out of conditions of colonialization. As Emma LaRocque so insightfully commented in her testimony to the Aboriginal Justice Inquiry of Manitoba, the squaw stereotype regulates relations between Aboriginal men and women as it does between Aboriginal women and white society. Emma LaRocque, "Written Presentation to Aboriginal Justice Inquiry Hearings, 5 February 1990," cited in Manitoba, *Report of the Aboriginal Justice Inquiry,* p. 479. See also Sherene Razack, *Looking White People in the Eye: Gender, Race, and Culture in Courtrooms and Classrooms* (Toronto: University of Toronto Press, 1998), p. 69.

21. Manitoba, *Report of the Aboriginal Justice Inquiry of Manitoba: The Deaths of Helen Betty Osborne and John Joseph Harper,* vol. 2 (Winnipeg: Queen's Printer, 1991), p. 52.

22. Razack, "Race, Space, and Prostitution."

23. Malek Alloula, *The Colonial Harem* (Minneapolis: University of Minnesota Press, 1986) cited in R. Bishop and L. S. Robinson, *Night Market: Sexual Cultures and the Thai Economic Miracle* (London: Routledge, 1998), p. 151.

24. Laura Robinson, *Crossing the Line: Violence and Sexual Assault in Canada's National Sport* (Toronto: McClelland and Stewart, 1998), pp. 39, 120, 151–2.

25. "Transcript," pp. 846–910.

26. "Transcript," pp. 3574, 3888.

27. For example, Sander Gilman shows how prostitutes in nineteenth-century Europe were depicted with African features even though they were nearly all white. Sander Gilman, "Black Bodies, White Bodies: Toward an Iconography of Female Sexuality in Late Nineteenth-Century Art, Medicine, and Literature," in J. Donald and A. Rattansi, eds., *"Race," Culture, and Difference* (London: The Open University Press, 1992), p. 171. Similarly, McClintock discusses the racialization of the Irish poor, routinely depicted with Black skin in nineteenth-century England. A. McClintock, *Imperial Leather* (New York: Routledge, 1995), pp. 52–3.

28. "Transcript of Sentencing," p. 40.

29. Justice Malone, "Response to the Honourable Chief Justice Allan McEachern." Emphasis added.

30. "Transcript," p. 5023.

31. Ibid, p. 60. While I do not take a position on the value of long prison terms, I note here that they have been traditionally understood by society as an indicator of the severity of the crime.

CHAPTER SEVENTEEN

The Social Construction of a "Drop-out": Dispelling the Myth

George J. Sefa Dei

The narratives assembled in this ethnography draw from experiential frames of reference to give meaning to the term "drop-out." The collective meaning which emerges is a composite of behavioural traits, attitudes, and socially constructed notions which are often at odds with one another. These notions speak to the fact that the term "drop-out" represents different things to different people, all of whom speak from particular vantage points. The various perspectives which emerge emanate from specific ideologies and world-views, including some which challenge the "conventional wisdom" regarding drop-outs and others which reinforce standard misconceptions. By employing race as a factor, the stereotypes and stigmas of dropping out of school take on different meanings and are seen to affect students in specific ways.

Students were asked specifically to define a drop-out. Black and non-Black students generally agreed that the term refers to someone who stops coming to school. However, some students also included in their definition of a drop-out students who are still officially "at" school, but who are involved in the process of "fading out" or disengagement. These students were characterized as skipping classes, hanging out, "acting out," and not being involved in the formal aspects of the school. These behaviours often represent the first stage in a process of disengagement, yet many of these warning signs are ignored or inappropriately addressed by school agents. In this way, the term "drop-out" does not adequately capture the students' experience of schooling and why they leave school prematurely. The term "fade-out" may be more appropriate because students may be there in body but not in spirit.

The question of whether the students who change schools may be considered drop-outs also became relevant. The implication of the question is whether failing in a particular environment qualifies as "dropping out." Student narratives were unanimous—a drop-out is someone who completely disengages from the system, not one who changes environments. Students who transfer to different schools were understood generally to have experienced failure or other problems at the previous school—conflicts with administration, teachers, or students—and were seeking an alternative environment in which they could succeed. In fact, when students actively seek out alternative school environments and succeed, this serves to validate their assessment of the problems they felt they were facing previously.

The ways in which students framed their understanding of why some students drop out of school can be related to certain ideological positions. Some responses conceptualized drop-outs as "push-outs," implicating outside forces such as adverse economic conditions, realities of the social structure, and personal problems, all of which conspire to force individuals out of school. Kin, a grade 12 student, was clear about the existence of barriers which compel some students to drop out:

> Drop-outs are ... students who have some kind of personal problems or anything socially that doesn't allow them to actually continue school or even work. They can't, whatever the problem may be, they can't actually continue school. *They have no other choice.* (File W01: lines 24–32)

Other responses provided examples of individualized and meritocratic world-views in which individuals are implicated as the sole architects of their success or failure. These views can be said to form the basis of popular notions of what is known as the "conventional wisdom" regarding drop-outs. Suneel, an OAC student, framed the decision to drop out as a free choice, not a reaction to circumstance:

> ... it's like if ... you drop out, it means that you don't want to come to school or you choose not to come to school. And *it's up to you*, it's your decision. Nobody won't force you to go. (File B04: lines 22–8)

Conversely, some students isolated factors related to the notion of a "hidden curriculum," that is, the attitudes and behaviours of teachers and other school agents which may affect a student's decision to leave school. Fema, a Black grade 10 general level student, identified interpersonal relationships as a factor in the decision-making process:

> I understand that lots of people dropped out because some of them are saying how much a teacher don't like them and stuff like that. (File D27: lines 11–14)

Fema addresses the powerful effect of the interpersonal relationship between teachers and students and the repercussions which can occur if this relationship is perceived to be negative.

Coupled with ideological factors, it becomes apparent that "drop-out" is a loaded term and commonly embodies aetiology. When causes are connected to individual shortcomings, they contribute to negative stereotypes and the stigmatization of leaving school, rather than implicating the school and society as part of the problem. When race is accounted for as a factor, these stereotypes are seen by Lea, another grade 10 general level student, to contribute to the low expectations held for Black students:

> I feel so angry; I get so bitter inside for them because it's like this is what people expect of some Black people, that they can't accomplish nothing. They can't be a doctor or a lawyer ... they're not capable. They're ignorant, as "they" put it. They always say we're ignorant, and it just, it makes us look so low. (File W17: lines 100–20)

The anger expressed here is empathetic and directed, not towards the drop-outs, but rather to their predicament. This young woman not only identifies the negative stereotypes associated with dropping out, but highlights how those stereotypes are connected with racial and cultural biases. In other words, for a White student, dropping out may carry the stigma of perceived failure but it is not automatically ascribed to racial or cultural factors, which is what is understood to occur when the student is Black. The preceding quotation is evidence of how the stigma associated with Black students who drop out affects even those students who remain in school, since it legitimizes perceived notions of the inferiority of all Black people. Therefore, the negative stereotypes and social stigmas carried by Black students who drop out affect not only themselves but, in effect, the status and perception of all Blacks in society.

Students expressed a range of feelings from sadness to empathy to anger. In response to the question of why students drop out of school, students frequently began with statements like "It's too bad, I feel sorry for them." Many students spoke in terms which did not blame drop-outs, but rather empathized with their reality. Lesline, an OAC level student, shared her insight into this reality:

> I don't scorn them, because I feel my friends ... would be considered drop-outs. But because I know them, I understand that there's politics involved when they say you are a drop-out or when you decide to. Some people, they're bored, and you say that's not a valid reason, but after being bored for two years and you haven't gotten let's say eight credits, and ... you're like, "I'll be in school longer and longer and it'll get more boring and more frustrating" ... a lot of friends have left because of that. Some people leave because they just can't, they can't find themselves in school ... (File O03: lines 73–95)

Lesline talks about the need to understand the reality faced by students and the importance which that understanding has for legitimizing their experiences. The references to not being able to "find themselves in school," and to the sense of "frustration" and "boredom," reveal the emotional and psychological conditions which are seen as contributing to the process of disengagement. These feelings are understood as the result of the "politics" of schooling, in which students who are unable to conform to the demands of the education system feel marginalized and eventually fade out of school.

The narratives addressed varying problems facing students. Financial concerns, "family problems," pregnancy, problems in the school related to racism, relationships with teachers, lack of academic success, and how some students simply cannot cope were identified as the primary issues affecting the lives of students. This reveals an identification with the complex and varied experiences of disengagement, both through personal experience and association.

When students talked about the future for drop-outs, it was frequently associated with negative activities such as dealing drugs, hanging out, collecting welfare, and so on. Yet at times some students mentioned the positive outcome of getting work, despite not having finished school. In this regard, a practical understanding of how drop-outs might assess their immediate future is expressed by Susan, an OAC student:

> They don't think after high school they're going to have anything else so they want to go pursue something that will give them some economic benefit right now. (File B19: lines 24–8)

Despondency over future employment prospects reflected an understanding of the changing realities of work in late capitalist society. Students questioned the practical benefits of education in a limited and fluctuating labour market. At times negative and somewhat fatalistic attitudes about future options were expressed. In this context, the exploitation of short-term gains at the expense of long-term goals such as continued education appeared more pragmatic.

More often students were critical of abandoning long-term goals, arguing that drop-outs are myopic in not seeing the connection between work and school. Some students empathized with wanting to leave school, but felt it was not practical. The repeated comment "Even to be a garbage-man you need grade 12" among students still in school indicated their awareness that one had to "play the game" in order to succeed. Education was understood as a means to an end rather than an end in itself. This understanding highlights the clear connection made between education and future economic opportunities.

Students were generally sympathetic towards drop-outs, empathizing with the disadvantage they feel drop-outs have in society, as a result of their lack of education. As Danielle, a Jamaican-born grade 12 student, indicated, these difficulties are compounded by the issue of race:

> I think it's sad and I think that [Black students] can do better. It's hard enough being the most obvious minority and having to live with that, but the lack of education will only hurt them more. (File D24: lines 139–45)

The discrimination and difficulty experienced in being Black is clearly described by this student as being intensified when a Black student drops out of school. Dropping out therefore creates a double impediment: racial discrimination compounded by a lack of education. As this student explained, Black students who drop out are generally regarded by some of their peers as following a course of action, whether or not it is of their own volition, which will serve to further disadvantage them within society.

Black students tended to speak about symptoms of disengaging rather than specific characteristics. They expressed a deep identification with the experience of not feeling as though they "belonged." Kenneth, a Caribbean-born student in the advanced stream of grade 11, related the feelings of alienation felt by students who eventually drop out:

> Mostly it's just the person who's, like, being stretched out, stretching him or herself out, and saying that they don't feel like they belong. They don't feel like they belong in the school ... (File B07: lines 356–62)

The notion of "stretching him or herself out" implies a certain incongruence of the reality of the student with that of the school and the pressures felt to conform. For Black and minority students this sense of not "belonging" is often related to the centrality of White middle-class norms and values within the educational system (see Ogbu 1982; Delpit 1988). An inability or unwillingness to conform serves to marginalize the culture and realities of minority students, and in effect the students themselves. When the interests of these students remain peripheral to mainstream education, the students themselves will feel similarly situated outside the boundaries of social acceptance. This process of marginalization can be seen to engender a school culture and climate that is perceived as unresponsive and excluding.

A few of the students interviewed had dropped out or had come close to dropping out. These students shared anecdotes and insights into their experiences. Wendy, a grade 10 advanced level student, discussed the feelings of dissonance and anomie experienced when she could not relate to other Black students after starting at a new school where the majority of students were White:

> After I moved up here, I didn't really like the area. I thought that I didn't really fit in because nobody was really the same as me. Even the Black students were different from me ... they were a bit more White to me than what I was used to and I just didn't really

like the school. I didn't fit in ... I didn't feel like going because to me there was no reason to go. I had nothing to look forward to going there. (File R02: lines 1476–90)

Wendy expressed a sense of detachment from members of her own race and ethnic background who acted "a bit more White." This detachment addresses the paradox of cultural conformity, in which, as individuals become culturally and socially more integrated into the mainstream, they often distance themselves from members of their own ethno-cultural group. In this instance, the student feels a sense of double alienation, from mainstream society and from members of her own community who have conformed to the status quo. The importance of school culture and the social aspects of schooling therefore cannot be underestimated in terms of their impact on student disengagement.

Students who had not given serious consideration to dropping out cited family influences as the main reason for not doing so. Responses such as "Oh yeah, I've thought about it, but my Mom would kill me" were prevalent when the students discussed their own situations. This suggests that parents and the values they hold are powerful deterrents to leaving school. People within the school (teachers, counsellors, administrators, etc.), however, were not mentioned as persons students could or would approach. In fact, students did not relate to them as people who they felt would care or try to intervene in a positive way. This view reveals the perception many students have of school agents and their inability to provide the kind of support students require.

The topic of disengagement elicited discussions of parental relationships, values, and responsibilities. Students talked about their connection to a parent and their desire to make the parent (and others in the family) proud. Many young males also spoke about being able to provide for their mothers in the future. As well, the limited opportunities experienced by their parents and how this affects their own motivation to stay in school was mentioned by male and female students alike. Rana, a grade 10 advanced student of Caribbean descent, stated:

... I'm just kind of holding back because of my dad ... he had a chance to get his education but he didn't actually do that. He was supporting his younger brothers and sisters and stuff. And now today he's got a good job and everything but he could have done better ... So, I'm kind of, you know, just staying on. (File O30: lines 133–44)

Many students said they would not even discuss the idea of dropping out with their parents. Rather, siblings and peers, if anyone, were indicated as people they would confide in if they were thinking about dropping out. In fact, for all students, the people who they indicated would most likely serve as confidants were friends.

When those who have been through the process of disengagement from school conceptualize, interpret, and give meaning to the term "drop-out," they invariably do so from a radically different vantage point than do students still in the system. The latter, whether "at risk" or not, talked hypothetically about what dropping out might mean, whereas for actual drop-outs, the years (or the months) of experience after leaving school had put a different "spin" on the meanings and interpretations they gave to the term "drop-out."

Drop-outs tended to discuss dropping out as a personal loss—as a decision which had resulted in lost time, lost chances, and/or lost status in society. In this way, their narratives could coincide with those of many of the students. Yet drop-outs tended not to blame themselves for dropping out and still maintained that their decision made sense at the time. They defined the process of dropping out as one of gradual disengagement from school, a process which, for some, began as early as grade 2. Drop-outs were able to reach back into their early memories of schooling to locate experiences that related to the beginning of their own process of disengagement. Jennifer talked about how racial discrimination and isolation laid the groundwork for her decision to drop out:

> ... it was in the fourth grade ... I had a teacher, she blatantly did not want to teach me anything. And I was the only Black kid there in the school, in the neighbourhood, in the whole area ... yeah, she was something else. (File F03: lines 254–61)

Jennifer's comment also makes connections to the broader impact of the local community and social relations, and the alienation which permeated her experiences in and out of school. Later in the same interview, these early negative experiences are described as having had a constraining effect on her future aspirations:

> ... by the time I got to high school, I didn't think I was smart for anything so university was never, ever, ever in my dreams ... (File F03: lines 315–18)

This shows how low expectations, negative reinforcement, and alienation associated with dropping out are internalized and can place limits on self-esteem and ultimately life chances.

Students tended to say that drop-outs do not feel that school is "for them." Drop-outs echoed this sentiment as they talked about a drop-out as someone for whom the school is an unfriendly, uncomfortable, and unwelcoming place:

> They're not comfortable, you know, the environment that they're in is not really for them, and they're feeling sort of, like discouragement about not going to school anymore. (File F10: lines 60–4)

Here Robert exemplifies the personal and academic constraints that result from a negative school environment. The social aspects of schooling are therefore important to the level of students' satisfaction with their educational experience and can ultimately influence their decision of whether or not to remain in school.

Drop-outs tended to relate dropping out as a failure on the part of the school rather than as a failure on the part of the individual who leaves. Darren, a drop-out himself, spoke directly to this issue:

> I don't see them as people who failed. I see them as people that the system failed ... (File F13: lines: 2594–8)

Perhaps because of a lack of confidence in the system within which they had once been marginalized, the drop-outs were concerned that their voices would not be heard. They, more than any other group interviewed in this study, questioned whether anyone would listen or truly respond to their concerns.

Non-Black students did not have a clear image or stereotype regarding drop-outs—anyone can and does drop out. These students also spoke of dropping out as a process, and among the factors they mentioned which they believed led to dropping out, the most notable was negative attitudes towards school. Peter, an OAC level student, was unequivocal in his opinion:

People who don't want to learn, just don't want to be in school, they just decide to take a hike and leave. (File CG05: lines 10–12)

This type of response, which attributes responsibility for dropping out to the individual, who is someone who "does not want to learn" or does not like school, was a common one for non-Black students. Whereas Black students were usually able to acknowledge certain outside forces which impact negatively on a student's ability to remain in school, non-Black students were less cognizant of such factors (e.g., racism). Although they might acknowledge that some students dropped out of school as a result of financial difficulties, their vantage point did not seem to equip them with a clear understanding of how systemic barriers may hinder the progress of those who are less privileged on the basis of their racial or ethnic identity.

The understandings and opinions held by teachers about the meanings and interpretations associated with dropping out of school and other related issues can be said to reflect different locations on an ideological spectrum. These views may be characterized as ranging from "conservative" to "progressive." Although social location (gender, race, class, age, etc.) frequently influenced the ideological position held by individuals, it was not necessarily a determining factor. Generally speaking, older White males who described themselves as having life experiences which did not include close relationships with Black/African Canadians would be defined as being conservative. Conversely, younger female, and non-White teachers, or White males who had had life experiences involving Black/African Canadians, had what we defined as more progressive attitudes. Conservative responses were consistent with a belief in meritocracy and denied the saliency of race as an organizing principle for differential treatment within educational institutions. They were similarly unsupportive of anti-racism and multicultural initiatives in education. More progressive opinions, however, usually reflected a deeper understanding or appreciation of Black students' experiences and acknowledged the need for more inclusive schools.

Teachers with more conservative views tended to conceptualize dropping out as a choice made solely by students who chose not to be focused. They pointed to several other contributory factors, such as becoming pregnant, acting out generalized adolescent alienation, frustration as the result of not being taught the basics earlier on in school, lack of motivation, lack of a belief in the possibility of success, unstable family homes, and an absence of certain attitudes needed in order to succeed. In particular, these teachers saw dropping out as related to a societal attitude of "taking the easy way out" or "not taking responsibility." They often spoke of a lack of "work ethic" in students, how students want instant gratification and don't realize that one has to work to get things.

Teachers expressing opinions corresponding with the conservative end of the spectrum recognized that drop-outs might "blame the institution" for their lack of success, but saw this blame as misplaced. Andrew, who had been teaching history for thirty years, referred directly to a faulty interpretation of responsibility on the part of students:

You don't have to be responsible. And so I think they end up here, many of them without having thought anything out, without putting any effort into anything. And when they find that seven different teachers treat them seven different ways and there doesn't seem to be any consistency in that, then they look at the institution and they say, "The institution sucks. It doesn't know what it's doing. Why should I be here? Why should I do what they say? They don't even know what they're doing." And so they sort of give up. It's almost as if they come wanting to give up before they even start. (File T01: lines 472–87)

Here Andrew implies that drop-outs are somehow predisposed to having negative attitudes about schooling. However, this interpretation does not account for why these students have negative attitudes in the first place. It therefore holds the student accountable without first subjecting other factors related to schooling to the same critical examination.

Other teachers saw the drop-out dilemma as the result of inappropriate placement. They argued that students with a history of failure are frustrated when they come up against the reality of their failure. Some teachers suggested that certain students cannot function within the rigid structures of the school system and would do better in co-op programs. This explanation once again reduces the issue to an individual's failure to meet the demands of the system. It does not, however, confront the issue of whether the system has failed the student. Thus, in cases in which individual ability or academic aptitude is of concern, this should be a demonstrated concern rather than a foregone conclusion.

Some teachers viewed the family as the key to a student's dropping out. The ability of a single-parent household to provide the necessary support to students was seen as problematic. It was frequently held that single parents have less time and often a lack of education, and that children in these environments take advantage of their parents' ignorance of the school system. The perceived dysfunctional nature of such families was seen by these teachers as a primary factor in student disengagement. While families in crisis are of concern, the drop-out problem cannot be reduced to this issue. Implicating the "dysfunctional family" as the source of educational difficulties for the child, in a sense, divests the school from responsibility and fails to interrogate the difficulty many parents feel in engaging with the educational system. Parents from non-White backgrounds, in particular, often feel alienated by the school environment (Dehli 1994). Language difficulties and cultural notions which lead to feelings of intimidation by the authoritative structure of schooling, as well as a lack of minority representation within school administrations, are specific impediments to parental involvement. Therefore, in order to achieve a mutually beneficial partnership, schools must confront the barriers which distance home from school and create the means for parents to effectively engage with the school system.

A number of teachers described the drop-outs as someone lacking the requisite work ethic needed for academic success—an individual for whom school is unimportant and socializing is of primary importance. For most teachers, the absence of discipline and respect for the school system was seen as a problem. Interestingly, this was a view also held by many students. Yet the feeling was prevalent among those teachers defined as conservative that there are plenty of support services of which students may choose to take advantage if they are experiencing difficulty—it is the student's choice. Disengagement, then, is understood as related to a lack of motivation and desire on the part of the students.

These attitudes contrast sharply with the views of drop-outs themselves, who felt incumbered by the system and by the low expectations of teachers, rather than by their sense of apathy. This explanation also does not correspond to the depth of emotion many drop-outs exhibited when discussing their decision to leave school. From the narratives of drop-outs, it was clear that it was not a decision taken lightly as some teachers may believe. In their narratives, teachers did not address what, for students and drop-outs, may be considered deterrents to accessing the support services provided by the schools.

A decided minority of teachers, who were more progressive in their understanding of the difficulties facing Black youth, viewed possible reasons for disengagement as lodged in the school system. In this way, they conceptualized dropping out as a process, as opposed to an isolated decision based on an individualized notion of failure. Although these teachers also tended to see dropping out as a specific choice, they cited reasons which included not only personal and family variables but school variables as well. Some of these teachers also noted that the schools are not adequately addressing the needs of students who feel that school is meaningless and boring. They felt that the problems students have outside the school are intensified by the lack of support within the institution.

For their part, as stakeholders in the educational system, parents see the drop-out problem as a major issue for the Black/African-Canadian community. They are concerned about their children "making the grade," and particularly about youth who no longer see education as a tool to achieve their life ambitions and dreams. When asked to describe students who have dropped out, parents used images which appear to reflect both systemic difficulties in the school system and individual issues with students. Marilyn, a mother, responded to the term "drop-out" with the following:

> It means to me that they're kids who the system has failed and it has turned them off of school … because … when you look at the kids who are drop-outs and they turn around and do something and then succeed at it, it means that they had the capability but it was not tapped … if the system had provided the necessary nurturing for those kids, they would have made it. (File P04: lines 6–27)

Marilyn argues that the educational system has to address the students' need for nurturing and focus on identifying the abilities and potential of students. By addressing these needs, she believes the level of achievement for Black students would be positively affected.

The idea that more could be done to ensure that students complete high school is prevalent throughout the parent narratives. Amma, a Black woman who works with youth on a regular basis, interpreted the term "drop-out" as referring to students who have somehow "lost their way":

> When I think about that person I think about someone who is … alienated … disillusioned … frustrated. Somebody who has just basically given up in believing the school system can work for them or that it can make a difference. Yeah, when I hear that term, I put it in that context right away, in terms of issues … I see it as something that is prevalent within our community … as a matter of fact, some of the kids that I've come in contact with are some kids who are finished grade eleven, grade twelve and who are not even aware that they can go beyond that, or that there's assistance for them to go on beyond that. It just boggles my mind that they feel, "This is as far as I'm going to get." (File CW1: lines 25–28)

Students who leave school early are seen by parents to be those who have lost interest in the school system for a variety of reasons. These students are seen, through a combination of their school experiences and personal lives, as having become disconnected with an educational system that does not strive to engage them.

The contrast that exists between the ideological vantage points of conservative teachers and non-Black students, on the one hand, and those of Black students, drop-outs, and Black parents and community workers, on the other, represents a clear dichotomy in the way drop-outs are conceptualized by these groups. For example, the conservative perspective tends to individualize reasons for dropping out and to point to factors such as negative attitudes towards schooling, lack of a work ethic, and low scholastic achievement. Conservative responses do not include implicating schools or the educational system for contributing to the drop-out problem, except for a decided minority, which cited some culpability on the part of schools and educators. The issue of race was not mentioned. While there may be a tendency to interpret such an omission as positive, it actually points to a disregard or lack of understanding of how issues of race can contribute to the process of disengagement for Black and other minority students. Although, ideally, race would not be a factor related to educational success, the students' and drop-outs' narratives show that it is.

Narratives from the other side of the ideological spectrum (most Black students, drop-outs, Black parents, and community workers) generally highlighted alienation, failure of the school system, and lack of support within schools as being some of the preconditions for Black students' disengagement from school. It was felt that family values in the Black community were conducive to greater perseverance in school than suggested by those teachers who viewed drop-outs as the product of dysfunctional homes. While "family problems" can certainly impact negatively on a student's school life and may ultimately affect the process of disengagement, this should not overshadow the positive effects of family ethics and values, which many students carry with them into their educative experiences. Black students stated that it was concern for their parents and the thought of how the repercussions of their dropping out would affect their parents that helped give them the impetus to remain in school. While some teachers and non-Black students tended to locate the epicentre of the drop-out phenomenon within the family structure and within the individual themselves, drop-outs, Black students, and Black parents and community workers generally implicated racism and the inefficiencies of the educational system as the co-determinants of Black students' disengagement.

The fact that many Black students stay in school and complete their education "successfully" gives the false impression that systemic barriers within the educational system do not exist or, at the very least, are overstated. Some students are successful in spite of genuine educational problems, and many do in fact give something up, specifically in terms of their identity, in order to "succeed" (see Fordham 1988). The issue is framed in another way by Fine (1991, 7), who states in her study of drop-outs in an urban New York high school that for her, after "uncovering layers of systemic, widespread school failure, the question was no longer why a student would drop out. It was more compelling to consider why so many would stay ..." The narratives suggest that once students get on the track of fading out (e.g., skipping classes, sitting in the back of class, hanging out in hallways, "acting out," being truant), schools often help them "out the door." These behaviours may be symptoms of a larger problem and can often tell us something about the process of schooling rather than simply about the individual. "Acting out" and other forms of anti-school behaviour among Black and minority students is often viewed as a means of resistance to school authority (Giroux 1983a, 1983b; Solomon 1992; Willis 1977). It is important to recognize the limits of resistance theories and that all oppositional behaviours cannot necessarily be connected to defiance of school authority; still, an understanding of the socio-political implications of such behaviour among Black and minority youth does often lead to this conclusion.

As the narratives in this chapter have shown, understanding student disengagement involves redefining ideologically conditioned notions of failure and misapprehensions regarding "dropouts" through an examination of the lived realities of students who must contend with what Fine (1991, 6) characterizes as "the rationalized policies and practices of exclusion" within public schooling. Contrary to the conventional wisdom surrounding the issue of student disengagement, Black respondents did not associate low scholastic achievement with dropping out. Dropping out was recognized as a process which had broader social and cultural implications.

There is no simple cause-effect relation which characterizes Black students' disengagement from school. Dropping out is the final act of a series of school and out-of-school developments/experiences that define the student's ability to engage and disengage in a school's culture. Students drop out of school when it appears, in their view, there is no other appropriate recourse or action to take.

REFERENCES

Dehli, K. 1994. *Parent Activism and School Reform in Toronto*. Toronto: Ontario Institute for Studies in Education.

Delpit, L.D. 1988. "The Silenced Dialogue: Power and Pedagogy in Educating Other People's Children." *Harvard Educational Review* 58(3): 280–98.

Fine, M. 1991. *Framing Dropouts: Notes on the Politics of an Urban Public High School*. New York: State University of New York Press.

Fordham, S. 1988. "Racelessness as a Factor in Black Students School Success: Pragmatic Strategy or Pyrrhic Victory?" *Harvard Educational Review* 58(1): 54–84.

Giroux, H. 1983a. *A Theory of Resistance in Education: A Pedagogy for the Opposition*. South Hadley, MA: Bergin and Harvey.

———. 1983b. "Theories of Reproduction and Resistance in the New Sociology of Education." *Harvard Educational Review* 53: 257–93.

Ogbu, J.U. 1982. "Equalization of Educational Opportunity and Racial/Ethnic Inequality." In *Comparative Education*. Ed. P.G. Allbach, R.F. Arnove, and G.P. Kelly. New York: Macmillan.

Solomon, P. 1992. *Black Resistance in High School: Forging a Separatist Culture*. New York: State University of New York Press.

Willis, P. 1977. *Learning to Labour*. Farnborough: Saxon House.

CHAPTER EIGHTEEN

Individual Freedom as a Social Commitment

Amartya Sen

Bertrand Russell, who was a firm atheist, was once asked what he would do if, following his death, he were to encounter God after all. Russell is supposed to have answered, "I will ask him: God Almighty, why did you give so little evidence of your existence?"[1] Certainly the appalling world in which we live does not—at least on the surface—look like one in which an all-powerful benevolence is having its way. It is hard to understand how a compassionate world order can include so many people afflicted by acute misery, persistent hunger, and deprived and desperate lives, and why millions of innocent children have to die each year from lack of food or medical attention or social care.

This issue, of course, is not new, and it has been a subject of some discussion among theologians. The argument that God has reasons to want us to deal with these matters ourselves has had considerable intellectual support. As a nonreligious person, I am not in a position to assess the theological merits of this argument. But I can appreciate the force of the claim that people themselves must have responsibility for the development and change of the world in which they live. One does not have to be either devout or nondevout to accept this basic connection. As people who live—in a broad sense—together, we cannot escape the thought that the terrible occurrences that we see around us are quintessentially our problems. They are our responsibility—whether or not they are also anyone else's.

As competent human beings, we cannot shirk the task of judging how things are and what needs to be done. As reflective creatures, we have the ability to contemplate the lives of others. Our sense of responsibility need not relate only to the afflictions that our own behavior may have caused (though that can be very important as well), but can also relate more generally to the miseries that we see around us and that lie within out power to help remedy. That responsibility is not, of course, the only consideration that can claim our attention, but to deny the relevance of that general claim would be to miss something central about our social existence. It is not so much a matter of having the exact rules about how precisely we ought to behave, as of recognizing the relevance of our shared humanity in making the choices we face.[2]

INTERDEPENDENCE BETWEEN FREEDOM AND RESPONSIBILITY

That question of responsibility raises another. Shouldn't a person herself be entirely responsible for what happens to her? Why should others take responsibility for influencing her life? That thought, in one form or another, seems to move many political commentators, and the idea of self-help fits well into the mood of the present times. Going further, some argue that dependence on others is not only ethically problematic, it is also practically defeatist in sapping individual initiative and effort, and even self-respect. Who better to reply on than oneself to look after one's interests and problems?

The concerns that give force to this line of reasoning can indeed be very important. A division of responsibility that places the burden of looking after a person's interests on another person can lead to the loss of many important things in the form of motivation, involvement, and self-knowledge that the person herself may be in a unique position to have. Any affirmation of social responsibility that *replaces* individual responsibility cannot but be, to varying extents, counterproductive. There is no substitute for individual responsibility.

The limited reach and plausibility of an exclusive reliance on personal responsibility can best be discussed only after its essential role has first been recognized. However, the substantive freedoms that we respectively enjoy to exercise our responsibilities are extremely contingent on personal, social, and environmental circumstances. A child who is denied opportunity of elementary schooling is not only deprived as a youngster, but also handicapped all through life (as a person unable to do certain basic things that rely on reading, writing, and arithmetic). The adult who lacks the means of having medical treatment for an ailment from which she suffers is not only prey to preventable morbidity and possibly escapable mortality, but may also be denied the freedom to do various things—for herself and for others—that she may wish to do as a responsible human being. The bonded laborer born into semislavery, the subjugated girl child stifled by a repressive society, that helpless landless laborer without substantial means of earning an income are all deprived not only in terms of well-being, but also in terms of the ability to lead responsible lives, which are contingent on having certain basic freedoms. Responsibility *requires* freedom.

The argument for social support in expanding people's freedom can, therefore, be seen as an argument *for* individual responsibility, not against it. The linkage between freedom and responsibility works both ways. Without the substantive freedom and capability to do something, a person cannot be responsible for doing it. But actually having the freedom and capability to do something does impose on the person the duty to consider whether to do it or not, and this does involve individual responsibility. In this sense, freedom is both necessary and sufficient for responsibility.

The alternative to an exclusive reliance on individual responsibility is not, as is sometimes assumed, the so-called nanny state. There is a difference between "nannying" an individual's choices and creating more opportunity for choice and for substantive decisions for individuals who can then act responsibly on that basis. The social commitment to individual freedom need not, of course, operate only through the state, but must also involve other institutions: political and social organizations, community-based arrangements, non-governmental agencies of various kinds, the media and other means of public understanding and communication, and the institutions that allow the functioning of markets and contractual relations. The arbitrarily narrow view of individual responsibility—with the individual standing on an imaginary island unhelped and unhindered by others—has to be broadened not merely by acknowledging that role of the state, but also by recognizing the functions of other institutions and agents.

JUSTICE, FREEDOM, AND RESPONSIBILITY

Central to the challenges we face in the contemporary world is our idea of an acceptable society. Why are some social arrangements hard to cherish? What can we do to make a society more tolerable? Underlying such ideas lie some theories of evaluation and—often implicitly—even some basic understanding of social justice. This is not, of course, the occasion to investigate theories of justice in any detail, which I have tried to do elsewhere.[3] I have, however, used in this work some general evaluation ideas that make use of notions of justice and their informational requirements. It may be useful to examine the connection of those ideas with what has been discussed in the intermediate chapters.

First, I have argued for the primacy of substantive freedoms in judging individual advantage and in evaluating social achievements and failures. The perspective of freedom need not be merely procedural (though processes do matter, inter alia, in assessing what is going on). The basic concern, I have argued, is with our capability to lead the kind of lives we have reason to value.[4] This approach can give a very different view of development from the usual concentration on GNP or technical progress or industrialization, all of which have contingent and conditional importance without being the defining characteristics of development.[5]

Second, the freedom-oriented perspective can accommodate considerable variations within that general approach. Freedoms are inescapably of different kinds, and in particular there is the important distinction, already discussed, between the "opportunity aspect" and the "process aspect" of freedom. While these different constituent components of freedom often go together, sometimes they may not, and much will then depend on the relative weights that are placed on the different items.[6]

Also, a freedom-oriented approach can go with different emphases on the relative claims of efficiency and equity. There can be conflicts between (1) having less inequality of freedoms and (2) getting as much freedom as possible for all, irrespective of inequalities. The shared approach permits the formulation of a class of different theories of justice with the same general orientation. Of course, the conflict between equity-oriented and efficiency-oriented considerations is not "special" to the perspective of freedoms. It arises no matter whether we concentrate on freedoms or on some other way of judging individual advantage (for example by happiness or "utilities," or by "resources" or "primary goods" that the persons respectively have). In standard theories of justice this conflict is addressed by proposing some very specific formula, such as the utilitarian requirement to maximize the sum total of utilities irrespective of distribution, or the Rawlsian Difference Principle that requires maximizing the advantage of the worst off, no matter how this may affect the advantages of all others.[7]

In contrast, I have not argued for a specific formula to "settle" this question, and have concentrated instead on acknowledging the force and legitimacy of both the aggregative and distributive concerns. That acknowledgment itself, along with the need to pay substantial attention to each of these concerns, draws our attention forcefully to the relevance of some basic but neglected issues in public policy, dealing with poverty, inequality, and social performance *seen in the perspective of freedom*. The relevance of both aggregative and distributive judgments in assessing the process of development is quite central to understanding the challenge of development. But this does not require us to rank all development experiences in one linear order. What is, in contrast, indispensably important is an adequate understanding of the informational basis of evaluation- the kind of information we need to examine in order to assess what is going on and what is being seriously neglected.

In fact, as discussed elsewhere[8] at the level of the pure theory of justice, it would be a mistake to look prematurely into one specific system for "weighting" some of these competitive concerns, which would severely restrict the room for democratic decision making in this crucial resolution (and more generally in "social choice," including the variety of processes that relate to participation). Foundational ideas of justice can separate out some basic issues as being inescapably relevant, but they cannot plausibly end up, I have argued, with an exclusive choice of some highly delineated formula relative weights as being the unique blueprint for "the just society."[9]

For example, a society that allows famines to occur when prevention is possible is unjust in a clearly significant way, but that diagnosis does not have to rest on a belief that some unique pattern of distribution of food, or of income, or of entitlements, among all the people in the country, will be maximally just, trailed by other exact distributions (all completely ordered vis-à-vis one another). The greatest relevance of ideas of justice lies in the identification of *patent injustice*, on which reasoned agreement is possible, rather than in the derivation of some extant formula for how the world should be precisely run.

Third, even as far as patent injustice is concerned, no matter how inescapable it may look in terms of foundational ethical arguments, the emergence of a shared recognition of that "injustice" may be dependent in practice on open discussion of issues and feasibilities. Extreme inequalities in matters of race, gender, and class often survive on the implicit understanding—to use a phrase that Margaret Thatcher made popular (in a different but somewhat related context)—that "there is no alternative." For example, in societies in which antifemale bias has flourished and been taken for granted, the understanding that this is not inevitable may itself require empirical knowledge as well as analytical arguments, and in many cases, this can be a laborious and challenging process.[10] The role of public discussion to debate conventional wisdom on both practicalities and valuations can be central to the acknowledgment of injustice.

Given the role that public debates and discussions must have in the formation and utilization or our social values (dealing with competing claims of different principles and criteria), basic civil rights, and political freedoms are indispensable for the emergence of social values. Indeed, the freedom to participate in critical evaluation and in the process of value formation is among the most crucial freedoms of social existence. The choice of social values cannot be settled merely by the pronouncements of those in authority who control the levers of government. [...] [W]e must see a frequently asked question in the development literature to be fundamentally misdirected: Do democracy and basic political and civil rights help to promote the process of development? Rather, the emergence and consolidation of these rights can be seen as being *constitutive* of the process of development.

This point is quite separate from the *instrumental* role of democracy and basic political rights in providing security and protection to vulnerable groups. The exercise of these rights can indeed help in making states more responsive to the predicament of vulnerable people and thus, contribute to preventing economic disasters such as famines. But going beyond that, the general enhancement of political and civil freedoms is central to the process of development itself. The relevant freedoms include the liberty of acting as citizens who matter and whose voices count, rather than living as well-fed, well-clothed, and well-entertained vassals. The instrumental role of democracy and human rights, important as it undoubtedly is, has to be distinguished from its constitutive importance.

Fourth, an approach to justice and development that concentrates on substantive freedoms inescapably focuses on the agency and judgment of individuals; they cannot be seen merely as patients to whom benefits will be dispensed by the process of development. Responsible adults must be in charge of their own well-being; it is for them to decide how to use their capabilities. But the capabilities that a person does actually have (and not merely theoretically enjoys) depend on the nature of social arrangements, which can be crucial for individual freedoms. And there the state and the society cannot escape responsibility.

It is, for example, a shared responsibility of the society that the system of labor bondage, where prevalent, should end, and that bonded laborers should be free to accept employment elsewhere. It is also a social responsibility that economic policies should be geared to providing widespread employment opportunities on which the economic and social viability of people may crucially depend. But it is, ultimately, an individual responsibility to decide what use to make of the opportunities of employment and what work options to choose. Similarly, the denial of opportunities of basic education to a child, or of essential health care to the ill, is a failure of social responsibility, but the exact utilization of the educational attainments or of health achievements cannot but be a matter for the person herself to determine.

Also, the empowerment of women, through employment opportunities, education arrangements, property rights, and so on, can give women more freedom to influence a variety of matters such as intrafamily division of health care, food and other commodities, and work arrangements as well as fertility rates, but the exercise of that enhanced freedom is ultimately a matter for the person herself. The fact that statistical predictions can often be plausibly made on the ways this freedom is likely to be used (for example, in predicting that female education and female employment opportunity would reduce fertility rates and the frequency of child-bearing) does not negate the fact that it is the exercise of the women's enhanced freedom that is being anticipated.

WHAT DIFFERENCE DOES FREEDOM MAKE?

The perspective of freedom, on which this study has concentrated, must not be seen as being hostile to the large literature on social change that has enriched our understanding of the process for many centuries. While parts of the recent development literature have tended to concentrate very much on some limited indicators of development such as the growth of GNP per head, there is quite a long tradition against being imprisoned in that little box. There have indeed been many broader voices, including that of Aristotle, whose ideas are of course among the sources on which the present analysis draws (with his clear diagnosis in *Nicomachean Ethics*: "wealth is evidently not the good we are seeking; for it is merely useful and for the sake of something else").[11] It applies also to such pioneers of "modern" economics as William Petty, the author of *Political Arithmetick* (1691), who supplemented his innovation of national income accounting with motivating discussions on much broader concerns.[12]

Indeed, the belief that the enhancement of freedom is ultimately an important motivating factor for assessing economic and social change is not at all new. Adam Smith was explicitly concerned with crucial human freedoms.[13] So was Karl Marx, in many of his writings, for example, when he emphasized the importance of "replacing the domination of circumstances and chance over individuals by the domination of individuals over chance and circumstances."[14] The protection and enhancement of liberty supplemented John Stuart Mill's utilitarian perspective very substantially, and so did his specific outrage at the denial of substantive freedoms to women.[15] Friedrich Hayek has been emphatic in placing the achievement of economic progress within a very general formulation of liberties and freedoms, arguing: "Economic considerations are merely those by which we reconcile and adjust our different purposes, none of which, in the last resort, are economic (except those of the miser or the man for whom making money has become an end in itself)."[16]

Several development economists have also emphasized the importance of freedom of choice as a criterion of development. For example, Peter Bauer, who has quite a record of "dissent" in development economics (including an insightful book called *Dissent on Development*) has argued powerfully for the following characterization of development:

> I regard the extension of the range of choice, that is, an increase in the range of effective alternatives open to the people, as the principal objective and criterion of economic development; and I judge a measure principally by its probable effects on the range of alternatives open to individuals.[17]

W.A. Lewis also stated, in his famous opus *The Theory of Economic Growth*, that the objective of development is increasing "the range of human choice." However, after making this motivational point, Lewis decided, ultimately, to concentrate his analysis simply on "the growth of output per head," on the ground that this "gives man greater control over his environment and thereby increases his freedom."[18] Certainly, other things given, an increase in output and income would expand the range of human choice—particularly over commodities purchased. But, as was discussed earlier, the range of substantive choice on valuable matters depends also on many other factors.

WHY THE DIFFERENCE?

It is, in this context, important to ask whether there is really any substantial difference between development analysis that focuses (as Lewis and many others choose to do) on "the growth of output per head" (such as GNP per capita), and a more foundational concentration on expanding human freedom. Since the two are related (as Lewis rightly points out), why are the two approaches to development—inescapably linked as they are—not substantively congruent? What difference can a focal concentration on freedom make?

The differences arise for two rather distinct reasons, related respectively to the "process aspect" and the "opportunity aspect" of freedom. First, since freedom is concerned with *processes of decisions making* as well as *opportunities to achieve valued outcomes*, the domain of our interest cannot be confined only to the outcomes in the form of the promotion of high output or income, or the generation of high consumption (or the other variables to which the concept of economic growth relates). Such processes as participation in political decisions and social choice cannot be seen as being—at best—among the *means* to development (through, say, their contribution to economic growth), but have to be understood as constitutive parts of the *ends* of development in themselves.

The second reason for the difference between "development as freedom" and the more conventional perspectives on development relates to contrasts within the *opportunity aspect* itself, rather than being related to the process aspect. In pursuing the view of development as freedom, we have to examine—in addition to the freedoms involved in political, social, and economic processes—the extent to which people have the opportunity to achieve outcomes that they value and have reason to value. The levels of real income that people enjoy are important in giving them corresponding opportunities to purchase goods and services and to enjoy living standards that go with those purchases. But as some of the empirical investigations presented earlier in this book showed, income levels may often be inadequate guides to such important matters as the freedom to live long, or the ability to escape avoidable morbidity, or the opportunity to have worthwhile employment, or to live in peaceful and crime-free communities. These non-income variables point to opportunities that a person has excellent reasons to value and that are not strictly linked with economic prosperity.

Thus, the *process* aspect and the *opportunity* aspect of freedom require us to go well beyond the traditional view of development in terms of "the growth of output per head." There is also the fundamental difference in perspective in valuing freedom *only for* the use that is to be made of that freedom, and valuing it *over and above* that. Hayek may have overstated his case (as he often did) when he insisted that "the importance of our being free to do a particular thing has nothing to do with the question of whether we or the majority are ever likely to make use of that possibility."[19] But he was, I would argue, entirely right in distinguishing between (1) the *derivative* importance of freedom (dependent only on its actual use) and (2) the *intrinsic* importance of freedom (in making us free to choose something we may or may not actually choose).

Indeed, sometimes a person may have a very strong reason to have an option precisely for the purpose of rejecting it. For example, when Mahatma Gandhi *fasted* to make a political point against the Raj, he was not merely *starving*, he was rejecting the option of eating (for that is what fasting is). To be able to fast, Mohandas Gandhi had to have the option of eating (precisely to be able to reject it); a famine victim could not have made a similar political point.[20]

While I do not want to go down the purist route that Hayek chooses (in dissociating freedom from actual use altogether), I would emphasize that freedom has many aspects. The *process* aspect of freedom would have to be considered in addition to the *opportunity* aspect, and the opportunity aspect itself has to be viewed in terms of *intrinsic* as well as *derivative* importance. Furthermore, freedom to participate in public discussion and social interaction can also have a *constructive* role in the formation of values and ethics. Focusing on freedom does indeed make a difference.

HUMAN CAPITAL AND HUMAN CAPABILITY

I must also briefly discuss another relation which invites a comment, to wit, the relation between the literature on "human capital" and the focus in this work on "human capability" as an expression of freedom. In contemporary economic analysis the emphasis has, to a considerable extent, shifted from seeing capital accumulation in primarily physical terms to viewing it as a process in which the productive quality of human beings is integrally involved. For example, through education, learning, and skill formation, people can become much more productive over time, and this contributes greatly to the process of economic expansion.[21] In recent studies of economic growth (often influenced by empirical readings of the experiences of Japan and the rest of East Asia as well as Europe and North America), there is a much greater emphasis on "human capital" than used to be the case not long ago.

How does this shift relate to the view of development—development as freedom—presented in this book? More particularly, what, we may ask, is the connection between "human capital" orientation and the emphasis on "human capability" with which this study has been much concerned? Both seem to place humanity at the center of attention, but do they have differences as well as some congruence? At the risk of some oversimplification, it can be said that the literature on human capital tends to concentrate on the agency of human beings in augmenting production possibilities. The perspective of human capability focuses, on the other hand, on the ability—the substantive freedom—of people to lead the lives they have reason to value and to enhance the real choices they have. The two perspectives cannot but be related, since both are concerned with the role of human beings, and in particular with the actual abilities that they achieve and acquire. But the yardstick of assessment concentrates on different achievements.

Given her personal characteristics, social background, economic circumstances, and so on, a person has the ability to do (or be) certain things that she has reason to value. The reason for valuation can be *direct* (the functioning involved may directly enrich her life, such as being well-nourished or being healthy), or *indirect* (the functioning involved may contribute to further production, or command a price in the market). The human capital perspective can—in principle—be defined very broadly to cover types of valuation, but it is typically defined—by convention—primarily in terms of indirect value: human qualities that can be employed as "capital" in *production* (in the way physical capital is). In this sense, the narrower view of the human capital approach fits into the more inclusive perspective of human capability, which can cover both direct and indirect consequences of human abilities.

Consider an example. If education makes a person more efficient in commodity production, then this is clearly an enhancement of human capital. This can add to the value of production in the economy and also to the income of the person who has been educated. But even with the same level of income, a person may benefit from education—in reading, communicating, arguing, in being able to choose in a more informed way, in being taken more seriously by others, and so on. The benefits of education, thus, exceed its role as human capital in commodity production. The broader human-capability perspective would note—and value—these additional roles as well. The two perspectives are, thus, closely related but distinct.

The significant transformation that has occurred in recent years in giving greater recognition to the role of "human capital" is helpful for understanding the relevance of the capability perspective. If a person can become more productive in making commodities through better education, better health, and so on, it is not unnatural to expect that she can, through these means, also directly achieve more—and have the freedom to achieve more—in leading her life.

The capability perspective involves, to some extent, a return to an integrated approach to economic and social development championed particularly by Adam Smith (both in the *Wealth of Nations* and in *The Theory of Moral Sentiments*). In analyzing the determination of production possibilities, Smith emphasized the role of education as well as division of labor, learning by doing and skill formation. But the development of human capability in leading a worthwhile life (as well as in being more productive) is quite central to Smith's analysis of "the wealth of nations."

Indeed, Adam Smith's belief in the power of education and learning was peculiarly strong. Regarding the debate that continues today on the respective roles of "nature" and "nurture," Smith was an uncompromising—and even a dogmatic—"nurturist." Indeed, this fitted in well with his massive confidence in the improvability of human capabilities:

> The difference of natural talents in different men is, in reality, much less than we are aware of; and the very different genius which appears to distinguish men of different professions, when grown up to maturity, is not upon many occasions so much the cause, as the effect of division of labour. The difference between the most dissimilar characters, between a

philosopher and a common street porter, for example, seems to arise not so much from nature, as from habit, custom, and education. When they came into the world, and for the first six or eight years of their existence, they were, perhaps, very much alike, and neither their parents nor play-fellows could perceive any remarkable difference.[22]

It is not my purpose here to examine whether Smith's emphatically nurturist views are right, but it is useful to see how closely he links *productive* abilities and *lifestyles* to education and training and presumes the improvability of each.[23] That connection is quite central to the reach of the capability perspective.[24]

There is, in fact, a crucial valuational difference between the human-capital focus and the concentration on human capabilities—a difference that relates to some extent to the distinction between means and ends. The acknowledgment of the role of human qualities in promoting and sustaining economic growth—momentous as it is—tells us nothing about *why* economic growth is sought in the first place. If, instead, the focus is, ultimately, on the expansion of human freedom to live the kind of lives that people have reason to value, then the role of economic growth in expanding these opportunities has to be integrated into that more foundational understanding of the process of development as the expansion of human capability to lead more worthwhile and more free lives.[25]

The distinction has a significant practical bearing on public policy. While economic prosperity helps people to have wider options and to lead more fulfilling lives, so do more education, better health care, finer medical attention, and other factors that causally influence the effective freedoms that people actually enjoy. These "social developments" must directly count as "developmental," since they help us to lead longer, freer, and more fruitful lives, *in addition* to the role they have in promoting productivity or economic growth or individual incomes.[26] The use of the concept of "human capital," which concentrates only on one part of the picture (an important part, related to broadening the account of "productive resources"), is certainly an enriching move. But it does need supplementation. This is because human beings are not merely means of production, but also the end of the exercise.

Indeed, in arguing with David Hume, Adam Smith had the occasion to emphasize that to see human beings only in terms of their productive use is to slight the nature of humanity:

> … it seems impossible that the approbation of virtue should be of the same kind with that by which we approve of a convenient or a well-contrived building, or that we should have no other reason for praising a man than that for which we commend a chest of drawers.[27]

Despite the usefulness of the concept of human capital, it is important to see human beings in a broader perspective (breaking the analogy with "a chest of drawers"). We must go *beyond* the notion of human capital, after acknowledging its relevance and reach. The broadening that is needed is additional and inclusive, rather than, in any sense, an *alternative* to the "human capital" perspective.

It is important to take note also of the instrumental role of capability expansion in bringing about *social* change (going well beyond *economic* change). Indeed, the role of human beings even as instruments of change can go much beyond economic production (to which the perspective of "human capital" standardly points), and include social and political development. For example, as was discussed earlier, expansion of female education may reduce gender inequality in intrafamily distribution and also help reduce fertility rates as well as child mortality rates. Expansion of basic education may also improve the quality of public debates. These instrumental achievements may be ultimately quite important—taking us well beyond the production of conventionally defined commodities.

In looking for a fuller understanding of the role of human capabilities, we have to take note of:

1. their *direct* relevance to the well-being and freedom of people;

2. their *indirect* role through influencing *social* change; and

3. their *indirect* role through influencing *economic* production.

The relevance of the capability perspective incorporates each of these contributions. In contrast, in the standard literature human capital is seen primarily in terms of the third of the three roles. There is a clear overlap of coverage, and it is indeed an important overlap. But there is also a strong need to go well beyond that rather limited and circumscribed role of human capital in understanding development as freedom.

FINAL REMARK

I have tried to present, analyze, and defend a particular approach to development, seen as a process of expanding substantive freedoms that people have. The perspective of freedom has been used both in the evaluative analysis for assessing change, and in the descriptive and predictive analysis in seeing freedom as a casually effective factor in generating rapid change.

I have also discussed the implications of this approach for policy analysis as well as for the understanding of general economic, political, and social connections. A variety of social institutions—related to the operation of markets, administrations, legislatures, political parties, nongovernmental organizations, the judiciary, the media, and the community in general—contribute to the process of development precisely through their effects on enhancing and sustaining individual freedoms. Analysis of development calls for an integrated understanding of the respective roles of these different institutions and their interactions. The formation of values and the emergence and evolution of social ethics are also part of the process of development that needs attention, along with the working of markets and other institutions. This study has been an attempt to understand and investigate this interrelated structure, and to draw lessons for development in that broad perspective.

It is a characteristic of freedom that it has diverse aspects that relate to a variety of activities and institutions. It cannot yield a view of development that translates readily into some simple "formula" of accumulation of capital, or opening up of markets, or having efficient economic planning (though each of these particular features fits into the broader picture). The organizing principle that places all the different bits and pieces into an integrated whole is the overarching concern with the process of enhancing individual freedoms and the social commitment to help to bring that about. That unity is important, but at the same time we cannot lose sight of the fact that freedom is an inherently diverse concept, which involves—as was discussed extensively—considerations of processes as well as substantive opportunities.

This diversity is not, however, a matter of regret. As William Cowper puts it:

Freedom has a thousand charms to show,
That slaves, howe'er contented, never know.

Development is indeed a momentous engagement with freedom's possibilities.

ENDNOTES

1. I heard this account from Isaiah Berlin. Since these lectures were delivered, we have lost Berlin, and I take this opportunity of paying tribute to his memory and recollecting how very much I have benefited over the years from his gentle critique of rudimentary ideas on freedom and its implications.

2. On this subject, see also my "The Right Not to Be Hungry," in *Contemporary Philosophy* 2, edited by G. Floistad (The Hague: Martinus Nijhoff, 1982); "Well-being, Agency and Freedom: The Dewey Lectures 1984," *Journal of Philosophy* 82 (April 1985); "Individual Freedom as a Social Commitment," *New York Review of Books*, June 16, 1990.

3. See my "Equality of What?," in *Tanner Lectures on Human Values*, volume 1, edited by S. McMurrin (Cambridge: Cambridge University Press, 1980), reprinted in my *Choice, Welfare, and Measurement* (Oxford: Blackwell; Cambridge, Mass.: MIT Press, 1982; republished, Cambridge, Mass: Harvard University Press, 1997); "Well-being, Agency, and Freedom" (1985); "Justice: Means versus Freedoms," *Philosophy and Public Affairs* 19 (1990); *Inequality Reexamined* (Oxford: Clarendon Press; Cambridge, Mass.: Harvard University Press, 1992).

4. The principal issues in characterizing and evaluating freedom—including some technically problems—are considered in my Kenneth Arrow Lectures, included in *Freedom, Social Choice, and Responsibility: Arrow Lectures and Other Essays* (Oxford: Clarendon Press, forthcoming).

5. Development is seen here as the removal of shortfalls of substantive freedoms from what they can potentially achieve. While this provides a general perspective—enough to characterize the nature of development in broad terms—there are a number of contentious issues that yield a class of somewhat different exact specifications of the criteria of judgement. On this, see my *Commodities and Capabilities* (Amsterdam: North-Holland, 1985); *Inequality Reexamined* (1992); and also *Freedom, Rationality, and Social Choice* (forthcoming). The concentration on the removal of shortfalls in some specific dimensions has also been used in UNDP's annual *Human Development Reports*, pioneered in 1990 by Mahbub ul Haq. See also some far-reaching questions raised by Ian Hacking in his review article on *Inequality Reexamined*: "In Pursuit of Fairness," *New York Review of Books*, September 19, 1996. See also Charles Tilly, *Durable Inequality* (Berkeley, Calif.: University of Californis Press, 1998).

6. On this see my *Commodities and Capabilities* (1985); *Inequality Reexamined* (1992); and "Capability and Well-being," in *The Quality of Life*, edited by Martha Nussbaum and Amartya Sen (Oxford: Clarendon Press, 1993).

7. See John Rawls, *A Theory of Justice* (Cambridge, Mass.: Harvard University Press, 1971); John Harsanyi, *Essays in Ethics, Social Behaviour, and Scientific Explanation* (Dordrecht: Reidel, 1976); and Ronald Dworkin, "What Is Equality? Part 2: Equality of Resources," *Philosophy and*

Public Affairs 10 (1981). See also John Roemer, *Theories of Distributive Justice* (Cambridge, Mass.: Harvard University Press, 1996).

8. This is discussed in my *Inequality Reexamined* (Oxford: Clarendon Press, 1992; Cambridge, Mass.: Harvard University Press, 1992), and more fully in my "Justice and Assertive Incompleteness," mimeographed, Harvard University, 1997, which is a part of my Rosenthal lectures at Northwestern University Law School, given in September 1998.

9. There is a similar issue relating to competing ways of judging individual advantage when our preferences and priorities diverge, and there is an inescapable "social choice problem" here too, which calls for a shared resolution [...].

10. On this see my paper "Gender Inequality and Theories of Justice," in *Women, Culture, and Development: A Study of Human Capabilities*, edited by Martha Nussbaum and Jonathan Glover (Oxford: Clarendon Press, 1995). There are a number of other papers in this Nussbaum-Glover collection that bear on this issue.

11. Aristotle, *The Nicomachean Ethics*, translated by D. Ross (Oxford: Oxford University Press, revised edition 1980), book 1, section 6, p. 7.

12. On the relevance of freedom in the writings of pioneering political economists, see my *The Standard of Living*, edited by Geoffrey Hawthorn (Cambridge: Cambridge University Press, 1987).

13. This applies to *Wealth of Nations* (1776) as well as to *The Theory of Moral Sentiments* (revised edition, 1790).

14. This particular statement is from *The German Ideology*, jointly written with Friedrich Engels (1846); English translation in D. McLellan, *Karl Marx: Selected Writings* (Oxford: Oxford University Press, 1977), p. 190. See also Marx's *The Economic and Philosophical Manuscript of 1844* (1844) and *Critique of the Gotha Programme* (1875).

15. John Stuart Mill, *On Liberty* (1859; republished: Harmondsworth: Penguin Books, 1974); *The Subjection of Women* (1869).

16. Friedrich Hayek, *The Constitution of Liberty* (London: Routledge and Kegan Paul, 1960), p. 35.

17. Peter Bauer, *Economic Analysis and Policy in Underdeveloped Countries* (Durham, N.C.: Duke University Press, 1957), pp.113–4. See also *Dissent on Development* (London: Weidenfeld & Nicolson, 1971).

18. W. Arthur Lewis, *The Theory of Economic Growth* (London: Allen & Unwin, 1955), pp. 9–10, 420–1.

19. Hayek, *The Constitutions of Liberty* (1960), p. 31.

20. These and related issues in "the evaluation of freedom" are discussed in my Kenneth Arrow Lectures, included in *Freedom, Rationality, and Social Choice* (forthcoming). Among the questions that are addressed there is the relation between freedom, on the one hand, and preferences and choices, on the other.

21. On this and related issues, see Robert J. Barro and Jong-Wha Lee, "Losers and Winners in Economic Growth," Working Paper 4341, National Bureau of Economic Research (1993); Xavier Sala-i-Martin, "Regional Cohesion: Evidence and Theories of Regional Growth and Convergence," Discussion Paper 1075, CEPR, London, 1994; Robert J. Barro and Xavier Sala-i-

Martin, *Economic Growth* (New York: McGraw-Hill, 1995); Robert J. Barro, *Getting It Right: Markets and Choices in a Free Society* (Cambridge, Mass.: MIT Press, 1996).

22. Adam Smith, *An Inquiry into the Nature and Causes of the Wealth of Nations* (1776), republished, edited by R.H. Campbell and A.S. Skinner (Oxford: Clarendon Press, 1976), pp. 28–9.

23. See Emma Rothschild, "Condorcet and Adam Smith on Education and Instruction," in *Philosophers on Education*, edited by Amélie O. Rorty (London: Routledge, 1998).

24. See, for example, Felton Earls and Maya Carlson, "Toward Sustainable Development for the American Family," *Daedalus* 122 (1993), and "Promoting Human Capability as an Alternative to Early Crime," Harvard School of Public Health and Harvard Medical School, 1996.

25. I have tried to discuss this issue in "Development: Which Way Now?" *Economic Journal* 93 (1983), reprinted in *Resources, Values, and Development* (Cambridge, Mass.: Harvard University Press, 1984; 1997), and also in *Commodities and Capabilities* (1985).

26. To a considerable extent the annual *Human Development Reports* of the United Nations Development Programme, published since 1990, have been motivated by the need to take a broader view of this kind. My friend Mahbub ul Haq, who died last year, played a major leadership role in this, of which I and his other friends are most proud.

27. Smith, *The Theory of Moral Sentiments* (1759; revised edition, 1790), republished, edited by D.D. Raphael and A.L. Macfie (Oxford: Clarendon Press, 1976), book 4, chapter 24, p. 188.

CHAPTER FIFTEEN, *Punam Khosla*

Further Reading

Callaghan, M., L. Farha, and B. Porter. (2002). *Women and Housing in Canada: Barriers to Equality.* Toronto: Centre for Equality Rights in Accommodation.

This is a national report that addresses widespread homelessness in Canada in both urban and rural areas and its impact on women. The report discusses federal government programs and policies from the standpoint of the particular barriers facing low-income women in meeting their housing needs. The report situates women's homelessness within the context of women's poverty and it thus assesses not only programs and policies related to housing, but also those related to income support.

Lochhead, C., and K. Scott. (2000). *The Dynamics of Women's Poverty in Canada.* Ottawa: Canadian Council on Social Development.

This report examines gendered dimensions of movements into and out of poverty, drawing on the new longitudinal *Survey of Labour and Income Dynamics* (SLID) for 1993–1994.

Sherkin, S. (2004). *Community-Based Research on Immigrant Women: Contributions and Challenges.* Joint Centre of Excellence for Research on Immigration and Settlement—Toronto Working Paper No. 32. Toronto: CERIS.

This paper explores the profuse amount of community-based research being conducted about and with immigrant women, primarily in Toronto. Its objectives include highlighting both the growing and stagnant number of collaborative academic-community partnerships. Despite the fact that research on immigrant women is excelling in depth and scope, academic and community efforts remain relatively discrete, as each world is often unaware of the other's interests and pursuits. Multi-tiered collaboration is vital in bridging this gap, including greater and ongoing communication between all researchers working in this field, as well as direct participation of community members in project development and implementation.

Related Web Sites

Centre on Housing Rights and Evictions
www.cohre.org/view_page.php?page_id=147

Women are also the majority of the world's refugees and internally displaced people. Despite international laws and norms protecting a woman's right to adequate housing, women are commonly systematically excluded from decision making or control over household resources. This web site offers information on women's housing rights program from an international context.

Institute for Gender Research at the University of Calgary
www.ucalgary.ca/gender/reports.htm

This site contains reports and resources in the areas of women's issues in Canada, which include women's views on poverty and feminization and racialization of poverty in Canada.

Prairie Women's Health of Centre of Excellence
www.uwinnipeg.ca/admin/vh_external/pwhce/program_poverty.htm

This site provides information and research reports on reducing women's poverty by many means, including good housing policy. This web site also works on raising public awareness and broadening the base of support for progressive policy alternatives.

CHAPTER SIXTEEN, *Sherene H. Razack*

Further Reading

Canada. (1996). *Report of the Royal Commission on Aboriginal Peoples: Perspectives and Realities.* Ottawa: Supply and Services Canada.

This five-volume report was released on November 21, 1996. The report included Vol. 1: *Looking Forward, Looking Back*; Vol. 2: *Restructuring the Relationship* (2 parts); Vol. 3: *Gathering Strength*; Vol. 4: *Perspectives and Realities*; and Vol. 5: *Renewal: A Twenty-Year Commitment.* The main conclusion of the report was the need for a complete restructuring of the relationship between Aboriginal and non-Aboriginal peoples in Canada. Some of the broader recommendations included the proposal for a new Royal Proclamation; that is, governmental commitment to a new set of ethical principles respecting the relationship that acknowledged and respected Aboriginal cultures and values, the historical origins of Aboriginal nationhood, and the inherent right to Aboriginal self-determination.

Monture-Angus, P. (1999). *Thunder in My Soul: A Mohawk Woman Speaks.* Halifax: Fernwood Publishing.

This book contains the reflections of one Mohawk woman and her struggles to find a good place to be in Canadian society. The essays, written in accessible language, document Aboriginal peoples struggles against oppression, as well as the success and change that have come to Aboriginal communities. It speaks to both the mind and the heart.

Paul, D. (2000). *We Were Not the Savages: A Mi'kmaq Perspective on the Collision between European and Native American Civilization.* Halifax: Fernwood Books.

According to this book, it was common for historians to downplay or even deny the violence inflicted on the Mi'kmaq people by European and Euro-American colonizers. As recently as 1989 the conveners of a conference on "The Northeastern Borderlands" summarized what they thought was an emerging consensus on the colonization process in the Maritimes. Scalp-bounty policies are now recognized as a historical problem worthy of investigation.

Related Web Sites

Amnesty International Canada
www.amnesty.ca/campaigns/sisters_overview.php

Stolen Sisters: A Human Rights response to discrimination and violence against Indigenous Women in Canada, October, 2004.

"Equality, Not Multiculturalism"
By Carol Goar, *Toronto Star*, January 2007.
www.thestar.com/article/170338

An article on White privilege and issues of equality.

Women's Health
Surveillance Report
www.phac-aspc.gc.ca/publicat/whsr-rssf/chap_21_e.html
Article: Violence against Canadian Women
By Marsha Cohen and Heather MacLean

Overview of violence against women in Canada, both physical and systemic violence.

CHAPTER SEVENTEEN, *George J. Sefa Dei*

Further Reading

Brown, J., D. Ford, and J.W. Richardson. (2004). "African Americans and Multicultural Education." *Education and Urban Society* 36 (3), 304–341.

This article examines the root causes for the overrepresentation of African-American students in special education classes and their underrepresentation in gifted and talented programs in America's public schools. It provides a historic overview of the legal struggles for educational equity, examines key issues surrounding the academic status of African-American students, discusses multicultural education as a remedy, and recommends an appropriate course of action for educators and policy makers.

Brown, M., K. Higgins, T. Pierce, E. Hong, and C. Thoma. (2003). "Secondary Students' Perceptions of School Life with Regard to Alienation: The Effects of Disability, Gender, and Race." *Learning Disability Quarterly* 26 (4), 227–238.

A considerable amount of research has focused on factors that distinguish between students who are engaged in the learning process and those who are not. This study examined the relationship between students and their perceptions of school life. A survey was distributed to over 200 students at two high schools in a large, urban school district in the southern United States. Results suggest that gender, race/ethnicity, and placement in special education are all strong factors in influencing whether students perceive school and/or life in general as alienating.

Henze, R., A. Katz, and E. Norte. (2000). "Rethinking the Concept of Racial or Ethnic Conflict in Schools: A Leadership Perspective." *Race, Ethnicity, and Education* 3 (2), 195–206.

Racial or ethnic conflict is often conceptualized as overt hostility such as fighting or name calling between groups defined as Black, White, Asian, etc. In a study of school leaders who worked proactively to improve race/ethnic relations, the authors of this article found that leaders' understandings of racial/ethnic conflict were far more complex, including an awareness of root causes or precursors of overt conflict as well as recognition of the many dimensions of student identity. Leaders who viewed conflict in these complex ways were able to develop proactive, rather than only reactive, approaches to addressing conflict and building positive interethnic relations.

Related Web Sites

Canadian Education Association
www.cea-ace.ca/home.cfm

This site initiates and sustains dialogue throughout the country influencing public policy issues in relation to education. It also provides statistics of provincial dropout rates in Canada.

Human Resources and Social Development Canada
hrsdc.gc.ca

A number of research reports on school dropouts and completion rates can be found in this web site. One of the relevant reports is *Leaving School: Results from a National Survey Comparing School Leavers and High School Graduates 18 to 20 Years of Age—January 1995*. It provides a model of the causes and consequences of departing at the high school level.

Partnership Table for School Retention in Montreal
www.perseverancescolairemontreal.qc.ca/english/english.html

This site provides information on the regional collaborative process undertaken to lower dropout numbers by encouraging youth in the Montreal region to stay in school.

CHAPTER EIGHTEEN, *Amartya Sen*

Further Reading

Sen, A. (1999. *Commodities and Capabilities*. New York: Oxford University Press.

This monograph explores the foundations of welfare economics, in particular the assessment of personal well-being and advantage. Arguments are presented against the usual concentration on "utility" (as in traditional welfare economics) and on "opulence" (as in "real income" estimations and other normative measurements). An alternative framework is developed for the analysis of personal well-being based on assessing "functionings" and the "capability to function," i.e., what a person can do or can be. The functionings considered vary from such basic biological performances as "being well-nourished" to such social achievements as "being able to take part in the life of the community." This exercise of comparing achievements and capabilities provides a structure for interpersonal comparisons of well-being. The book's critical appraisal of traditional methods, combined with a newly developed framework, throws new light on comparisons of well-being, and aids assessment of some international contrasts.

Sen, A. (2004). *Rationality and Freedom*. Cambridge: Belknap Press.

The author scrutinizes and departs from the standard criteria of rationality, and shows how it can be seen in terms of subjecting one's values as well as choices to the demands of reason and critical scrutiny. This capacious approach is utilized to illuminate the demands of rationality in individual choice (including decisions under uncertainty) as well as social choice (including cost benefit analysis and environmental assessment). Identifying a reciprocity in the relationship between rationality and freedom, the author argues that freedom cannot be assessed independently of a person's reasoned preferences and valuations, just as rationality, in turn, requires freedom of thought. Sen uses the discipline of social choice theory (a subject he has helped to develop) to illuminate the demands of reason and the assessment of freedom. This work contributes to our understanding of the connections among rationality, freedom, and social justice.

Tilly, C. (1998). *Durable Inequality*. Berkeley: University of California Press.

The author presents a powerful new approach to the study of persistent social inequality. How, the author asks, do long-lasting, systematic inequalities in life chances arise, and how do they come to distinguish members of different socially defined categories of people? Exploring representative paired and unequal categories, such as male/female, Black/White, and citizen/non-citizen, the author argues that the basic causes of these and similar inequalities greatly resemble one another. In contrast to contemporary analyses that explain inequality case by case, this account is one of process. Also, the book illustrates the social mechanisms that create and maintain paired and unequal categories with a rich variety of cases, mapping out fertile territories for future relational study of durable inequality.

Related Web Sites

Ian Hacking's review article of *Inequality Reexamined*, "In Pursuit of Fairness," *New York Review of Books*, September 19, 1996
www.nybooks.com/articles/article-preview?article_id=1427

UN Annual Human Development Reports
hdr.undp.org/reports/

> Featuring the Human Development Index, every report presents agenda-setting data and analysis and calls international attentions to issues and policy options that put people at the centre of strategies to meet the challenges of development today—economic, social, political, and cultural.

World Social Forum: Another World Is Possible
www.forumsocialmundial.org.br/index.php?cd_language=2&id_menu

> The World Social Forum is an open meeting place where social movements, networks, NGOs, and other civil society organizations opposed to neo-liberalism and a world dominated by capital or by any form of imperialism come together to pursue their thinking, debate ideas democratically, formulate proposals, share their experiences freely, and network for effective action. Since the first world encounter in 2001, it has taken the form of a permanent world process, seeking and building alternatives to neo-liberal policies. (See the WSF's guiding document, its Charter of Principles.)

A National Strategy to Address the Racialization and Feminization of Poverty

Maria A. Wallis and Siu-ming Kwok

The increasing poverty in Canada is an urgent reality that must be addressed by us all. In addition, the racialized and gendered characteristic of this structural poverty also requires immediate public policy attention. There is evidence that these issues can be reduced given the wealth and resources of Canada as the ninth largest economy of 183 nations in 2005 in terms of GDP (Yalinizyan, 2007:9)

In 2001, the federal government made a commitment to end poverty. However, this commitment was not followed through. Advocates calling for the eradication of poverty point to the fact that poverty costs all Canadians. Both economic growth and human well-being need to be measured to assess a nation's progress. Since the 1970s, gross domestic product (GDP) has risen a great deal, but human well-being has not. According to the National Council of Welfare, "population health evidence points to the increased costs to the health care system, and the decreases in the academic achievements, health and life spans, of those populations at the bottom end of the socio-economic scale" (National Council of Welfare, 2002). Costs to the justice system (through the criminalization of poverty), as well as the negative effects on individuals' productive capacity and on child development, are additional costs to Canadian society. The growing gap between the rich and poor in Canada is a failure of a democratic society. This failure includes higher education costs, unsafe drinking water in some communities, fewer public services, and the increased use of food banks (National Council of Welfare, 2002). The National Council of Welfare concludes:

> This polarization increases societal tensions. It undermines the public good and the human dignity of people who are treated as clients ... rather than as citizens. This costs society the creative and productive capacity of a large portion of the population, it costs governments the trust and support of the public and it costs a society its humanity. (2002:5)

Solving the racialization and feminization of poverty is a long-term task. It requires the determination and political will of all Canadians who would like to make Canada a better place to live. With this aim in mind, this book supports the four recommendations suggested by the National Council of Welfare (2007) to address the problem of structural poverty in Canada. These four recommendations include an inclusive definition of poverty, a comprehensive anti-poverty strategy, practical action plans, and an accountable reporting system. Also, these four suggestions should be understood in the context of the interdependence between individual freedom and social responsibility. Before further elaborating on the above suggestions, it should be noted that these suggestions are being put forward to identify key areas for further discussion and research rather than providing a definitive solution to the problem.

INCLUSIVE DEFINITION OF POVERTY

First, Canada should have an inclusive definition of poverty. Canada does not have an official poverty line. Statistics Canada's Low-Income Cut-Offs (LICOs), which is commonly used, shows how many people in Canada spend significantly more than average on the necessities of life. Economic indicators currently in use do not measure the distribution of wealth or the well-being of all citizens. Poverty is usually measured in terms of income, but people can be impoverished by lack of access to other resources such as by social exclusion and the stress of insecurity (National Council of Welfare, 2002). The United Nations report on poverty titled *Overcoming Human Poverty* calls for a comprehensive view of poverty:

> One that recognizes that it is more than a shortage of income.... [It is also] the denial of opportunities and choices most basic to human development to lead a long, healthy, creative life and to enjoy a decent standard of living, freedom, dignity, self-esteem, and the respect of others. (Townson, 2000:5–6)

Critical effects of structural inequality or social exclusion, such as gender and race, are also taken into account by this United Nations' definition.

Access to resources such as adequate and affordable housing is critical. Housing is not just a matter of physical shelter; it is a site of other activities such as where children are raised and community ties are built. The access to sports, recreation, culture, and other activities are important too. These activities help individuals build confidence, friendships, and other positive social relationships. In particular, new immigrant women of colour with children and lone parents too will find the access to resources invaluable.

There is no internationally recognized set of social indicators to measure human well-being comparable to the way GDP is accepted as a measure of the market economy. But there is growing interest and there have been significant developments in this field (National Council of Welfare, 2002), including government and non-government work in Canada. While GDP has one common indicator—money—social indicators should include various measures of health, education, paid and unpaid work time, leisure and rest, earning and other income, participation in public life, and safety and security. In designing a new measure to determine the poverty rate, Canada should also include social indicators in its calculation.

INDIVIDUAL FREEDOM AND RESPONSIBILITY

A comprehensive view of poverty demonstrates the interdependence of individual freedom and social responsibility. A society can be assessed by what it deems to be its goal of an acceptable society. The choice of social values cannot be settled merely by the pronouncements of those in authority who control different levels of government; it should be formulated in public debates and discussion. According to Amartya Sen, the general enhancement of political and civil freedoms is central to the process of economic and social development of society itself. The argument for social support in expanding people's freedom is an argument for individual responsibility, not against it. In other words, responsibility requires freedom (Sen, 1999:284). Further, the capabilities that a person does have depend on the nature of social arrangements, which is crucial for individual freedoms. And the state and the society cannot escape responsibility (Sen, 1999:288).

In this way, people could lead the lives they have reason to value and to enhance the real choices they have. At the same time, society will benefit as a whole. The human capability will be improved and individuals will be empowered to take up their responsibilities and contribute back to society. In the context of this book, if society could address the problem of racialization and feminization of poverty, vulnerable groups such as people of colour, low-income immigrant women, and all other marginalized populations will be able to deal with the cycle of deprivation and to make valuable contributions to society.

With the interdependence of individual freedom and responsibility in mind, it is clear that the Canadian state, and society as a whole, must make critical interventions now to begin the eradication of poverty in this country.

NATIONAL ANTI-POVERTY STRATEGY

To substantiate our commitment to end poverty in Canada, we should have a national anti-poverty strategy with a long-term vision and measurable targets and timeline. We have never had a national anti-poverty strategy. However, other countries with a national plan have successfully lowered the poverty rate of certain populations.

In 1999, the U.K. government set the target of halving child poverty in Britain by 2010. In addition, the U.K. has also set specific program targets, including affordable child care for all children aged three to fourteen years, by 2010 (National Council of Welfare, 2007:6).

These strategic responses have included focuses on lone parents, people with disabilities, members of ethnic minorities, and older workers. These strategies bear results (National Council of Welfare, 2007).

> Although the UK still has a great deal of work to do, it is making progress. The proportion of children living in a household at-risk-of-poverty has gone from being the highest in Europe at 27% in 1997/98 to 22% in 2004/05, closer to the EU average of 20%. (National Council of Welfare, 2007:6)

In the case of Ireland, the government has set targets to reduce the kind of basic deprivation it calls "consistent" poverty. In 1997, a 10-year National Anti-Poverty Strategy (NAPS) was launched. It plans to reach the targets, which include a combination of new and existing measures focused on children. Other measures included the coordination of immigration service; the design of an action plan against racism; and a range of health, education, and housing services for minority groups. Ireland's results are impressive (National Council of Welfare, 2007:6).

> The rate of people experiencing consistent poverty dropped from 15.1% in 1994 to 5.2% in 2001. In the year between 2003 and 2004, the rate for children under age 15 dropped from 12.2 % to 9.5%. (National Council of Welfare, 2007:7)

Around the globe, the fight against poverty is the highest priority for the majority of countries. Canada should not discount what it can learn from these successful examples as the problems they faced are more severe than ours. The success of any effort to reduce poverty will depend on the engagement of the federal government. The root causes of poverty discussed in this book include systemic racism, non-recognition of foreign credentials, and gender equity in employment, in particular of women of colour and new immigrants. These structural causes require a national strategy. Such a strategy could be in the best interests of all Canadians. For example, the creation of the national health care system demonstrates how effective governments can be when they work together toward common goals. We think that a national anti-poverty strategy in Canada could provide the vehicle for similar progress for vulnerable populations to break the cycle of deprivation and social exclusion.

ACTION PLAN

All levels of government must work toward common objectives and provide adequate and appropriate human and financial resources to implement the anti-poverty strategy. An action plan is essential. Using the successful examples of anti-poverty action plans in other countries, most of these countries have committed resources to prioritize and implement action plans. For example, Ireland has made ongoing efforts to set up an Irish National Women's Strategy, coordinated across government and aimed at enhancing the socio-economic status of women, their well-being, and their participation in decision making and civil society. The Irish Office for Social Inclusion has been charged with monitoring and reporting on social inclusion matters across the range of strategies and will coordinate a single national social inclusion report on an annual basis (National Council of Welfare, 2007:7).

At home, an Anti-poverty and Income Security Questionnaire conducted by the National Council of Welfare in late 2006 found that most respondents rated an action plan with goals, commitments, and accountability for results and better coordination across governments of the highest importance. Further, there is a strong agreement among respondents in this survey that a comprehensive strategy with an action plan is needed in order to address the root cause of poverty, instead of just helping those whose incomes are just under the poverty line. These actions include a guaranteed livable income, affordable housing, child care, and education and training. As such, we support the National Council of Welfare's call for all levels of government to make coordinated efforts and commit resources for action plans to address the challenges faced by vulnerable populations covered by various chapters of this book instead of the current fragmented and patchwork solutions implemented by different levels and departments of government.

ACCOUNTABLE REPORTING SYSTEM

As a way to show their determination and to encourage civic participation, the governments should consult various stakeholders, especially people living in poverty, as strategies and plans are being developed, implemented, and evaluated over time. Before the launch of the National Anti-poverty Strategy (NAPS) in 1997, the government of Ireland consulted widely with stakeholders, including people experiencing poverty. In the report of *Solving Poverty: Four Cornerstones of a Workable National Strategy for Canada*, the National Council of

Welfare also suggested setting up a government accountable structure for ensuring results and for consulting Canadians in the design, implementation, and evaluation of the action that will affect the stakeholders.

> Accountability can take many forms—legislation, ministerial responsibility for the strategy, public reporting on progress in meeting targets and timelines, specific policy and program targets and measures tied to goals or an independent oversight agency. (National Council of Welfare, 2007:10)

In conclusion, a reporting system is a good way of fostering accountability and ensuring an effective long-term plan.

It is not by chance that poverty will be resolved; it is by social responsibility, political will, and good design. This book is a call for those who are concerned with the racialization and feminization of poverty in Canada to make this a priority item in the political agenda of this country. The development of both the nation and individuals are at stake. We agree with the inspiring vision of Amartya Sen: "Development is indeed a momentous engagement with freedom's possibilities" (Sen, 1999:298).

REFERENCES

National Council of Welfare. (2002). "The Cost of Poverty." Retrieved March 20, 2007, from http://www.ncwcnbes.net/en/publication-list.html

———. (2007). "Solving Poverty: Four Cornerstones of a Workable National Strategy for Canada." Retrieved March 20, 2007, from http://www.ncwcnbes.net/en/home.html

Sen, A. (1999). *Development as Freedom.* New York: Random House.

Townson, M. (2000). "A Report Card on Women and Poverty." Retrieved March 20, 2007, from the Canadian Centre for Policy Alternatives Web site: http://policyalternatives.ca/index.cfm?act=news&call=426&do=article&pA=BB736455

Yalnizyan, A. (2007). *The Rich and the Rest of Us: The Changing Face of Canada's Growing Gap.* Ottawa: Canadian Centre for Policy Alternatives.

Canada's Action Plan against Racism

Executive Summary

A Canada for All: Canada's Action Plan against Racism outlines issues and approaches for the Government of Canada with the aim of eradicating racism and racial discrimination from society. This document consists of three parts:

PART I: Breaking down Barriers sets out the general context for the action plan.

PART II: Six-Point Action Plan identifies six key priority areas that guide existing government-wide activities. Each priority section identifies steps taken to date as well as new ones proposed by the government and its partners.

PART III: Reporting Back to Canadians outlines the ways in which each action item will be evaluated.

Serving the common good, so that everyone is valued and respected for who they are—that is the Canadian approach to diversity and multiculturalism. Indeed, it serves Canada well—helping to build a more resilient, harmonious, and creative society. The country's ongoing success and its prospects for the future hinge on being able to bring together people of all backgrounds—ethnic, racial, and religious—to build a society where no one's identity or cultural heritage is compromised.

Diversity in Canada has increased significantly over the past decade and will continue to expand. There are more than 200 ethnic groups living in Canada. Visible minorities comprise 13 percent of the population and 18 percent of Canadians are foreign-born. Immigration accounts for 53 percent of population growth and visible minorities will account for 20 percent of the population by 2016.

In the context of this growing diversity, Canada has developed an evolving approach to citizenship based on shared core values, rights, and responsibilities, anchored in a robust legislative and policy framework. This model is based on deeply held principles: acceptance, fairness, equality of opportunity, and respect for human rights and rule of law. These rights are balanced against an expectation that individuals live up to basic responsibilities of citizenship.

Over the past forty years, Canada's legal framework has served to promote the rights of citizens and protect them from discrimination. Canada is also recognized internationally as a leader in human rights. As one illustration, our country is the birthplace of John Peters Humphrey—one of the principal authors of the Universal Declaration on Human Rights (1948). Moreover, Canada has ratified the six major United Nations international human rights treaties and many supporting instruments.

Although racism erodes Canada's social foundations and runs counter to the values of Canadian citizens, recent public-opinion surveys confirm that racism and discrimination continue to exist. A 2003 Ipsos-Reid survey, commissioned by the Centre for Research and Information on Canada and *The Globe and Mail*, reports that 74 percent of Canadians polled believe that racism is prevalent in Canada. Analysis of Statistics Canada's 2002 Ethnic Diversity Survey reveals disturbing levels of reported discrimination and unfair treatment experienced by visible minorities, and particularly by Blacks, in the last five years. Moreover, domestic and international events have focused greater attention on issues of hate, racial bias, systemic discrimination, allegations of racial profiling, and weaker citizen engagement.

The Government of Canada is taking decisive steps to eliminate racism and remove barriers in society. This strong, public commitment—reaffirmed in the October 2004 Speech from the Throne—is a promise to reach out to all Canadians "in a manner that recognizes Canada's diversity as a source of strength and innovation." It has also pledged that the Government will "take measures to strengthen Canada's ability to combat racism, hate-speech and hate crimes, both here at home and around the world."

The federal response is building momentum through programs, initiatives and legislation. To ensure all Canadians have equal opportunity to participate fully in society, federal departments and agencies have launched a wide range of initiatives, many of them in partnership with various sectors of society.

A Canada for All: Canada's Action Plan against Racism is a key component of the Government of Canada's response. It is a collaborative effort aimed at eliminating racism in Canada. It seeks to enhance policies, programs, and actions across federal departments and sets out a plan for the future.

CANADA'S SIX-POINT ACTION PLAN TO COMBAT RACISM AND DISCRIMINATION

1. Assist victims and groups vulnerable to racism and related forms of discrimination
2. Develop forward-looking approaches to promote diversity and combat racism
3. Strengthen the role of civil society
4. Strengthen regional and international cooperation
5. Educate children and youth on diversity and anti-racism
6. Counter hate and bias

A five-year investment of $56 million, included in the 2005 Federal Budget, strengthens the government's ability to move ahead on implementation of the anti-racism action plan. Developed from extensive consultations with Canadians, it is dynamic and inclusive. It invites all sectors of society—governments, organizations, ethno-racial and ethno-cultural communities, and individuals—to embrace action against racism as a *shared task*.

Through partnerships with various sectors of society, the Government of Canada continues to address issues relevant to ethnic, racial and religious diversity, where there is joint responsibility. It will also help coordinate and share information among governments. As a part of this process, the Minister of State (Multiculturalism), supported by the Multiculturalism Program within the Department of Canadian Heritage, will annually consult with stakeholders to assess progress and to help renew efforts towards a cohesive and racism-free society.

A Canada for All is not just about inclusion—it is a call to action to combat racism. It represents a major step for Canada in its ongoing efforts to strengthen social cohesion. It complements the outstanding work being done throughout the country at the community level by organizations committed to fighting racism.

APPENDIX B

UN Definition of Poverty

THE CONCEPT OF POVERTY AND HUMAN RIGHTS

The Need for an Appropriate Concept of Poverty

In trying to incorporate the human rights perspective into the strategy for poverty reduction, it is first necessary to address a basic conceptual issue: How can we think of poverty in a way that is most appropriate for a human rights approach? There is an emerging view that poverty constitutes a denial or non-fulfilment of human rights. But does this mean that poverty is the same thing as non-fulfilment of human rights in general—i.e., does the non-fulfilment of any kind of human rights constitute poverty? Or should only certain kinds of human rights matter in the context of poverty? If so, how are we to decide which ones, and can the discourse on poverty be indifferent to the rest? These are the kinds of question that need to be addressed.

The simplest approach to take would be the all-embracing one—i.e., to define poverty as non-fulfilment of any kind of human right. This approach would obliterate any conceptual distinction between poverty and non-fulfilment of human rights by definition, but it would not be appropriate to do so. For it would clearly be odd to characterize certain cases of non-fulfilment of rights as poverty, no matter how deplorable those cases may be. For instance, if a tyrant denies his political opponent the right to speak freely, that by itself would not make the latter poor in any plausible sense. Certainly a deprivation has occurred in this case, but it seems implausible to characterize this deprivation as poverty. The reason it seems implausible is that when viewed as a social problem, and in the context of practical policy-making, the concept of poverty has acquired a specific connotation that ties it closely with lack of command over economic resources.[1]

Of course, in our day-to-day life, we tend to use the word "poor" in many diverse ways. For example, we might refer to the "poor chap" who has narrowly missed a lottery jackpot, or to the "poor old man" who has no heir to whom to bequeath his vast wealth, and so on. The common element in all these cases is some kind of deprivation that evokes the description "poor." However, when poverty is discussed as a social problem, the concept has a much more restricted domain because of its well-established link with deprivation caused by economic constraints. We cannot deny this link.[2]

These considerations suggest that we need a definition of poverty that refers to the non-fulfilment of human rights, but without delinking it from the constraint of economic resources. It is argued below that Amartya Sen's "capability approach" provides a concept of poverty that satisfies these twin requirements. The capability approach has already inspired a significant broadening of the concept of poverty—replacing a narrow focus on low income with a multi-dimensional view of poverty. Most of the current discussions of poverty in academic circles, as well as in international organizations such as the World Bank and the United Nations agencies that deal with poverty, draw upon this approach either explicitly or implicitly. As a rule, these discussions do not use the language of rights. But a little reflection shows that there exists a natural transition from capabilities to rights. Most human rights are concerned with the human person's rights to certain fundamental freedoms, including the freedoms from hunger, disease, and illiteracy. The capability approach requires that the goodness of social arrangements be judged in terms of the flourishing of human freedoms. The focus on human freedom is thus the common element that links the two approaches. Looking at poverty from the perspective of capability should, therefore, provide a bridge for crossing over from poverty to human rights.

The Capability Approach to Poverty

Underlying the capability approach is a specific conception of what constitutes human well-being. At a very basic level, well-being can be thought of as the quality or the "well-ness" of a person's being or living, and living itself can be seen as consisting of a set of interrelated "functionings"—the things that a person can do or be. The level of well-being thus depends on the level of those functionings, i.e., how well a person can do or be the things she has reasons to value—for example, to what extent can she be free from hunger or take part in the life of a community, and so on. The concept of "capability" refers to a person's freedom or opportunities to achieve well-being in this sense.

To see the relevance of capability for understanding poverty, we may begin by noting that the defining feature of a poor person is that she has very restricted opportunities to pursue her well-being. Poverty can thus be seen as low levels of capability, or, as Sen puts it, "the failure of basic capabilities to reach certain minimally acceptable levels."[3] A couple of properties of this concept of poverty are worth noting.

First, not all kinds of capability failure would count as poverty. Since poverty denotes an extreme form of deprivation, only those capability failures would count as poverty that are deemed to be basic in some order of priority. Different communities may of course have different orders of priority and hence a different listing of what would qualify as "basic" capabilities. To that extent, there is some degree of relativity in the concept of poverty. But from empirical observation it is possible to identify certain basic capabilities that would be common to all—for example, being adequately nourished, being adequately clothed and sheltered, avoiding preventable morbidity, taking part in the life of a community, and being able to appear in public with dignity.

Second, once poverty is seen to consist in the failure of a range of basic capabilities, it immediately becomes a multidimensional concept. Poverty can no longer be defined uni-dimensionally as lack of adequate income, as has traditionally been done. In fact, in this conception inadequate income ceases to be a dimension of poverty at all because income is not a capability and hence not an aspect of well-being in itself, although it may contribute to the achievement of capabilities.

It is nonetheless important to acknowledge that the concept of income—more generally, command over economic resources—does play an important role in defining poverty. The way it does so is not by adding a dimension to poverty but by helping to distinguish the phenomenon of poverty from a low level of well-being in general. This distinction is important because while poverty implies a low level of well-being, not every case of a low level of well-being can be regarded as poverty. For example, while the absence of the capability to live a healthy life is certainly a case of a low level of well-being, the specific case of ill-health caused by a genetic disorder (for which no remedy currently exists) will not in itself be recognized as poverty;[4] whereas ill-health caused by lack of access to basic health-care resources will be. In general, for poverty to exist, lack of command over economic resources must play a role in the causal chain leading to a low level of well-being.

Several clarifications should, however, be made at this point so as to avoid misunderstanding. First, while the concept of poverty does have an irreducible economic connotation, the relevant concept here is not low income but the broader concept of *inadequate command over economic resources*, of which inadequate personal income is only one possible source. Other sources include insufficient command over publicly provided goods and services, inadequate access to communally owned and managed resources, inadequate command over resources that are made available through formal and informal networks of mutual support, and so on. If a person's lack of command over any of these resources plays a role in precipitating basic capability failures, she would be counted as poor.

Second, the recognition that poverty has an irreducible economic connotation does not necessarily imply the primacy of economic factors in the causation of poverty. For example, when discrimination based on gender, ethnicity, or any other ground denies a person access to health-care resources, the resulting ill-health is clearly a case of capability failure that should count as poverty because the lack of access to resources has played a role here. But causal primacy in this case lies in the sociocultural practices as well as the political-legal frameworks that permit discrimination against particular individuals or groups; lack of command over resources plays merely a mediating role. However, as argued before, the existence of this mediating role is crucial in distinguishing poverty from a low level of well-being in general.

Third, it is important to emphasize that even though the link with economic resources must be maintained, this does not render the capability-based concept of poverty equivalent to a uniformly low level of command over economic resources. The two would be equivalent only if everyone had the same capacity to convert resources into capabilities, but that is not the case. For instance, people with different biological characteristics may require different amounts of food and health care in order to acquire the same degree of freedom to live a healthy life. Similarly, people living in different cultural environments might feel that they need different amounts of clothing in order to have the capability to be clothed at a minimally acceptable level. In other words, the degree of command over resources that may be adequate for one person may not be adequate for another. It would, therefore, be a mistake to define and measure poverty in terms of a uniformly low level of command over economic resources, when the fundamental concern is with a person's capabilities.

* * * * *

ENDNOTES

1. That is why Amartya Sen, who has done more than anyone else to broaden the concept of poverty, insists that "there are some clear associations that constrain the nature of the concept, and we are not entirely free to characterize poverty in any way we like." See, A. Sen, *Inequality Re-examined*, Cambridge, Harvard University Press, 1992, p. 107.

2. The implications of this link are explored more fully below.

3. A. Sen, op. cit., p. 109.

4. Once ill-health has been caused by a genetic disorder, this may of course lead to a state of poverty, for example, by preventing the afflicted person from taking up any productive activity, but the point is that ill-health in this case will have played an instrumental role in causing poverty rather than constituting a dimension of poverty in its own right.

Copyright Acknowledgements

Chapter 1: Peter S. Li, "The Market Value and Social Value of Race," from *Racism and Social Inequality in Canada: Concepts, Controversies and Strategies of Resistance*, edited by V. Satzewich. Copyright © Thompson Educational Publishing 1998. Reprinted with permission of the publisher.

Table 1.1: *Multiculturalism and Canadians: Attitude Study 1991 National Survey Report.* Copyright © Angus Reid Group, 1991.

Chapter 2: Rose Baaba Folson, "Representation of the Immigrant," from *Calculated Kindness: Global Restructuring Immigration and Settlement in Canada*, edited by Rose Baaba Folson. Copyright © Fernwood Publishing 2004. Reprinted with permission of the publisher.

Chapter 3: Yasmeen Abu-Laban and Christina Gabriel, "Selling (out) Diversity in an Age of Globalization," from *Selling Diversity: Immigration, Multiculturalism, Employment Equity, and Globalization*. Copyright © by Yasmeen Abu-Laban and Christina Gabriel. Reprinted by permission of Broadview Press

Chapter 4: Bonita Lawrence, "Regulating Native Identity." Reprinted with permission of the publisher from *'Real' Indians and Others* by Bonita Lawrence. © University of British Columbia Press 2004. All rights reserved by the Publisher.

Chapter 5: Grace-Edward Galabuzi, "Social Exclusion: Socio-economic and Political Implications of the Racialized Gap," from *Canada's Economic Apartheid: The Social Exclusion of Racialized Groups in the New Century* by Grace-Edward Galabuzi. Copyright © Canadian Scholars' Press Inc. 2006. Reprinted with permission of the publisher.

Chapter 6: Roxanna Ng, "Homeworking: Dream Realized or Freedom Constrained? The Globalized Reality of Immigrant Garment Workers," *Canadian Woman Studies* 19, no. 3 (November 1999): 110–114. Reprinted with permission of the author.

Chapter 7: Jo-Ann Lee, "Immigrant Women Workers in the Immigrant Settlement Sector" in *Canadian Woman Studies* 19, no.3 (Fall 1999): 97–103. Reprinted with permission of the author.

Chapter 8: Nandita Sharma, "Home(lessness) and the Naturalization of Difference," from *Home Economics: Nationalism and the Making of 'Migrant Workers' in Canada* by Nandita Sharma. Copyright © University of Toronto Press 2006. Reprinted with permission of the publisher.

Chapter 9: Lorne Foster, "Foreign Credentials in Canada's Multicultural Society," from *The Professionalization of Work*, edited by Merle Jacobs and Stephen E. Bosanac. Copyright © 2006 by Lorne Foster. Reprinted with the permission of the author.

Table 9.1: Source: Statistics Canada, Ethnic Diversity Survey, 2002.

Chapter 10: Tania Das Gupta, "Racism/Anti-racism, Precarious Employment, and Unions," from *Precarious Employment: Understanding Labour Market Insecurity in Canada*, edited by Lead Vosko. Copyright © McGill-Queen's University Press 2006. Reprinted with permission of the publisher.

Chapter 11: Kiran Mirchandani and Wendy Chan, "The Racialized Impact of Welfare Fraud Control in British Columbia and Ontario." Printed with permission from *DIRECTIONS: Research and Policy on the Elimination of Racism*, vol. 2, no. 2 (2006), titled "Facing Institutionalized Racism." *DIRECTIONS* is the flagship journal of the Canadian Race Relations Foundation (CRRF). More information available at www.crrf-fcrr.ca.

Chapter 12: Scot Wortley and Julian Tanner, "Data, Denials, and Confusion: The Racial Profiling Debate in Toronto," *Canadian Journal of Criminology and Criminal Justice* 45, no. 3 (2003): 367–389. Copyright © Canadian Criminal Justice Association. Reprinted with permission of Canadian Criminal Justice Association.

Chapter 13: Siu-ming Kwok and Dora Tam, "Deliquency of Asian Youth in Canada," *Asian Pacific Journal of Social Work and Development*, vol. 2 (2004): 5–18. Reprinted with permission.

Chapter 14: Sunera Thobani, "War Frenzy," *Atlantis: A Women's Studies Journal* 27, no. 1 (2004). Reprinted with permission of *Atlantis*, www.msvu.ca/atlantis.

Chapter 15: Punam Khosla, excerpted from "If Low Income Women of Colour Counted in Toronto," from *If Low Income Women of Colour Counted in Toronto*. Published by the The Community Social Planning Council of Toronto, 2003. Copyright © Punam Khosla. Reprinted with permission of the author.

Chapter 16: Sherene H. Razack, "Gendered Racial Violence and Spacialized Justice: The Murder of Pamela George," in *Race, Space and the Law: Unmapping a White Settler Society*, edited Sherne H. Razack. Copyright © Between the Lines, 2002. Reprinted with permission of the publisher.

Chapter 17: George J. Sefa Dei, "The Social Construction of a 'Drop-Out': Dispelling the Myth," from *Reconstructing 'Drop-Out': A Critical Ethnography of the Dynamics of Black Students' Disengagement from School*, edited by George J. Sefa Dei et al. Copyright © University of Toronto Press 1997. Reprinted with the permission of the publisher.

Chapter 18: Amartya Sen, "Individual Freedom as a Social Commitment," from *Development as Freedom* by Amartya Sen, copyright © 1999 by Amartya Sen. Used by permission of Alfred A. Knopf, a division of Random House, Inc.

Appendix A: Executive Summary, *Canada's Action Plan against Racism*. Copyright © 2005 Department of Canadian Heritage.

Appendix B: *Human Rights and Poverty Reduction: A Conceptual Framework*. Copyright © United Nations, New York and Geneva, 2004.